Politics Without Parties

Politics

Without

Parties

Massachusetts, 1780–1791

VAN BECK HALL

University of Pittsburgh Press

Library of Congress Catalog Card Number 78-158186
ISBN 0-8229-3234-2
Copyright © 1972, University of Pittsburgh Press
Henry M. Snyder & Co., Inc., London
Manufactured in the United States of America

To Paula

Contents

Acknowledgments

I am, first of all, indebted to my wife for without her love, concern, and assistance this book would never have been begun, much less completed. Three scholars played an important role in motivating my interest in history, in teaching me research skills, and in giving me new ideas that could be applied in the book. I have indeed been fortunate to have been a student of Thomas H. LeDuc and Merrill Jensen and a colleague of Samuel P. Hays. In addition to these men many individuals who have read either parts of or the entire manuscript have given me valuable insights. My colleagues in Dr. Jensen's seminar at the University of Wisconsin were extremely helpful, and I borrowed a great deal from the work of Stephen Patterson and the bibliographical knowledge of Gaspar Saladino. Julius Rubin, Robert Doherty, Seymour Drescher, and Joel Silbey, my colleagues at the University of Pittsburgh, have read parts of the manuscript and have given some invaluable advice. Samuel P. Hays read the entire work and gave me a critique that led me to rework and reorganize much of the material. Jackson Turner Main read the manuscript twice and supplied useful criticism, and Alfred Young pointed out sections that seemed weak or might cause difficulties.

The editors at the University of Pittsburgh Press have been extremely helpful. Mrs. Eleanor Walker read the entire manuscript and helped me whip the prose and footnotes into a hopefully acceptable condition. I am also grateful to Mrs. Louise Craft for her editorial contributions and to Miss Margot Barbour, who provided the artwork for the maps.

I was aided and encouraged by many people I met while engaged in research. No scholar could glean much from the Massachusetts Archives without the aid of Leo Flaherty and his wife. The staff at the Boston Public Library's newspaper and manuscripts divisions

were extremely helpful, and the staff at the Massachusetts Historical Society also gave valuable assistance. Dr. Patrick J. Riley of the
Massachusetts Historical Society gave me permission to use the
Benjamin Lincoln papers while he was engaged in arranging them
for archival use. A pleasant afternoon with Hiller B. Zobel cleared
up many questions concerning court structure and legal terminol-
ogy for the 1780s. The staffs of the Wisconsin State Historical
Society, the American Antiquarian Society, and Dedham Historical Society, the Library of Congress, the Hillman Library of the
University of Pittsburgh, and the clerk of the supreme judicial
court of Suffolk County were uniformly courteous and helpful.

Finally, I must thank all those scholars who have worked in this
period of Massachusetts history. I hope the footnotes will reflect
their contributions.

Introduction

P O L I T I C S without parties seems a contradiction in terms. Yet even in modern states, governments, representative or not, can make vital decisions affecting millions of people without or outside of the ministrations or influence of parties. What tends to be exceptional today was the rule in the eighteenth century. There were, of course, *parties*, if the term is extended to include factions, ideological divisions, and the loose and transitory confederations which united to sponsor certain, usually broad, programs. But the modern institutionalized party had not yet emerged.

This fact places the historian studying the eighteenth century at a serious disadvantage. Scholars studying the nineteenth or twentieth centuries have been able to correlate tremendous amounts of social, economic, religious, and cultural data to a definite number of well-organized, relatively stable parties. The availability of data and the finite number of parties enable them to describe the differences among the parties in terms of leadership and voting support and permit them to study changes in these categories over time. Many, after developing this description, have pushed on to analyze rhetoric, issues, and changes in party positions and have attempted to show how these factors are interrelated with party support and leadership. But the eighteenth-century historian faces two serious and related problems: (1) the absence of parties which provide a ready-made structure for his analysis, and (2) the lack of massive quantities of social, economic, and other types of data that can be used to describe the society and can then be used to compare the support for various parties.

Most political historians working in the eighteenth century have avoided these difficulties by their choices of approach and research techniques. Many have concluded that politics, both in Britain and in the colonies, revolved around countless numbers of factions united by personality, by family alliance, or by narrowly

defined economic, social, or religious interests. With indefatigable
energy they have ransacked genealogical and manuscript sources to
build up biographical data banks for leading politicians and legislators and have used roll calls and division lists to prove the incredi-
bly complex nature of parliamentary and legislative politics. An
older, but now resurgent, interpretation finds ideological and intellectual conceptions and divisions at the root of political decision.
Scholars of this persuasion have made exhaustive studies of partisan rhetoric and the development of political ideologies to underline the differences among certain articulate individuals and groups
within the population. Many of these historians have found evidence showing the continuity of these intellectual traditions over
time which, to some, seems almost partylike. Several historians
have gone beyond this point in arguing that parties, although unor-
ganized in a modern sense, did exist in early eighteenth-century
Britain and in the new United States. Division lists and roll call
analysis prove that certain groups and individuals voted together
on a relatively wide range of issues and, at least at the legislative
level, this reflects a significant degree of party regularity. Finally, a
few have attempted to show political divisions based upon the
varying desires of large sections within a given society. These men
found that the western areas of many states tended to support
different policies than the eastern sections. All of these approaches
have been valuable and have yielded useful descriptions of political
differences and developments over time in preparty societies.

Just as scholars have used certain intellectual constructs in which
to place their research, they have also tended to narrow their
attention to certain types of evidence. Ideologically oriented
scholars have directed their attention to pamphlets, newspapers,
and manuscript evidence produced by a relatively small but articulate elite. The Namierists, or students of faction, have collected
massive amounts of data about members of Parliament or legislators, another small elite group within the total society. Those
interested in early parties have examined manuscript evidence and
roll call votes to define the issues and describe the divisions between their parties. But again their evidence usually comes from
the legislators or from small but articulate groups. Finally the
sectionalists and regionalists have collected data that describe the
differences among large geographical areas within a society and
then analyzed legislative records to find evidence of political debate and division related to these sectional differences.

This book is, in part, an attempt, using Massachusetts politics between 1780 and 1791 as an example, to suggest some new methods and approaches for analyzing preparty politics. Ideally the new methodology should enable the scholar to relate political divisions over time to the social, economic, cultural, and other characteristics of the total population. Indeed, in that best of all possible worlds, the scholar could analyze and measure the characteristics of every politically active person within the society, a feat which is obviously impossible. This means that the smallest possible political units in the society must be analyzed and related to each other on the basis of available data. In many societies these units either were too large to serve as meaningful subjects of analysis or failed, in any significant way, to control or influence the activities of their legislative representatives. Even in many of the American colonies and states, large and diverse counties became the basis of the representative system; and although careful analysis of these units sharpens the description of political and other differences within these states and colonies, the very size and diversity of the counties obscure many important differences. In some colonies and states these units also had relatively little control over their elected representatives. But in certain colonies and states, notably in New England, representation and political participation rested on individual towns, generally much smaller and much less diverse than the larger county units. Of course many of these communities contained large, diversified populations, but an analysis of towns in Massachusetts in the 1780s and early 1790s permits differentiation among more than three hundred forty political entities that had some control over their representatives. The economic, social, and other differences among them can be described and related to their political responses over time.

But how can these small political units be analyzed in any meaningful fashion? What types of materials are available that can be used to differentiate them? And how can this analysis be related to their varied political responses over time? In Massachusetts, at least, masses of data that can be quantified and related to these small political units are available for the period. The General Court, for example, listed and evaluated the property of every town in the commonwealth in over thirty different categories. Official and unofficial registers give the names and denominations of all ministers in each community; standard reference works give the number of newspapers, books, and pamphlets printed in each of them; other sources give the names of judges, lawyers, doctors, justices of the peace, attorneys, securities holders, merchants, senators, representatives, national congressmen, and scores of other important and unimportant office holders who resided in them. Archival materials show the amount of taxes collected and the towns that fell behind in their collections, the number of ships built in individual communities, the number of fishermen and whalers, and the number and tonnage of ships operating from them. Thus a multitude of sources yields massive amounts of cultural, economic, political, financial, and administrative information that can be used to differentiate these communities.

In order to use this data several scales which measure the relative commercial, social, and other characteristics of the communities are developed in chapter 1. The towns are then divided into three major groups, each containing about one-third of the state's total population. The first, group A or the most commercial-cosmopolitan towns, comprises the fifty-three communities that controlled the commercial activities of the state and had the greatest number of institutional, intellectual, and social contacts with other towns. The second, group B or the less commercial-cosmopolitan category, includes eighty-six towns with some commercial and social connections, while the two hundred four group C towns had little or no commercial activity and the fewest connections with a wider society. These three groups of towns can then be related to various demographic, economic, social, and cultural variables in order to give a concise description of the entire commonwealth.

The next step is to relate these groups of communities to the political divisions and questions of the period 1780 to 1791. Fortunately massive amounts of political data based on these same communities exist and can be used to relate political behavior to the economic and cultural characteristics of the individual towns. The lower house took over eighty roll call votes on important political questions between 1780 and 1791. Although the turnover in membership discourages statistical analysis of the voting patterns of individual legislators, the voting patterns of the towns are remarkably consistent throughout the period. Voting data for governor, lieutenant governor, county senator, and after 1788 for the national House of Representatives also provides additional insights into the operation of the political system. Thus the constituencies, rather than the representatives, become the means of analysis and the approach shows that important political divisions during the

1780s were related to the varied characteristics of the three groups of towns.

This new method supplements rather than replaces the approaches described earlier. Political leaders supported by personal factions struggled for power and position at the highest levels. Ideological differences became important especially after 1788, and many of the factions quarreled with each other on ideological issues. By 1788 it seemed that parties were beginning to develop as ideologically oriented leaders appealed to communities on the basis of their reactions to the national Constitution. Finally, votes on many important issues and questions did reflect regional differences. Thus a complete description must use the techniques of careful analysis of small constituencies and at the same time incorporate these other pertinent approaches.

The new methodology, in conjunction with these older approaches, suggests a new approach to American preparty politics which can be used to describe Massachusetts politics between 1780 and 1791. In a preparty political system such as the one in Massachusetts, the relationship of constituencies to divisive issues can be studied if two conditions exist: first, an issue must be considered important to a large number of towns that shared similar characteristics; and second, the towns had to be able to at least partially control their representatives. From 1780 through 1787 these conditions were met as the fiscal and taxation problems bequeathed by the Revolution divided the towns accordingly to their socioeconomic differences and the representatives of these communities tended to vote for their town's interests. At the same time factional politics continued as James Bowdoin and his followers attempted to force John Hancock out of the governorship and as local and county leaders fought for positions in the state senate or as judicial placeholders. Ideological debates also flared up in which various factions and leading politicians attempted to discredit their enemies as Tories, as aristocratic conspirators, or as corrupters of republican morality. These three causes of political division seldom overlapped before 1787. The least commercial-cosmopolitan communities that opposed the consolidation and refunding of the state debt failed to attract any of the leading factions to their cause and ideological and constitutional questions played only a minor role in their efforts to change the policies of the commonwealth. But in 1787 and 1788 the situation changed. The least commercial-cosmopolitan towns feared the new Constitution and opposed ratification while at the same time some of the members of the factions active in the earlier 1780s also opposed the new charter for ideological reasons. Between 1788 and 1790 it seemed that a type of party politics would develop. The Antifederalist politicians picked up broad popular support from those towns that opposed ratification in early 1788 and the newspaper rhetoric began to point out ideological differences between the Federalists and Antifederalists. But in 1790 and 1791 the assumption of the state debt and the failure of the national government to levy direct taxes or run roughshod over the rights of the less commercial-cosmopolitan towns removed the basic issues of Massachusetts politics. Thus when parties developed in the 1790s, their leaders would come from the two opposing Antifederalist and Federalist factions of the 1788-1790 period but their rank and file support would be almost completely different from what it was when ratification was at issue. The Massachusetts experience thus suggests three propositions about political behavior in a preparty period: (1) if the voters or the smallest political corporate groups in the society either failed to control their representatives or did not respond to issues, then factions of leaders at the local, state, and national levels machinating for power and place would control politics; (2) if the voters and units did recognize the importance of issues, whether ideological, economic, religious, or cultural, and had a minimal amount of control over their representatives, divisions would result that can be analyzed by studying the economic, cultural, ideological, or religious background of the communities involved; and (3) if the factions of important leaders began to identify themselves with these divisions based upon issues, a party type of situation began to emerge. But unlike authentic political parties, these protoparties depended upon the persistence of the underlying issues that had divided the community. In other words, these protoparties failed to develop their own identity and were kept alive only by the continuation of issues that had already developed and divided the society.

Thus preparty politics involved more than the scramble for power and prestige by numerous factions and more than the ideological debates of the intellectual or cultural elite. In Massachusetts, at least, real divisions within the wider society developed into well-defined political battle lines on issues related to the commonwealth's fiscal problems.

The book is divided into four sections and eleven chapters.[1] The first section of three chapters describes the social, economic, and cultural differences among the three groups of towns; the various economic, social, financial, and administrative interests operating throughout the commonwealth; and the way politics worked in such a system. The second section describes the political divisions of the earlier 1780s that flowed from the economic and fiscal problems created by the Revolution and illustrates how these divisions widened with the passage of time. The third section places Shays's Rebellion in this context and shows how both the rebellion and the reaction to the Constitution resembled the earlier divisions. Finally the last section describes the development of protoparties based on the newer ideological differences in addition to the older socioeconomic ones. However, these protoparties fall apart when the assumption of the state's debt finally solves the fiscal problems that had plagued the commonwealth since the 1770s.

The book begins with the first session of the General Court after the adoption of the 1780 constitution and ends with the disintegration of the divisions resulting from the fiscal issue. It makes no attempt to explain the eventual development of organized parties during the 1790s or the reasons for the adoption of the 1780 constitution. It accepts the constitution as a framework for politics and it leaves the later parties to historians who have studied their creation. This book attempts instead to explain how preparty politics worked and how bitter divisions could and did result from the explosive mixture of issues that tended to divide the society along social and economic lines. It has little to say about the concept of democracy except that it does show how minority interests could control political institutions while at the same time the usually apolitical majority, when aroused, could accomplish a great deal through voting, extralegal activities, and rioting. Since even the leaders of this majority left few manuscripts, we often know them only through the opinions of their very articulate enemies. But at least roll call votes and other data do show that they existed and that their often ineffectual and sometimes desperate challenges to the policies of the men of property and intelligence could, on occasion, succeed.

1. Statistical appendices to this book are available. See Notice to Readers on page xviii.

NOTICE TO READERS

Several photocopies and microfilms of three statistical appendices to this book have been catalogued and shelved at the Hillman Library, University of Pittsburgh, Pittsburgh, Pennsylvania 15213. Readers who would like to examine these appendices may borrow them through interlibrary loan from Hillman Library.

These appendices contain the following information:

Appendix 1 gives the commercial index number for each of the 343 towns by ranking each one in terms of (1) inventory, (2) money lent at interest, (3) specie, and (4) vessel tonnage.

Appendix 2 gives the social index rating of each town by ranking each one according to (1) number of newspapers and years of publication, (2) court sessions, (3) number of barristers, (4) number of lawyers, (5) number of years between 1780 and 1790 it was represented in the lower house of the General Court, and (6) number of ministers in 1780, 1786, and 1790.

Appendix 3 combines the first two appendices, assigns a commercial-cosmopolitan index number, and places each town in one of the three commercial-cosmopolitan groups.

Politics Without Parties

1

Economy and Society:
The Commercial-Cosmopolitan
Continuum

T H E description of politics in a preparty period requires the careful reconstruction of the economic and social characteristics of the society, relating the resulting structure to a wide range of demographic, social, cultural, economic, and religious variables. In order to accomplish this task, I have divided the 343 towns, districts, and plantations in Massachusetts, as of 1784, into three socioeconomic groups.[1] The first, group A or the most commercial-cosmopolitan, comprises the 54 towns that controlled the commercial activities of the commonwealth and had the greatest number of social and institutional connections with other communities. The second, group B or the less commercial-cosmopolitan, includes 88 towns with some commercial wealth and a few social and institutional connections, while the third, group C or the least commercial-cosmopolitan towns, includes the remaining 201 communities with little or no commercial activity and the least connection with the wider society. These three groups of towns, each with roughly one-third of the population and with relatively equal potential political power, have then been related to various demographic, regional, economic, social, cultural, and

1. The best description of the legal characteristics of the towns, districts, and plantations is found in Samuel Freeman, *The Town Officer, or the Power and Duty of Selectmen, Town Clerks, Town Treasurers, Overseers of the Poor . . . As Contained in the Laws of the Commonwealth* (Portland, 1791), pp. 111-21 for the town, pp. 122-24 for the parish, and pp. 126-27 for the plantations. The districts and plantations could not send representatives to the General Court but they could and did vote for the governor, lieutenant governor, national congressmen (after 1788), and county senators.

religious variables. The resulting description of the economy and society of the state serves as the basis for studying political behavior during the 1780s and early 1790s.

I have then related these three groups of towns to the politically important interest groups operating in the commonwealth and have measured their political behavior by analyzing their popular voting patterns and the political positions taken by their delegates in the General Court. This analysis has enabled me to describe the political divisions within the state in terms of economic, social, and cultural differences among the towns. Thus, in the absence of organized political parties, the towns themselves and their controlling interests are related to the political and financial issues created by the Revolution.

The vast differences in commercial activity among the towns can be measured by placing all 343 communities on a commercial continuum that ranges from Boston at one extreme to towns like rural Mount Washington in the Berkshire hills at the other. In order to construct this continuum I have analyzed the data collected by the General Court as a basis for apportioning taxes among the various towns. The court required all towns, districts, and plantations to submit lengthy lists of the various types of property held by their citizens which a special committee analyzed, reviewed, and sometimes revised. The court then used the resulting valuation lists to assign a specific proportion of the total tax bill to each of the towns. In 1782 the court decided that Boston should pay 5.7 percent of the state's taxes while Mount Washington escaped with a contribution of less than 0.05 percent.[2] The court drafted these evaluations in 1781-1782, 1784-1786, and 1792-1793, but since the 1781-1782 lists reflect a wartime economy and the 1792-1793 lists have unfortunately disappeared, the 1784-1786 lists have been used to measure the relative commercial wealth of all 343 towns.[3] Four items on this 1784-1786 list—inventory (or stock in trade), silver, money lent at interest, and vessel tonnage—

2. This 1782 valuation list gives the proportion paid for every £1000 of taxes levied on the entire commonwealth. See *Acts and Laws of the Commonwealth of Massachusetts*, 1780-1797, 11 vols. (Boston, 1890-1897) (cited hereafter as *Acts and Laws*), 6 Mar. 1782, 1:903-06.

3. The 1782 list is in ibid. The best single source for the lists for 1786 and 1793 is in the *Abstract of the Report of the Committee on the Valuation* (Boston, 1793), pp. 1-13, which lists both the later valuations.

have been used as a basis for constructing the commercial continuum. I have ranked all 343 towns from first to last in all four of these items, added each town's rankings, and divided them by three or four (depending upon whether the town possessed shipping tonnage), and the resulting figure became that town's commercial index number with the more commercial towns ranking the lowest. Boston, for example, ranked first in all four items and had a commercial index number of one, while Mount Washington ranked 213 in inventory, 226 in silver, 248 in money lent at interest, and had no vessel tonnage for a commercial index number of 229.00. The towns were then arranged by these index numbers, from lowest to highest, and divided into deciles of 33 to 36 towns each.[4] Table 1 shows the tremendous concentration of commercial wealth in the most commercial deciles. A comparison of

4. The evaluation called for in 1784 and completed in 1786 is found in the Evaluation, 1784/86 in vols. 162 and 163 of the unpublished Massachusetts Archives, Office of the Secretary, Boston. Volume 162 contains the returns sent to the General Court by the towns. Volume 163 contains the taxable valuation assigned to this property by the committee. This committee also rated several plantations that had not submitted returns and increased the taxable property returned by several communities. In both volumes each town occupies an individual page on which the types and amounts of property are listed. These included: polls both rateable and nonrateable, houses, barns, warehouses, various types of mills, distilleries, potash factories, iron works, stock in trade (inventory), money lent out at interest, silver, money on hand, number and value of shops, five categories of improved land, unimproved land, various types of livestock (sheep and goats are reported in vol. 162 but not rated in vol. 163), vessel tonnage, wharfage, factorage, etc. Totals of these valuations are given in Thomas Fleet and John Fleet, *Fleet's Pocket Almanack for the Year of Our Lord 1791 . . . to Which Is Annexed the Massachusetts Register* (Boston, 1790), p. 57. (This series with slight changes in title extended throughout the 1780s. It will be cited hereafter as Fleet, *Register*, with the year and date of publication.) This states that the valuation was supposed to be 20 percent short. However, this shortage did not affect the relative holdings of property within the commonwealth. Another summary, with slightly different totals for some items, is in the *American Museum*, Jan. 1790, p. 541. The totals in both these sources often differ from the totals I computed from Evaluation, 1784/86, apparently due to the fact that the computations in Fleet, *Register* and the *American Museum* are based on the data in vol. 162 and not the revised totals in vol. 163. If their totals are changed to reflect the increases in vol. 163, my computations are quite close to theirs. For an earlier use of this type of data, based on the evaluation lists for 1801, see Percy W. Bidwell and John I. Falconer, *History of American Agriculture in the Northern United States, 1620-1860* (New York, 1941), pp. 90, 105, and 112.

TABLE 1
The Commercial Deciles

Decile	Number of Towns	Polls	Inventory	Silver	Tonnage	Money Lent	Money on Hand
First	34	23.4%	88.4%	76.1%	77.5%	68.0%	80.5%
Second	34	15.8	5.1	10.4	8.6	12.7	6.2
Third	34	14.0	3.3	5.0	3.7	8.2	3.9
Fourth	35	10.1	1.6	3.8	5.2	4.2	3.0
Fifth	33	8.3	0.7	2.6	1.9	3.0	2.0
Sixth	34	7.1	0.4	1.1	1.9	2.2	2.0
Seventh	34	6.0	0.3	0.6	1.2	0.9	1.1
Eighth	34	6.5	0.1	0.3	0.0	0.7	0.8
Ninth	35	5.9	0.0	0.1	0.0	0.2	0.6
Tenth	36	2.8	0.0	0.0	0.0	0.0	0.1

SOURCE: Evaluation, 1784/86, in vol. 163 of the unpublished Massachusetts Archives, Office of the Secretary, Boston (cited hereafter as Evaluation, 1784/86).

the per-poll holdings of these various types of commercial wealth in the first as compared with the last four deciles shows the same concentration of wealth. (See table 2.)

TABLE 2
Amount of Commercial Property Held per Poll

	Amount and Types of Property				
Decile	Inventory (£)	Silver (ounces)	Tonnage (tons)	Money Lent (£)	Percentage of Polls
First	£22.35	2.91	2.26	£12.95	23.40%
Last four	0.11	0.04	0.04	0.35	21.20

SOURCE: Evaluation, 1784/86. The property per poll is determined by dividing the amount of various types of commercial wealth in each decile by the total number of polls included within the same decile.

This concentration of commercial wealth and activity in a relatively few towns had important social and political consequences. The commercially oriented interest groups that controlled these towns cooperated with outsiders to advance a wide range of commercial, financial, and economic programs.[5] But commercial dif-

5. Chapter 2 contains a detailed description of these interest groups and their relationships with the three categories of towns. It should be understood that this cooperation was not simply by towns but by men within these towns.

ferences, important as they are, are only one segment of the complex socioeconomic continuum.

Differences among the communities in their involvement in the broader society can be gauged by measuring the social, cultural, and institutional activities of each of the towns. All 343 towns were placed on a nine-point scale depending upon the presence or absence of: (1) newspapers, (2) sessions of the county courts of common pleas and general sessions of the peace or of the state supreme judicial court, (3) barristers present in either 1786 or 1791, (4) two or more lawyers in either 1786 or 1791, (5) one lawyer in either 1786 or 1791, (6) the presence of a minister of any denomination in the town for two of the three years, 1780, 1786, or 1791, (7) representatives in the lower house of the General Court for at least nine of the twelve years between 1780 and 1792, and (8) representatives in the lower house for at least six of the same twelve years. The presence or absence of these eight indicators gauges the involvement of the town in the wider society and its influence, in turn, on other communities. Newspapers gave local readers political and economic information and spread the ideas of editors and essayists. Court sessions provided opportunities for wider social and political contacts because they brought into the towns circuit-riding judges and lawyers from all over the state. Lawyers and barristers, who were often politicians, had extensive legal, social, political, economic, and cultural contacts with outsiders and their presence contributed to the cosmopolitan character of many towns. A town's record in sending representatives to the lower house is a measure of its involvement and interest in state politics; moreover, the representatives often returned from Boston with significant political, economic, financial, and

TABLE 3
The Social Groups

	Social Group Number								
	1	*2*	*3*	*4*	*5*	*6*	*7*	*8*	*9*
Number of indicators present	8	7	6	5	4	3	2	1	0
Towns in each group Total towns = 343	6	3	7	10	34	89	62	61	71

SOURCES: See the data in note 6.

social information. Finally the ministers corresponded with one another and frequently met at conventions, thus providing another conduit through which information and outside influences could · reach the local community. Based on this data each town was assigned to one of nine social groups. Boston in the first group had all eight indicators; Mount Washington in the ninth had none.[6] Table 3 shows the number of towns in each one of the nine groups ranging from group 1, the most cosmopolitan, to group 9, the most localistic.

Finally I merged the commercial and social scales into a single continuum that measures both the commercial and cosmopolitan characteristics of each town. Every town was assigned from one to ten points depending upon its commercial decile and from one to eight points according to the number of social indicators present. This puts Boston, with a total of eighteen points, at the most com-

6. The scale of eight items is based on the following sources: Clarence S. Brigham, comp., *History and Bibliography of American Newspapers, 1690-1820*, 2 vols. (Worcester, 1947), 1:196-217 for Maine and 1:311-415 for Massachusetts. This source gives the name of the paper, years of publication, location, and editor. Court sessions are available in Isaiah Thomas, comp., *The Perpetual Laws of the Commonwealth of Massachusetts from the Establishment of the Constitution of 1780 to the First Session of the General Court, A.D. 1788* (Worcester, 1788). This compilation prints on p. 133 the act of 1783 that established sessions of the supreme judicial court and on pp. 130-31 the act of 1787 concerning the sessions of the common pleas and general sessions of the peace. Legislation for the early 1780s is available in the *Acts and Laws*, 10 March 1783, 2:126-28, and 14 Mar. 1783, 2:141-43. For sessions in the newly created counties of Washington and Hancock see ibid., 25 June 1789, 5:426-29, and 21 June 1790, 6:126-29, for a later law listing the courts of common pleas and general sessions for the entire state. Also notice: Fleet, *Register, 1787* (1786), pp. i-ii, and ibid., *1792* (1791), n.p., in the calendar section. Barristers are listed in Fleet, *Register, 1792* (1791), pp. 139, and ibid., *1787* (1786), p. 106. Lawyers are listed in ibid., *1792* (1791), pp. 139-40, and ibid., *1787* (1786), p. 106. Ministers and Friend's meetings are listed in ibid., *1792* (1791), pp. 98-105 and ibid., *1787* (1786), pp. 51-58. The list for 1780 is in ibid., *1781* (1780) which has no pagination. Representatives in the lower house are listed in the *Acts and Laws* at the beginning of each annual series of laws. See, for 1780, 1:130-33; for 1781, 1:602-04: for 1782, 2:184-86; for 1783, 2:670-73; for 1784, 3:198-201; for 1785, 3:622-25; for 1786, 4:266-70; for 1787, 4:664-67; for 1788, 5:172-75; for 1789, 5:520-23; for 1790, 6:92-95; and for 1791, 6:378-81. These lists must be used with care and compared with the annual lists of representatives in the manuscript journals of the house since the latter source gives the names of representatives who arrived after the first session who are frequently omitted from the published lists. These Unpublished Journals of the House of Representatives of the Commonwealth of Massachusetts are available at the Office of the Secretary, Boston, and are cited hereafter as House Journals.

mercial-cosmopolitan end of scale as opposed to Mount Washington, with only one point, at the other extreme. The 54 towns with over twelve points become the group A, or the most commercial-cosmopolitan, category; the next 88 towns with nine through twelve points become the group B, or the less commercial-cosmopolitan, category; while the remaining 201 towns with fewer than nine points become the least commercial-cosmopolitan group C category.[7] Each of these three groups of towns contained roughly one-third of the total population of the commonwealth. Their political power was, therefore, potentially equal. Table 4 shows the location of the three groups of towns within the three geographic regions of the state.

TABLE 4
Location of Groups Within the State

Towns	Number of Towns in:			
	Eastern Region	*Western Region*	*Maine*	*Total*
Group A	31	20	3	54
Group B	35	42	11	88
Group C	19	107	75	201
Total	85	169	89	343

NOTE: Eastern Massachusetts included the counties of Essex, Suffolk, Bristol, Plymouth, Barnstable, Nantucket, and Dukes. Western Massachusetts included Worcester, Hampshire, Berkshire, and Middlesex counties. Maine consisted of York, Cumberland, and Lincoln counties. Other divisions could have been made but this one enables me to use county data and still shows the differences among the three groups of towns within the same region.

The distribution of population among three groups of towns and three geographical regions contributed to the political polarization of the 1780s. Although state-wide each of the three groups had roughly one-third of the population, the group A towns accounted for three-fifths of the population of the eastern counties while the

7. The cut-off points between the groups were chosen so that each of the three would contain about one-third of the 1784 polls. Thus the three groups reflect divisions located along a commercial-cosmopolitan continuum which can be compared with and related to one another. For some other methods of analyzing social and economic differences in a preindustrial society, see Charles Tilly, *The Vendee: A Sociological Analysis of the Counterrevolution of 1793* (New York, 1967), pp. 38-81; Jackson T. Main, *The Social Structure of Revolutionary America* (Princeton, 1965), pp. 7-67; Manning J. Dauer, *The Adams Federalists* (Baltimore, 1953), pp. 3-34; David Hackett Fischer, *The Revolution of American Conservatism: The Federalist Party in the Era of Jeffersonian Democracy* (New York, 1969), pp. 201-26.

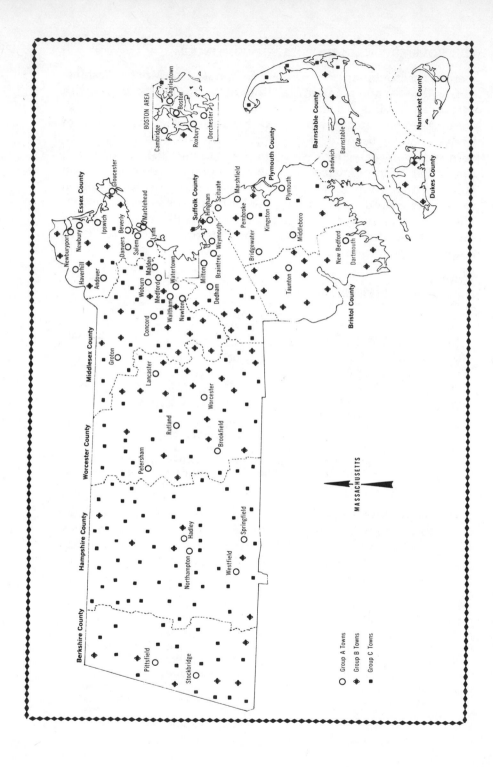

MASSACHUSETTS

BOSTON AREA

Charlestown
Boston
Cambridge
Roxbury
Dorchester

Barnstable County
Barnstable
Sandwich

Nantucket County

Dukes County

Essex County
Gloucester
Newburyport
Newbury
Ipswich
Beverly
Marblehead
Danvers
Salem
Lynn
Haverhill
Andover

Suffolk County

Plymouth County
Marshfield
Scituate
Hingham
Weymouth
Pembroke
Plymouth
Kingston
Bridgewater
Middleboro

Bristol County
New Bedford
Dartmouth
Taunton

Middlesex County
Woburn
Medford
Malden
Watertown
Waltham
Newton
Concord
Milton
Dedham
Braintree
Groton
Lancaster

Worcester County
Worcester
Rutland
Brookfield
Petersham

Hampshire County
Hadley
Northampton
Westfield
Springfield

Berkshire County
Pittsfield
Stockbridge

○ Group A Towns
◆ Group B Towns
■ Group C Towns

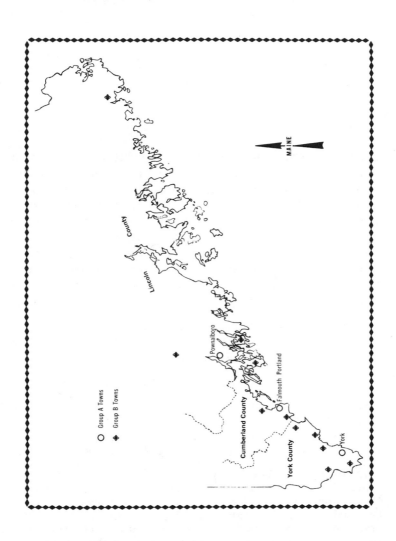

MAINE

Lincoln County

Pownalboro

Cumberland County

Falmouth Portland

York County

York

○ Group A Towns
◆ Group B Towns

TABLE 5
Towns and Population by Groups and Regions, 1784

| | Percentage of Polls in | | | |
	Eastern Region	Western Region	Maine	State
Group A	60%	18%	12%	34%
Group B	31	32	31	32
Group C	9	50	57	34
Regional Totals	42%	43%	15%	

SOURCE: Evaluation 1784/86.

group C communities held over one-half the population of the four western counties and the District of Maine. This skewed distribution gave the commercial-cosmopolitan interests a natural base in the eastern region while their more localistic opponents possessed their greatest potential in the western and Maine counties. (See table 5). The concentration of almost one-half the total population in the two most politically diverse regional groups of towns—the eastern group A and the western group C—intensified this sectional difference and increased the impact of fiscal and other issues.[8]

8. The number of polls per town is given in the Evaluation, 1784/86. The following table gives the percentage of polls within each group and region:

| | Regions | | | |
	East	West	Maine	Total
Group A	24.9%	7.6%	1.8%	34.3%
Group B	13.0	14.1	4.6	31.7
Group C	3.6	21.7	8.7	34.0
Total[a]	41.6%	43.3%	15.1%	100.0%

NOTE: Eastern Massachusetts included the counties of Essex, Suffolk, Bristol, Plymouth, Barnstable, Nantucket, Dukes, and Middlesex. Western Massachusetts included Worcester, Hampshire, and Berkshire counties. Maine consisted of York, Cumberland, and Lincoln counties. Other divisions could have been made, but this one enables me to use county data and still shows the differences among the three groups of towns within the same region.

a. Totals may not add because of rounding.

These percentages indicate the proportion of the total polls in the state that resided within a specific group of towns in any of the three regions. For example, almost one-fourth of the total polls lived within the eastern group A towns while only about one-fiftieth resided in the group A communities in Maine.

Varied rates of population growth had almost no political consequences during the decade. The group C towns grew more rapidly than the more commercial-cosmopolitan communities, but they did not send a higher proportion of representatives to the General Court or cast a higher percentage of votes in state elections. Thus, at least for the short term, they failed to parlay their more rapid growth into increased political power. Maine's extremely rapid population growth had some political effect during the period because her representation in the lower house increased from around 6 percent of the membership in 1780 to over 14 percent by 1790.[9] But even so she did not send her proportionate share of representatives and her additional delegates did not change the balance of political power within the commonwealth.

The concentration of inventory, silver, loans, and money in the group A towns gave them almost complete control over the commercial economy of the commonwealth. The group A towns held over nine-tenths of the inventory, or stock in trade, four-fifths of the silver, vessel tonnage, and money on hand, three-quarters of the money lent at interest, and about one-half of the total taxable value of industrial and semiindustrial enterprises.[10] At the other extreme, group C towns held less than one-twentieth of the inventory and silver, one fifteenth of the money at interest and money on hand, one-twelfth of the tonnage, and one-fourth of the value of industrial and semiindustrial enterprises. Table 6 shows the enormous difference in the various types of commercial wealth held in the three groups of towns. The average poll living in a group A town held £16.0 worth of inventory, 2.2 ounces of silver, £1.6 of money, had loaned out £9.7 and held £0.2 worth of tax-

9. See ch. 3 for a detailed discussion of representation. The three sections sent the following proportion of the total members in the lower house between 1780 and 1790: east, 38.1 percent; west, 51.5 percent; Maine, 10.4 percent. Between 1780 and 1787 Maine sent 10.1 percent of the members. Between 1787 and 1791 she sent 10.9 percent of the total.

For the increase of rateable polls between 1784 and 1792 in the three regions and among the three groups of towns; see for 1784 the Evaluation, 1784/86, and for 1792, Fleet, *Register*, 1794 (1793), pp. 52-64.

10. Notice table 6 which is based upon the Evaluation, 1784/86. The fractions are based upon the percentages of inventory (stock in trade), tonnage, money lent out at interest, money on hand, and the taxable value assigned to tanneries and slaughter houses, ropewalks, potash factories, grist and saw mills, other mills, and iron works, all of which were totaled to become the "value of industrial and semi-industrial enterprises."

TABLE 6
Commercial Wealth Held by Groups of Towns

Towns	Inventory	Silver	Money Lent	Tonnage	Money on Hand	Value of Enterprises
Group A	92.7%	82.4%	75.0%	81.3%	84.8%	50.6%
Group B	5.5	13.1	19.0	10.7	8.6	25.1
Group C	1.7	4.5	6.0	7.9	6.5	24.3

SOURCE: Evaluation, 1784/86.

TABLE 7
Holdings of Commercial Wealth by Region

		Percentage of			
Towns	Polls	Inventory	Silver	Money at Interest	Money on Hand
Eastern					
Group A	60%	98%	92%	85%	94%
Group B	31	2	7	14	5
Group C	9	0	1	1	1
Western					
Group A	18	59	56	58	40
Group B	32	33	31	29	30
Group C	50	8	13	13	30
Maine					
Group A	12	38	21	16	33
Group B	31	32	52	43	20
Group C	58	30	27	41	48

	Holdings of Average Poll in			
Towns	Inventory	Silver	Money at Interest	Money on Hand
Eastern				
Group A	£20.4	2.5 oz.	£10.3	£2.2
Group B	0.7	0.3	3.2	0.2
Group C	0.1	0.2	1.1	0.2
Western				
Group A	4.2	1.3	9.7	0.4
Group B	1.2	0.4	2.7	0.2
Group C	0.2	0.1	0.8	0.1
Maine				
Group A	3.8	0.4	1.3	0.6
Group B	1.2	0.5	1.4	0.1
Group C	0.6	0.1	0.6	0.2

SOURCE: Evaluation, 1784/86.

able property in manufacturing and semimanufacturing activities. His country cousin in a group C community possessed less than £0.3 worth of inventory and about 0.1 of an ounce of silver, lent out less than £0.8, and held about £0.1 worth of taxable manufacturing and semimanufacturing property.[11]

The same concentration of commercial wealth in the most commercial-cosmopolitan towns occurred in each one of the three geographical regions of the commonwealth. (See table 7.) The inhabitants of the eastern group A towns held over 85 percent of the specie, inventory, money lent at interest, and money on hand in their seven counties. In the four western counties the 18 percent of the polls who lived in group A towns, held over 56 percent of that region's inventory, specie, and money lent at interest, and possessed more than twice as much of these items per poll than did residents of the group B and C communities. In Maine the inhabitants of the three group A towns had less control over the district's commercial wealth.[12] Yet even there, where many commercial centers had failed to attract judicial and social institutions, the group A and B towns together controlled the commercial wealth of the district.[13]

Naturally this concentration of commercial wealth had economic, social, and cultural consequences with important political ramifications. The group A, most commercial, towns and their citizens developed and became enmeshed in a range of fiscal, economic, and commercial connections that were progressively less important in the group B and C communities. This involvement created the requirement for courts and lawyers and encouraged religious and cultural institutions which intensified the social distinctions among the three groups of towns. Given the magnitude of these commercial-economic differences and their social effects, it is not surprising that financial and economic issues would

11. Sources are in Evaluation, 1784/86. The figures are based upon the amount of inventory (stock in trade), money lent at interest, silver, money on hand, and the taxable value of industrial and semiindustrial enterprises described in fn. 10 above, divided by the number of polls within each of the three groups of towns.

12. Ibid.

13. The following table shows the number of towns in each commercial decile, for Massachusetts and for Maine, that were assigned to each one of the three commercial-cosmopolitan groups of towns. It shows that, generally speaking, the Maine towns in the higher commercial deciles had less chance to be included in the two highest commercial-cosmopolitan groups. This re-

TABLE 8
Location of Manufacturing and Processing Activities

	Percentage of Taxable Wealth of						
Towns	Distilleries	Rope-Walks	Tanneries and Slaughterhouses	Other Mills	Iron Works	Pot-ashes	Grist and Saw Mills
Group A	100%	100%	55%	66%	30%	23%	29%
Group B	0	0	31	28	33	37	34
Group C	0	0	15	7	37	40	38

SOURCE: Evaluation, 1784/86. This table shows the proportion of the taxable valuation of the listed types of enterprises held in each of the three groups of towns.

separate the more commercial-cosmopolitan towns from the less commercial and more isolated communities.

Even preindustrial manufacturing and processing activities differentiated the three groups of towns. The group A communities held almost 100 percent of the taxable value of ropewalks and distilleries and over 50 percent of the value of tanneries, slaughterhouses, and other mills, while they held less than one-third of the taxable value of iron works, potash factories, and grist and saw mills. Table 8 gives the percentages of the taxable value of certain

flected the fact that many of these towns had not yet developed the social and cultural institutions that would have given them a higher position on the commercial-cosmopolitan continuum.

The number of towns within the various deciles located within the indicated groups is as follows:

	Massachusetts			
Towns	1st-2d	3d-4th	5th-6th	7th-10th
Group A	48	3	0	0
Group B	15	49	13	0
Group C	0	0	44	82
Total	62	52	57	82

	Maine			
Towns	1st-2d	3d-4th	5th-6th	7th-10th
Group A	2	1	0	0
Group B	3	8	0	0
Group C	0	8	11	56
Total	6	17	15	56

manufacturing operations in the three groups of towns. These variations in the location of manufacturing and processing activities intensified the economic differentiation of the three groups of towns since the least commercial communities had almost no investment in the distilleries and rope walks which were directly dependent upon commercial development. Their potash factories, iron works, and mills depended upon local raw materials and the availability of convenient water power.

In agricultural wealth, too, the group C towns lacked the resources of the more commercially oriented communities. (See table 9.) The group B towns, with some commercial wealth, held

TABLE 9
Agricultural Wealth per Poll

Towns	Improved Acreage	Taxable Value of Acreage	Value of Barns
Group A	13.30	£3.95	£0.36
Group B	16.74	4.41	0.35
Group C	13.13	3.59	0.28

SOURCE: Evaluation, 1784/86, which gives the total amount of acreage and its taxable value for: (a) tillage, (b) English meadow, (c) salt marsh and meadow, (d) upland or highland meadow, and (e) pasturage. The lists also give the number and taxable value of houses and barns. The per-poll figures for the three groups of towns are calculated by adding the taxable value of the various types of land and property for all of the towns in a particular group and dividing that figure by the number of polls who resided in the same groups of towns.

the most valuable land and had the highest per-poll acreage. Even group A, which includes such completely urbanized towns as Boston, Newburyport, Salem, Marblehead, and Plymouth, had more acreage per poll at a higher valuation than did the group C towns. These least commercial group C towns held the least valuable land and their citizens owned the smallest amount of improved acreage.

The same conditions persisted even in the four western counties and the District of Maine. (See table 10.) In the west the average holding of a poll in a group A or B town was three improved acres larger and £1.6 more valuable than the holding of a typical poll in a group C town. In Maine the holdings of the group C towns also lagged behind. Only in eastern Massachusetts did the group C communities, with a mere 9 percent of the region's polls, have higher

TABLE 10

Agricultural Wealth by Region

| | Eastern Region | | | Western Region | | | Maine Region | | |
| | | Per Poll | | | Per Poll | | | Per Poll | |
Towns	Polls	Improved Acreage	Taxable Value[a]	Polls	Improved Acreage	Taxable Value[a]	Polls	Improved Acreage	Taxable Value[a]
Group A	60%	12.35	£3.54	18%	16.55	£5.34	12%	12.58	£3.80
Group B	31	17.21	4.00	32	16.85	4.92	31	15.06	4.03
Group C	9	17.37	4.17	50	13.61	3.79	58	10.17	2.84

SOURCE: Evaluation, 1784/86.

NOTE: In this table the results are broken down by region and by group within the region. The value of barns is not included. The percentage in the polls column gives the proportion of rateable polls residing within each group of towns within each of the three regions. For example 60 percent of the total polls in the eastern region lived in the group A towns within only 12 percent of the polls in the District of Maine lived in the group A towns while

a. Taxable value of the improved acreage.

amounts of per-poll acreage and valuation than did the more commercial towns.

As can be seen, the comparative lack of agricultural wealth intensified the economic backwardness of the group C communities. Both the group B and C towns lacked commercial wealth, but the agricultural potential of the group B communities integrated them into a complex network of commercial agriculture that excluded most of the group C towns. In addition to all their other deficiencies, these least commercial communities, with the exception of the handful of group C towns in the eastern counties, were also land poor and so lacked a stable base for commercial agriculture. Thus shut out in both the commercial and agricultural sectors, these towns often opposed the political and economic programs sponsored by the wealthier communities.

Social, cultural, and institutional differences which made the wealthier towns more cosmopolitan helped push the three groups of communities further apart. The group A towns were favored in more than just raw wealth and wide contacts. They were comparatively large and old. Their populations were almost twice the size of the group B and four times the size of the group C towns, and most of them had been incorporated since the seventeenth century. (See table 11.) They had the political experience that

TABLE 11
Population, Age, and Political Involvement

Towns	Average Population (1784 Polls)	Percentage Incorporated			Percentage Between 1780–91 with Reps for		
		Between 1600–99	Between 1700–50	After 1750	9–11 Yrs.	6–8 Yrs.	0–5 Yrs.
Group A	577	78%	13%	10%	98%	2%	0%
Group B	325	39	39	23	70	24	6
Group C	153	3	18	82	14	25	61

SOURCES: To get the average size, the number of towns within each group is divided into the total number of 1784 polls living within that group. For the 1784 polls, see Evaluation 1784/86. For the incorporation dates of the towns, see Oscar Handlin and Mary Handlin, eds., *The Popular Sources of Political Authority: Documents on the Massachusetts Constitution of 1780* (Cambridge, Mass., 1966), pp. 933–42, with the sources cited on p. 933. Also see Thomas Fleet and John Fleet, *Fleet's Pocket Almanack for the Year of Our Lord 1792 . . . to Which Is Annexed the Massachusetts Register* (Boston, 1791), pp. 50–74 (cited hereafter as Fleet, *Register*, with the year and date of publication).

comes with age and the tax base to pay for sending numbers of representatives to the General Court as well as more talent to draw upon. Thus 53 of the 54 group A towns sent representatives to the lower house of the General Court for eight or more of the eleven years between 1780 and 1790 while, at the other extreme, three-fifths of the much newer group C towns sent representatives for less than five years during the eleven-year period.

Naturally these larger, older, and politically active group A towns became the institutional, cultural, and information centers. Between 1780 and 1791 they published all the commonwealth's newspapers, magazines, and imprints and thus controlled the flow of information and ideas out into the less commercial-cosmo-politan communities. (See table 12.) The same towns attracted

TABLE 12
Sociocultural Differences

Towns	Newspapers (1780–91)	Lawyers (1786)	Court Sessions (1786–91)	Magazines	Post Offices (1786)	Post Offices (1791)
Group A	100%	81%	64%	100%	100%	70%
Group B	0	14	18	0	0	13
Group C	0	5	18	0	0	17

SOURCES: Newspapers are in Clarence S. Brigham, comp., *History and Bibliography of American Newspapers, 1690–1820* (Worcester, 1947), 1:196–217, 311–416. Lawyers for 1786 are given in Fleet, *Register, 1787* (1786), p. 106. Court sessions for 1786 and 1792 are in ibid., *1787* (1786), pp. i–ii, and *1793* (1792), n.p., calendar section. Magazines are from Albert Matthews, "Lists of New England Magazines of the Eighteenth Century," in Colonial Society of Massachusetts, *Publications*, 13:69–74. Post offices are in Fleet, *Register, 1793* (1792), p. 63, and *1786* (1785), pp. 51–52.

over four-fifths of all the lawyers and held almost two-thirds of all the local and state court sessions that sat between 1780 and 1791, another factor extending their influence. Even at the most per-sonal level, a resident of a B or C town would usually have to come into an A town to pick up his mail because 70 to 100 per-cent of the post offices were located in the group A towns.

The fact that over four-fifths of the subscribers to the first Bos-ton edition of John Adams's *Defense of the Constitutions of Government* lived in these group A towns merely underlines the differences in outside intellectual and cultural interests that marked the citizens of the three groups of communities.[14]

Even in the less commercial regions of Maine and the west, the group A towns dominated social and cultural life. The commercial-cosmopolitan centers contained all the newspapers, had a longer corporate identity, and evidenced more political involvement than did the other two groups of towns. In both regions the group C, least commercial-cosmopolitan towns, had the least political involvement, the fewest lawyers, and the shortest history.

The degree and diversity of religious involvement serves as a final factor in describing the three groups of towns. The fact that all the group A towns had Congregational ministers and that over two-fifths housed competing denominations gave these communities greater contact with organized religious groups and made their citizens more tolerant of varied theological and denominational ideas. In Boston even the opening of a Roman Catholic church in 1789 created little stir. But in the more isolated group B and C communities, fewer towns had ministers and those communities which had churches generally had churches of only one denomination. (See table 13.) These less commercial-cosmopolitan towns

TABLE 13
Religious Differences

Towns	No Minister	Congregational Only	Congregational and Other	Non-Congregational Only
Group A	0%	57%	43%	0%
Group B	3	60	33	3
Group C	31	52	10	7

SOURCES: Fleet, *Register, 1792* (1791), pp. 98–105; *1787* (1786), pp. 51–58, and *1781* (1780), n.p.

remained either unaffected by theological and religious ideas or became intolerant of the religious practices of outside groups. Thus religious diversity underlined the economic, social, and cultural divisions among the groups of towns since the most cosmopolitan communities, having the most contact with differing religious traditions, became more liberal in their religious outlook.

14. John Adams, *A Defense of the Constitutions of Government of the United States of America* (Boston, 1788), contains a complete list of subscribers, by town, at the beginning of the volume.

The group A towns, with roughly one-third of the population, contained most of the commercial wealth, dominated most of the social and institutional activities within the state, and had the most contact with organized religion and the most denominational diversity. These 54 communities with wide-ranging economic, legal, cultural, social, and religious contacts and connections contained the lawyers, the courts, the newspapers, the commercial wealth, took the most active role in politics, and served as the headquarters for the political interest groups with the widest ranging political, social, and religious programs. At the other extreme the 201 least commercial-cosmopolitan towns had no newspapers, few lawyers, the least political involvement, the least commercial wealth, less agricultural wealth, and the fewest economic, social, cultural, political, or legal contacts with the wider society. These relatively isolated communities would become the base of operations for political interest groups that frequently opposed the programs of the politicians from the most commercial-cosmopolitan centers. The 88 group B towns with some commercial wealth, the greatest agricultural development, and some institutional and social connections with the outside society stood between the group A and C towns, not only in their contacts with the rest of the world, but also in their reactions to the crucial political questions that would divide the commonwealth during the 1780s.

2

Economy and Society: The Political Interest Groups

FOUR broad and vaguely defined categories of interests controlled the politics of these three groups of towns. These categories, ranging from most to least commercial and cosmopolitan, used the political power of the towns to secure their economic, political, and financial goals and to defend their vested judicial, religious, and institutional interests. The merchants, shipowners, fishermen, whalers, manufacturers, shipbuilders, traders, shopkeepers, investors, speculators, placeholders, lawyers, and ministers involved in wide-ranging commercial and social activities formed the most commercial-cosmopolitan category of interests with the greatest political strength in the 54 group A towns. The least commercial farmers with the fewest cultural, economic, or social contacts with the wider society controlled the political responses of many of the 201 least commercial-cosmopolitan communities. The artisans, sailors, and smaller manufacturers, generally concentrated in the group A towns, usually followed the political lead of the most commercial-cosmopolitan interests, while commercial farmers, strongest in the group B towns, fluctuated between the two extreme categories.

The most commercial-cosmopolitan interests, already strengthened by the Revolution, sought to improve their financial and economic status and defend the judicial, administrative, and political systems established by the commonwealth's new 1780 constitution. They demanded the refunding and repayment of the state and national debts, supported the judiciary, upheld the sanctity of private and public contracts, and defended the religious, political, and institutional arrangements that had been effected by the 1780 charter. The least commercial farmers opposed these programs when they appeared to attack their particular interests, became more and more disgruntled by their failure to defeat or influence legislation, and began to fear a shadowy conspiracy plotted by the most commercial-cosmopolitan interests to destroy their economic position and political power. The artisans and commercial farmers also fought to protect their interests, but their more commercial orientation made the programs of the merchants, placeholders, and speculators more palatable to their political and economic tastes.

The political responses of the three groups of towns reflected the concerns of their controlling interests. The 54 group A towns, represented by merchants, placeholders, and speculators, spearheaded efforts to consolidate and refund the state debt, pay the interest on the national debt, rely on heavy direct taxes levied on real property, and defend the established credit and judicial systems. The 201 group C communities, generally controlled by subsistence farmers, opposed these plans, usually with limited success, while the group B towns, typically controlled by commercial farmers, were in the middle.

The most commercial-cosmopolitan category of interests, strongest in the group A towns and comprising a multiplicity of commercial and professional groups with complex political goals, cooperated on a wide range of issues ranging from taxation and finance through the defense of the 1780 constitution. The commercial-cosmopolitan interest's political strength was augmented by the ministers and placeholders who frequently represented the B and C towns but who cooperated with the commercial interests instead of supporting policies favored by their constituents. On vote after vote between 1780 and 1791 the representatives of the group A towns and placeholders from the group B and C communities supported the demands, the programs, and the political aims of the commercial-cosmopolitan interests.

The merchants and shipowners with their local, national, and international social and economic connections played a leading role among the most commercial-cosmopolitan category of interests. They faced serious challenges from the policies of other nations and states but their greatest political differences with less commercial-cosmopolitan groups in the commonwealth resulted from their support of taxation, credit, and judicial policies that seemed to trespass on the interests of these other groups. Their wide-ranging activities, their control over shipping, their need to find markets for the great variety of Massachusetts exports, and their imports of a large range of foreign commodities made them the most commercial and cosmopolitan of all the varied interests. By the 1790s they controlled over 25 percent of the tonnage of the entire American merchant marine and owned 40 percent of the tonnage involved in the nation's coastal trade. Their ships accounted for 71 to 98 percent of the total tonnage of all ships plying between the commonwealth and the rest of the world.[1] Their markets spread from Rhode Island to China. In 1787 30 percent of their exports went to Europe, 30 percent to other parts of the United States, 25 percent to the West Indies, and 15 percent to Africa and the East Indies.[2] Although they dispatched a wide range of commodities to these far-flung shores, in 1787 fishing and whaling products accounted for 40 percent, timber for 15 percent, manufactured products for 14 percent, and tropical and West Indian reexports for about 9 percent of the total value of their exports.[3] In exchange for these, they imported coffee, sugar, molasses, and cocoa from the West Indies, manufactured goods from Great Britain, wines from Iberia and the Atlantic islands, iron from Russia, and tea from China and the islands of the Indian

1. The ownership of tonnage for Massachusetts during the early 1790s may be found in the *American State Papers: Documents Legislative and Executive*, 38 vols. (Washington, 1832-61), *Commerce*, 1:26, 27, 29, 39, for the years 1789-1792 with a general table on 1:896. For coastal trade see: 1:39, 41, 43, 44. For foreign and domestic tonnage engaged in importing goods into the state see 1:52 for 1789, 1:207 for 1790, 1:255 for 1791. [Leonard Jarvis], "Report of the Comptroller-General" [1787], in *Massachusetts Magazine*, March 1789, pp. 167-69, gives data for 1787. The Reports of Naval Officers filed among the Treasurer's Papers, Office of the Secretary, Boston (in early 1964 located in the attic of the capitol building), especially those for Salem and Newburyport for the years 1787-1789, give a detailed picture of the comparative lack of foreign shipping using these ports.

2. [Jarvis], "Report," pp. 167-69, gives an excellent statistical survey of Massachusetts exports for 1787. His data is broken down by product and region. For additional data see *Essex Journal*, 8 Apr. 1789, which gives estimates for trade in 1788, and James Swan, *National Arithmetick, or Observations on the Finances of Massachusetts* (Boston, 1786), pp. 2-5, for a good general survey. According to data in the *Hampshire Gazette*, 23 July 1788, Boston accounted for almost 50% of the total value of goods exported during 1787.

3. [Jarvis], "Report," pp. 167-69.

Ocean.[4] During the 1780s they developed new trading patterns as their captains began to arrive at a number of new ports of call ranging from St. Petersburg to Canton.[5] Individual merchants, often engaged in trade with several different areas, kept informed of their complex affairs by the reports of their factors, supercargoes, and captains. All of these contacts, connections, and interests gave them knowledge about economic, political, cultural, and religious developments throughout the nation and the entire world.[6] These hardheaded, hard-working businessmen thus be-

4. Imports for the early 1790s may be found in *American State Papers: Commerce*, 1:66-72, 163-65, 320-21, and 927.

5. The following secondary sources give an excellent overview of the wide-ranging nature of Massachusetts trade during the 1780s: Samuel Eliot Morison, *The Maritime History of Massachusetts* (Boston, 1941), pp. 27-94; James Duncan Phillips, *Salem and the Indies* (Boston, 1947) and *Salem in the Eighteenth Century* (Boston, 1937), both passim; Benjamin W. Labaree, *Patriots and Partisans: The Merchants of Newburyport, 1764-1815* (Cambridge, Mass., 1962), pp. 54-66, 97-98; John J. Babson, *History of the Town of Gloucester, Cape Ann, Including the Town of Rockport* (Gloucester, 1860), pp. 565-71; "Notes on Commerce," in *The Papers of Thomas Jefferson*, ed. Julian P. Boyd et al. (Princeton, 1950-), 6:339-46, 349; Rhoda Dorsey, "The Resumption of Anglo-American Commerce" (Ph.D. diss., University of Minnesota, 1956), passim, especially pp. 345, 354½, 362, 383; Richard H. McKey, "Elias Haskett Derby and the Founding of the Eastern Trade," in Essex Institute, *Historical Collections* 98:1-26, 65-84; Hamilton Andrews Hill, *The Trade and Commerce of Boston, 1630-1890* (Boston, 1895), pp. 71-87; James R. Pringle, *History of the Town and City of Gloucester, Cape Ann, Massachusetts* (Gloucester, 1892), pp. 83-84.

6. For the activities of individual merchants see McKey, "Derby and the Eastern Trade," 98:1-26, 65-84; K. W. Porter, *The Jacksons and the Lees*, 2 vols. (Cambridge, Mass., 1937), 1:24-25, 47-49. For some examples of activities covered in manuscript materials see Lee and Cabot to Captain Joshua Ellinwood, 20 Mar. 1787, Lee-Cabot Papers, Massachusetts Historical Society. For examples of the activities of a single Boston merchant see Bills of Lading in the Caleb Davis Papers, Massachusetts Historical Society. These include: *William* (to the West Indies), 24 Apr. 1787; *Juno* (to Great Britain), 12 Apr. 1787; *Union* (to Wilmington, N.C.), 4 Mar. 1786; *Hawk* (to Newfoundland), 16 Sept. 1783; *William* (to Ireland), 23 Oct. 1792. For the complexities of mercantile business see Thomas Sarjeant, *An Introduction to the Counting House; or a Short Specimen of Mercantile Precedents, Adapted to the Present Situation of the Trade and Commerce of the United States of America* (Philadelphia, 1789), pp. 5-14, 19, 27-29. The statistics in Dorsey, "Resumption," p. 383, show both the complexity and the changing patterns of Boston's trade during the 1780s.

came more commercial and more cosmopolitan than the other interests in the commonwealth.

This hustling, capable, and cosmopolitan group constantly provided openings for the young and ambitious and welcomed into its ranks many persons not considered as merchants in the strict eighteenth-century definition of that term. In Boston, for example, only 14 percent of the 236 men who owned shares in five or more ships between 1789 and 1795 had been listed as merchants in the 1789 *Boston Directory*. The artisans, traders, and professionals who owned these shares became integrated into the interest and thus increased its political power in the eastern and Maine port towns.[7] Yet even the more exclusive ranks of the merchants were opened because of vacancies left by the Revolution, death, or bankruptcy. In Boston only 72 of the 123 merchants listed in the 1789 *Directory* had appeared in the "Assessor's Taking Books" for 1780, and of those 72 only 25 had been listed as merchants.[8]

This broadly based, dynamic interest group faced a complex series of economic and political problems. Foreign regulations worried the merchants and interfered with their trade. Britain regulated commerce with the new United States through a series of orders in council which could be changed at will, levied high duties on American whaling imports, closed her colonial ports to American bottoms, and refused to make a commercial treaty with

7. These figures are based upon a comparison of John Norman, ed., *The Boston Directory, Containing a List of the Merchants, Mechanics, Traders and Others of the Town of Boston* (Boston, 1789) (cited hereafter as Norman, *Directory*), which gives the names and occupations of about 1,400 residents with the indexes in the Survey of Federal Archives, Division of Professional and Service Projects, Works Progress Administration, *Ship Registers and Enrollments of Boston and Charlestown, 1789-1795*, 2 vols. (Boston, 1941), which gives the names of all the persons holding interests in ships between 1789 and 1796.

8. Labaree, *Patriots and Partisans*, pp. 84-91, 94-97, describes these changes in an important "outport." Boston data is based upon the occupations given in the Norman, *Directory*, compared with the "Assessor's Taking Books of the Town of Boston" [1780], in Bostonian Society, *Publications*, 9:9-59, that lists the names of all Boston taxpayers in 1780 and gives occupations for the residents of about three-quarters of Boston's twelve wards. For a general view of urban mobility in America during this period see Jackson T. Main, *The Social Structure of Revolutionary America* (Princeton, 1965), pp. 185-96.

the infant republic.[9] France experimented with a monopolistic tobacco contract, changed port regulations in the West Indies, and attempted to lure Nantucket whalers to Dunkirk.[10] The Barbary powers seized American ships, enslaved sailors, and demanded payment of tribute.[11] At home other states established imposts and duties, passed inspection laws, and adopted tonnage and shipping regulations that troubled many merchants.[12] But the merchants had little difficulty within Massachusetts in finding support for

9. British restrictions are covered in Dorsey, "Resumption," pp. 345-54. The *American Museum*, July 1792, pp. 54-56, gives a complete list of the numerous British restrictions and regulations. The restrictions on the important trade to Nova Scotia are covered in John Hird [Hurd] to John Adams, 17 Apr. 1790, Adams Papers, pt. 4, Adams Manuscript Trust. John Temple to Lord Walsingham, 11, 12 Mar. 1784, in Bowdoin-Temple Papers, Massachusetts Historical Society, *Collections*, 6th ser., vol. 9 (1897) and 7th ser., vol. 6, (1907); 7th ser., vol. 6, pp. 33-36, gives an informative protest against British regulations. Edmund C. Burnett's two articles, "Note on American Negotiations for Commercial Treaties," *American Historical Review* 16:579-87, and "Observations of London Merchants on American Trade, 1783," ibid., 18:769-80, are also informative.

10. An excellent account of the French regulations during the 1780s is found in George Cabot to Alexander Hamilton, 18 Dec. 1791, in Henry Cabot Lodge, *The Life and Letters of George Cabot* (Boston, 1877), pp. 49-51. An example of newspaper interest is found in the *American Herald*, 6 Dec. 1784, and in the *Massachusetts Centinel*, 3 Oct. 1787. For an overview see Henri Sée, "Commerce Between France and the United States, 1783-1784," *American Historical Review* 31:732-52. For the Nantucket whalers see Alexander Starbuck, *The History of Nantucket County, Island and Town Including Genealogies of First Settlers* (Boston, 1924), pp. 393-400, and Gerald S. Graham, "The Migration of the Nantucket Whale Fishery: An Episode in British Colonial Policy," *New England Quarterly* 8:179-202.

11. The Barbary menace is covered in Thomas Jefferson to John Adams, 27 Nov. 1785; ibid., 11 and 30 May 1786; and John Adams to Jefferson, 6 June 1786, all in Boyd, ed., *Papers of Jefferson*, 9:64, 506, 594-95, and 611. For other reactions see Rufus King to Caleb Davis, 7 Nov. 1785, Caleb Davis Papers, Massachusetts Historical Society, and Otto to Vergennes, 8 Oct. and 25 Dec. 1785, in George Bancroft, *History of the Formation of the Constitution of the United States of America*, 2 vols. (New York, 1882), 1:460, 474-75. For a newspaper reaction see *Salem Gazette*, 1 Nov. 1785.

12. For the importance of the inspection laws of the various states see Stephen Higginson to John Adams, 21 Dec. 1789, Adams Papers, pt. 4. For the effort in 1785 to form some sort of joint front among the states in response to British policy see ch. 5. Notice especially the discussion with the New Hampshire delegates in *Acts and Laws of the Commonwealth of Massachusetts, 1780-1797*, 11 vols. (Boston, 1890-1897) (cited hereafter as *Acts and Laws*), 16 June 1785, 3:718-19.

programs designed to meet these problems. Even the least commercial-cosmopolitan farmers and towns supported anti-British navigation acts, tonnage duties that favored Massachusetts shipowners, the granting of additional commercial powers to the confederation, the construction of lighthouses, and the payment of bounties on exported whale oil.[13] All of this important legislation passed the General Court without the formality of a roll call vote and even during the debates over the new national constitution in the years 1787 and 1788 both the farmers and the antifederalists had no objections to the commercial provisions in the proposed charter.[14]

The critical political differences between the merchants and the less commercial-cosmopolitan interests developed over domestic financial, economic, and institutional questions. The merchants supported taxation that discriminated in favor of commercial and liquid property. In 1784 the ten leading shipowning towns contained only 12 percent of the total taxpaying males who held two-thirds of the state's inventory, 72 percent of her vessel tonnage, and 87 percent of her wharfage facilities, but were assessed for only 14 percent of the state's total tax bill.[15] One-third to two-fifths of the taxes levied between 1780 and 1786 were assessed on rateable polls alone and the remainder on personal and real property. These taxes had to be paid in specie or paper money

13. The best secondary account of the wide range of economic legislation passed during the early 1780s is in Oscar Handlin and Mary Handlin, *Commonwealth—A Study of the Role of Government in the American Economy: Massachusetts, 1774-1861* (New York, 1947), pp. 53-92. The Handlins did not give enough attention to the commonwealth's efforts to regulate foreign commerce although some of the most important legislation is noted here. See *Acts and Laws*, 23 June 1785, 3:439-43, for the basic anti-British legislation. The act of 29 Nov. 1785, ibid., 3:489, modified this for all except British ships. The act of 5 July 1786, ibid., 4:36, suspended the act of 23 June 1785 against British shipping. Tonnage duties were established in the act of 1 July 1784, ibid., 3:34-41 and 52-57. Light money, collected to finance the construction and repair of lighthouses is covered in the act of 22 Oct. 1783, ibid., 2:543-45; 2 July 1784, ibid., 3:46; and 8 July 1786, ibid., 4:66. Whale oil bounties were authorized in an act of 28 Nov. 1785, ibid., 3:795-97.

14. The absence of political divisions over these commercial policies is discussed in ch. 4 and the debates over the new national Constitution are covered in chs. 8 and 9.

15. Evaluation, 1784/86, in vol. 163 of the unpublished Massachusetts Archives, Office of the Secretary, Boston, contains the amount of the taxable value of wharfage, inventory, and vessel tonnage of the shipowning towns. The 1781 evaluation is in *Acts and Laws*, 6 Mar. 1782, 1:903-06.

and securities. The commercial towns, with more liquid assets, could pay them, but by early 1787 many other towns had fallen so far behind in their collections that the treasurer had issued legal executions against them for the payment of back taxes. The ten leading shipowning towns, with the exception of Dartmouth, accounted for less than 2.5 percent of all the uncollected back taxes out on execution.[16] In addition to defending the tax system, the merchants opposed tender laws and the suspension of suits for debt and defended the judges who upheld the sanctity of contracts and the prompt repayment of debts. They supported these policies and institutions because their prosperity depended upon the free flow of credit and they feared reforms which would dam this stream and create a commercial recession.[17]

The political stronghold of the merchants lay in these ten leading shipowning towns. (See table 14.) Men classified as merchants served over 50 percent of the terms as representatives in the lower house for Boston, Newburyport, Salem, and New Bedford, and in Boston they held over 42 percent of the terms of selectmen and

16. The uncollected back taxes for which legal executions had been issued are given for every town in "Executions at the Death of the Late Treasurer Ivers" (Early 1787), in Papers of the Treasurer, Office of the Secretary, Boston.

17. The best secondary account of inland trade connections is in Margaret E. Martin, "Merchants and Trade of the Connecticut River Valley, 1750-1820," Smith College Studies in History, 34:40-42, 133-66. Robert A. East, Business Enterprise in the American Revolutionary Era (New York, 1938), pp. 52-53, gives some of the interstate connections. The Caleb Davis Papers contain five lists of excise accounts for loaf sugar sales covering the periods May 1788 to Nov. 1788, Nov. 1788 to May 1789, May 1789 to Nov. 1789, Nov. 1789 to May 1790, and May 1790 to Nov. 1790. For the importance of British credit see "Notes on Commerce," in Boyd, ed., Papers of Jefferson, 7:339; Harrison Ansley and Company to John Hancock, 26 Apr. 1784, Hancock Papers, Massachusetts Historical Society; Labaree, Patriots and Partisans, pp. 61-62; Porter, Jacksons and Lees, 1:45-46.

For the dangers of a specie drain to Britain, see Massachusetts Centinel, 14 May, 24, 31 Aug., 10 Sept. 1785; Independent Chronicle, 18 Mar. 1784; Worcester Magazine, July 1787, p. 237; Swan, National Arithmetick, pp. 81-83. Forrest McDonald, The Formation of the American Republic, 1776-1790 (Baltimore, 1965), p. 131, especially fn. 48, gives another discussion. McDonald fails to note that the data in vol. 163 of the Massachusetts Archives give the amounts of money loaned out by citizens of various communities. Thus these statistics do not show the debts owed by local citizens but instead indicate the debts that were payable to them.

TABLE 14
The Merchants

			Percentage of			
Towns	*Num-ber*	*Polls*	*Ton-nage*	*Value of Wharf-age*	*Senators (1780-91)*	*Repre-sentatives (1780-90)*
Eastern and Western						
Ten leading	10	12%	72%	86%	16%	11%
Other shipowning	90	31	28	14	31	25
Nonshipowning	243	57	0	0	53	64
Maine						
Shipowning	42	68	100	100	83	75
Nonshipowning	47	32	0	0	17	25

SOURCES: *Acts and Laws of the Commonwealth of Massachusetts, 1780-1797*, 11 vols. (Boston, 1890-1897) (cited hereafter as *Acts and Laws*); Thomas Fleet and John Fleet, *Fleet's Pocket Almanack for the Year of Our Lord [1780-1790] . . . to Which Is Annexed the Massachusetts Register* (Boston, 1779-1789) (cited hereafter as Fleet, *Register*, with the year and date of publication); and the polls, wharfage, and tonnage are from the Evaluation, 1784/86, in vol. 163 of the unpublished Massachusetts Archives, Office of the Secretary, Boston (cited hereafter as Evaluation, 1784/86).

72 percent of the terms as overseers of the poor.[18] Many merchants served in the state senate, the confederation and national congresses, and two of them, John Hancock and James Bowdoin, held the governor's office for the entire period between 1780 and 1791. The ten leading shipowning towns sent about 16 percent of the total membership of the state senate and 11 percent of the total representatives to the lower house between 1780 and 1791.

18. Representatives from these communities may be identified in the annual lists in the *Acts and Laws* and in the unpublished Journals. of the House of Representatives, available at the Office of the Secretary, Boston. (See ch. 1, fn. 6, for details.) Names of the selectmen and overseers of the poor for Boston are listed in *Reports of the Record Commissioners of the City of Boston*, 39 vols. (Boston, 1876-1909), vols. 26 and 31. Occupations and business activities of representatives from the various commercial towns may be found in the following sources· Gardner W. Allen, "Massachusetts Privateers of the Revolution," in Massachusetts Historical Society, *Collections*, vol. 77, lists most of the persons who were involved in privateering during the war; Norman, *Directory*, and the "Assessor's Taking Books" [1780] give occupations for Boston; Phillips, *Salem in the Eighteenth Century* and *Salem in the Indies*, gives the occupations of many Salem representatives; Labaree, *Patriots and Partisans*, does the same for Newburyport. Other useful local histories include Charles B. Hawes, *Gloucester by Land and*

The representatives sent by the ninety other towns with some shipping tonnage swelled the strength of the mercantile interest to 47 percent of the senators and 36 percent of the total membership of the lower house during the same twelve-year period. In Maine, which was often considered a frontier area, the forty-two towns with some tonnage sent 83 percent of the senators and 75 percent of the representatives who sat in the General Court as delegates from the district. [19]

The fishermen and whalers depended on the merchants to finance their operations and to market their catch. Since the fishing and whaling industry provided over 40 percent of the total value of the commonwealth's exports in 1787, the merchants had a considerable interest in the development of that industry, many of them actually owning fishing and whaling vessels. Almost two-thirds of the fishermen as of 1786 lived in the ten leading ship-owning towns where they followed the political lead of the local merchants. [20] Even the fishermen in the poorer B and C fishing

---

Sea: The Story of a New England Sea Coast Town (Boston, 1923); Thomas F. Waters, Ipswich in the Massachusetts Bay Colony, 2 vols. (Ipswich, 1917), especially 2:600 ff.; D. Hamilton Hurd, ed., History of Essex County, Massachusetts, with Biographical Sketches of Many of Its Pioneers and Prominent Men, 2 vols. (Philadelphia, 1888), esp. 1:754, 756, 762; D. Hamilton Hurd, ed., History of Plymouth County, with Biographical Sketches of Many of Its Pioneers and Prominent Men, 2 vols. (Philadelphia, 1889), esp. 1:150, 156, 157; Daniel Ricketson, The History of New Bedford, Bristol County, Massachusetts, Including a History of the Old Township of Dartmouth (New Bedford, 1858); D. Hamilton Hurd, ed., History of Bristol County, Massachusetts, with Biographical Sketches of Many of Its Pioneers and Prominent Men (Philadelphia, 1883), pp. 53-55, 141-43; Samuel Roads, Jr., The History and Traditions of Marblehead (Boston, 1880). Several newspapers were also helpful: Plymouth Journal, Jan.-June 1786; Salem Gazette, 1782-1784, Jan.-Nov. 1785; Salem Mercury, Jan.-Mar. 1787 and Oct.-Dec. 1787; Essex Journal, July-Dec. 1784 and all of 1785.

19. Lists of representatives were compiled from the sources in ch. 1, fn. 6. Names of the senators are found in the Acts and Laws immediately preceeding those of the representatives. The residence of the senators may be determined by comparing the list of senators with the lists of justices and place-holders which were published each year in Thomas Fleet and John Fleet, Fleet's Pocket Almanack for the Year of Our Lord [1780-1790] . . . to Which Is Annexed the Massachusetts Register (Boston, 1779-1789) (cited hereafter as Fleet, Register, with the year and date of publication) between 1779 and 1789.

20. The best single account for the fisheries is [Thomas Jefferson], "Report on the Fisheries," American State Papers: Commerce, 1: 8-13, which gives the number of fishermen, the catch, tonnage of fishing vessels, etc., by

communities, if interested in politics at all, supported the programs initiated by the most commercial interests in the leading commercial-cosmopolitan centers.[21]

Shipbuilders extended the influence of the most commercial-cosmopolitan interest groups into many towns that had little or no shipping tonnage in 1784. Between 1783 and 1795 at least 67 Massachusetts towns built ships and these yards employed local artisans who constructed the vessels and fabricated their equipment, local farmers and laborers who provided the muscle and a few skills, and lumbermen who cut and transported the required timber.[22] These builders, whether capitalists, artisans, laborers, or

---

town. [Jarvis], "Report," 167-69 gives the exports of fishing products from Massachusetts. *American Museum*, Mar. 1789, pp. 257-59, and Apr. 1789, p. 358, covers whaling. Other information is available in *American Museum*, May 1791, pp. 283-84; *Massachusetts Magazine*, Feb. 1791, pp. 73-76, and Mar. 1791, pp. 149-51. Swan, *National Arithmetick*, pp. 5-12, gives further details. For Barnstable County see Frederick Freeman, *History of Cape Cod*, 2 vols. (Boston, 1858-1862), 2:399-402; for oyster fishery at Eastham see Charles F. Swift, *Cape Cod, the Right Arm of Massachusetts* (Yarmouth, Mass., 1897), pp. 314, 319, and Henry C. Kitteridge, *Cape Cod—Its People and Their History* (Cambridge, Mass. 1930), pp. 172-73, 184-91. For whaling at New Bedford see Hurd, ed., *Bristol County*, pp. 66-69.

21. Chapter 4 describes the voting patterns of the Barnstable and Maine group B and C shipbuilding and fishing towns. The General Court often abated taxes on these communities because of their poverty during and immediately after the war; see *Acts and Laws*, 2 Dec. 1780, 1:202 for Marblehead; 31 Jan. 1781, 1:246-47 for Chatham, Eastham, Yarmouth, Manchester, and Harwich; 9 May 1781, 1:449 for Truro, Wellfleet, Eastham, Harwich, Yarmouth, Chatham, Barnstable, Sandwich, and Falmouth (Barnstable); 19 June 1781, 1:630 for Dukes County.

22. Statistics on shipbuilding are compiled from: *Ship Registers and Enrollements of Boston and Charlestown, 1789-1795* for Boston; Survey of Federal Archives, Division of Professional and Service Projects, Works Progress Administration, *Ship Registers of the District of Plymouth, Massachusetts, 1789-1908* (Boston, 1939); "Gloucester Ship Registers" in Essex Institute, *Historical Collections*, 77:363-78; 78:42-64, 177-92, 265-80, 387-404; 79:65-80, 177-92, 293-308, 387-402; 80:71-78, 180-91; "Salem Ship Registers" in ibid., 39:185-208; 40:49-72, 177-200, 217-40, 314-36; 41:141-64, 309-32, 357-80; 42:89-110; "Newburyport Ship Registers" in ibid., 70:60-92, 185-200, 283-314, 387-418; 71:81-96, 167-98, 267-98, 351-66; 72:159-74, 261-76; 73:88-99. Unfortunately these computations do not include vessels registered in southern Massachusetts or in the District of Maine, but they still give a good sample of the spread of the shipbuilding industry since all the registration data gives the town at which the registered vessel was constructed.

farmers, had a vested interest in commercial prosperity. Moreover, with an income from wages they escaped many of the taxation and credit problems that plagued some commercial and many subsistence farmers.[23] Due to its dependence upon local supplies of timber the industry spread up and down the coast of the commonwealth. The ten leading shipowning towns owned 70 percent but built only one-fourth of the total ships, while 21 group B towns constructed 37 percent of the total ships built between 1780 and 1795. Seven towns with absolutely no shipping tonnage in 1784 produced 7 percent of the total ships and communities with less than 100 tons of shipping slid almost one-fifth of the new vessels into the water.[24] Thus this industry extended the influence of the most commercial category of interests into many of the smaller coastal towns of the commonwealth.

The wealthier manufacturers and the most valuable factories clustered in the ten leading shipowning towns. These ten communities possessed 90 percent of the value of all the distilleries and 100 percent of the value of all ropewalks. In Boston, Salem, and Newburyport, a number of distillers became relatively wealthy and engaged in commerce as well as in manufacturing, and in Boston and Salem merchants chartered corporations to produce glass and cotton cloth. Merchants exported the rum and used the rigging produced by these commercially oriented manufacturers who thus became tightly integrated with the mercantile interest.[25]

23. The best account of the impact of shipbuilding on the local economy is in L. Vernon Briggs, *History of Shipbuilding on the North River, Plymouth County, Massachusetts, 1640-1872* (Boston, 1889), especially pp. 47-49, 66-68, 89, 93, 129, 164-74. Also see Hurd, ed., *Bristol County*, pp. 112, 170, 229; Morison, *Maritime History*, 105. For some data on the Maine industry see Samuel Parkman to Henry Knox, 24 July 1788, Knox Papers, Massachusetts Historical Society; Benjamin Lincoln to Daniel Little, 15 Dec. 1788, Miscellaneous Papers, Massachusetts Historical Society; William Hutchinson Rowe, *The Maritime History of Maine: Three Centuries of Shipbuilding and Sea Faring* (New York, 1948), pp. 66-67. The *American Museum*, May 1787, p. 436, claimed that ships could be built in New England for one-third the English price.

24. For ships built between 1780 and 1795 see fn. 22. The amount of tonnage owned in each town is from Evaluation, 1784/86.

25. The location and taxable value of distilleries and ropewalks are given in the Evaluation, 1784/86. For an excellent description of Boston in the early 1790s see Thomas Pemberton, "A Topographical and Historical Description of Boston, 1794," in Massachusetts Historical Society, *Collections*, 1st ser., 3:241-301. For an overview of manufacturing see East, *Business Enterprise*, pp. 312-13; Handlin and Handlin, *Commonwealth*, pp. 81-82, 110-12; Main,

If these merchants, shipowners, fishermen, whalers, shipbuilders, and larger manufacturers were the backbone of the mercantile interest, the large number of shopkeepers and traders in the inland A and B towns were the ribs. These traders and shopkeepers did not belong to a single socioeconomic class. Many who resided in Boston and other leading mercantile centers were wealthier than some merchants, and a few in the Connecticut valley and the western shire towns had contracts with national networks of financiers and speculators.[26] But the majority of traders scattered from Stockbridge to Machias ran their small shops and taverns on a financial shoestring.[27] All of the inland traders and shopkeepers needed contacts with eastern or coastal merchants or wholesalers who provided the markets for western produce and a supply of manufactured and West Indian goods. The ten leading shipowning towns, which contained 93 percent of the taxable value of all warehouse facilities, served as the headquarters for the wholesale trade with the smaller traders. These traders also required a constant supply of credit from their wholesalers and, in turn, had to extend loans to the small farmers and artisans who purchased goods at their mills, stores, and taverns. This gave them, too, a

---

Social Structure, pp. 38-39; George Cabot to Alexander Hamilton, 6 Sept. 1791, in Lodge, *Cabot*, pp. 43-46. Exports of rum are given in [Jarvis], "Report," pp. 167-69. Charters for the new manufacturing activities may be found in *Acts and Laws*, 6 July 1787, 4:567-69, for glass; 3 Feb. 1789, 5:71-73, for cotton.

26. The location of stores is from the Evaluation, 1784/86. For the connection between a city merchant and a retail trader see Articles of Agreement, dated 6 April 1784, in the Caleb Davis Papers.

27. The best secondary account of the importance of credit to inland storekeepers is in Martin, "Merchants and Trade," pp. 16-17, 40-42, 114, 118, 119, 133-37. Private History, 10 Dec. 1791 (but located in the box for 1785), Miscellaneous Papers, Massachusetts Historical Society, gives an interesting account of a western trader during the 1780s. A large number of advertisements in the western papers, especially the *Western Star, Worcester Spy, Worcester Magazine, Hampshire Gazette, Hampshire Chronicle*, and the *Massachusetts Gazette* (Springfield) often give the types of goods sold by the traders and the local produce accepted by them. Some correspondence also deals with questions of credit and debts. See especially Mrs. Abigail Dwight to Mrs. Martin, 10 Jan. 1785, Sedgwick Papers, Massachusetts Historical Society, and Mrs. Martin to Mrs. A. Dwight, 26 July 1785, ibid. Some of the problems in collecting debts are described in Samuel Sewall to George Thatcher, 25 June 1787, Miscellaneous Papers, Massachusetts Historical Society; Samuel Dexter to Rev. William Lyman, 25 Jan. 1785, Miscellaneous Papers; Artemas Ward, Jr., to Samuel P. Savage, 4 Apr. 1788, Samuel P. Savage Papers, Massachusetts Historical Society.

vested interest in upholding the sanctity of contracts and in defending the judicial system that protected credit. They naturally opposed measures such as stay laws or legislation suspending the collection of debts that would dry up the flow of credit.[28] They had little to complain about with the tax system that bore heaviest on real property and undervalued their inventories and accounts receivable.

In all sections of the state the shopkeepers and traders with the most valuable stores and the largest inventories located their businesses in the 54 most commercial-cosmopolitan towns. Only 22 percent of all stores were located in the ten leading shipowning towns, but these were housed in the most valuable and best equipped buildings (worth 48 percent of the total value of stores) and were by far the best stocked (contained 80 percent of the state's total inventory). By contrast the comparable 18 percent of the total stores located in the group C towns were worth 9 percent of the total and held less than 2 percent of the inventory, and this paucity was divided among 201, not 10, communities.

The same pattern prevailed in the four western counties. The twenty most commercial-cosmopolitan towns contained 98 percent of the value of all western warehouses and one-third of the stores worth nearly one-half of the western total with almost three-fifths of the inventory. At the other extreme the one-third of stores located in the 107 western group C towns were worth only one-fourth of the total western valuation and had less than one-tenth of the total western inventory, but were nevertheless expected to serve over 50 percent of the region's polls.[29]

This concentration of commercial wealth in the relatively small number of western group A towns caused these towns to identify with the eastern mercantile interests rather than the local agrarian ones. Their representatives supported the programs of the mercantile interests rather than those of the less commercial farmers and towns in their own region.[30]

28. The number and taxable value of warehouses is given in Evaluation, 1784/86. East, *Business Enterprise*, pp. 84-85, 105, 114, 122, gives information about the wider connections of the Connecticut valley traders. Also note Martin, "Merchants and Trade," pp. 149-54, 156-62.

29. The Evaluation, 1784/86, contains the number of stores, their taxable value, the amount of inventory, and the number and taxable value for warehouses in all of the towns in the state.

30. See ch. 4 for the manner in which the representatives of the western group A towns consistently voted in opposition to delegates from the western B and C communities on a wide range of issues in the 1780s.

Another speculative interest overlapped the mercantile and trading concerns. Many merchants and traders also invested and speculated in banks, internal improvements, land, and governmental securities. Everyone with spare cash—from wealthy merchants to farm laborers—loaned money, often at usurious rates. These speculators generally supported mercantile political goals at the same time as they pursued a program designed to force the refunding and payment of the national and state debts and to protect the collection of interest and principal on private loans.

Banking, as such, created little political dissension during the 1780s. The commonwealth's one bank, chartered in 1784 by Boston merchants, catered to their credit requirements and those of their allies, the shipowners, while refusing long-term loans to farmers, artisans, and manufacturers. This emphasis on commercial credit paid off in handsome dividends amounting to over 29 percent annually by the early 1790s. The fact that the Phillips family, which had controlled the bank since 1785, was collecting these dividends and spurning noncommercial borrowers made banking an important political issue after 1791.[31]

The lending policies of the moneyed men in the ten leading mercantile towns reinforced the credit policy of the commonwealth's single bank. With their better contacts they were in a position to know about and invest in potentially more profitable ventures involving government securities, insurance, and land. Consequently, they loaned out a smaller proportion of the money at interest than their holdings of silver and cash would have allowed. The more isolated capitalists in the remaining 44 group A and the 88 group B towns with less liquid wealth loaned out 54 percent of the total money at interest, a much greater proportion than their relative share of silver and cash.[32] This meant that the smaller group A and most of the group B towns had as much, if not more, interest in the problem of collecting private debts than did the residents of the ten leading shipowning communities.

These moneylenders and usurers, the only source for private

31. An excellent account of the early history of this bank is in N. S. B. Gras, *Massachusetts First National Bank of Boston* (Boston, 1937), pp. 17-30, 34-39, 538-40; dividends are listed on p. 581 and lending policies are described on pp. 45-58. Also see Handlin and Handlin, *Commonwealth*, pp. 107-08. For insurance, note East, *Business Enterprises*, pp. 69-70. There are some examples of insurance policies in the Caleb Davis Papers; see An Agreement dated 1 Sept. 1788, from Edward Payne's Office.

32. Evaluation, 1784/86 gives the amount of money lent at interest, money on hand, and ounces of silver for all the towns in the state.

loans, were especially important in the western counties. Concentrated in group A and B towns, they loaned out more than 85 percent of the region's money lent at interest. They serviced farmers who needed cash to buy land and livestock, to repair their houses and barns, to breed their cattle, or to pay their taxes, and they often charged exorbitant interest rates. Their ranks included representatives from all the important social and economic groups in the region—shopkeepers, placeholders, traders, and even yeoman farmers, ministers, and occasional farm laborers. With much less available capital, the westerners managed to lend 29 percent of the total money at interest, a fact that would make the creditor-debtor struggle as important in the west as in the east. The western money-lending interest would often complement the political strength of the western shopkeepers and traders to prevent many western communities from supporting stay legislation, reforms in the judiciary, and the suspension of debts favored by the majority of the region's polls.[33]

Acrimonious political disputes over internal improvements usually reflected factional quarrels among competing groups of investors who attempted to secure state charters or local approval for their schemes. The proposed bridge between Boston and either Charlestown or Cambridge resulted in a bitter struggle between the Cabot group based in the Beverly-Salem area and the local Boston merchants. The Cabots, after being rebuffed in Boston, secured a charter for the Salem-Beverly bridge in 1787.[34] Other investors

33. See ibid., for money lent out at interest from the western towns. Credit and usury are discussed in the *Massachusetts Centinel*, 26 Oct. 1785; *Continental Journal*, 26 Apr. 1782; *Independent Chronicle*, 27 Oct. 1785. Notice also James Sullivan to Rufus King, 25 Oct. 1785, Sullivan Papers, Massachusetts Historical Society (this is a collection of copies of Sullivan's correspondence); Samuel Dexter to William Cushing, 28 Jan. 1785, Robert Paine Papers, Massachusetts Historical Society. See *Acts and Laws*, 16 Mar. 1784, 2:637-39, for usury legislation.

34. The best secondary account is in Handlin and Handlin, *Commonwealth*, pp. 108-10. Primary sources include a massive collection of documents in the Public Papers Concerning the Act of 9 March 1785 in the Office of the Secretary, Boston. Petition of Cambridge, 11 Feb. 1785, supported Cabot's plan to build a bridge from west Boston to Cambridge. It is opposed by Petition of Charlestown, 12 Feb. 1785, and Petition of Medford, 9 Feb. 1785. Discussion of the Beverly Bridge may be located in Henry Jackson to Henry Knox, 18 Nov. 1787, Knox Papers; *Worcester Magazine*, Nov. 1787, p. 87; *Salem Mercury*, 26 June, 11 Sept., and 6 Nov. 1787. The 26 June 1787 issue states that 351 citizens voted on the proposal. This was more than voted for representatives to the ratification convention.

followed the lead of these large operators and secured charters for bridges located throughout the state.[35] When several of these enterprises paid high dividends and the refunding and assumption of the national and state debts in 1791 made additional capital available, speculators prevailed upon the General Court to approve a rash of projects ranging from a canal cut through Cape Cod to an inland waterway designed to link the Atlantic with the Connecticut valley.[36] These schemes never threatened the noncommercial interests, and the General Court was able either to approve or to reject them without resorting to roll call votes.

At both the national and the state levels, land speculators used political leverage to acquire more land or to defend their previous grants. Former Revolutionary officers demanded grants throughout the 1780s. The most important was Rufus Putnam who in 1786 organized the Ohio Company from former officers and speculators willing to finance their claims.[37] During the next year these Massachusetts claimants and investors joined forces with bigger operators from other states and secured a large chunk of Ohio from the Confederation Congress.[38] Another speculative coup was

35. For these other improvements see *Massachusetts Magazine*, Mar. 1792, p. 200; Lysander S. Richards, *History of Marshfield* (Plymouth, Mass., 1901), p. 128; Joseph Merrill, *History of Amesbury Including the First Seventeen Years of Salisbury, to the Separation in 1654; and Merrimac from Its Incorporation in 1876* (Haverhill, Mass., 1880), pp. 306-07. Also note Handlin and Handlin, *Commonwealth*, p. 109.

36. L. Vernon Briggs, *History and Genealogy of the Cabot Family, 1475-1927*, 2 vols. (Boston, 1927), 1:167, states that the Beverly Bridge paid a dividend of 28% per year.

For the flurry of interest in canals see Handlin and Handlin, *Commonwealth*, pp. 116-17. Also note *Massachusetts Magazine*, July 1792, p. 470, and *Hampshire Gazette*, 11 May 1791. *Massachusetts Magazine*, Jan. 1791, pp. 25-27, gives a support for a Cape Cod canal.

37. William Parker Cutler and Julia Perkins Cutler, *Life, Journals, and Correspondence of the Reverend Manasseh Cutler, LL.D.*, 2 vols. (Cincinnati, 1888), 1:152-54, 159-67, 173, 179-86. Sidney Kaplan, "Veteran Officers and Politics in Massachusetts, 1783-1787," *William and Mary Quarterly*, 3d ser. 9:29-57.

38. Cutler and Cutler, *Life of Cutler*, 1:191, 196, 293-94, 296. For action by Congress see Worthington C. Ford et al., ed., *Journals of the Continental Congress, 1774-1789*, 34 vols. (Washington, D.C., 1904-1937), 14 July 1787, 32:345-46; 17 July 1787, 32:350; 20 July 1787, 32:376-77. Also note Nathan Dane to Rufus King, 16 July 1787, in Cutler and Cutler, *Life of Cutler*, 1:371-72. See *Massachusetts Centinel*, 25 Jan. 1786, for the formation of the Ohio Company. Notice the "Articles of Agreement," 3 Mar. 1786, in Cutler and Cutler, *Life of Cutler*, 1:181-86.

engineered by Nathaniel Gorham, an influential merchant-politician, and Oliver Phelps, a Connecticut valley trader, when they purchased land in southwestern New York State that had been surrendered by the New Yorkers to the commonwealth in 1786. The land was to be paid for in state securities which they had yet to purchase. When these bonds rose in value beyond the price Phelps and Gorham were able to pay, they were forced to disgorge the grant which was then snapped up by Robert Morris and some Dutch associates.[39]

Land speculation in Maine involving many leading Massachusetts capitalists and politicians added to the chaos in the district's land system and helped build sentiment for secession from the commonwealth. During the seventeenth century and early eighteenth century, Massachusetts speculators had acquired disputed titles to large areas of Maine. By the 1780s a large number of important figures including the two governors, Hancock and Bowdoin, owned shares in these grants. These politicians and speculators created political tension in the district when they defended their claims against squatters and illegal timber cutters. During the 1780s the General Court granted additional lands, and in some areas serious disputes broke out between the speculators and the actual settlers.[40] Despite this friction, the constant disputes over land titles, and the threats of secession, the General Court con-

---

39. For an overall view see Ray Allan Billington, *Westward Expansion: A History of the American Frontier* (New York, 1949), pp. 251-55; Julius Goebel, Jr., ed., *The Law Practice of Alexander Hamilton, Documents and Commentary* (New York, 1964-), 1:553-84. The grant to Phelps and Gorham is in *Acts and Laws*, 1 Apr. 1788, 4:900-01. The court granted an extension in ibid., 23 June 1789, 5:579-80. The agreement with New York is in ibid., 16 Dec. 1786, 4:463-67. Also note East, *Business Enterprise*, pp. 320-21; Thomas C. Amory, *Life of James Sullivan with Selections from His Writings*, 2 vols. (Boston, 1859), 1:158-63, 172-74.

40. The best modern study of the Maine situation in the 1780s is Lawrence D. Bridgham, "Maine Public Lands, 1781-1795, Claims, Trespasses and Sales," (Ph.D. diss., Boston University, 1959). A short survey is in Douglas E. Leach, *The Northern Colonial Frontier, 1697-1763* (New York, 1966), pp. 172-75. A contemporary analysis is Benjamin Lincoln, "Observations on the Climate, Soil, and Value of the Eastern Counties in the District of Maine; Written in the Year 1789," in Massachusetts Historical Society, *Collections*, 1st ser., 4:150-52. Ronald F. Banks, *Maine Becomes a State: The Movement to Separate Maine from Massachusetts, 1785-1820* (Middletown, 1970) is the best political survey.

tinued to protect the older speculative interests and even promoted new ones throughout the 1780s.[41]

The greatest political dissension resulted from the efforts of the state and national securities holders to increase the value of their bonds and to secure interest payments. Massachusetts investors, who had by 1790 accumulated about $5.0 million worth of securities, agitated for the refunding and repayment of the national debt throughout the 1780s. Their local campaign succeeded in the spring of 1786 when they convinced the General Court to grant the confederation the use of "supplemental funds," levied by direct state taxes, for the purpose of paying interest on their securities. But defeat at the national level followed when New York rejected the 1783 congressional impost and several other states declined to provide the "supplemental funds." The confederation government's failure to discover revenue sources for funding its debt led many speculators to support the new national Constitution which provided the federal government with the necessary tax revenue for the payment of interest and even the principal on their large holdings.[42]

The state securities holders faced even greater political and financial problems. At first they scored several major victories: the General Court consolidated the state's debt at a high value, paid the interest in specie, determined to retire the principal during the later 1780s, and established a state impost and excise system that serviced the interest charges. In 1786 these investors won their last victory when the court assigned revenues from direct taxes to service interest payments. Then Shays's Rebellion cut tax receipts and increased the state's debt; the court used the revenues from the impost and excise to pay general state expenses; and the commonwealth made no effort to find new revenue sources to service its securities. By 1788 it seemed that the speculators in state securities might have to paper their walls with valueless bonds.[43]

41. The best secondary account is Bridgham, "Maine Public Lands." A section of Ch. 4 discusses the development of this issue during the early 1780s.

42. See E. James Ferguson, *The Power of the Purse: A History of American Public Finance, 1776-1790* (Chapel Hill, 1961), pp. 289-325 for holdings and passim for the financial developments of the 1780s.

43. The political role of the state's debt will be discussed in chs. 4, 6, 7, and 9. Estimates of the total debt at various periods are given in "Address to the People," in *Acts and Laws*, 14 Nov. 1786, 4:142-43, in which the General

Alexander Hamilton's assumption and funding program and the settlement of accounts between the commonwealth and the United States saved both groups of speculators and had a tremendous impact on the political economy of the state. The market value of state and national securities held by Massachusetts investors skyrocketed from $1.5 million in 1788 to over $5.5 million in later 1791, giving the commonwealth and its speculators a tidy profit of over $4.0 million. The least commercial farmers and the group C towns, who had opposed the use of direct taxes for paying the state and national debts and the constitution because of their fear of heavier direct taxes, appreciated the new national financial program that lifted the state debt from their shoulders and funded the new combined debt through relatively painless impost and excise duties.[44] Thus by the early 1790s everyone appeared content. The investors had their money and the nonspeculative farmers would not have to pay for the servicing of the new national debt.

The concentration of speculators in the group A towns, the over-

---

Court estimated a total debt of £1,631,791 of which £1,326,447 remained due. Swan, *National Arithmetick*, 53, estimated the debt at £1,394,809 in 1786. Ferguson, *Power of the Purse*, 245, estimated it at $4.6 million. "Report of the Committee of Finance of the Massachusetts General Court," 10 June 1789, in Fleet, *Register, 1790* (1789), p. 58, estimated the debt at £1,489,599 which included back interest. *The Independent Chronicle*, 29 Dec. 1785, estimated the debt at £1.4 million. Some of the debt was still outstanding, despite assumption, in 1794. See *Acts and Laws*, 1 Feb. 1794, 10:433-36.

44. Market values for the various types of securities are given in the *Massachusetts Magazine* for each month between July 1789 and June 1792. During this period the value of the state's consolidated securities rose from 20% of their par value to almost 72% of par while national securities soared from 24% to 112% of par. This represented a profit of almost £800,000 on state securities alone. When combined with the rise of national securities, profits must have amounted to nearly four million dollars, a sum almost as great as the total value of the state's exports in 1787.

Ferguson, *Power of the Purse*, pp. 326-43, shows how the settlement of accounts was related to the refunding program. [Thomas Davis], *Report of Thomas Davis, Treasurer, on the Public Debt of the Commonwealth* (Boston, 1794), pp. 1-4, estimated that almost £690,000 was still outstanding after assumption. The settlement of accounts with the United States reduced this amount when the national government paid Massachusetts a considerable sum supposedly owed to her by the confederation. See Ferguson, *Power of the Purse*, pp. 332-33; Paul B. Trescott, "Federal-State Financial Relations, 1790-1860," *Journal of Economic History* 15:227-45, especially 227-33. Chapter 11 describes the impact of assumption on Massachusetts politics.

lapping of their holdings of national and state securities, and the large proportion of merchants who held these securities gave this particular speculative interest a great deal of political power in the most commercial-cosmopolitan towns. In 1779 when the Continental emissions of May 1777 and April 1778 were called in, 170 persons who held over $5,000 worth of currency accounted for 55 percent of the total amount retired and over three-fourths of these large holders lived in Boston or Salem.[45] At the ratification convention of January and February 1788, over two-thirds of the security holders selected as delegates represented the group A towns and these men held over nine-tenths of the value of all securities held by convention members. (See table 15.) In Boston, a comparison of the treasury registers and the state interest books with the 1789 *Boston Directory* shows that one-fourth of the 123 merchants owned over $10,000 worth of securities in 1790-1791 and that almost one-third received over £25 worth of interest on their state bonds in 1786 and 1787.[46] Many individuals held large

45. William H. Dumont, "A Short Census of Massachusetts in 1779," *National Genealogical Society Quarterly* 49:14-20, 96-100, 137-41, and 50:26-28, 207-14, gives a list of individuals who retired certain issues of Continental currency in 1779. The lists record the name, amount retired, and residence of the holder.

46. A good secondary description of the concentration of holdings in Massachusetts is in Ferguson, *Power of the Purse*, pp. 273-75. There are also four other sources for analysis: The Old Loans-Register of Stock Owners, Records of the Bureau of the Public Debt, Massachusetts Loan Office Records Relating to the Loan of 1790, The Old Loan Book of Stock Owners, vol. 1119, lists the stocks on which interest was paid during the early 1790s. (It does not include holdings of deferred stocks.) This means that the totals from this source differ from those of Ferguson and McDonald, but the pattern of concentration is much the same. Roughly 1,400 persons and corporations held a total of $4.2 million worth of these securities. The 83 individuals and corporations who held over $10,000 each accounted for about 59% of the total value. A second source is the Interest Payment Books, Treasurer's Papers, Office of the Secretary, Boston, of which vols. 11 through 15 cover the payments made between 1 Mar. 1786 and Mar. 1787. During this period the 145 leading holders of state securities received about £41,200 in interest which represented nearly 46% of the total payments made during the period. A third source consists of the original vouchers filed as Papers Concerning the State Debt in 1794, in the Office of the Secretary, Boston. (There were also located in the attic of the capitol building in early 1964.) The final source is Norman, *Directory*, which gives the occupations of many of the Boston security holders as of 1789. Massachusetts investors held little of the debt of the southern states; see Whitney K. Bates, "Northern Speculators and Southern State Debts, 1790," *William and Mary Quarterly*, 3d ser., Jan. 1962, pp. 30-48, especially p. 48.

TABLE 15
Security Holders at the Ratification Convention of 1788

Towns	Number of Security Holders	Value of Securities	Towns in Group Represented by Security Holders
Ten leading shipowning towns	31%	78%	90%
Other group A	35	14	49
Group B	18	7	15
Group C	16	1	6

SOURCE: Based on the data assembled by Forrest McDonald in *We the People: The Economic Origins of the Constitution* (Chicago, 1958), pp. 199-200.

amounts of both national and state securities. One-third of the 83 investors who held over $10,000 worth of the new national debt had received over £100 of interest on their state holdings between March 1786 and April 1787.[47] Other investors held only state or national paper, a situation which caused some friction, especially during the early 1780s when both groups vied to have their holdings refunded. These differences tended to dissipate after 1787 when it became obvious that only a more powerful national government would possess the fiscal resources to bail out both the state and national securities holders.[48] Thus, despite a potentially serious division between the state and national creditors, the investors' common residential patterns, occupational similarities, and the failure of both the commonwealth and the confederation to develop a workable funding system after 1786 and 1787 united them, especially after 1787, and made them one of the most dynamic political groups in the most commercial category of interests.

47. Based on the Interest Payment Books for 1786 and 1787, several important politicians received large sums of interest. These included: James Bowdoin, the governor, over £1000; Elbridge Gerry, congressman, delegate to the Philadelphia Convention, and future Antifederalist leader, £440; Samuel Adams, Jr., the only son of Samuel Adams, president of the senate and future governor, £111; Nathaniel Gorham, speculator and politician, £228; Benjamin Lincoln, fervent nationalist and militia major general, £104; William Phillips, politician, state senator, and merchant, £1201; James Swan, the author of *National Arithmetick*, £145, and many others appeared in these records, in the records of the Old Loans-Register of Stock Owners, and in the Papers Concerning the State Debt in 1794.

48. Chapters 9, 10, and 11 discuss the political importance of these issues and programs.

In addition to these commercially involved individuals ranging from merchants and traders to usurers and speculators, the most commercial-cosmopolitan interests also included several professional occupations that had wide-ranging social and economic contacts and vested interests that had to be politically defended. Lawyers and placeholding judges were concentrated in the 54 most commercial-cosmopolitan towns, while ministers and justices of the peace lived in all three groups of towns where they often differed with their neighbors in the less commercial communities on a wide range of financial and social issues. These issues involved the defense of contracts, upholding the judiciary, supporting the fee system, and retaining the establishment of religion written into the 1780 constitution. Lawyers, placeholders, and ministers joined to combat inflation and to assail the immorality of stay legislation while the placeholders fought to uphold the judiciary and the fee system, and the ministers tried to defend town support of the established churches.

The increasing fraternity of lawyers produced several new economic, social, and political leaders during the 1780s. The rapid rise to political and social prominence of lawyers like James Sullivan, Harrison Gray Otis, Fisher Ames, and Theodore Sedgwick showed others the obvious advantages of a legal career. Over four-fifths of these attorneys practiced in the 54 group A towns, where they prospered by handling cases for merchants, traders, investors, and other members of the most commercial interest groups.[49] Many of them speculated in land and securities and the ones who entered politics held considerably more than their share of political offices, especially in the Confederation and National Congresses.[50] These rising lawyers defended their newly won positions

49. Fleet, *Register, 1781* (1780), n.p., or p. 47; ibid., *1787* (1786), pp. 105-06; ibid., *1792* (1791), pp. 139-40, gives the names and residences of attorneys. Between 1780 and 1791 the number of barristers increased from 12 to 16 while the number of attorneys soared from 22 to 109.

50. Business activities of the Boston bar are outlined in John Q. Adams to John Adams, 21 Sept. 1790, in Worthington C. Ford, ed., *Writings of John Quincy Adams*, 7 vols. (New York, 1913-1917), 1:56-59. The growing connections of a young lawyer are illustrated in Harrison Gray Otis to William Case, 24 Sept. 1789; Otis to John Pringle, 24 Sept. 1788; Otis to Andrew Craigie, 29 Sept. 1788, all in Harrison Gray Otis Letterbook, Massachusetts Historical Society. The connections of western lawyers with Boston merchants may be followed in William Cranch to Richard Cranch, 20 Sept. 1791, Cranch Papers, Massachusetts Historical Society, and Samuel A. Otis to Theodore Sedgwick, 10 Jan. 1785, Sedgwick Papers. For early careers of two of the younger and more important lawyers see E. A. Bernhard, *Fisher Ames,*

of power and prestige by organizing professional associations
which set standards for admission to the bar and in a few instances
even established fees.[51] As individuals and as a corporate group,
they opposed efforts to reform the commonwealth's prolix and
disorganized laws and defended the judiciary and the fee system.[52] They naturally cooperated with other commercial-cosmopolitan interests in opposing closure of the courts, stay legislation,
and the suspension of debts. In short, despite their own dynamic
rise, they defended the commercial interests and the sociolegal
status quo.

The placeholders included many of the commonwealth's leading
politicians who controlled the judicial and administrative machinery of the state. In an era lacking a professional bureaucracy,
these social and economic leaders filled the judicial and administrative posts and performed governmental functions for fees and
occasional salaries. These placeholders included an entire company
of judicial officials ranging from the judges of the supreme judicial
court to the local justices of the peace. Many others collected

---

Federalist and Statesman, 1785-1808 (Chapel Hill, 1965), pp. 37-54, and
Richard E. Welsh, Jr., *Theodore Sedgwick, Federalist; A Political Portrait*
(Middleton, Conn., 1965), pp. 27-41. *Biographical Directory of the American
Congress; 1774-1961*, 85th. Cong., 2d sess., House doc. no. 442 (Washington,
D.C., 1961), shows that seven of the twenty-two men who represented Massa-
chusetts in the Continental Congress were lawyers as were five of the first ten
representatives in the national Congress and one of the first three senators.

51. These early bar associations may be studied in George Dexter, ed.,
"Record Book of the Suffolk Bar," in Massachusetts Historical Society, *Proceedings*, 1st. ser., 19:141-79. Also see Minutes of Theodore Sedgwick, Sept.
1792 term, Lenox [Berkshire County], in Sedgwick Papers. Handlin and
Handlin, *Commonwealth*, pp. 79-80, gives a concise secondary account.

52. There were two major periods of agitation against lawyers. The first in
1786 sparked by the "Honestus" essays is covered in ch. 7. The second in
early 1791 was occasioned by John Gardner's efforts at legal reform. This is
discussed in ch. 11. Theodore Sedgwick to Henry Van Schaack, 24 May 1790,
Sedgwick Papers, vol. 3, blames the problems of lawyers on the poverty of
the people. John Adams to William Cranch, 14 Mar. 1790, Cranch Papers, in
which Adams, irritated by the attacks on lawyers, expresses his hopes that the
bar associations will retain their high standards and will prevent ill bred persons from becoming attorneys. *Boston Magazine*, Feb. 1784, pp. 164-65,
gives the address by Supreme Court Justice William Cushing upon the admission of new barristers. Cushing not only defended the traditional legal and
judicial systems but also commented upon the honesty and morality of paying the state debt in specie. For a brief secondary account of the Gardner
affair see Thomas C. Amory, *Life of James Sullivan with Selections from His
Writings*, 2 vols. (Boston, 1859), 2:13-14.

taxes and enforced laws and inspection regulations. Appointed by the governor or elected by the General Court and unchecked by an efficient bureaucracy or by popular election, most of the place-holders received fees or commissions collected in specie which gave them a cash income they were anxious to retain.[53] Their ranks included men of varied economic and social origin, but most of the more important resided in the group A towns where they had close contact with merchants, traders, speculators, and other members of the most commercial-cosmopolitan category. Their defense of the judiciary, the obligation of contracts, and the pay-ment of their fees dovetailed with the interests of other members of the most commercial-cosmopolitan group.

The judges of the supreme judicial court, resplendent in their scarlet gowns, sat at the peak of the pyramid of judges and place-holders. This court, composed of four judges, handed down final decisions in civil and criminal cases as they rode circuit throughout the commonwealth. Of the eight men who staffed this court be-tween 1780 and 1791, all resided in the group A towns, all pos-sessed important commercial or speculative connections, and all but James Sullivan had graduated from Harvard. In addition to their judicial powers, their addresses to the grand juries in the various counties gave them an opportunity to propagandize the local citizenry on a wide variety of political issues.[54]

53. Important fee acts of the 1780s include *Acts and Laws*, 2 Nov. 1781, 1:535, which continues the act of 1773; 27 July 1782, 2:10-14; and 28 Feb. 1787, 4:226-27.

54. Information about the supreme judicial court is compiled from: Fleet, *Register*, for the years 1780 through 1791 which gives the names of the judges each year. These are included in a complete civil list giving not only the supreme court judges but also the judges of common pleas, the justices of the peace, registers of probate, and almost all other important county or state placeholders. See Fleet, *Register*, *1781* (1780), n.p.; *1782* (1781), n.p.; *1783* (1782), pp. 49-63; *1784* (1783), pp. 50-67; *1785* (1784), pp. 63-80; *1786* (1785), pp. 75-95; *1787* (1786), pp. 86-105; *1788* (1787), pp. 80-101; *1789* (1788), pp. 111-132; *1790* (1789), pp. 119-141; *1791* (1790), pp. 92-115; *1792* (1791), pp. 115-138. L. Kinvin Wroth and Hiller B. Zobel, ed., *Legal Papers of John Adams*, 3 vols. (Cambridge, Mass., 1965), 1:cxv-cxix, give biographical information. Dress is described in Memorial of Lawyers, 4 Oct. 1783, and William Cushing to Robert T. Paine, 24 Aug. 1784, both in the Robert Paine Papers. At least four of the eight judges who sat during this period had security holdings in 1786-1787. Judges Nathan Cushing, N. P. Sargeant, Robert Treat Paine, and David Sewall all appear in the Interest Payment Books between Mar. 1786 and Apr. 1787. An excellent survey of the supreme judicial court is found in: John D. Cushing, "A Revolutionary Conservative: The Public Life of William Cushing, 1732-1810," (Ph.D. diss., Clark University, 1959), pp. 204-09.

Every county had a court of common pleas, composed of four judges, with only civil jurisdiction and from whose decisions most parties appealed to the supreme judicial court. In practice, this court mainly served the judges themselves who received fees for all cases heard before them. The hapless plaintiffs, however, complained about the existence of an institution that settled few cases at a heavy cost.[55] Residents of the group A towns held over one-half of all the positions on these courts between 1780 and 1791. Many of these judges loaned money, speculated, or traded, and several served long terms in the state senate where they used their considerable political influence to protect their court and income and helped to promote many of the programs sponsored by other members of the most commercial-cosmopolitan interests.[56]

In addition to these judges each county had numerous justices of the peace who possessed individually and corporately a considerable amount of legislative, judicial, and executive authority. These justices sat together on the county court of general sessions of the peace which handled criminal cases and served as the county's governing body. At these sessions the judges tried criminal cases, laid out roads, approved the bylaws of the county towns, granted licenses to tavern keepers, and recommended the county tax rate to the General Court. In addition to these corporate powers each individual justice tried minor civil and criminal cases and received fees for all these services. Between 1780 and 1790 over half of the justices of the quorum and almost half of the total justices resided in the group A towns (see table 16), but no matter where they lived justices supported the judicial and fee systems. Moreover, on many important roll calls justices representing the less commercial towns voted with the most commercial-cosmopolitan interests rather than with the other representatives from their towns.[57]

55. Wroth and Zobel, eds., *Legal Papers of Adams*, 1:xxxviii-lii, have an excellent description of the legal and court system. For the statutory basis of the court of common pleas see *Acts and Laws*, 3 July 1782, 2:28-30.

56. The civil list is in Fleet, *Register*. (See fn. 54, this chapter.) If residence is not given, it may be determined by referring to the lists of justices of the peace in the various counties. Membership in the senate is given in the *Acts and Laws* at the beginning of each legislative year. Each county usually had four judges assisted by a number of special judges who sat if the regular judges had their personal interests involved in a case. For these special judges see *Acts and Laws*, 16 May 1784, 2:627-28.

57. There were three types of justices of the peace. The first, usually important state politicians, held commissions good in any county within the commonwealth. The second, or justices of the quorum, was composed of

TABLE 16
The Professionals and Placeholders

	Percentage of Polls (1784)	Percentage in 1786 of			Percentage of Terms in Common Pleas (1780–91)	Professionals per 1,000 Polls		
		Lawyers	Justices of Quorum	Total Justices[a]		Lawyers	Justices of Quorum	Total Justices[a]
Towns								
Group A	34%	84%	65%	47%	52%	2.1	3.0	10.1
Group B	32	13	27	28	35	0.3	1.4	6.5
Group C	34	4	9	25	13	0.1	0.4	5.5
State						0.9	1.6	7.4

SOURCES: Polls are from the Evaluation, 1784/86; lawyers and barristers from Fleet, *Register, 1787* (1786), pp. 105–06; justices of the quorum, ibid., pp. 86–105; total justices, ibid.; terms in common pleas compiled from citations in note 54.

a. Total justices include the two types: justices of the peace and justices of the quorum.

Congregational ministers played an important religious, social, and political role in many Massachusetts towns during the 1780s. In 1786 there were about 3.3 ministers for every thousand polls and over two-thirds of all the towns and plantations had a resident Congregational preacher. Over four-fifths of the state's polls resided in communities with Congregational ministers and only Bristol, Hampshire, and the Maine counties had fewer than three ministers per thousand polls.[58] Many of these 297 ministers had a vested interest in the local town establishment of religion continued by the 1780 constitution which permitted the use of local

TABLE 17
The Congregational Ministers

	Ministers per 1,000 Polls (1786)	*Percentage Without Congregational Minister of*	
		Towns (1780–90)	*Polls*
Towns			
Group A	3.2	0%	0.0%
Group B	3.3	6	6.2
Group C	3.4	38	23.3
State	3.3	24	9.9

SOURCES: Ministers are from Fleet, *Register, 1787* (1786), pp. 51–58; polls, from Evaluation, 1784/86.

appointees, a certain number of whom had to be present at sessions of the court of general sessions of the peace. The third, or regular justices, could sit on the court of general sessions and possessed limited authority within their towns. For the legal basis of these positions see Isaiah Thomas, comp., *The Perpetual Laws of the Commonwealth of Massachusetts from the Establishment of the Constitution of 1780 to the First Session of the General Court, A. D. 1788* (Worcester, 1788), 11 March 1784, pp. 107-09; 16 March 1784, pp. 105-106; 30 June 1784, pp. 109-11; 19 Oct. 1782, p. 112; 3 July 1782, p. 122; 28 Feb. 1787, pp. 57-63; 2 Nov. 1781, pp. 185-86; 27 Feb. 1787, pp. 54-56. All three types of justices are listed in the civil list in Fleet, *Register.* (See fn. 54, this chapter.) Justices may be identified in the lower house by their titles of Esquire that are printed in the lists in the *Acts and Laws* and in the House Journals. See chs. 4 and 9 for examples of how these justices and placeholders often voted differently from other representatives from the same groups of towns.

58. Figures are based on Fleet, *Register, 1787* (1786), pp. 51-57 for the names and residences of ministers. (Non-Congregational ministers are listed on p. 58.)

taxes to pay ministerial salaries. (See table 17 for ministers, 1780-1790.) Since these payments were often made in specie at a relatively fixed annual rate, the ministers were unreceptive to inflationary programs, and since the laws excused them from paying taxes on their polls and property, they had little concern over heavy direct taxes.[59] Many ministers became integrated with the more commercial-cosmopolitan interests through lending money or serving as officers, along with merchants and placeholders, in charitable, social, and religious organizations.[60] Many of them preached the political, social, and financial gospel of the most

59. Two good recent studies are John D. Cushing, "Notes on Disestablishment in Massachusetts, 1780-1833," *William and Mary Quarterly*, 3d ser., 26:169-90, and William McLoughlin, *Isaac Backus and the American Pietistic Tradition* (Boston, 1967), pp. 136-66. The older Conrad Meyer, *Church and State in Massachusetts from 1740 to 1833; A Chapter in the History and Development of Individual Freedom* (Cleveland, 1930), pp. 10, 17, 112, 114, 116, 118-19, 122-24, 134-36 is still valuable. The 1780 constitution provided that all previous legislation remain in force until specifically modified by new laws; see Francis N. Thorpe, ed., *Federal and State Constitutions, Colonial Charters, and Other Organic Laws*, 7 vols. (Washington, D.C., 1909), 2:1910. For examples of local disputes see Donald G. Thrayser, *Barnstable: Three Centuries of a Cape Cod Town* (Hyannis, Mass., 1939), pp. 64-65; *Independent Chronicle*, 17 Aug. 1780; *Boston Gazette*, 7, 19 Feb., 7 May 1781; *Continental Journal*, 22 Feb. 1781; Amory, *Sullivan*, 1:181-84. All the *direct* tax legislation exempted ministers; see *Acts and Laws*, 22 Mar. 1782, 1:153-54 for an example. In the *Continental Journal*, 29 May 1783, a writer protested because ministers had to pay the excise tax on cider. For the income of ministers see Main, *Social Structure*, pp. 95-97.

60. Some examples of the business connections of ministers may be seen in Samuel Dexter to Rev. William Lyman, 1 Nov. 1782, Miscellaneous Papers, Massachusetts Historical Society, and Dexter to Lyman, 23 Oct., 19 May, and 27 Feb. 1781 in ibid. James Sullivan and Rev. Peter Thatcher conducted a heated debate on the condition of the clergy during 1783 and 1784. Thatcher argued that ministers were relatively poor and that the towns should not have the right to dismiss ministers without the consent of a ministerial council. Sullivan contended that the ministers were well paid and upheld local and town control of the clergy. Main, *Social Structures*, pp. 96-97, agrees with Sullivan about their economic position. The debate may be followed in Peter Thatcher, *Observations Upon the Present State of the Clergy in New England with Strictures Upon Power of Dismissing them* (Boston, 1783); James Sullivan, *Strictures on the Rev. Mr. Thatcher's Pamphlet* . . . (Boston, 1783); and Thatcher, *A Reply to the Strictures of Mr. J. S. A Layman* (Boston, 1784). Five of the sixteen clergymen who attended the ratification convention in 1788 held governmental securities; see Forrest McDonald, *We the People: The Economic Origins of the Constitution* (Chicago, 1958), pp. 194, 198, 200.

commercial-cosmopolitan interests. Their presence alone brought outside influences into the more isolated communities.[61]

These merchants, shipbuilders, manufacturers, speculators, investors, shopkeepers, and professionals were, to use Henry Knox's phrase, the "persons of property, position and intelligence." Hardworking, aggressive, cosmopolitan, and linked with one another through economic, social, religious, and institutional contacts, these groups and individuals became the most dynamic political force in the commonwealth. They used the political strength of the group A towns to initiate new policies that would be of financial benefit to themselves and to defend their privileged religious and legal positions. They refunded the state debt at a high value and serviced it with specie; they protected the commerce and shipping of the commonwealth; they worked for internal improvements and speculative schemes; and they defended the religious establishment, the placeholders, and the constitution of 1780. They needed no political party to control the commonwealth's intricate preparty political system.

Naturally the vast majority of the commonwealth's citizens were not by their own or Knox's standards persons of property, position, and intelligence. Nevertheless artisans, sailors, urban laborers, and commercial farmers often found themselves sharing the interests of the commercial-cosmopolitan leaders and supporting their programs, while on other issues they allied themselves with the poorer and less commercial agrarians. Their differences in outlook and political response so divided the urban artisans and the commercial farmers that they seldom could join together with enough momentum to take the political initiative. This group of interests sympathized with parts of the program sponsored or defended by the most commercial-cosmopolitan groups, but often opposed the

61. Ministers could and did sit in the lower house; see Luther S. Cushing, *Reports of Controverted Elections in the House of Representatives of the Commonwealth of Massachusetts from 1780 to 1852* (Boston, 1852), p. 28. For ministers at the 1788 convention see McDonald, *We the People*, pp. 194, 198, 200. For the annual election sermon preached by a minister elected by the General Court, see the listings in Charles Evans, ed., *American Bibliography: A Chronological Dictionary of All Books, Pamphlets, and Periodical Publications Printed in the United States . . . 1639 . . . 1820*, 12 vols. (Chicago, 1903-1934). Volumes 6, 7, and 8 cover 1779 through 1792. Also note Roger P. Bristol, *Supplement to Charles Evans' American Bibliography* (Charlottesville, 1970), pp. 289-449.

more commercial-cosmopolitan interests on taxation, the suspension of debts, and other important political questions.

The artisans and smaller manufacturers, depending upon their occupations, tended to be either concentrated in the ten most mercantile communities or scattered throughout the entire commonwealth. Practically all the artisans and laborers engaged in rope-making or distilling lived in the ten most mercantile towns and at least two-fifths of the tanners, slaughterers, and shipbuilders worked in the 54 group A communities.[62] Outside these centers scattered artisans made iron and potashes, ran mills, fabricated a wide variety of products, and worked at numerous trades ranging from house-building to blacksmithing.[63] Decentralization diluted their political power and their entrepreneurial outlook often made them politically sympathetic to programs backed by traders and small shopkeepers. They had little interest in inflation, wanted to collect their debts, had little objection to the tax system, and had been irritated by the farmer's opposition to agricultural price controls during the War of Independence.[64] Their desire for protec-

62. Evaluation, 1784/86 gives the number and taxable value of all slaughter houses, tanneries, distilleries, and ropewalks for every town in the state. For shipbuilding see fn. 22, this chapter. The artisans played an important role in Boston and represented a high proportion of the population in several other Massachusetts coastal towns. See Main, *Social Structure*, pp. 38-39; Labaree, *Patriots and Partisans*, pp. 10-14; Ricketson, *New Bedford*, pp. 108-09, 140. Samuel Roads, Jr., *The History and Traditions of Marblehead* (Boston, 1880), pp. 341-54; Babson, *Gloucester*, pp. 448, 455, 463; Hurd, ed., *Plymouth County*, 1:156-57.

In Boston a writer in the *Gazette*, 4 Apr. 1787, estimated that artisans cast about 40% of the total vote in Boston. In the "Assessor's Taking Books" [1780], pp. 9-59, the artisans accounted for over 40% of the total taxpayers in the four northern wards of the city. According to the same source several artisans were among the wealthiest men in the city. Distillers, ropewalk owners, apothecaries, goldsmiths, tailors, and chaise makers accounted for almost one-fifth of those among the highest 5% of the Boston taxables in 1780.

63. Evaluation, 1784/86 lists the number and taxable value of all iron works, sawmills, grist mills, other mills, potash factories, etc., for every town in the commonwealth.

64. For artisans outside the mercantile centers see Peter Whitney, *The History of the County of Worcester in the Commonwealth of Massachusetts, with a Particular Account of Every Town* (Worcester, 1793), passim, since he noticed artisans in almost every town in the county. Millers, potash makers, carpenters, and many others often served as shopkeepers or operated farms. *Massachusetts Magazine*, Jan. 1792, pp. 9-13; Feb. 1791, pp. 73-76; Mar. 1791, pp. 149-50, published descriptions of the towns in Barnstable and Essex counties that also give some information about local artisans. For some political action see *American Magazine*, Oct. 1788, pp. 347-48. For the reac-

tive tariffs differentiated them from some of the groups in the most commercial-cosmopolitan category, but the latter interests compromised on this question and adopted protective legislation in 1785.[65]

The sailors, urban laborers, and poor fishermen, located in the coastal and most mercantile towns, also performed chores that tied them to the most commercial-cosmopolitan group of interests. During the 1780s they remained apathetic or supported these more dynamic groups. Many lacked sufficient property to vote, were not assessed for taxes, and had little incentive for a continued involvement in state or even local affairs. Since these workers could be incited to violence or riot if they believed their interests were threatened, the calm of the port towns during the 1780s, compared with the riots of the sixties, seventies, and nineties, reflects their apathy and lack of interest in the political questions of the 1780s.[66]

---

tion of some artisans to certain financial and political questions see Joseph G. Cranch to Richard Cranch, 20 May 1786, 13 and 16 July 1786, Cranch Papers. Cranch did not care for either paper money or inflation. An analysis of suits for debt in Worcester County in 1785 shows that twice as many artisans were entered as plaintiffs than as defendants in debt actions. For battles over price control that tended to divide artisans from farmers see Andrew McFarland Davis, "On the Limitation of Prices in Massachusetts, 1776-1779," Colonial Society of Massachusetts, *Publications*, 10:119-35. For high food prices near the end of the war see William Tudor, ed., *Deacon Tudor's [John Tudor] Diary: A Record of More or Less Important Events in Boston from 1732 to 1793, by an Eyewitness* (Boston, 1896), pp. 79-80, 82.

65. The best secondary account about the Massachusetts tariff is in William F. Zornow, "Massachusetts Tariff Policies, 1775-1789," Essex Institute, *Historical Collections*, 90:194-215. See ch. 6, this book, for successful artisan opposition to a structural change in the Boston town government.

66. It is difficult to determine the number of urban laborers and sailors. Norman, *Directory*, gives the names of 1,404 persons, 10 of whom were listed as truckmen and only 3 as laborers. A total of 41 others had no listed occupation. In 1790 the city contained 4,325 males over 16. If we calculate that about 25% of these were between 16 and 21 years of age, this leaves us with 3,244 men over 21 with only 1,404 listed in the directory. See Department of Commerce and Labor, Bureau of the Census, *Heads of Families at the First Census of the United States Taken in the Year 1790* (Washington, 1908), *Massachusetts*, pp. 9-10; *Maine*, pp. 9-10. Thus about 1,800 adult males could have been apprentices, laborers, seamen, etc. This would amount to around 50 percent of the total adult male population. According to a writer in the *Boston Gazette*, 4 Apr. 1787, laborers cast 30 percent of the town's vote in the 1787 election. This would also indicate a sizeable population of laborers, seamen, etc., at least in Boston. Portage bills for several vessels available in the Caleb Davis Papers give the typical wage of a seaman at around £29 per year if he found steady, year-round employment. Also see

The commercial farmers, the largest and politically most powerful group included in these less commercial interests, possessed
their greatest political power in the commercially oriented agrarian
towns that had been integrated into a wider economic network
because of their sale of various agricultural commodities. In order
to be incorporated into this system, the farmers and towns had to
secure markets, find transportation facilities, and produce a sur-
plus. Markets could be found in the nonagrarian mercantile towns
in eastern Massachusetts, in several cities located on the perimeters
of the commonwealth, or in foreign nations. Within the state
about 7 percent of the total polls resided in five mercantile towns
that had almost no agricultural wealth. The other group A towns
with relatively high indexes of agricultural wealth served only as
markets for farmers who resided in these communities or as collection points for agricultural commodities exported to the east or to
other states and nations.[67] In order to reach these more distant
markets, Berkshire farmers drove livestock to the Hudson valley and

---

Main, *Social Structure*, p. 39. A study of local histories and newspaper accounts of the 1780s uncovered only one incident involving an urban mob. In
1784 a Marblehead crowd threatened the returning Robie family, which was
formerly Tory. See Roads, *Marblehead*, p. 134 for this incident. The first
serious riot after the Revolution in Boston was apparently the antitheater riot
of 1792; see William T. Ball, "The Old Federal Street Theatre," Bostonian
Society *Publications*, vol. 8, pp. 45-48; and John Q. Adams to John Adams,
22 Dec. 1792, in Ford, ed., *Writings of J. Q. Adams*, 1:131-32. The complete
absence of any mob action or violence directed at the establishment of the
first Roman Catholic church in Boston is described in Robert H. Lord, John
E. Sexton, and Edward T. Harrington, *History of the Archdiocese of Boston
in the Various Stages of Its Development*, 3 vols. (New York, 1934),
1:375-78. Compared with the 1760s, 1770s, and 1790s, the Boston of the
1780s was a remarkably quiet community.

67. The importance of the eastern port towns as markets for agricultural
produce is shown in the *American Museum*, May 1790, p. 229, where a writer
notes that Boston imported almost 12% of the total wheat and flour exported
from Philadelphia in 1786. Salem, Nantucket, Falmouth (Portland) were also
listed as importers of Pennsylvania breadstuffs. The *Plymouth Journal*, 7 Mar.
1787, describes the arrival of corn ships from the south. The Evaluation,
1784/86 gives polls and the taxable value of all types of improved land and
livestock. It lists five categories of improved land: (1) tillage land, (2) English
meadow or mowing land, (3) upland meadow or mowing land, (4) salt marsh
and meadow, and (5) pasture. The English meadow land had the highest value
per acre and pasture the lowest. These tax valuations on land varied considerably from town to town throughout the state. Livestock, on the other hand,
had a constant value regardless of location. The lists included horses and
colts, oxen, neat cattle, cows, and swine, but sheep and goats were not
evaluated.

transported provisions to Albany. Farmers in the Connecticut valley drove their cattle overland to the eastern ports and shipped produce down the river. Some towns in Worcester, Plymouth, and Suffolk counties supplied the Rhode Island ports.[68] Foreign nations also provided markets. In 1787 agricultural produce accounted for about one-eight of the commonwealth's exports and Massachusetts merchants dispatched a wide range of commodities to various foreign and American ports.[69] The lure of foreign markets interested many commercial farmers in the development of a wide variety of crops and animal products that could be shipped abroad.

But the farmers often faced serious difficulties in transporting their surpluses to these distant markets. Eastern farmers supplying the mercantile centers had the easiest chore. They often personally marketed their crops and livestock to city dwellers and avoided both commissions to middlemen and the high expenses of overland transportation.[70] Farmers living in the coastal towns of

68. A secondary survey is in Martin, "Merchants and Trade," pp. 7, 11-17, 134-35, 154. Some detailed accounts for individual towns are in Timothy Dwight, *Travels in New England and New York* . . . , 4 vols. (New Haven, 1822), 1:317-21, 2:376, 379, 382, 386, 387, 389, 502. Also see Richard D. Birdsal, *Berkshire County: A Cultural History*, (New Haven, 1959), pp. 27-30, and for some examples of advertisements see the following issues of western papers: *Hampshire Gazette*, 13 Nov. 1787, 30 July 1788, 30 Dec. 1789, 27 Jan. 1790, 14 Sept. 1791; *Hampshire Herald*, 22 Mar. 1785, *Massachusetts Gazette* [Springfield], 8 Apr., 6 May 1783; *Berkshire Chronicle*, 25 Sept. 1788, 20 Feb., 24 Apr. 1789; *Western Star*, 30 Mar., 28 Sept., 2 Dec. 1790, 11, 25 Jan., 12 Apr. 1791.

69. Based on the export data in [Jarvis] "Report," 167-69.

70. For information and data regarding eastern agriculture and the marketing of crops in the coastal towns and cities, see Freeman, *Cape Cod*, 1:493, 504-05; John S. Barry, *A Historical Sketch of the Town of Hanover, Massachusetts, with Family Genealogies* (Boston, 1853), pp. 138-40, 144; Hurd, ed., *Plymouth County*, 1:186-87, 216, 240, 418, 465, 1023-24, 1123; Hurd, ed., *Bristol County*, pp. 182, 227-28, 235-36, 559, 565, 823, 827-29; Briggs, *Hanover*, p. 24; Dwight, *Travels*, 1:383, 389, 399-400, 2:10, 16, 23, 25-27, 201, 3:117. Henry S. Griffith, *History of the Town of Carver, Massachusetts: A Historical Review, 1637-1910* (New Bedford, 1913), pp. 192-209; William Jones, "A Topographical Description of the Town of Concord," Massachusetts Historical Society, *Collections*, 1st ser., 1:237; D. Hamilton Hurd, ed., *History of Middlesex County, Massachusetts, with Biographical Sketches of Many of Its Prominent Men*, 3 vols. (Philadelphia, 1890), 1:266-67 and ibid., *History of Norfolk County, Massachusetts, with Biographical Sketches of Many of Its Prominent Men* (Philadelphia, 1884), pp. 181, 604-06, 857. For examples of farmers selling fodder to Boston merchants notice the number of hay tickets in the Caleb Davis Papers, especially those for 20 Oct., 16 Nov., 22 Dec. 1789 and 2 Apr. and 3 Oct. 1790.

Maine and eastern Massachusetts and in the river plantations in Maine sent their commodities to market through middlemen who employed coasters that carried potashes, livestock, vegetables, and especially timber to eastern and Canadian markets.[71] In the western valleys the Berkshire and Hampshire farmers dealt through merchants and traders who used the Connecticut River or drove cattle overland to the Hudson valley, Connecticut, Rhode Island, or to eastern Massachusetts.[72] The farmers most limited by the high costs of transportation lived in the hill farming towns located in the four western counties. They had to either develop high value but lightweight products such as potashes and flaxseed or drive their livestock overland to available markets.[73]

Markets and availability of transportation thus influenced the development of commercial agriculture. Farmers living near the eastern mercantile or in the other group A communities possessed an available market while those hidden in the Hampshire and Worcester hills had few markets, less agricultural wealth, and much less involvement in a broader pattern of economic and commercial relationships. Generally the farmers in the group A and B towns, already involved in other commercial activities, were the most completely integrated into the system of commercial farming.

In the state as a whole the residents of the group A and B towns possessed a higher per-poll average of agricultural wealth and owned more expensive barns than did the less commercially oriented inhabitants of the group C communities. (See table 18.) This meant that the wealthier and more commercially oriented farmers

71. For the economy of the District of Maine see Lincoln, "Observations," pp. 149-56; Francis G. Butler, *A History of Farmington, Franklin County Maine, 1776-1885* (Farmington, 1885), pp. 24-28, 45-52; William C. Hatch, *A History of the Town of Industry, Franklin County, Maine* (Farmington, Maine, 1893), pp. 27, 66; *Boston Gazette*, 15 Jan., 11 Feb. 1782; *Massachusetts Magazine*, Jan. 1792, p. 58; Harry H. Cochrane, *History of Monmouth and Wales*, 2 vols. (East Winthrop, Maine, 1894), 1:71, Petition to Henry Knox, dated 18 Oct. 1788, Knox Papers; E. H. Quincy to John Hancock, 16 Apr. 1791, Hancock Papers; John P. Farrow, *History of Isleborough, Maine* (Boston, 1893), p. 16. Many of the newer and rawer towns in the district produced only lumber and imported their foodstuffs from eastern Massachusetts. An example is given in Caleb Coolidge to Caleb Davis, 10 Nov. 1791, Caleb Davis Papers.

72. Martin, "Merchants and Trade," pp. 7, 11, 12-17, 134-35, 139-44.

73. The town of Worcester sometimes imported flour from the east. See advertisement of Samuel B. Baker, *Worcester Spy*, 23 Sept. 1784. For some general comments on agriculture see Whitney, *Worcester County*, pp. 51, 52, 61, 62, 79, 179. For the barter trade see advertisements in the *Worcester Spy*, 12, 26 Aug., 16 Sept. 1784; 19 Feb., 3 June, 1 July, 7 Oct., 16 Dec. 1784.

TABLE 18
Agricultural Wealth

| | Taxable Value per Poll of | | | |
	Land	Livestock	Barns	Total
Towns				
Group A	£3.95	£0.59	£0.36	£4.90
Group B	4.41	0.84	0.35	5.60
Group C	3.59	0.86	0.28	4.73
State	3.98	0.76	0.33	5.07

SOURCE: Evaluation, 1784/86. The taxable values of all types of improved land, livestock, and barns were calculated for every town, and the total sum for each group of towns was divided by the number of polls that resided in those communities.

tended to be located in the same towns that had other connections with the commercial network.

The same general pattern held true for each of the three regions of the state. In the east, the five mercantile towns with little agrarian wealth ranked at the bottom but the other 26 group A communities led the B and C towns in their per-poll valuation of agricultural property. Because of their market opportunities, the eastern group C towns, unlike the C towns in any other section of the state, did have a slightly higher valuation than the group B communities. In the more typical western counties, the residents of the group A and B towns possessed considerably more agrarian wealth per poll than did the least commercial residents of the group C communities. In Maine the group B towns led both other groups but even in the district the group A towns had a considerably higher valuation per poll than did the much more numerous group C towns and plantations.[74]

The commonwealth contained 112 towns with a valuation of over £5.00 per poll on land and £1.00 per poll on livestock. These wealthiest agricultural towns accounted for one-third of the total communities in the state and contained 34 percent of the total polls.[75] Almost one-half of the group A, almost half of the

74. Based on the materials in Evaluation, 1784/86. The values are computed for each of the three groups of towns within each of the three regions.

75. I used the cutoff point of £5.00 for land and £1.00 for livestock because this resulted in a group of towns that accounted for almost exactly one-third of the total population. In other words if the towns had been arranged in terms of their per capita agricultural wealth, these 112 communities would have been the group A agricultural towns. The data are available in Evaluation, 1784/86, but I computed the totals and holdings per poll for every town in the state.

group B, but only one-fourth of the group C towns were included among these 112 communities. The same leading agrarian communities accounted for 32 percent of the polls in the most commercial and only 26 percent of those living in the least commercial or group C towns. In the four western counties an even greater differential existed among the three groups of communities. In the west over two-thirds of the group A, over one-half of the group B, and one-fourth of the group C towns were included among the 112 leading agrarian communities. Thus the analysis of the 112 leading agricultural towns reinforces other evidence to show the lesser involvement of the group C towns in commercial agriculture.

This concentration of the most commercial farmers in the group A and B towns had some serious political implications. The farmers in the group A towns tended to be either overshadowed by or integrated with the most commercial-cosmopolitan interests, while in the group B communities they possessed more political power in relation to the most commercial interests. In the least commercial-cosmopolitan communities, the farmers faced only the opposition of scattered ministers and placeholders and the more massive numbers of the least commercial farmers. Although partially integrated into the commercial system, these more commercial farmers had several interests that set them apart from other more commercial categories. They often disliked the taxation system, they had less personal involvement in defending the credit and judicial systems, and they could be irritated by excessive fees and heavy direct taxes. Even in the east and Maine, important commercial towns often were divided because of the conflicts between these more commercial farmers and the merchants, tradesmen, artisans, and shopkeepers in the urbanized sections of the townships. Newburyport separated from Newbury in the 1750s, and during the 1780s two very important mercantile communities —Portland and New Bedford—separated themselves from the more agrarian communities of Dartmouth and Falmouth.[76] But these most commercial farmers did not consistently oppose the most commercial-cosmopolitan interests. Many farmers speculated and loaned money and all of them had become at least partially involved in the complex web of commercial relationships that ran from Boston and other important centers to their local farms. Thus politically these farmers divided on many issues pushed by

76. New Bedford was separated from Dartmouth on 23 Feb. 1787 and Portland from Falmouth on 4 Jan. 1786. In both cases the commercial core was separated from a surrounding commercial farming area.

the most or the least commercial interests and towns. On vote after vote during the 1780s they and the group B towns occupied a median position between the representatives of the group A and the group C communities.

The least commercial farmers, the largest single element in the least commercial-cosmopolitan category of interests, had their greatest strength in the western group C towns. With almost no commercial activities these farmers depended upon the sale of agricultural products. But marketing and transportation difficulties made it hard for them to become integrated into the pattern of commercial agriculture. Almost two-thirds of the polls who resided in the least commercial towns lived in the 110 communities located in the four western counties. In every one of these four counties, these towns ranked considerably below the group A and B towns in their holdings of agricultural wealth, with the greatest differentials occurring in Berkshire and Hampshire counties. (See table 19). Only in the eastern counties did the group C towns hold relatively high per-poll quantities of agrarian wealth. In the District of Maine their proportion was even lower than in the west.

TABLE 19
Agrarian Wealth in the Western Region

	Total Per-Poll Holdings of Taxable Value of Land, Livestock, & Barns in					
Towns	Middlesex Co.	Worcester Co.	Hampshire Co.	Berkshire Co.	West	State
Group A	£6.47	£6.73	£6.24	£7.21	£6.58	£4.90
Group B	6.10	6.11	6.27	6.63	6.25	5.60
Group C	5.50	5.58	4.43	4.90	4.97	4.73

SOURCE: Based on the Evaluation, 1784/86. The computations were made for each of the three groups of towns within each of the four western counties.

These least commercial farmers concentrated in the group C communities found themselves in serious financial and economic difficulties during the 1780s. The Revolution had created a heavy state and national debt, caused increased taxation, and led to the formation of speculative groups that wanted land, charters, and high returns on their bonds. During the 1780s these least commercial farmers fought with the most commercial-cosmopolitan interests on a wide range of economic and financial issues that included the consolidation and refunding of the state debt, the payment of interest on state securities, taxation, and the suspension of suits for debts. Generally the farmers wanted lower direct taxes, cheap and rapid justice, the suspension of suits for debts in bad times, and a few even pushed for the issuing of paper currency.[77] On issue after issue during the 1780s these farmers found themselves at the opposite end of the political spectrum from the merchants, speculators, and tradesmen who formed the most commercial-cosmopolitan interests.[78]

77. The average income of Massachusetts farmers is difficult to ascertain. Most authorities believe it to have been between £25 and £50 per year, an income which would have compared favorably with the income of a Boston sailor. However, the farmer, if he owned land, had to make investments in land, livestock, housing, etc. Often he became indebted to the local money-lender or ran up "book debts" at the local store or tavern. Main, *Social Structures*, pp. 2-23 and 42-43, gives an overview of subsistence and commercial farmers. Percy W. Bidwell and John I. Falconer, *History of American Agriculture in the Northern United States, 1620-1860* (New York, 1941), p. 115-41, gives an overview of rural conditions and trading patterns. Swan, *National Arithmetick*, p. 5, estimated the average annual living expenses of a Massachusetts citizen at £23 lawful money per year. This is about the same as the income of a consistently working seaman (see fn. 66 above). Robert J. Taylor, *Western Massachusetts in the Revolution* (Providence, 1954), p. 115, estimated that a farm laborer in the western part of the state received from two to three shillings per day. This would have given him an income of £20 to £30 per year if he worked 200 days. Some writers also estimated income by acre or by farm. Swan, *National Arithmetick*, p. 35, estimated that an acre of corn grown in the best prepared ground would give the farmer about £6 13s. a year. Since the state average for tillage came to around two and one-half acres per poll (there would be about three acres per poll, excluding Boston and the other four nonagricultural communities) and there were about one and one-half polls per family, this would give an annual income from corn crops, i.e., wheat, barley, rye, etc., of £30 per year. This would not include income from dairy produce, livestock sales, sales of hay and fodder, orchard products, timber, potashes, or labor on other farmers' lands. "A Farmer in Plymouth County," *Massachusetts Magazine*, July 1790, pp. 409-11, estimated that a well-run efficient farm would yield 6% per year on its capital value. He estimated that with proper rotation an acre of farm land would yield a profit of £14 4s. over a five year period. He also noted that it required £1600 to establish a good 150 acre farm. Douglas S. Robertson, ed., *An Englishman in America 1785: Being the Diary of Joseph Hadfield* (Toronto, 1933), p. 219, observed that a tenant farmer near Providence, Rhode Island, made an annual profit of £31 14s. on a 76 acre farm. Many of these accounts mention the presence of agricultural laborers. See also *Independent Chronicle*, 27 Oct. 1785; Samuel Dexter to William Cushing, 28 Jan. 1785, Robert Paine Papers; and *Continental Journal*, 26 Apr. 1782.

78. Voting patterns of the group C towns for all three regions, are described and discussed in chs. 4, 5, and 7 through 11.

The interrelationships of the three categories of interests with the three groups of towns and the development of political issues that revolved around financial and economic questions made the split between the most and least commercial-cosmopolitan interests the central feature of Massachusetts politics between 1780 and 1788. The dynamic, most commercial-cosmopolitan interests, strongest in the group A towns with scattered support in the other communities, developed a wide range of political programs and defended certain institutions that alienated the least commercial farmers who were strongest in the western group C towns. The artisans and commercial farmers, scattered throughout all three groups but with their greatest strength in the group B towns, joined with one side or the other depending upon their interest in a particular issue. But the socioeconomic differences among the three groups of towns and categories of interests need not have led to such bitter divisions. No society has ever been socially or economically homogeneous. In order to explain the bitterness and depth of the political struggles of the 1780s it is necessary to examine how the Commonwealth's preparty political system exacerbated these divisions.

3

The Mechanics
of Preparty Politics

ALTHOUGH the basis of Massachusetts preparty politics was the conflict of interests resulting from social and economic differences, the influence of a number of other factors such as the formal structure of government and popular political ideology also must be considered. During the 1780s these factors generally worked to the advantage of the group A towns and the most commercial-cosmopolitan interests while, at the same time, they helped wedge the most and the least commercial-cosmopolitan groups and towns further apart. Residents of the group A towns held the important state and national offices and controlled the upper house of the General Court. In the lower house the group A towns' considerable power was augmented by the support of placeholders from the less commercial towns. All in all the group A towns and the interests they represented had a tremendous political advantage over their less commercial-cosmopolitan competitors. Their success in controlling the formal institutions was largely due to the outsiders' failure to develop organizations that could effectively push their political objectives. In desperation these groups finally resorted to holding extraconstitutional conventions and to violence in order to bring pressure to bear on the state government. Since all the voluntary social and cultural institutions of the commonwealth were also controlled by these most commercial-cosmpolitan interests and towns, the outsiders could not even count on the support of established, nongovernmental organizations. In addition the group A towns and the more dynamic interests had the advantage of being able to obtain fresher political and financial information than the poorer and more localistic group C communities and farmers.

Other factors accelerated the tendency to political polarization. The constant use of inflamatory political rhetoric and the pervasive moralizing of orators and pamphleteers led many to view politics as a struggle between the forces of good and evil which made compromise even more difficult. Paradoxically the universal lip service paid to so-called republican institutions did nothing to relax tensions since each group defined *republic* to suit its own vested interests. Tremendous fluctuations in voting patterns both reflected and widened these divisions. When politics ran smoothly, few voted. But when issues exploded, the newspapers filled with inflamatory rhetoric, and voters, many of whom had never bothered to cast a ballot, swarmed to their town meetings and upset established political patterns.

Finally the mechanics of the preparty system worked to the advantage of the more commercial-cosmopolitan elements and towns with the concomitant exacerbation of their opponents. When serious economic and social divisions overlaid this already divisive political system and important issues resulting from the Revolution drove in a few more wedges, politics in the commonwealth quickly moved toward a condition of almost complete polarization.

The mechanics of politics under the new 1780 constitution gave the commercial-cosmopolitan towns and interests considerable advantages. Members of this group and residents of the group A towns held almost all the important state and federal offices between 1780 and 1791. The constitution of 1780 provided for the annual, direct election of a governor, with considerable veto powers, and a lieutenant governor who sat on the council.[1] Every year the electors selected residents of the group A towns and members of the commercial-cosmopolitan interests to serve in these key positions. (See table 20.) James Bowdoin, Thomas Cushing, Benja-

1. Francis N. Thorpe, ed., *Federal and State Constitutions, Colonial Charters, and Other Organic Laws*, 7 vols. (Washington, D.C., 1909), 3:1893-94, 1900-01, 1903-04, gives the formal requirements and powers. For additional background on the constitution see J. R. Pole, *Political Representation in England and the Origins of the American Republic* (New York, 1966), pp. 190-226; Oscar Handlin and Mary Handlin, eds., *The Popular Sources of Political Authority; Documents on the Massachusetts Constitution of 1780* (Cambridge, Mass., 1966), pp. 1-54; Elisha P. Douglas, *Rebels and Democrats: The Struggle for Equal Political Rights and Majority Rule During the American Revolution* (Chicago, 1965), pp. 187-213.

TABLE 20
Holders of Major Offices, 1780-1791

	Governor	Lieutenant Governor	Judges of Supreme Court	President of Senate	Speaker of House	Confederation Congress	National Congress	Governor's Council
From group A	100%	100%	100%	100%	91%	84%	69%	62%
From group B	0	0	0	0	9	16	31	20
From group C	0	0	0	0	0	0	0	18
Held by Harvard/Yale graduates	100	91	94	n.a.	n.a.	79	77	n.a.

SOURCES: Governors and lieutenant governors are from Allen Johnston and Dumas Malone, eds., *Dictionary of American Biography*, 22 vols. (New York, 1928-1944); council, president of the senate, and speaker of the house from *Acts and Laws of the Commonwealth of Massachusetts, 1780-1797*, 11 vols. (Boston, 1890-1897) (hereafter cited as *Acts and Laws);* and members of the supreme judicial court from L. Kinvan Wroth and Hiller B. Zobel, eds., *Legal Papers of John Adams*, 3 vols. (Cambridge, Mass., 1965), 1:cxv-cxix. In doubtful cases, residence may be determined from Thomas Fleet and John Fleet, *Fleet's Pocket Almanack for the Year of Our Lord [1780-1790] . . . to Which Is Annexed the Massachusetts Register* (Boston, 1779-1789) (cited hereafter as Fleet, *Register*, with the year and date of publication).
n.a. = not applicable.

min Lincoln, John Hancock, and Samuel Adams each served either as governor or lieutenant governor between 1780 and 1791. With the sole exception of Lincoln, a former Continental major general, confederation secretary of war, and land speculator who held office for only one year, they all had been important Whig leaders during the earlier 1770s, had graduated from Harvard College, and resided in Boston.[2] During the 1780s the General Court elected delegates to the Confederation Congress cast from the same mold.

2. Allen Johnson and Dumas Malone, eds., *Dictionary of American Biography*, 22 vols. (New York, 1928-1944), contains the following essays: Carl L. Becker, "Samuel Adams," 1:100-01; William A. Robinson, "James Bowdoin," 2:499-500; Edgar A. J. Johnson, "Thomas Cushing," 3:633; James T. Adams, "Benjamin Lincoln," 11:259-61; and ibid., "John Hancock," 8:218-19.

Over four-fifths of these congressmen lived in the group A towns
and three-quarters had graduated from Harvard.[3] The shift to popular election of national congressmen beginning in 1788 made
little difference. Between 1788 and 1791 69 percent of these new
congressmen lived in the group A towns and 77 percent had attended Harvard or Yale. Judges with the same background filled
the seats on the supreme judicial court. Every member between
1780 and 1791 lived in the most commercial-cosmopolitan towns
and only one man, James Sullivan, had not attended Harvard. All
the presidents of the senate during the decade and all but one
speaker of the house resided in group A towns. The exception, a
former Continental major general and member of the Worcester
County Court of Common Pleas, was a typical small town ally of
the commercial-cosmopolitan interests. Residents of the 54 group
A towns also held over one-half of all the seats on the annually
elected, nine-member governor's council during the same eleven-
year period.[4]

In addition to controlling the state's executive and judicial and
the national legislative offices, residents of the group A towns and
placeholders controlled the state senate and had considerable influence in the house of representatives. The commercial-cosmopol-

3. Biographical information for all these individuals may be found in *Biographical Directory of the American Congress, 1774-1961*, 85th Cong., 2d
sess., House doc. no. 442 (Washington, D.C., 1961).

4. Ibid. gives the data for national congressmen. L. Kinvin Wroth and Hiller
B. Zobel, eds., *Legal Papers of John Adams*, 3 vols. (Cambridge, Mass., 1965),
1:cxv-cxix, gives biographies of most of the men on the bench of the state
supreme court during the 1780s. Membership in the court may also be ascertained from Thomas Fleet and John Fleet, *Fleet's Pocket Almanack for the
Year of Our Lord* [1780-1790] . . . *to Which Is Annexed the Massachusetts
Register* (Boston, 1779-1789)(cited, hereafter as Fleet, *Register*), with the
year and date of publication for the 1780s.

Presidents of the senate and speakers of the house of representatives are
listed in the *Acts and Laws of the Commonwealth of Massachusetts,
1780-1797*, 11 vols. (Boston 1890-1897) (cited hereafter as *Acts and Laws*)
at the beginning of each legislative year.

For the selection and power of the council, see Thorpe, ed., *Constitutions*,
pp. 1902, 1904, 1906. Membership in the council is given in the *Acts and
Laws* at the beginning of each legislative year. The council possessed the
power of advising and consenting to the Governor's appointments to all
judicial offices, the attorney general, the solicitor general, sheriffs, coroners,
and registers of probate. It, as a body, heard appeals from the registers of
probate. During the period of Shays's Rebellion in 1786 and 1787, it often
played an important role. See chs. 7 and 8.

itan control of the senate cannot be attributed to the provision of
the 1780 constitution which apportioned senators on the basis of
taxable wealth instead of population because a reapportionment
of the upper house on the basis of population instead of tax
assessments would have resulted in the shift of only three of forty
seats in 1784 and four of forty by 1790. (See table 21.) The

TABLE 21
Apportionment of Senators

Regions	Total Population (1790)	Polls (1784)	Senators Allotted by 1780 Constitution
Eastern	40%	42%	50%
Western	40	43	40
Maine	20	15	10

SOURCES: Population for 1790 is from Department of Commerce and
Labor, Bureau of the Census, *Heads of Families at the First Census of the
United States Taken in the Year 1790* (Washington, D.C., 1908), *Maine*,
pp. 9-10, and *Massachusetts*, pp. 9-10. Polls in 1784 are from the Evalua-
tion, 1784/86, in vol. 163 of the unpublished Massachusetts Archives, Of-
fice of the Secretary, Boston (cited hereafter as Evaluation, 1784/86).
The apportionment of senators among the various counties is in Francis
N. Thorpe, ed., *Federal and State Constitutions, Colonial Charters, and
Other Organic Laws*, 7 vols. (Washington, D.C., 1909), 3:1896.

inhabitants of the District of Maine found themselves underrepre-
sented, but the western Massachusetts counties had no cause to
complain about their share of senators.[5]

Despite this relatively equitable apportionment, the most commercial-cosmopolitan interests controlled the upper house. (See
table 22.) Residents of the group A towns or judges of the courts

5. Thorpe, ed., *Constitutions*, 3:1895-97. Senators had to possess a freehold worth £300 or personal estate valued at £600 or other types of property
valued at £600. They had to reside in Massachusetts for five years and be
residents of their senatorial district. Election for the state senate were held on
the same day as elections for governor and lieutenant governor. Senators had
to be elected by a majority of the voters in their districts. If no candidate
received a majority of the popular vote, the members of the house met with
the elected members of the senate and selected a senator from among those
who had received the highest number of votes. (There were two men auto-
matically nominated for each vacancy.) Due to the fact that most of the
councillors were elected from the senate, the upper house never had a full
complement of forty senators during the entire eleven-year period.

TABLE 22
Membership of the Senate

| | | | | Senators Who
Voted on
National Constitution | | | |
Towns	Total Population (1790)	Senate Seats (1780-91)	Served as Judges of Court of Common Pleas	Yes	No	Not Present	Percentage of Total Judges' Seats[a]
Group A	33%	47%	23%	48%	3%	49%	n.a.
Group B	29	38	39	43	18	49	15%
Group C	39	16	38	44	9	47	6
Total			31%	46%	6%	47%	68%[b]

SOURCES: Population for 1790 is from *Heads of Families, Maine*, pp. 9-10, and *Massachusetts*, pp. 9-10. Senators actually serving in the upper house [i.e., those serving in the council are not listed] are listed in the *Acts and Laws* at the beginning of each legislative year. Their residences may be determined from the lists of justices and placeholders in Fleet, *Register*. This same source also gives the names, and sometimes the residences, of the judges and special judges of the courts of common pleas. The vote on ratification in 1788 is from *Debates and Proceedings in the Convention of the Commonwealth of Massachusetts, Held in the Year 1788, and Which Finally Ratified the Constitution of the United States* (Boston, 1856), 6 Feb. 1788, pp. 87-92.

a. Figures are for those seats in the senate held by judges from group B and C towns.

b. This includes the total percentage (47%) of senators living in group A towns plus the percentage (21%) of those living in group B and C towns who served as judges or special judges of the courts of common pleas. The prohibition against plural office-holding (see Thorpe, *Constitutions*, 3:1909) did not prevent persons from serving as common pleas judges and senators at the same time. The table shows the proportion of total years in office, between 1780 and 1791 held by men from the three groups of towns. For example senators from the group A towns held 47 percent of the total seats occupied in the senate between 1780 and 1791. Senators who favored the ratification of the Constitution in 1788 held 46 percent of the total senate seats during the same period.

n.a. = not applicable.

of common pleas held over 70 percent of the total seats in the senate between 1780 and 1791. The fact that politicians who would support the new Constitution in 1788 held almost one-half of the seats while the Antifederalist senators held less than one-tenth is another indication of commercial-cosmopolitan political power in the senate. These interests used their control time after time during the 1780s to emasculate, defeat, or shelve measures passed by the lower house that might damage their plans and programs. The senate refused to repeal the suspension of legal tender notes in 1781, and it dug in against tax reform, the suspension of suits for debt, and more lenient terms for the "Regulators," or rioters, of 1786.

The lower house, which was more fairly apportioned than many present-day legislatures, became a storm center precisely because the commercial-cosmopolitan interests were unable to dominate it. The four most overrepresented counties which contained 48 percent of the total polls in 1784 could send only 52 percent of the total potential members.[6] But many towns failed to send delegates and few of the larger communities sent their full complements, so theoretical membership did not coincide with actual voting strength. (See table 23.) In practice, Maine, as usual, was severely underrepresented, while the western counties and group C towns sent more members than their relative population entitled them. Between 1780 and 1790 the group C towns with 34 to 40 percent of the total polls or population sent 33 percent of the members and the western counties with 44 percent of the 1784 polls sent almost 52 percent of the total delegates. Maine, at the other extreme, contained 15 to 20 percent of the total polls and population but accounted for only 10 percent of the actual membership in the lower house.[7] Thus the towns and interests least likely to

6. Thorpe, ed., *Constitutions*, 3:1898. Representatives in the lower house had to reside in the town that elected them and in the commonwealth for at least one year, had to possess a freehold worth £100 or a total estate valued at £200, and were elected during the month of May. Each town received one representative for its first 150 polls and one additional one for every 225 polls over 375. All towns incorporated before 1780 could send representatives, regardless of their size. Potential membership is based on the composition of the lower house if every town sent its full complement of members.

7. Actual representation is based on the number of members who attended any of the sessions of the General Court. These men are listed in the *Acts and Laws* at the start of each legislative year. Those who appeared later are often listed in the unpublished Journals of the House of Representatives of the Commonwealth of Massachusetts, Office of the Secretary, Boston (cited hereafter as House Journal), at the beginning of the legislative year.

TABLE 23
Membership of the House of Representatives

Towns	Polls (1784)	Theoretical Members 1781	Theoretical Members 1786	Actual Members 1780-91	Justices as Percentage of Membership
Group A	34%	34%	33%	33%	52%
Group B	32	32	31	34	33
Group C	34	35	36	33	25

SOURCES: *Acts and Laws* for the legislative year, and the Evaluation, 1784/86, for the number of polls and the theoretical membership in 1784. Theoretical membership for 1781 is based upon the list of 1781 polls in E. B. Greene and Virginia Harrington, *American Population Before the Federal Census of 1790* (New York, 1932), pp. 40-45. Justices of the peace are identified by representatives entitled Esquire in the lists of the *Acts and Laws* and house journals. These may be checked against the lists of justices in Fleet, *Register*.

NOTE: The proportion of total seats held by members from the various groups of towns is also given. For example, men from the group A towns held 33 percent of the total seats between 1780 and 1791, and 52 percent of the seats held by men from these communities were held by justices of the peace.

support the programs of the most commercial-cosmopolitan interests actually secured overrepresentation in the popular branch of the General Court. The large number of justices of the peace elected to the lower house tended to reduce the power of these less commercial-cosmopolitan interests. These justices accounted for over one-third of the seats in the house and the combination of justices with representatives of the group A towns accounted for over half the membership.[8] But these justices, often susceptible to local pressures, were never as dependable allies of the most commercial-cosmopolitan interests as the judges in the senate. Thus the house became the scene of some of the bitterest political battles of the 1780s, battles which sometimes ended with the

8. Voting behavior of the justices on several important issues is described in chs. 4 and 9. Robert M. Zemsky's study, "Power, Influence, and Status: Leadership Patterns in the Massachusetts Assembly, 1740-1755," *William and Mary Quarterly*, 3d series. 26:502-20, underlines the importance of the representatives from the commercial towns on important committees of the assembly. This pattern continued into the 1780s. The total number of seats held by representatives from group A towns and justices from the other two groups accounted for 52% of the total seats in the lower house between 1780 and 1791.

defeat of proposals advanced by the most commercial-cosmopolitan interests.

Since the apportionment system did not guarantee the commercial-cosmopolitan interests control of the legislature, the real reason for their power must be sought in the actual operation of the complex preparty political system. This system made it practically impossible for the less commercial-cosmopolitan interests to develop state or even county-wide organizations or programs. The absence of organized parties made it difficult if not impossible to coordinate the state, county, and town campaigns and made it almost impossible for a constituency to completely control its representative. This situation favored the commercial-cosmopolitan interests and towns which were generally represented by the state's best known politicians.

At the state and national levels various commercial-cosmopolitan factions competed with one another for congressional and the higher state offices. In the elections for governor and lieutenant governor during the earlier 1780s these factions usually coalesced around Hancock or Bowdoin, both of whom resided in Boston and had commercial connections. Contests for these offices had little relationship to the voting patterns in the General Court. After the ratification of the Constitution in 1788, patterns emerged that corresponded to the Federalist-Antifederalist division over the new charter, but by 1791 these distinctions had disappeared. The elections of delegates to the Confederation Congress illustrate the same interplay of factions since the court elected leading politicians with commercial and cosmopolitan connections regardless of their stands on significant state issues. This factionalization resulted partly from the fact that the voters electing the governor or lieutenant governor and the legislators selecting the congressmen could not use party labels or platforms to guide their choices. Instead, for personal reasons, they tended to vote for the better-known candidates who almost without exception had commercial-cosmopolitan interests and connections.[9]

9. There is a complete discussion of gubernatorial politics between 1780 and 1786 in ch. 5. The 1787 election are covered in ch. 8; the elections from 1788-91, in chs. 10 and 11. For other examples of faction, especially concerned with job-seeking, see Theodore Sedgwick to Caleb Davis, 25 May 1781, Caleb Davis Papers, Massachusetts Historical Society; Seth Paddelford

The lack of party organization also helped the commercial-cosmopolitan interests at the county level at which state senators and after 1788 national congressmen were elected. In the senatorial elections lawyers, placeholders, social and economic leaders, and residents of the more commercial-cosmopolitan communities in the counties had the tremendous advantage of being better known than their localistic opponents. Occasionally factions of county politicians struggled for control or geographical divisions within the county or a congressional district influenced an election, but on the whole the better-known men won election with little difficulty. Since no information about voting patterns in the senate was available and since the newspapers seldom published campaign information in senatorial contests, the voters had to choose their senators on the basis of personal knowledge of the various candidates. If the electors failed to give a majority of their ballots to any candidate, the General Court filled the vacancies from the two highest contenders for each position. In either case, well-known placeholders and lawyers generally won the elections. The same thing happened in the national congressional elections after 1788.[10]

to Robert Treat Paine, 7 Feb. 1785, Robert Paine Papers, Massachusetts Historical Society; James Warren to Thomas Cushing, 1, 14 Mar. 1783, Cushing Papers Massachusetts Historical Society; and William Cushing to John Hancock, 21 Dec. 1789, in ibid. For an example of requested assistance to become sheriff, see the interchange between Nathaniel Paine and Dwight Foster, 27 Nov. 1788, Dwight Foster Papers, Massachusetts Historical Society. For debate over appointment of justices see "A True Republican," *Salem Gazette*, 17 Jan. 1782, which attacked Hancock for appointing unneeded justices in order to create an "influence." "A True Republican" continued in ibid., on 24 Jan. 1782, while "True Patriot" in the *Independent Chronicle*, 24 Jan. 1782, defended Hancock. For examples of judicial and court appointments see John Cotton to William Cushing, 2 Oct. 1782, Cushing Papers. For a wonderful story of Hancock as a political operator see the account in Charles W. Jenkins, *Three Lectures on the Early History of the Town of Falmouth [Barnstable County] Covering the Time of Its Settlement to 1812, Delivered in the Year 1843*. (Falmouth, Barnstable County, Mass., 1889), p. 92.

10. There is a detailed examination of national congressional elections in ch. 10 and 11. These elections were held at different times. The governor, lieutenant governor, and state senators were selected in early April, the town representatives to the lower house in May, and the national congressmen during the fall. The lists of senators in the *Acts and Laws* show that 102 men served 348 terms in the senate between 1780 and 1791. Eight of these men sat for 72 terms. (These figures *do not* include several men who were con-

The less commercial-cosmopolitan interests had their greatest success in electing town representatives to the General Court. Even at these elections many voters tended to send minor placeholders such as justices of the peace and militia officers to the house and these men often voted with the more commercial-cosmopolitan interests instead of representing the opinions of their constituencies. Towns attempted to retain control over their representatives by drafting instructions for them and the local electors could at least determine how they voted on critical questions. Yet, even at the town level, the less commercial-cosmopolitan interests met political frustration since the voters in one community could not influence the electors in nearby towns unless they could develop some sort of organization that could unify the political responses of the local communities in regard to either programs or candidates.[11]

The less commercial-cosmopolitan interests recognized their political weaknesses and attempted to remedy them by creating

---

stantly reelected but who usually resigned their senate seats to serve on the council.) Five of the eight long-termers lived in the group A towns and the other three served as judges or special judges of the court of common pleas. Six of the eight long-term senators voted for ratification of the national Constitution in Feb. 1788 and not a single one opposed it. See the vote in *Proceedings in the Convention of the Commonwealth of Massachusetts, Held in the Year 1788 and Which Finally Ratified the Constitution of the United States* (Boston, 1856) 2 Feb. 1788, pp. 82-83. Lists of judges and their residences may be compiled from Fleet, *Register* (see fn. 54 in ch. 2 for a list showing annual citations.)

11. Thomas Crafts to John Adams, 7 May 1790, Adams Papers, pt. 4, Adams Manuscript Trust, gives an amusing picture of a chaotic Boston election with only 200 voters, twenty candidates, and no lists or tickets presented or prepared. For other election problems see Luther S. Cushing, *Reports of Controverted Elections in the House of Representatives of the Commonwealth of Massachusetts from 1780 to 1852* (Boston, 1852), p. 13, for the town of Adams, which featured a double return made by two different town clerks; p. 16, for Holliston, where the notice of elections was posted too late to enable many voters to attend; p. 17, for Mansfield, in which the elected representative was accused of bribing electors with liquor; p. 7, for Woburn, where the voters failed to receive timely warning of the election; p. 3 for Cambridge, where petitioners charged that the town clerk double counted a vote in an election where the elected representative won by one vote; p. 26, for Hopkinton and another double return; and p. 32, for Westminister, where petitioners charged that the town meeting was called only to decide if the town wanted to send a representative but that the meeting went ahead and actually elected a member.

rudimentary political organizations or by resorting to "regulation" (riots) and violence. Individual towns did elect men who voted against programs sponsored by the most commercial-cosmopolitan interests and many communities petitioned the General Court to take action on their problems. But these methods usually failed: concessions forced from the lower house would be ignored by the senate and the court tabled the petitions. The towns were forced to turn to extraconstitutional political methods designed to increase their political leverage.[12] Many towns mobilized sentiment by calling and holding county conventions of delegates from many towns which could hammer out a political program and might even nominate candidates for the state senate. Although all the western counties held such conventions between 1781 and 1787, they could not construct a state-wide list of candidates and they often failed to integrate their demands.[13] Too divided to unite to push specific legislative reforms, they were once again frustrated. After elections, petitions, and conventions failed, many westerners turned to violence. They mobbed tax collectors if the General Court failed to reduce taxes or they blocked or "regulated" the courts if the General Court failed to grant relief to debtors. This eventual resort to violence and "regulation" showed the frustration of many westerners—a frustration growing from their inability to obtain any leverage over the governmental institutions of a preparty period.

These less commercial-cosmopolitan interests could expect almost no assistance from the large numbers of social, intellectual, and economic institutions that had been organized throughout the commonwealth before, during, and after the Revolution. The commercial-cosmopolitan interests controlled almost all these groups and either used them for their own political advantage or made them unavailable for use by the less commercial-cosmopolitan interests. The Masons, who in many societies supported revolutionary sentiments, had been integrated into the most commercial-cosmopolitan interests within the commonwealth, and by 1792 the group A towns contained all but one of the eighteen lodges. Several important merchants, artisans, and brokers served as leading Masonic officials.[14] The marine societies located in the leading

12. See chs. 6 and 7.
13. See chs. 6 and 7.
14. Fleet, *Register, 1793* (1792), pp. 80-81, lists the lodges and state officers for 1792. Machias was the only B or C community with a Masonic lodge.

mercantile towns naturally supported the programs of the merchant-shipowning interests.[15] The various professional associations of doctors and lawyers drew most of their membership and practically all of their officers from the group A towns.[16] The commercial-cosmopolitan interests also controlled the entire range of social, religious, educational, and charitable associations that sprang up in the state during the 1780s. The American Academy of Arts and Sciences, led by merchants, placeholders, and ministers, supported philosophical and scientific studies; the Massachusetts Historical Society, founded by politicians, ministers, and merchants, furthered the study of the commonwealth's past; several missionary and charitable societies, organized by merchants and ministers, spread the gospel and assisted the poor; the merchants, placeholders, and ministers founded academies where their sons could receive a better, more socially correct education.[17] The

15. For the various marine societies see Fleet, *Register, 1788* (1787), pp. 8-9; *1786* (1785), p. 62; *1792* (1791), p. 87. Also see William Bently, *The Diary of William Bently, D.D., Pastor of the East Church, Salem, Massachusetts*, 4 vols. (Salem, 1905-1914), 1:144-45, for the Salem society. Also see Lawrence W. Jenkins, "The Marine Society at Salem in New England," Essex Institute, *Historical Collections*, 76:199-220. For contemporary data see [Salem Marine Society], *Laws of the Marine Society at Salem . . . [24 July 1784]* (Boston, 1784), passim.

16. Fleet, *Register, 1792* (1791), p. 84, gives the officers of the Massachusetts Medical Society, the Middlesex Medical Society, the Bristol Medical Society, and on p. 85 there is a list of surgeons and doctors in Boston. John Norman, ed., *The Boston Directory, Containing a List of the Merchants, Mechanics, Traders and Others of the Town of Boston* (Boston, 1789) (cited hereafter as Norman, *Directory*) also lists doctors. Fleet, *Register, 1789* (1788), p. 108., gives the officers of the Massachusetts Medical Society, and *1786* (1785), pp. 66-67; *1783* (1782), pp. 22-23; and *1782* (1781), n.p., give a list of the officers and members of the same organization.

17. These societies are listed for selected years in Fleet, *Register*, as follows: Massachusetts Historical Society, *1792* (1791), p. 76; Massachusetts Humane Society, *1792* (1791), p. 83; *1786* (1785), p. 78; Society to Propagate the Gospel, *1792* (1791), p. 86; Scots Charitable Society, *1790* (1789), p. 97; Massachusetts Congregational Society, *1790* (1789), p. 97. For schools see the following: Phillips Academy (Andover), *1786* (1785), p. 67; Williamstown Free School, *1786* (1785), p. 74; Derby School (Hingham), *1786* (1785), p. 72; Leicester Academy, *1786* (1785), p. 69; Ipswich Grammar School, *1788* (1787), p. 8. For Humane Society see *Massachusetts Centinel*, 8 Mar. 1785; for Historical Society see Charles C. Smith, *A Short Account of the Massachusetts Historical Society . . .* (Boston, 1918), p. 23, and *Massachusetts Magazine*, Dec. 1791, p. 783. Information on the American Academy is available in Fleet, *Register, 1792* (1791), p. 86, and *1787* (1786), pp. 65-67; a complete list of members is available in *1782* (1781) and *1781* (1780), n.p. See also *Massachusetts Magazine*, Aug. 1791,

leading merchants and placeholders even staffed the Massachusetts Agricultural Society which naturally met in the least agrarian of all Massachusetts towns—Boston.[18]

The location of all these organizations in the group A towns and their control by the most commercial-cosmopolitan interests further weakened the potential political influence of the less commercial-cosmopolitan communities. Unlike the situation in modern politics, many interests including the less commercial farmers lacked even rudimentary organizations that could function as effective pressure groups and provide the funds and personnel for lobbying and political action. Existing institutions were all controlled by the more commercial-cosmopolitan interests. Occasionally such groups as the Society of the Cincinnati, conventions of ministers, or maritime societies officially backed programs sponsored by the most commercial-cosmopolitan interests, but the use of these organizations for political ends was less important than the fact that the less commercial-cosmopolitan interests that lacked political organization also had little control over the more informal social, cultural, and intellectual institutions in the commonwealth.

While the structure and nature of preparty politics played into the hands of the most commercial-cosmopolitan interests, a whole series of factors ranging from education to voting turnout tended to increase the bitterness of political divisions within the commonwealth. The state had, over time, developed an educational system that taught the masses to read and at the same time trained the social and political elite to rule. State law required all towns to provide primary schools for their children and forced the larger communities to establish grammar schools for advanced students. Naturally many towns ignored or violated these laws, but enough

---

p. 591, and *Massachusetts Spy* [Worcester], 9 Aug. 1781. For organizations in Boston see Thomas Pemberton, "Topographical and Historical Description of Boston, 1794," in Massachusetts Historical Society, *Collections*, 1st ser., 3:273-75. For a convenient list of the dates of incorporation see Fleet, *Register, 1789* (1788), pp. 100, 105-06; *1788* (1787), pp. 8-14.

18. For the Massachusetts Agricultural Society see Fleet, *Register, 1792* (1791), p. 75; *1794* (1793), p. 32. The officers included Thomas Russell, a leading securities holder, as president; John Lowell, a merchant, as vice president; Moses Gill, placeholder, securities holder, and judge, as second vice president; and John Avery, Jr., a placeholder, as recording secretary.

education seeped down to make the population highly literate for a preindustrial society.[19] The schools, pervaded by clerical influence, inculcated the principles of Protestant public and private morality together with reading, writing, and arithmetic. Ministers inspected the primary schools, checked on the morals of the teachers, approved grammar school instructors, and often prepared advanced students for Harvard. Students studied Bible stories and the Westminster Confession and learned that the Republic rested on a foundation of religion and morality.[20] While the masses learned to read, write, and moralize, the sons of the "better people" were integrated into the political and social elite at Harvard.

19. The school laws current in the 1780s are abstracted in Fleet, *Register, 1786* (1785), p. 61. For examples of interest in education in various towns, see *The System of Public Education Adopted by the Town of Boston, 15 Oct. 1789* (Boston, 1789), passim; *Reports of the Record Commissioners of the City of Boston*, 39 vols. (Boston, 1876-1909), 5 March 1784, 31:16-18; 23 May 1785, 31:79; 10 Mar. 1788, 31:166: 21 Sept. 1789, 31:205-06; 8 May 1790, 31:218-19; Henry F. Jenks, *Catalogue of the Boston Public Latin School, Established in 1635, with an Historical Sketch* (Boston, 1886), pp. 7, 34, 41, 43; John S. Barry, *A Historical Sketch of the Town of Hanover, Massachusetts, with Family Genealogies* (Boston, 1853), p. 92; George F. Clarke, *A History of the Town of Norton, Bristol County, Massachusetts from 1669 to 1859* (Boston, 1859), p. 263; Lysander S. Richards, *History of Marshfield* (Plymouth, 1901), p. 154; *Hampshire Gazette*, 21 July 1790; Bently, *Diary of William Bently*, 1:188; Abijah P. Marvin, *History of the Town of Lancaster, Massachusetts from the First Settlement to the Present Time, 1643-1879* (Lancaster, 1879), pp. 35-53. For an example of the enforcement of the education laws, see Docket Books, Supreme Judicial Court, Barnstable County, June 1787 term (available from Suffolk County Court House, Boston, Mass.) in which the judges fined Falmouth, Sandwich, Harwich, Yarmouth, and Eastham £10 each for not providing grammar schools. For a statistical report on the Boston schools see Fleet, *Register, 1791* (1790), p. 59.

20. *Acts and Laws*, 25 June 1789, 5:416-21; this act stated that it was the duty of all teachers to instruct youth in a "sacred regard to truth, love of the country, humility and universal reverence, sobriety, industry, and frugality." All teachers had to possess certificates of good moral character from a local minister or selectman if they were not residents of the towns in which they taught. The local ministers were responsible for inspecting the schools and for overseeing the attendance of the pupils. See also *The New England Primer . . . to Which Is Added the Assembly of Divines and Mr. Cotton's Catechism* (Boston, 1781), passim, and especially the sections with Bible stories, questions and answers about the Bible, Watt's hymns, and the Westminster Catechism. For public instruction see "C" in the *Hampshire Gazette*, 27 Apr. 1791, "S.C.A." in ibid., 11 May 1791; "A Friend to Education" in *Independent Chronicle*, 27 Nov. 1789; and "Observer" in ibid., 23 Dec. 1790.

During the 1780s Harvard graduates accounted for less than one-sixtieth of the state polls, but these few men held over four-fifths of the seats in the Confederation and National Congresses and served over nine-tenths of the terms of the justices of the supreme judicial court.[21] During the 1780s merchants, placeholders, and other wealthier members of the most commercial-cosmopolitan interests established academies to give their children even more advantages over those from other social and economic groups.[22]

The educational system provided a massive audience for the discussion of political and public morality that deepened divisions among political opponents already divided along social and economic lines. Literacy naturally increased the political potential of the citizens, enabling them to read writers promoting all sorts of varied interests. In 1780, even the most isolated towns debated the new state constitution in an intelligent manner and often proposed lengthy and complex amendments.[23] The pervasive interest in morality, however, led many citizens to concern themselves with theological and moral matters and to view political differences in moral terms. Puritanism may have been dead in the commonwealth by the 1780s, but the Yankees continued to read religious tracts, sermons, theological treatises, and religious polemics that poured from the presses during the decade. Highly sophisticated thinkers argued that the republican system rested upon the virtue of its leaders and citizens and practically all the home-grown political theorists began their treatises with a nod to the importance of

21. Fleet, *Register*, *1781* (1780), n.p., stated that 2,815 men had graduated from Harvard of whom 1,430 had died. This left 1,385 living graduates as of 1781. The costs of a Harvard education are described in Christopher Gore to Rufus King, 28 June 1790, in Charles R. King, *The Life and Correspondence of Rufus King*, 2 vols. (New York, 1894), 1:389.

22. The academies were attacked for their antirepublican tendencies; see "On Education," *Boston Magazine*, Apr. 1784, pp. 238-39, and ibid. Mar. 1784, pp. 171-73. For the creation of academies in Maine see J. T. Champlin, "Educational Institutions in Maine While a District of Massachusetts," Massachusetts Historical Society, *Collections*, 8:155-81. Fleet, *Register*, *1791* (1790), p. 73, gives a list of a dozen public and private grammar schools as of 1790. In the early 1790s, agitation began for the establishment of a college in Maine; see *Massachusetts Magazine*, Apr. 1791, p. 253.

23. See Handlin and Handlin, eds., *Popular Sources of Political Authority*, pp. 475-83, 500-04, 534-54, 564-71, 587-99, 600-05, 614-26, for the detailed responses of several group B and C communities in Hampshire and Berkshire counties.

the religious and moral foundations of the state.[24] This interest in religion and public morality led the political publicists and pamphleteers to discuss political and financial questions in moral terms. The payment of the state debt at its par value thus became not a question of economics but one that dealt with the eternal verities. The supporters of consolidation and refunding with specie argued that the state had a moral obligation to pay its debtors, while the opponents charged that immoral speculators had acquired all the securities and that repayment in specie would re-

24. For the influence of religion on some specific persons see Joseph Barrell [Sr.], to Joseph Barrell, Jr., 8 Dec. 1783, Miscellaneous Papers, Massachusetts Historical Society, and Samuel Adams to Thomas Wells, 22 Nov. 1780, in Henry Alonzo Cushing, ed., *The Writings of Samuel Adams*, 4 vols. (New York, 1908), 4:223-25. For examples of local political theory written during the 1780s which had a strong moral and ethical content, see Benjamin Lincoln, "Observations on the Climate, Soil, and Value of the Eastern Counties in the District of Maine; Written in the Year 1789," in Massachusetts Historical Society, *Collections*, 1st ser., 4:152-55; "Free Republican," *Boston Magazine*, Mar. 1784, pp. 192-95. Also note *Hampshire Gazette*, 1 Aug. 1787; David Hoar, *The Natural Principles of Liberty, Moral Virtue, Learning, Society, Good Manners, and Human Happiness*... (Boston, 1782), esp. pp. i-ii and 1-7; "On Society," *Hampshire Chronicle*, 11 and 18 June 1788; "Propriety," *Massachusetts Centinel*, 21 Mar. 1787; Jonathan Mason, Jr., *An Oration Delivered March 6, 1780* [Boston Massacre Oration] (Boston, 1780), p. 5; John Warren, *An Oration Delivered July 4th, 1782* . . . (Boston, 1783), pp. 6-9. For examples of the many attacks on luxury see "Observer," nos. 1 and 2, *Massachusetts Centinel*, 15 and 22 June 1785, and James Swan, *National Arithmetick or Observations on the Finances of Massachusetts* (Boston, 1786), pp. 21-22. For an excellent overview of this rhetoric see Edmund S. Morgan, "The Puritan Ethic and the American Revolution," *William and Mary Quarterly*, 3d ser., 24:3-43.

The following table is based on a survey of all Massachusetts imprints listed in Charles Evans, ed., *American Bibliography: A Chronological Dictionary of All Books, Pamphlets, and Periodical Publications Printed in the United States . . . 1639 . . . 1820*, 12 vols. (Chicago, 1903-1934), for the years 1781, 1786, and 1791; Roger P. Bristol, *Supplement to Charles Evans' American Bibliography* (Charlottesville, 1970), pp. 289-449.

Imprints	Number Published in		
	1781	*1786*	*1791*
Total number	64	102	144
Religious (sermons, tracts, hymns, convention reports, theological works)	13	24	58
Percentage of religious nature	20%	24%	40%

ward drones and evil men.[25] The casting of such questions in moral terms further increased political tensions throughout the commonwealth.

Almost universal literacy increased the importance of the newspapers and their editors. Most of the editors remained artisan printers, although a few like Isaiah Thomas of Worcester, John Mycall of Newburyport, and Benjamin Russell of Boston became either financially or politically involved with leading merchants and politicians. Most of the papers depended heavily on legal and personal advertising by the state or shopkeepers and traders, and all of them were located in the most important group A communities. Despite these obvious connections between the most commercial interests and the papers, the editors apparently attempted to be relatively impartial on many issues. Essays opposed to consolidation, favoring paper money, advocating legal and land reforms and constitutional amendments found their way into the papers throughout the 1780s. Many editors even published the proceedings of the county conventions that protested against many measures sponsored by the most commercial-cosmopolitan interests.[26]

25. For some examples of this type of rhetoric see *Independent Chronicle*, 20 Nov., 14 Dec. 1780, 3 Nov. 1786; 4, 25 Jan., 8 Feb. 1781; *Continental Journal*, 4, 11, 25 Jan. 1781; *Massachusetts Spy* [Worcester], 11 Jan. 1781; *Massachusetts Centinel*, 11, 22 Feb., 1 Mar., 23, 27 July, 2 Nov. 1785; *Salem Gazette*, 26 July 1785. Also see chs. 4, 6, and 7 for its effects on politics during the 1780s. For some examples in election sermons see Samuel Cooper, *A Sermon Preached Before His Excellency John Hancock, Esq., . . . October 25, 1780* (Boston, 1780), pp. 40-41. Zabdiel Adams, *A Sermon Preached Before His Excellency John Hancock, . . . May 29, 1782* (Boston, 1782, p. 33; and Henry Cummings, *A Sermon Preached Before His Honor Thomas Cushing, Esq., . . . 28 May 1783* (Boston, 1783), pp. 38-39.

26. Clarence S. Brigham, comp., *History and Bibliography of American Newspapers, 1690-1820*, 2 vols. (Worcester, 1947), 1:197-217 and 271-415, gives the location and publishers of these papers. For the importance of subscribers as a source of revenue see *Massachusetts Spy* [Worcester], 12 Apr. 1781; *Massachusetts Gazette* [Springfield], 14 May 1782; *Salem Gazette*, 6 Nov. 1783. One of the best sources on finances is Marcus A. McCorison, "A Day Book from the Office of the Rutland *Herald*, kept by Samuel William, 1798-1802," in American Antiquarian Society, *Proceedings*, 76:306-07, which estimated the various types of income received by a country printer.

For connections with the commercial interests see Isaiah Thomas, *The History of Printing in America with a Biography of Printers and an Account of Newspapers*, 2 vols. (Albany, 1874), 2:73-79; Samuel A. Green, "The Boston Magazine," in Massachusetts Historical Society, *Proceedings*, 2d ser., 18:326-29. For example of broad coverage see a discussion of the Maine land system in *Massachusetts Spy* [Worcester], 17, 24 May, 2 Aug. 1781; 21 Mar.

After 1786 a slight change occurred. The eastern papers printed almost nothing defending the conventions or the Regulators and during the struggle over the Constitution several papers took pronounced Federalist or Antifederalist positions. [27]

But serious deficiencies lurked beneath this editorial fairness, for the press failed to give the electors some extremely important political and financial information. The voter, for example, had almost no indication of how his representatives and senators had actually voted. The lower house of the General Court, with the exception of a few sessions during 1784, published neither its journals nor roll call votes and the senate did not even bother to record roll calls in its official journal. [28] The press, except for brief periods in 1784 and 1785 and later in 1790, made absolutely no effort to cover the proceedings and debates in the General Court. Thus, the typical voter could obtain only the printed session laws published at the end of each legislative session which gave him no information about roll calls, debates, or where defeated bills had been bottled up in committees or quietly ignored. The only way an interested elector could secure this information would be from his town representative who seldom attended all the sessions and who had to rely on his memory, hardly a trustworthy faculty in a

---

1782; *Boston Gazette*, 4 Feb., 11 Mar., 29 Apr. 1782. The judicial and legal system is covered in *Boston Gazette*, 6, 27 May 1782; *Salem Gazette*, 7 Nov., 4 July 1782. See imprisonment for debt in *Independent Chronicle*, 8, 22 Jan. 1784; *Worcester Spy*, 18 Mar. 1784; *Massachusetts Centinel*, 4, 7, 14, 21 Jan. 1785. For Maine secession see *Falmouth Gazette*, 5 Mar., 16 Apr., 7, 19 May, 11, 18, 25 June, 9, 16, 23 July, 6, 13, 20, 27 Aug. 1785.

27. Several western papers did cover the conventions during the Regulation. See *Worcester Magazine*, Sept. 1786, pp. 294-295; Aug. 1786, p. 246; Oct. 1786, p. 334. (The *Worcester Magazine* was a continuation of Thomas's *Spy*. He converted it into a magazine to avoid paying the advertising tax.) See *Massachusetts Gazette* [Springfield], 25 Aug., 5, 8 Sept., 6, 17 Oct. 1786; *Hampshire Gazette*, 15, 29 Nov. 1786. Also see chs. 7 and 8 for the eastern reaction.

28. Evans, *American Bibliography*, vols. 6-8, gives the citation for the sessions in which a journal was published. The house took roll call votes but these were seldom printed. See House Journal, 20 Nov. 1780, when the rule was adopted requiring a roll call vote if requested by fifteen members. The unpublished Journals of the Senate of the Commonwealth of Massachusetts, 1780-1790, Office of the Secretary, Boston (cited hereafter as Senate Journal) contain no roll call votes. Coverage of debates in the General Court is found in *Boston Magazine*, Mar., June, July, Oct., Nov. 1784, and Mar. 1785. For the later period see *Independent Chronicle*, Jan. and Feb. 1790.

politician of any age. The press also failed to publish information about the holders of the state debt, and the commonwealth, with two exceptions, issued no financial statements between 1780 and 1786.[29] Thus while the papers and pamphlets frightened the electors with the polemics of an "Aristides," a "Cato," or a "Convention Man," they failed to inform them of the activities of the General Court or of the financial situation of the commonwealth.

The lack of published information increased the value of public contacts and thus gave many individuals in the commercial-cosmopolitan interests an inside track in securing valuable information. The Boston speculators had easy access to the commonwealth's land office and many urban merchants and traders had connections with state officials who furnished them with information about the workings of the government that remained a mystery to other citizens. Merchants, traders, and speculators forwarded political and financial information to one another and lawyers and judges received and disseminated information through their state-wide network of contacts and acquaintances.[30]

29. Evans, *American Bibliography*, vols, 6-8, lists citations for the session laws and resolves. In most cases these did not include the messages of the governors and failed to print several resolves. For this reason the later edited *Acts and Laws* should be used for this period. The annually printed documents were in two series: (1) the *Acts and Laws*, printed for the entire legislative year, and (2) the *Resolves*, printed at the end of each legislative session. Important legislation was also printed in the official newspaper, usually the *Independent Chronicle* during this period. For examples of the lengthy legislative addresses to the people that gave some information about state finances, see *Acts and Laws*, 26 Feb. 1781, 1:310-18, and 1:309, that provided for the printing and distribution of 900 copies (about three per town). For action in 1786 see ibid., 14 Nov. 1786, 3:142-64. For an example of a resolve providing for the publication and distribution of session laws see ibid., 2 Mar. 1781, 1:323. A few other reports were also published; see *Independent Chronicle*, 29 Dec. 1785, for the report of the court's committee on finance, and Fleet, *Register, 1791* (1790), p. 58, for the report of a similar committee. Swan, *National Arithmetick*, passim, although unofficial, gave a great deal of inside information about finances. Pole, *Political Representation* pp. 231-32, has some interesting insights about the lack of information.

30. For the exchange of information between the state treasurer and the bank, see N. S. B. Gras, *Massachusetts First National Bank of Boston* (Boston, 1937), pp. 308-34. For exchange of information between the treasurer and an important speculator see Moses M. Hayes to [Treasurer] Hodgdon, 22 Dec. 1789, and Hodgdon to Hayes, 22 Dec. 1789, both in Treasurer's Letters, Office of the Secretary, Boston. At least one contemporary was aware of this situation; see Samuel Eliot Morison, ed., "William Manning's *The Key of Liberty*," *William and Mary Quarterly*, 3d ser., 13:205-54, especially

This lack of easily available financial and political information and the pervasive effects of an educational system that promulgated morality and virtue led to a consideration of political questions in moral terms and to an emphasis on the personal qualities of candidates running for the higher state offices. Well-educated, sophisticated theorists argued that a republic required virtue and that a successful republic had to be led by moral men who could recognize the universal validity of certain natural and divine laws. Political pamphleteers thus concluded that debts had to be repaid, contracts must be fulfilled, luxuries should be taxed, dancing, theaters, and other time-wasting activities should be avoided, or the moral foundations of the Republic would be undermined and some type of oligarchy or popular tyranny might result. Ministers joined the chorus and discussed the moral implications of political measures currently before the General Court in their annual election sermons. Political debate of complex political and fiscal issues thus frequently revolved around their morality or immorality. To some publicists the legislators who supported stay legislation, the suspension of suits for debt, or the issuing of paper currency became "degenerate, self-seeking bankrupts," who wished to destroy the moral foundations of the state. Publicists favoring such legislation pointed out that a failure to pass these measures would enrich cliques or juntos of aristocrats, stock-jobbers, or tory speculators who fed at the expense of the public instead of working for a living and whose immoral values naturally sabotaged the principles of republican virtue. This moralizing pervaded even the General Court which titled its most important piece of financial legislation during the early 1780s "An Act to Establish the Public Credit on the Basis of Justice and Morality." This constant moralizing unchecked by the facts pertinent to a given issue tended to deepen the divisions between the conflicting interests.[31]

In addition to moralizing the issues, the authors and political

---

pp. 220-22. For the presence of merchants on key standing committees that considered financial information, see Fleet, *Register, 1790* (1789), p. 45, for The Committee to Deface Public Securities, The Standing Committee to Examine and Pass on Accounts against the Commonwealth, The Managers of the State Lottery, and the Committee to Sell Unappropriated Land in the Eastern Part of Massachusetts [Maine]. Compare these names with those listed in Norman, *Directory*.

31. See chs. 4 and 6 for the constant use of this type of rhetoric between 1780 and 1786.

pamphleteers defended or attacked candidates in highly personal terms. Between 1780 and 1791 every contested election for one of the state's higher offices uncovered character assassins who blackened the reputation of every leading politician within the state. Bowdoin was portrayed as a Tory or a trimmer, as the leader of an aristocratic junto, or as a nepotist. Hancock was pilloried as immoral, incompetent, lazy, stupid, a secret Tory symphathizer, and as a poor businessman. Samuel Adams was execrated as a public embezzler, the enemy of George Washington, and a crusty autocrat. Thomas Cushing was pictured as a creature of Hancock, a nepotist, and a weakling. Benjamin Lincoln was shown to be another aristocrat, a militarist, and an admirer of monarchy. The high point of abuse, Stephen Higginson's "Letters of Laco," a vitriolic denunciation of Hancock, merely went a trifle further than similar defamations of character during the decade. The politicians took such assaults in stride and never brought suit against their defamers. By the end of the 1780s these personal attacks on persons running for minor offices were common and several writers even libeled John Gardner for suggesting a revision of the commonwealth's legal code.[32] This type of rhetoric, when projected on a background of limited information and constant moralizing on issues, subjected the voter to a great deal of heated discussion without shedding much light on the positions of the various candidates or the important issues confronting the commonwealth.

Man evidently cannot tolerate an informational vacuum. Lacking facts, he will invent suppositions and rumors. During the decade many Massachusetts citizens, denied the necessary facts of politics, spread outlandish rumors and came to believe that shadowy conspirators planned to seize the commonwealth. Even hardheaded placeholders like Artemas Ward and Henry Knox reported baseless fabrications in their private letters while the more isolated inhabitants of the western less commercial-cosmopolitan towns spread even wilder rumors. During 1787 many westerners apparently believed that the eastern militia on its march to the west, led by Lincoln, left a swath of rape and pillage behind it, and that the

---

32. See ch. 5 for the use of this personal abuse between 1780 and 1786. The best secondary account on freedom of the press in Massachusetts is in Leonard W. Levy, *Freedom of Speech and Press in Early American History* (New York, 1963), pp. 192-96, 207-09. For a criticism of this style of personal abuse see "Reformer," *Massachusetts Magazine*, Feb. 1789, p. 79.

arrest of Regulator leaders in Middlesex County had occasioned the bayonetting of innocent women and children. The people's gullibility encouraged a corps of writers who constantly uncovered all sorts of so-called conspiracies during the 1780s. The Tory conspiracy became one of the staples of writers who argued that Tories really controlled all sorts of activities ranging from county conventions, through the Maine secessionist movement, to the activities of the Regulators. Other writers, generally spokesmen for the less commercial-cosmopolitan interests, uncovered aristocratic juntos, often related to Toryism, that wanted to seize complete power, destroy the Republic, and crush the "little people." In 1783 and 1784 many pamphleteers flavored this basic conspiracy by injecting a dash of militarism growing out of the efforts of the Society of the Cincinnati to establish a special order within the society.[33] By 1787 many westerners and residents of the less commercial-cosmopolitan towns saw themselves as minnows that could be swallowed up by big, eastern, commercial-cosmopolitan fish who intended to crush the Republic by electing Bowdoin and by forcing through the new national Constitution. Thus constant moralizing, the abuse of personalities, and the lack of detailed political information created a climate of opinion where many electors firmly believed in the existence of conspiratorial groups who intended to destroy their rights.

Although the citizens differed on political ideology and religion, the almost universal belief in a republican form of government and

33. For rumors among placeholders see Artemas Ward to Bowdoin, 12 Sept. 1786, Massachusetts Archives, Office of the Secretary, Boston, 190:252; Thomas Clarke to Bowdoin, 8 Sept. 1786, ibid., 190:238; Henry Knox to [Theopolis] Parsons, 19 Nov. 1786, Knox Papers; *Massachusetts Gazette* [Springfield], 15 Sept. 1786. For rumors see *Salem Mercury*, 10 Feb. 1787; *Worcester Magazine*, Feb. 1787, pp. 532-33. *Hampshire Gazette*, 14, 28 Feb., 7, 14 Mar. 1787; *Massachusetts Centinel*, 21, 28, 31 Mar. 1787; *Essex Journal*, 28 Mar. 1787; *Independent Chronicle*, 29 Mar. 1787; *American Herald*, 2 Apr. 1787; *Independent Chronicle*, 26 July 1787; and *Massachusetts Centinel*, 1, 4 Aug. 1787.

Fears were also expressed by Amos Singletary in his speech before the ratification convention; see *Proceedings*, 25 Jan. 1788, p. 203. William Widgery took a similar position on the same day in ibid., p. 207. A contemporary account of fear of conspiracies is in Morison, ed., "Manning," pp. 220-22. For examples of conspiracies discovered by the press see *American Herald*, 2 Apr. 1787 and 7 Apr. 1788; *American Recorder*, 9 Mar. 1787; "Scrutiny" in the *Massachusetts Centinel*, 4 May 1785; *Independent Chronicle*, 27 Mar. 1788, and *Boston Gazette*, 9 Feb. 1789.

a Protestant-Christian form of religion saved the commonwealth from many of the worst effects of this moralizing and lack of information. Although many citizens disagreed as to how republicanism should be implemented all the groups and interests supported popular election of officials, short terms for office holders, geographical distribution of representatives, and the necessity of public and private virtue within the commonwealth. Even the rioters of 1782 and 1786 made no effort to overthrow the republican system and the most isolated agrarian opponents of the commonwealth's policies never believed themselves completely at odds with the wider society. The large number of conventions attempted to bring nonviolent pressure to bear on the General Court as they championed reforms which, they argued, would make the state even more republican. The most commercial-cosmopolitan interests also showed little interest in a nonrepublican government. A few men, discouraged by the events of 1786 and 1787, wrote private letters hinting at the need for a stronger and, in some cases, a semimonarchical form of government, but no one dared suggest such ideas publicly within the Commonwealth. Even when frightened by the Regulation and dismayed by the 1787 elections, these interests made no effort to seize control of the government through illegal methods.[34] Thus all the interests agreed that the political problems facing the commonwealth would have to be hammered out within the framework of republican institutions.

Naturally the interpretation of republicanism varied from person to person and from interest to interest. Generally these differences concerned the balance of power between the various regions and interests and had little to do with abstract notions of democracy. In their responses to the proposed state constitution of 1780, over 20 percent of the 182 towns whose returns have survived demanded the reduction of property qualifications for voters and five other changes that would have increased the politcal influence of the less commercial-cosmopolitan towns and interests. The

34. Some excellent secondary accounts may be found in Handlin and Handlin, eds., *Popular Sources of Political Authority*, pp. 1-54, and Pole, *Political Representation*, pp. 172-249. Notice the behavior described in E. J. Hobsbawm, *Primitive Rebels, Studies in Archaic Forms of Social Movement in the 19th and 20th Centuries* (New York, 1963), and how differently the less commercial-cosmopolitan towns and groups behaved in Massachusetts.

For the fearful reaction of many leaders to the 1787 election see the discussion in ch. 8.

other five alterations recommended included weakening the power of the governor, an officer elected by the entire state, but who would generally represent the more commercial-cosmopolitan interests; cutting down the power of the senate, a body elected by county districts that would also be much more receptive to the commercial-cosmopolitan interests; increasing the share of representatives from the rural towns and regions; granting the house, which was more influenced by local interests, more power over appointments; and changing the amendment procedures so that less commercial-cosmopolitan towns and interests would have an option to change the charter before the middle of the 1790s. Each of these five suggested changes drew much heavier support from the group B and C towns than from the group A communities both throughout the state and within the western region. On the other hand, the divisions over reducing the property requirement for voting, a distinctly democratic reform, showed little difference among the responses of the three groups of towns. (See table 24.)

After the approval of the 1780 constitution, the debate over these issues died down with only a brief flare-up in 1786. Since the constitution could not be amended until the mid-1790s, pro-

TABLE 24
Recommendations for Changes in the 1780 Constitution

Towns	Number Making Returns	Percentage Favoring the 6 Changes					
		1^a	2^b	3^c	4^d	5^e	6^f
Group A	39	10%	10%	15%	10%	33%	23%
Group B	59	32	31	27	24	37	15
Group C	84	37	25	26	31	39	27
State total	182	30%	24%	24%	24%	37%	23%
Western group A	19	11%	16%	16%	11%	26%	16%
Western group B	35	34	34	34	29	43	17
Western group C	73	40	21	27	34	41	26

SOURCE: Based upon the analysis of data presented in Steven Patterson, "Massachusetts Politics, 1763-1780" (Ph.D. diss., University of Wisconsin, 1968), pp. 657–73.
  a. Demanded a weaker governor.
  b. Demanded a weaker senate.
  c. Demanded representation that would favor rural interests.
  d. Demanded the reduction of the appointive power of the governor.
  e. Demanded changes in amendment procedures.
  f. Demanded the reduction of the property requirement for voting.

tests and the county conventions during the earlier 1780s took little notice of constitutional reforms. During the Regulation movement in the west conventions criticized the powers and composition of the senate and suggested other reforms, but these quickly died out when the General Court dismantled the state's refunding and taxation programs. Despite the fact that many of the less commercial-cosmopolitan towns protested the 1780 constitution, there is little evidence that this protest flowed from deeply rooted ideological differences between the two general interests. Each naturally desired as much political power as possible and attempted to rationalize its quest for power in republican and even democratic rhetoric.

The debates over the 1780 constitution also involved a bitter struggle over religion and the church establishment within the commonwealth. Almost all citizens agreed that their commonwealth required a foundation of Christian and Protestant religion and morality, and most of them favored some form of relationship between religion and the virtuous state. The real debate concerned the continuation of the establishment of individual Congregational churches by towns and parishes. This system permitted the local civil division to assess and collect for church purposes taxes from all its citizens. Legislation had been enacted that provided that members of certain specified denominations could pay these rates to their own ministers if they gave their local assessors or collectors a certificate signed by their particular minister. Many Baptists and some others refused to obey this law and in many towns collectors seized livestock and property for the nonpayment of church taxes.[35] These problems fomented local disputes that tore some communities apart. Most of the disputes were resolved at the local level and were seldom referred to the General Court. In 1780 these differences played an important role in the reaction of the various towns to the new state constitution. Indeed, the voters may even have rejected article three which continued the previous establishment.[36] A slightly different pattern appeared in the response of the towns to article three and to the absence of a religious qualification or test for the governor. (See table 25.) In both instances about two-fifths of the towns protested against both the

35. See ch. 2, especially fn. 59.
36. This is Samuel Eliot Morison's argument in "The Struggle over the Adoption of the Constitution of Massachusetts, 1780," in Massachusetts Historical Society, *Proceedings*, 50:353-411.

TABLE 25
Reaction of the Towns to the Religious Articles in the 1780 Constitution

| | Opposing | |
Towns	Article	Lack of Test
By group		
Group A	21%	28%
Group B	54	42
Group C	42	45
State total	41%	41%
By religious character		
With Congregational ministers only	31%	41%
All others	58	40
State total	41%	41%

SOURCE: Based on an analysis of the data in Patterson, "Massachusetts Politics," pp. 657–73. Towns with ministers may be determined from the lists of ministers in Fleet, *Register, 1781* (1780), n.p.

establishment and the lack of a Protestant test. Almost three-fifths of the towns that had no Congregational ministers or had Congregational and other ministers protested against article three, while only one-third of the communities with only Congregational ministers objected. Around two-fifths of both groups of towns protested against the lack of the test for the governor, so the reaction against the establishment had little correlation with the demands for a Protestant governor. After 1780 state-wide debate over these issues abated since the constitution could not be amended until the mid-1790s. Issues did crop up when some legislators attempted to pass Sabbatarian and sumptuary legislation, or when the inhabitants of Roxbury enforced the Sabbath Blue Laws against the enraged citizens of Boston, or even when in 1791 a Maine constable arrested the judges of the supreme judicial court for traveling on Sunday, but these local and minor disputes did not become the basis for state-wide political divisions during 1780s. Indeed during much of that decade, Bristol, the most religiously diverse county, voted with the solid Congregationalists from Worcester County on a wide range of important political questions. Religious differences remained important, towns continued to be torn apart by church controversies, and religion and morality were staples of political rhetoric. But since political and religious divisions seldom overlapped, political differences, at least at the state level, tended to

cut across rather than accentuate divisions based on religious differences.

Before 1787 most of the commonwealth's citizens, while accepting republican government in theory, voted erratically if at all.
With no organized parties attempting to get out the vote and with
different election dates for state, local, and (after 1788) national
offices, voting tended to fall off from relatively high returns for
the governor to lower results for state senators, the lieutenant
governor, and local representatives. Although Boston had, over
time, the highest turnout rate of any town in the commonwealth,
the group A towns generally did not have a significantly higher
rate than did the less commercial-cosmopolitan group B and C
communities. It is mainly the extremely low turnout in the Maine
frontier group C towns that depresses the rate for the group C
communities as a whole.

In election after election the voters cast a much higher proportion of their ballots at the April election for the governor than
for his lieutenant or for county senators. In 1785 only 11 percent
of the potential electors voted in the gubernatorial election and
only 9 percent voted for senators. In 1787 the turnout for governor soared to 28 percent and almost one-fourth of the electorate
voted for state senators. These rates then remained high throughout the later 1780s. This reflected popular interest in the regulation and its repression by the Bowdoin government and the
continued political quarrels revolving around Federalist and
Antifederalist candidates and measures between 1787 and 1790.
The first national congressional elections in 1788 drew out about
13 percent of the voters, but the obvious importance of the new
government and the important issues handled by Congress attracted almost 16 percent of the electors in 1790.[37] This reflected

37. The calculation of males over 21 was accomplished as follows: (1) Take
the 90,757 polls, as of 1784, in the Evaluation, 1784/86 in the unpublished
Massachusetts Archives, Office of the Secretary, Boston, vol. 163. (2) Subtract these from the 106,427 polls listed for 1792 in Fleet, *Register, 1794*
(1793), pp. 52-63. (3) Divide this figure by eight, giving an annual increase of
1,959 polls. (4) Subtract the two years' increment from the 1792 figure,
giving a total of 102,551 polls for 1790. (5) Compare this figure with the
figure in Department of Commerce and Labor, Bureau of the Census, *Heads
of Families at the First Census of the United States Taken in the Year 1790*
(Washington, D.C., 1908), *Maine*, pp. 9-10, and *Massachusetts*, pp. 9-10, giving 119,925 males over 16. Subtract 20 percent of these as being between 16
and 21 leaving 95,940 males over 21 compared with 102,511 polls. (6) Sub-

the growing importance of national politics and the increasing interest of the voters in national political questions.

The same pattern of lower turnout for more local offices and the growing importance of national elections held true for the town of Boston which usually had a higher turnout rate than any other town in the commonwealth.[38] Even the interested and relatively well-organized Bostonians neglected to vote for their town representatives and became much more interested in national elections between 1788 and 1790.

Differences in turnout rates among the three groups of towns remained relatively minor. The most commercial-cosmopolitan towns usually had a higher turnout but, except for the numerous group C Maine frontier towns, the group C least commercial-cosmopolitan communities had comparable turnouts. The voting changes in 1787 resulted in higher relative rates for both the Maine towns and the group C communities as a whole.[39]

---

tract 10 percent of the polls, leaving a figure of about 92,000. Thus I have computed the total number of polls for each county and each group of towns for every year between 1784 and 1792 and have subtracted 10 percent to arrive at the approximate number of males over 21. The resulting figures are almost identical to those computed by Pole, *Political Representation*, pp. 544-45. The number of voters is taken from the following sources: (a) Elections for governor and lieutenant governor, taken from "Abstract of votes for the Election of Governor and Lieutenant-Governor," Office of the Secretary, Boston. These are available for all years except 1783 and 1784 and give the returns of all candidates in every town. (b) Returns for senators are given in the Abstract of Votes for State Senators, also available in the office of the Secretary for all years between 1780 and 1790. The Senate Journal for every year between 1782 and 1791 gives the total vote for each county and the number of ballots received by elected or nominated candidates.

38. Boston turnout may be computed from the sources in fn. 37, and from the elections in the *Boston Town Records*, vols. 26 and 31. The returns for the 1788 Constitutional Ratification Convention come from the *Boston Town Records*, vol. 31. For congressmen see Abstracts of Votes for the house of Representatives, Office of the Secretary, Boston, for the returns for all national congressional elections after 1788.

39. Sources are contained in the Abstract of Votes for the Election of Governor and Lieutenant-Governor, for the years 1780, 1785, 1787, 1788 and 1789, and the Abstracts of Votes for House of Representatives, for the years 1788 and 1790. The abstracts may be located in the office of the Secretary, Boston. (In the last two instances the first elections in 1788 and 1790 were the only ones analyzed since these were the only elections that resulted in contests in all of the congressional districts.) For further details see chs. 10 and 11.

Two examples of significant voting behavior, aside from the low turnouts, were the failure of many towns to send in their returns and the propensity to cast over nine-tenths of their ballots for a single candidate. In 1780 and 1785 almost one-third of the towns and plantations in the commonwealth submitted no returns and, although this number fell to around one-fifth in the 1787 election, many towns had no elections or did not submit their votes. In the three contested gubernatorial elections in 1780, 1785, and 1787, over one-third of the towns that did vote submitted returns that gave one particular candidate over nine-tenths of their votes. This showed the importance of personal contacts of the candidates in the various communities as a local opinion leader could obviously sway the local voters into voting for the leader's choice. The group C, least commercial-cosmopolitan towns, were most negligent about submitting their returns and had the highest proportion of straight voting.[40]

Thus the patterns of preparty politics tended to keep voter participation low and reduced the political strength of the group C towns, especially in the District of Maine. Yet electors turned out in record numbers in 1787 and the rate remained generally high in the later 1780s. Low turnout may have aided the most commercial-cosmopolitan interests and their placeholding allies in many communities and sections of the state. Well-known placeholders were not hampered by the lack of printed advertising, and since each town had only one polling place, the residents of the village could vote much more easily than most of the farmers.[41]

Qualified electors failed to vote for a number of reasons. The lack of party organization meant a complete absence of platforms, ballots, or any other efforts to mobilize massive voting turnouts. The intricacies of the three-layered political system confused the voters who found it difficult to acquire political information from newspapers, pamphlets, and politicians. Only a crisis, such as the Regulation and the reaction of the Bowdoin government to the Shaysites, could spur a heavy turnout, and only the persistence of divisive issues could keep the voting rate high.

40. The number of towns submitting returns for lieutenant governor in 1780 and for governor in 1785 and 1787 and the voting patterns of these towns can be determined from Abstract of Votes for the Election of Governor and Lieutenant-Governor for the noted years.

41. Turnout rates are computed as noted in fn. 37 of this chapter.

Thus the three groups of towns and the two coalitions of interests struggled for control within a political system that gave several important advantages to the more commercial-cosmopolitan interests while at the same time widening the divisions among the towns and groups. Citizens of the most commercial-cosmopolitan towns and members of that interest controlled the important executive and judicial offices, held a stranglehold on the state senate, received more complete and detailed political and financial information, and controlled most of the nonpolitical social, religious, and cultural organizations throughout the commonwealth. With no organized political parties the less commercial-cosmopolitan towns had to organize themselves, surmount ideological and religious differences within their ranks, and develop broad policies that could win over a majority of the voters. This task, given the nature of the political system, was simply impossible. While the system was aiding the most commercial-cosmopolitan interests, other factors, such as the tendency to debate political questions as moral problems, the fear of conspiracies, and the tendency of the electors to vote in periods of trouble, increased the divisions among the various groups of towns and the conflicting interests. Between 1780 and 1786 when the financial issue, a legacy of the Revolution, split the interests and towns along economic and cultural lines, the less commercial-cosmopolitan interests and towns, who found themselves unable to control the political system through normal preparty methods, resorted to violence in order to achieve their political goals.

4

Conflict and Consensus
in the Commonwealth

THE serious political divisions generated by the economic and financial legacies of the Revolution placed a severe strain on the commonwealth's preparty political structure. In their efforts to promote financial and credit policies that would aid merchants, traders, investors, and speculators, the most commercial-cosmopolitan towns and interests drove the less commercial-cosmopolitan communities and occupations into a position of almost constant and consistent opposition. By 1786 these state issues had become related to certain questions concerning the finances of the confederation government leading the less commercial-cosmopolitan interests and towns to become more and more suspicious of programs designed to increase the financial and taxation powers of the confederation. Their lack of success in the General Court led some towns and farmers to attempt to apply political pressure outside the usual channels. Towns and counties held conventions and occasionally rioters attempted to block courts or prevent the collection of state taxes and private debts. Thus by 1786 state and national fiscal questions had effectively divided the commonwealth, and the less commercial-cosmopolitan interests had become more and more concerned over their lack of ability to control or even influence the political situation. Fortunately for the commonwealth these varied and conflicting interests did reach consensus on a wide range of social, economic, religious, and cultural questions so that the struggles over the state and national debt, taxation policies, and the enforcement of private contracts did not become directly related to other complex and potentially explosive issues.

A complex of national and state financial issues became critical

94

because of the economic changes wrought by the Revolution. During the War of Independence both the commonwealth and the confederation printed large quantities of paper currency, borrowed large sums from their citizens, levied taxes, and intervened in the economy by controlling prices and wages. The war also resulted in the rise of new mercantile and speculative groups, closely allied with the governments, who looked forward to ending paper currency and legal tender and who wanted their securities refunded, serviced, and repaid. These dynamic elements in the most commercial-cosmopolitan centers concentrated their efforts on these specific goals. Meanwhile the less commercial-cosmopolitan towns and groups mistakenly believed that the Revolution had democratized the government which they could now control by their numbers. They, of course, had little interest in paying heavy direct taxes for the benefit of speculators and commercial communities.[1] Economic developments during the early 1780s gradually awakened these less commercial-cosmopolitan elements to their real situation. As the commercial recession after the war deflated agricultural prices, less commercial farmers found it more and more difficult to pay their taxes or retire their private debts. More frustration resulted when the less commercial-cosmopolitan groups had difficulty securing information, controlling or influencing the political system, or preventing the more commercial-cosmopolitan interests from carrying out their programs. To many it seemed that the Revolution had been betrayed and in their suspicion and fear they turned to opposition, conventions, and eventually Regulation.[2]

1. The impact of the war on the Massachusetts economy may be studied in Robert A. East, *Business Enterprise in the American Revolutionary Era* (New York, 1938), pp. 49-71, 202-04; Oscar Handlin and Mary Handlin, *Commonwealth—A Study of the Role of Government in the American Economy: Massachusetts, 1774-1861* (New York, 1947), pp. 20-25, 59-62; Ralph V. Harlow, "Economic Conditions in Massachusetts During the American Revolution," Colonial Society of Massachusetts, *Publications*, 20:163-90; Andrew M. Davis, "The Limitations of Price in Massachusetts, 1776-1779," ibid., 10:119-34; Oscar and Mary Handlin, "Revolutionary Economic Policy in Massachusetts," *William and Mary Quarterly*, 3d ser., 4:3-26.

2. The best data on prices is from Ruth Crandall, "Wholesale Commodity Prices in Boston During the 18th Century," *Review of Economic Statistics*, 16:109-28; and Carroll D. Wright, "Comparative Wages, Prices and Cost of Living," *Tenth Annual Report of the Massachusetts Bureau for Statistics* (Boston, 1889), pp. 57, 60, 64-70.

The wide-ranging programs of the most commercial-cosmopolitan towns intensified and partially justified these fears. The speculators, merchants, placeholders, and other members of the most
commercial-cosmopolitan interests sponsored, supported, and
passed legislation that refunded the Massachusetts state debt at an
extremely high figure, provided for the servicing and eventual repayment of this debt in specie, furnished tax revenues from the
state impost and excise that could be used only to pay the state
debt, levied heavy direct taxes on polls and property to meet
Continental requisitions, struggled against any modification of
laws concerning private contracts for debt, pushed for voting the
confederation an annual sum collected by direct taxes, and tried
to tighten up the administration of the state's tax system. These
interests claimed that their program would enrich the commonwealth and that morality demanded the repayment of so-called
just state and private debts and the effective collection of taxes,
but many of the less commercial-cosmopolitan groups saw the
financial program as an effort to enrich usurers and speculators at
their expense. They found themselves constantly outmaneuvered
during the early 1780s. Their considerable strength in the lower
house was frequently undercut by the placeholder representatives
among them who often voted for the commercial-cosmopolitan
programs rather than as their constituents would have preferred.
Once a program had become law, the control of the senate by the
more dynamic commercial-cosmopolitan interests made it practically impossible to dismantle or repeal it. The more localistic
interests won a few victories: they passed a modified tender law
for debts in 1782 and they prevented the passage of measures
designed to improve the collection of direct taxes or the annual
grant of funds to the confederation, but on the whole the workings of the preparty political system gave most of the benefits to
the speculators, merchants, traders, and placeholders.

At the root of the conflict concerning the state debt and private
contracts and credit was the commonwealth's inequitable taxation

---

For personal observations about prices see: William Bently, *The Diary of
William Bently, D.D., Pastor of the East Church, Salem, Massachusetts*, 4 vols.
(Salem, 1905-1914), 11 Jan. 1790, 1:136; and William Tudor, ed., *Deacon
Tudor's Diary [John Tudor] A Record of More or Less Important Events in
Boston From 1732 to 1793, By an Eyewitness* (Boston, 1896), 7 Apr. 1780,
p. 82. For some general background see Richard D. Hershcopf, "The New
England Farmer and Politics, 1785-1787" (Masters Thesis, University of Wis-
consin, 1947); Robert A. Feer, "Shays' Rebellion" (Ph.D. diss., Harvard Uni-
versity, 1957-1958), pp. iv, 30-34.

system which most of the less commercial-cosmopolitan interests believed weighed heavily against them and their property. In typical times when taxes were low few towns or groups protested. But between May 1781 and April 1786 the General Court levied almost £1.4 million in direct taxes with the poll tax alone accounting for almost one-third of the total bill.[3] In addition to a poll tax of £6 per poll, the less commercial-cosmopolitan towns also discovered that their taxes had to be paid in specie or in other forms of liquid wealth that had migrated into the commercial centers. In addition to the high state taxes, they had to pay local and county rates that had been levied to pay bounties for recruits and to

3. The following table lists the tax acts, payable in specie or currency, for the period December 1780 through 1791.

Date of Act	Citation in Acts and Laws	Amount Levied	Poll Tax
18 May 1781	1:91-104	£207,863	£1 5s.
31 Oct. 1781	1:503-24	303,634	1 5
5 Mar. 1782	1:547-67	200,000	16s. 8d.
22 Mar. 1783	2:153-74	200,000	16 8
9 July 1784	3:62-83	140,000	11 8
23 Mar. 1786	3:580-605	300,439	1 5
Total (1781-86)		£1,351,936	£6 0s. 0d.
27 Mar. 1788	4:628-48	£ 65,000	5s. 5d.
14 Feb. 1789	5:131-50	32,606	2 6
3 Mar. 1790	5:476-97	25,360	1 9
5 Mar. 1791	6:33-55	25,365	11 5
Total (1787-91)		£148,321	11s. 5d.

NOTE: There was also a 4 Dec. 1780 levy for 4,626,178 pounds of beef and a levy of 22 June 1781 for beef, clothing, and shoes. These are in *Acts and Laws of the Commonwealth of Massachusetts, 1780-1797*, 11 vols. (Boston, 1890-1897) (cited hereafter as *Acts and Laws*), 1:207-10, and 1:639-56. Pre-Revolutionary taxes had been very low:

Date of Act	Citation in Acts and Resolves	Amount Levied	Poll Tax
29 June 1773	18:305-21	£29,458	2s. 6d.
17 June 1774	18:396-406	12,960	1 1

SOURCE: Citations are from *Acts and Resolves, Public and Private, of the Province of the Massachusetts Bay, 1692-1780*, 21 vols. (Boston, 1869-1922).

Of the £1,351,936 levied between 1780 and 1786 at least £450,000 was collected by the poll tax (which was equally levied on all ratable polls regardless of their wealth). (Approximately 90,000 polls in 1784 paying £6 per poll equals the £450,000.)

rebuild schools, courthouses, and other public buildings damaged by the war.[4] In order to escape some of the impact of these taxes, the less commercial-cosmopolitan interests attempted to force the court into servicing the state debt with the revenues from the impost and excise duties which, they believed, fell heaviest on the eastern commercial communities and occupations. Time after time they attempted to prevent using direct taxes to pay the interest or principal on the state and national debts, but since the impost and excise could not produce the needed revenue they found themselves paying direct taxes to meet interest requirements on state securities after early 1786.[5] Fear of even heavier direct taxes lurked beneath their opposition to schemes providing for the funding and reimbursement of both the national and state debts and would play an important role in their opposition to the Constitution in 1788.

4. Between October 1781 and April 1786 the court levied forty-seven taxes for county use. These had been requested by the county courts of general sessions but were levied by the General Court.

For local bounties see *Acts and Laws*, 2:744-45, 6 Oct. 1783, and Jonathan Smith, "How Massachusetts Raised Her Troups in the Revolution," Massachusetts Historical Society, *Proceedings*, 55:345-70.

For other local problems and examples of local taxation see D. Hamilton Hurd, ed., *History of Norfolk County Massachusetts, with Biographical Sketches of Many of Its Pioneers and Prominent Men* (Philadelphia, 1884), p. 347 for Braintree; Leonard B. Ellis, *History of New Bedford and Its Vicinity, 1602-1892* (Syracuse, 1892), pp. 142-44; "Civil Spy" in *Independent Chronicle*, 12 May 1785, for Harvard [Town]; Samuel Sewall, *The History of Woburn, Middlesex County, Massachusetts* (Boston, 1868), p. 379; John J. Babson, *History of the Town of Gloucester, Cape Ann, Including the Town of Rockport* (Gloucester, 1860), p. 447; D. Hamilton Hurd, ed., *History of Bristol County, Massachusetts, with Biographical Sketches of Many of Its Pioneers and Prominent Men* (Philadelphia, 1883), p. 709, for Raynham; Frederick Freeman, *History of Cape Cod*, 2 vols. (Boston, 1858), 2:129, 131, for Sandwich; *Records of the Town of Plymouth, 1636-1783*, 3 vols. (Plymouth, 1889-1903), 3:401-03, 429, 438. For some examples of taxes on specific property see *Independent Chronicle*, 7 Feb. 1782 for Dedham, 31 Jan. 1782 for Fryeburgh, 22 Jan. 1784 for Monson, 18 Oct. 1781 for Hubbardstown, 4 Oct. 1781 for Granville, and 6 June 1782 for Sunderland.

5. See tables 27, 28, 30, 32, 33, and 36. For the impost and excise, see Ledgers [of Treasurer Ivers] in Treasurer's Papers, Office of the Secretary, Boston, pp. 28, 72, 85, 94, 99, 124, 125, 101, 102, 104, 135, 139, 141, 142, 143, 148, which gives examples of impost and excise collections by various counties for the years 1782-1787. It reflects the high proportion of excise paid to collectors in the eastern and coastal counties. This naturally fell upon the consumer but the actual payments fell on the more commercial counties and towns.

The workings of the state's tax system substantiated many of the fears of these less commercial-cosmopolitan interests and towns. The 1781 valuation, which served as the basis for levying direct taxes between 1782 and 1786, hit the group C towns, especially those in western Massachusetts, relatively hard. (See table 26.) The 54 group A communities with 36 percent of the polls

TABLE 26
Assessed Taxes, 1781–1786

Towns	Polls 1781	Tax Valuation	Inventory	Silver	Tax per Poll on a Levy of £200,000
Group A	36%	42%	93%	82%	£2.88
Group B	33	32	6	13	2.42
Group C	30	27	2	5	2.22
Western group C	22	20	1	3	2.37

SOURCES: 1781 polls and tax valuation from *Acts and Laws of the Commonwealth of Massachusetts, 1780-1797* (Boston, 1890-1897), 1:903-06 (cited hereafter as *Acts and Laws*). "Inventory" and "Silver" are from the Evaluation, 1784/86, in vol. 163 of the Massachusetts Archives, Office of the Secretary, Boston (cited hereafter as Evaluation, 1784/86). "Tax per Poll on a Levy of £200,000" was determined as described in note 6.

but over four-fifths of the value of inventory and silver had been assessed for only 42 percent of the taxes, while the 30 percent of the polls living in the group C communities with less than one-twentieth of the inventory and silver had to provide 27 percent of the tax funds. The inhabitants of Maine escaped the brunt of the taxation system as an average poll in the district had to pay only £1.87 on each £200,000 levied, while the bill for eastern and western Massachusetts residents was £2.73 and £2.53 respectively. Table 26 shows the percentage of the total valuation assigned to the various groups of towns and the tax on each poll that would result from a levy of £200,000 in taxes.[6]

6. The figures and computations are based on the following sources. Polls, inventory, and specie, from Evaluation, 1784/86, vol. 163, Massachusetts Archives, Office of the Secretary, Boston. The 1782 valuation is in *Acts and Laws*, 6 March 1782, 1:903-06. The calculations are based on a £200,000 tax levied on the basis of the 1782 valuation paid by the number of polls listed in the 1784 valuation. This procedure reduces the amount paid per poll for 1782-1783 but the 1784 figure would be an average for the entire 1782-1786 period.

The unfairness of the tax structure resulted in heavy pressure on the less commercial-cosmopolitan communities. By early 1787 the state treasurer had issued executions against various towns for unpaid taxes amounting to over £150,000. The group C towns accounted for 37 percent of the value of these executions while the 54 wealthier group A communities had only 27 percent of the total. The western group C towns alone accounted for 29 percent of the value of outstanding executions and the group B and C communities in the two counties of Worcester and Hampshire accounted for 44 percent of all taxes out on execution by early 1787. While the typical poll in a group A town faced a total of £1.36 worth of back taxes on execution the polls from the unfortunate group B and C towns in the two western counties had to find £3.41 to meet the executions on their local communities.[7] Thus the less commercial-cosmopolitan communities, especially in the west, had good reason to fear any increase in direct taxes and this made them unreceptive to programs designed to fund or repay state or national securities with funds allocated from increased taxes on polls and property.

Fortunately for the commonwealth the various interests and groups of towns did not relate these struggles over finances and taxation to a number of other important economic questions during the 1780s. The less commercial-cosmopolitan towns had few objections to higher tariffs, navigation acts, chartering of banks and internal improvements, or bounties to whalers. They resisted only economic programs sponsored by the most commercial-cosmopolitan interests which promised to further undermine their financial stability. The same towns also had little interest in sponsoring constitutional, religious, social, judicial, or institutional reforms during the period. They had no intention of democratizing the commonwealth or letting the radicals take over, but would respond to direct assaults on their interest by the more dynamic commercial-cosmopolitan groups and towns who attempted to implement a wide-ranging financial program.

Financial and credit questions held the spotlight on the political stage of the General Court between 1780 and 1786. During this seven-year period almost three-quarters of the roll call votes re-

7. The book Executions at the Death of Treasurer Ivers [1787], Treasurer's Papers, Office of the Secretary, Boston, lists the executions, by tax, lodged against every town in the commonwealth with the exception of the four communities in the island counties of Nantucket and Dukes.

corded in the journals considered state or national credit or financial issues, and almost half of them dealt with state fiscal and credit problems. These questions ranged from the refunding and consolidation of the state debt in 1781 to efforts favoring the use of the commonwealth's impost and excise revenues to meet general expenses instead of to service the state debt. The representatives of the group A, most commercial-cosmopolitan towns, voted differently from the delegates from the group C, least commercial-cosmopolitan communities on nineteen of the twenty roll calls dealing with these diverse and divisive financial matters. Table 27 shows the proportion of representatives from each of the three groups of towns that favored the programs sponsored by the most commercial-cosmopolitan interests on these nineteen roll calls. The greatest polarization developed between the eastern group A and the western group C towns, which together accounted for nearly one-half of the total population of the commonwealth and whose representatives cast about one-half of the total votes in the General Court between 1780 and 1786.[8] In the west the group A towns, with only one exception, cast a much higher percentage of their votes in favor of these programs than did the western group C communities. Table 28 shows the difference between the votes of the western group C towns and those of the eastern and western group A communities. The only exception to this pattern was the vote on the 1781 Evaluation Act which reflected geographical differences among the counties.[9]

When we examine how the towns during the same period voted on five key financial issues, the same pattern emerges. (See table 29.) Over 63 percent of the group A communities that sent

(Text continued on page 104)

8. This analysis is based upon E. B. Greene and Virginia Harrington, *American Population Before the Federal Census of 1790* (New York, 1932), pp. 41-45 for the 1781 polls. Evaluation 1784/86, gives the 1784 polls; Department of Commerce and Labor, Bureau of the Census, *Heads of Families at the First Census of the United States Taken in the Year 1790* (Washington, D.C., 1908), *Maine*, pp. 9-10; *Massachusetts*, pp. 9-10, for the 1790 population. Five roll call votes covering the years 1780 through 1786 were taken from the note to table 27. These were numbers one, eight, eleven, fourteen, and fifteen.

9. This vote was in the unpublished Journal of the House of Representatives, available at the Office of the Secretary, Boston (cited hereafter as House Journal), 9 Oct. 1781, pp. 306-08. The vote to concur with the senate gave the following percentages voting in favor: group A, 56 percent; group B, 49 percent; group C, 50 percent; total, 52 percent.

TABLE 27

Votes on Financial Programs Sponsored by
Commercial-Cosmopolitan Interests, 1780–1786

	Percentage of Representatives Voting for Programs on 19 Roll Calls									
Towns	1	2	3	4	5	6	7	8	9	10
Group A	58%	76%	80%	78%	77%	75%	80%	60%	48%	69%
Group B	23	39	45	46	51	42	47	30	13	46
Group C	29	32	42	42	42	47	33	24	20	34
Total	37%	54%	58%	58%	59%	54%	54%	38%	26%	49%

	Percentage of Representatives Voting for Programs on 19 Roll Calls								
Towns	11	12	13	14	15	16	17	18	19
Group A	59%	58%	72%	78%	84%	38%	40%	84%	70%
Group B	40	42	24	50	32	26	24	74	35
Group C	14	15	30	53	29	25	34	63	26
Total	36%	38%	41%	58%	49%	30%	32%	73%	44%

SOURCES: For the roll call votes, see the unpublished Journal of the House of Representatives, Office of the Secretary, Boston (cited hereafter as House Journal), for the following descriptions and citations:

Vote One: "On the question whether the House will this session take into consideration the propriety of giving leave to bring in a bill for the repeal of any act or acts of any act or acts of this Commonwealth . . . which will oblige any creditor public or private to receive any Debtors demand, at a less sum than the just value thereof" (House Journal, 24 Nov. 1780, pp. 138–40. Percentage of Yes vote).

Vote Two: "And on the question of the report of Committee of Ways and Means . . . and that the several acts of government which now related to the currency of the state be altered and conform with the foregoing [a system reported by the Committee, 'founded in Justice and Equity', that would repeal any legal tender provisions of Massachusetts currency] principle upon such a plan that all Debts public and private that are already contracted or that may hereafter be contracted at the real current value of the passing money of the state such value must be determined from time to time by some Impartial Judges, except in case of special contracts" (Ibid., 11 Jan. 1781, pp. 203–05. Percentage of Yes vote).

Vote Three: "That all such Government Securities shall be liquidated by the scale of depreciation established by the state and that the sums so liquidated shall be paid in gold and silver or in current money of this Commonwealth at the real value of said liquidated sums" (Ibid., 16 Jan. 1781, pp. 218-19. Percentage of Yes vote).

Vote Four: "Be it therefore enacted by the authority aforesaid that the above mentioned Bills of Credit or such others may hereafter be emitted on the credit of this or the United States . . . shall be received in all payments within the same . . . but subject however to the . . . last cited clause at the true real value of current money compared with gold and silver . . . and shall avail as the tender had been in Gold and Silver" (Ibid., 16 Jan. 1781, pp. 220-21. Percentage of Yes vote).

Vote Five: "House resumed consideration of [the above] bill. Vote to 'assign tomorrow for a third reading" (Ibid., 17 Jan. 1781, pp. 225-26. Percentage of Yes vote).

Vote Six: Above bill passed to be engrossed, to "send up for concurrence" (Ibid., 18 Jan. 1781, pp. 228-29. Percentage of Yes vote).

Vote Seven: Above bill having had three readings, passed to be enacted (Ibid., 24 Jan. 1781, pp. 246-47. Percentage of Yes vote).

Vote Eight: "That a certain clause of an Act passed the 25th of Jan. last [the above] which authorizes the Judges to determine the value of paper money and another clause in said act which repeals the tender act so called be repealed" (Ibid., 13 June 1781, pp. 67, 68. Percentage of No vote).

Vote Nine: "That the issuing of another Tax Act be referred to the next session of the General Court" (Ibid., 14 Feb. 1782, p. 568. Percentage of No vote).

Vote Ten: Motion made to reconsider the vote of the house passed 26 June 1782 not to issue a tax upon the polls and estates of this commonwealth the present session (Ibid., 28 June 1782, pp. 140-41. Percentage of Yes vote).

Vote Eleven: "A Bill intitled an Act directing the appraising of certain articles of personal estate when taken to satisfy execution at the suit of any private person or persons . . . read a third time. . . . That it pass to be engrossed" (Ibid., 2 July 1782, pp. 150-51. Percentage of No vote).

Vote Twelve: "On the Report of Committee of Ways and Means . . . agreed to take the articles separately . . . 'Whether a duty of 1s per barrel shall be laid upon all cyder made or imported into this state' [with the revenue from the state impost and excise to be used to meet some general state expenses]" (Ibid., 3 March 1784, pp. 433-34. Percentage of No vote).

Vote Thirteen: House considered resolve of the senate for treasurer to issue executions against all collectors who have not returned tax money and to "make complaint against towns and plantations that have neglected to make return to him" (Ibid., 12 Nov. 1784, pp. 205-07. Percentage of Yes vote).

Vote Fourteen: House took up again a bill entitled "An Act Imposing duties on licensed vellum, parchment, and paper," should "bill pass to be engrossed" (Ibid., 10 March 1785, pp. 338-39. Percentage of Yes vote).

Vote Fifteen: House proceeded to consider the subject of a tax and the following was again made a question before the house: "Whether the appropriations of the monies arising from the Impost and Excise laws be altered and that said monies . . . be appropriated to comply with the requisitions of Congress" (Ibid., 3 March 1786, pp. 466-68. Percentage of No vote).

Vote Sixteen: When the question was called for to have the excise bill not to be engrossed (Ibid., 2 Nov. 1781, pp. 432-33. Percentage of Yes vote).

Vote Seventeen: Question that a committee be appointed to bring in a bill to repeal the excise act (Ibid., 31 Jan. 1782, p. 507. Percentage of Yes vote).

Vote Eighteen: "House took up the bill intitled . . . An Act imposing duties on licensed vellum, parchment, and papers . . . read a third time; . . . motion made to refer bill to the next session of the General Court . . . carried in the affirmative; . . . motion made to reconsider this vote so bill would lie open to debate" (Ibid., 8 March 1785, pp. 328-29. Percentage of Yes vote).

Vote Nineteen: "Committee on new draught of the bill in addition to the Act for laying a duty on licensed vellum and other articles . . . reported that the house agree to a new draught with a clause levying a duty of one shilling on every bond and writing under seal . . . not by law recorded in any office to give it full validity. Question then put as to whether the said new draught should be agreed to be inserting the above amendment reported by the committee" (Ibid., 1 July 1785, pp. 181-83. Percentage of No vote).

TABLE 28
Polarization on Financial Questions

	Percentage of Representatives Voting for Programs[a] on 19 Roll Calls									
Towns	1	2	3	4	5	6	7	8	9	10
Eastern group A	69%	85%	89%	86%	87%	83%	90%	70%	58%	78%
Western group A	40	55	69	69	60	64	67	13	17	55
Western group C	25	25	32	32	37	36	27	17	14	39

	Percentage of Representatives Voting for Programs[a] on 19 Roll Calls								
Towns	11	12	13	14	15	16	17	18	19
Eastern group A	75%	75%	86%	88%	91%	42%	37%	84%	80%
Western group A	40	29	38	56	69	38	44	82	40
Western group C	13	15	18	49	22	24	40	58	24

SOURCES: See sources for table 27.
a. Sponsored by commercial-cosmopolitan interests.

voting representatives during the seven-year period consistently favored the policies of the most commercial-cosmopolitan interests, while only 34 percent of the group B and 19 percent of the group C towns favored these programs. Again the greatest differences occurred between the patterns of the eastern group A and western group C towns as 83 percent of the former but only 10 percent of the latter group backed the financial programs favored by the most commercial-cosmopolitan interests. The voting patterns on these financial issues show a deep division between the group A and the other two groups of towns and a serious polarization between the eastern group A and the western group C communities. Within this framework of divisiveness, the General Court attempted to hammer out some solutions to the fiscal problems inherited from the Revolution. This process, complicated by the inadequacies of the preparty political system, increased the political tension within the commonwealth.

The commercial-cosmopolitan interests began to implement their programs as soon as the electors accepted the 1780 constitution. Between the fall of 1780 and the spring of 1781 these groups managed to secure legislation that refunded the state debt at a

TABLE 29
Voting Patterns by Towns on Five Key Financial Issues

Towns	Not Voting	Favorably	Divided	Opposed
Group A	4%	63%	15%	21%
Group B	7	34	9	57
Group C	52	19	18	64
Eastern group A	6	83	14	3
Western group A	0	40	20	40
Western group C	34	10	18	72

SOURCES: Based on the voting patterns of the towns on the following five roll call votes between 1780 and 1786 completely described in the source notes for table 27:

Vote one is vote seven, table 27. Vote two is vote eleven, table 27. Vote three is vote twelve, table 27. Vote four is vote thirteen, table 27. Vote five is vote fifteen, table 27.

NOTE: The figures represent the percentage of towns favoring, dividing on, or opposing commercial-cosmopolitan financial and economic programs (not of the total vote of these communities). Towns that voted with the commercial-cosmopolitan interests more than two-thirds of the time are listed in the "Favorably" column. Towns that voted against these interests more than two-thirds of the time are listed in the "Opposed" column. Towns that voted between these two extremes are listed in the "Divided" column, and towns whose representatives cast no votes on any of these five votes are listed in the "Not Voting" column. The percentages in the "Favorably," "Divided," and "Opposed" columns are for those towns whose representatives voted on these questions.

relatively high value, ended the legal tender provisions for the new emission currency, and provided for the servicing and repayment of the new state consolidated debt. Their first objective involved repealing the legal tender characteristics of the $1.5 million worth of new emission Continental currency that the state had issued during 1780. These notes had been issued in exchange for $60 million worth of old Continental currency, paid five percent interest to their holders, and had been declared legal tender by the General Court. [10] The new emission quickly depreciated and by

10. The best background for this is in E. James Ferguson, *The Power of the Purse: A History of American Public Finance, 1776-1790* (Chapel Hill, 1961), pp. 51-52, 65-66. The Massachusetts response is in *Acts and Resolves*, 21:1178-82 which gives the act of 5 May 1780. Also notice the resolves of 19 June 1780 and 29 Sept. 1780 in ibid., p. 1413.

The act of 5 May 1780 provided for the emission of £460,000 of these new bills, bearing 5 percent interest, that were to be redeemed in specie by 31 Dec. 1786. The same legislation established a fixed annual tax of £72,000 designed to retire the new bills. (£6,000 per year was to meet the interest and

the end of the summer of 1780 publicists began to attack the legal tender quality of the new currency and urged the court to abolish the unrighteous tender provision that "pauperized" widows and orphans and allowed "evil" debtors to retire their debts at a 50 percent discount.[11]

These developing plans ran into difficulties during the fall 1780 session of the General Court. Hancock advocated no financial reforms in his first message, and although the court decried the horrible plight of the state's creditors, widows, orphans, and others ruined by the depreciation of the new emission, it suggested no remedy for their distress.[12] The commercial-cosmopolitan interests introduced a measure permitting the introduction of a bill designed to change the legal tender characteristics of the new emission but the support of 58 percent of the representatives of the group A communities could not carry the day against the opposition of 77 percent and 71 percent of the delegates from the group B and C towns.[13]

This defeat was a minor setback. During the winter 1781 session of the court the commercial-cosmopolitan interests used their control of the committee of ways and means to draft a complex proposal that refunded and consolidated the state's debt and modified the legal tender characteristics of the new emission currency.

£66,000 was for redemption.) These bills could not be called in for taxes (or "sponged up" as the term was used in the 1780s). The legal tender provision read as follows: "That all the bills of credit to be emitted as aforesaid shall be received in all payment within this state, except for the annual tax of £72,000 . . . and a tender of same may be pleaded in any action brought for the recovery of any money or other demand, and shall avail as though the tender had been made of gold and silver, except for money due on special contract, expressly promising the payment of gold and silver, made since the 20th of May 1775." On 29 Sept. 1780, ibid., the court passed a resolve that repealed certain portions of the act of 13 April 1776 that had made it illegal to pass Continental [old emission] bills at less than face value. This provision was replaced by a measure making the old bills a "legal tender, at the nominal value" to creditors in other states.

    11. For some examples of the rhetoric see *Continental Journal*, 26 Oct. 1780, and *Independent Chronicle*, 20 Nov., 14 Dec. 1780. Also note "The People of Massachusetts Bay" in *Independent Chronnicle*, 19 Oct. 1780.

    12. "Address of Governor Hancock," in E. M. Bacon, ed., *Supplement to the Acts and Laws of the Commonwealth of Massachusetts* (Boston, 1896), 31 Oct. 1780, pp. 23-24. The "Reply of the General Court" is 7 Nov. 1780, pp. 27-31.

    13. The vote is in House Journal, 24 Nov. 1780, 138-40.

By taking advantage of the relative absence of representatives from the group C towns and by winning over most of the minor place-holders to their side, the commercial-cosmopolitan group finally passed a comprehensive refunding act on 24 January 1781. This major campaign opened with a barrage of essays that assailed the injustices of legal tender, bewailed the sufferings of the public creditors, and predicted disaster if the commonwealth did not perform its moral duty by placing its finances upon a firm and just foundation.[14] The committee of ways and means, controlled by the representatives from the most commercial-cosmopolitan inter-ests and towns, then reported a comprehensive measure that re-duced the legal tender characteristics of the new emission and consolidated the outstanding state securities at a level well above their market price.[15] Thanks to the support of over three-fourths of the representatives from the group A towns and the low propor-tion of delegates present from the group C communities, the court accepted the committee's report.

The acceptance of the report sparked the bitterest legislative struggle of the early 1780s. The house took five additional roll call votes before it passed the final bill by a vote of 75 to 65. Of the 172 representatives who cast votes on any of the six roll calls, 169 voted consistently for or against the measure. The representatives from the group A towns cast from 75 to 80 percent of their votes for passage while the group C delegates cast 53 to 68 percent of theirs against the bill. (See table 30.) The eastern group A and western group C towns occupied the two extreme positions as the easterners cast 83 to 90 percent of their votes for the measure while the westerners opposed it with 63 to 75 percent of theirs. Three factors permitted the most commercial-cosmopolitan inter-ests to push the measure through the lower house. The group C towns, most opposed to the act, found themselves underrepre-sented in the first five roll call votes; the representatives of the

14. For examples see "Aristides," *Independent Chronicle*, 4 Jan. 1781; "A Countryman," ibid., 25 Jan., 1 Mar. 1781. Also see *Independent Chronicle*, 11 Jan. 1781, and 8 Feb. 1781; *Continental Journal*, 4, 11, 25 Jan. 1781; "Sydney" and "A Massachusetts Farmer" in *Massachusetts Spy* [*Worcester*], 11, 18 Jan. 1781.

15. For the appointment of the committee, see the unpublished Journal of the Senate, Office of the Secretary, Boston (cited hereafter as Senate Jour-nal), 30 Nov. 1780, where the upper house refused to concur in the first selections and ibid., 2 Dec. 1780, for the final appointments. Tentative accep-tance of the report is in the House Journal, 11 Jan. 1781, pp. 203-05.

TABLE 30
Voting Patterns for the Act of 24 January 1781

Towns	Percentage of Votes Favoring Act on 6 Roll Calls						Percentage of Representatives by Roll Call		
	1	*2*	*3*	*4*	*5*	*6*	*1*	*3*	*6*
Group A	76%	80%	78%	77%	75%	80%	45%	39%	33%
Group B	39	45	46	51	42	47	37	41	36
Group C	32	42	42	42	47	33	18	20	31
Eastern group A	85	89	86	87	83	90	33	25	21
Western group A	55	69	69	60	64	67	11	14	11
Western group C	25	32	32	37	36	27	16	16	26
Total vote	54%	58%	58%	59%	54%	54%			

SOURCES: Based on the following six roll call votes, all listed in the House Journal (for additional information, see source notes to table 27): 11 Jan. 1781, pp. 203-05; 16 Jan. 1781, pp. 218-19; 16 Jan. 1781, pp. 220-21; 17 Jan. 1781, pp. 225-26; 18 Jan. 1781, pp. 228-29; 24 Jan. 1781, pp. 246-47.

group B communities divided their votes on the six roll calls; and the minor placeholders and representatives of the less commercial-cosmopolitan towns in Barnstable County and Maine voted with the most commercial-cosmopolitan interests. These justices who represented the group B and C towns and the delegates from the group B and C Cape Cod fishing and Maine shipbuilding communities played a vital role in the commercial-cosmopolitan victory. On the vote for the final passage of the act on 24 January 1781 over three-fourths of the justices and two-thirds of those from group B and C towns voted for the measure. Table 31 shows the importance of the justices and the votes of these communities to the final result. Thus the commercial-cosmopolitan interests took the initiative, drafted the bill, struck at a time when the group C towns were underrepresented, won over an important group of justices from the less commercial-cosmopolitan towns and the representatives of the shipowning and fishing communities, and passed the act by a narrow 4 percent margin. The senate, more under the thumb of these interests and towns, needed little persuasion to pass the measure by a healthy margin of 23 percent.[16]

16. The vote in the senate is given in the *Boston Gazette*, 5 Feb. 1781. The upper house cast 73 percent of its vote in favor of the act. (This was one of the very few senate roll calls that was either recorded or published during the entire decade.)

TABLE 31

Votes of Justices and the Representatives of Barnstable County Fishing and Maine Shipowning Towns

Towns	Total Representatives for Act[a]	Justices for Act[a]	Representatives for Act[a] From Maine & Barnstable Co.	All Others
Group A	80%	88%	n.a.	70%
Group B	47	65	100%	22
Group C	33	67	100	13
Totals	54%	77%	100%	33%

SOURCES: Based on sources in table 30. Justices are identified by their title of Esquire in the House Journal and are also listed in Thomas Fleet and John Fleet, *Fleet's Pocket Almanack for the Year of Our Lord 1781 . . . to Which Is Annexed the Massachusetts Register* (Boston, 1780), n.p. (cited hereafter as Fleet, *Register*, with the year and date of publication).
  a. Act passed on 24 January 1781.
  n.a. = not applicable.

The act laid the foundations for the commonwealth's fiscal structure. It refunded state securities and guaranteed the eventual payment of principal and interest in specie and modified the legal tender character of the new emission currency so that it would pass at its market instead of its face value.[17] During the same session £400,000 worth of state securities were refunded. In the next session the court decided to refund another £800,000 worth, specified an interest rate of 6 percent and provided for the repayment of the principal in specie between 1785 and 1788.[18] The

17. The final legislation is in *Acts and Laws*, 25 Jan. 1781, 1:6-10. It established two basic principles: (1) the refunding of the outstanding state debt and its eventual repayment in specie; and (2) modification of the legal tender provisions of the new emission notes by providing that they would pass not at their face value but at the valuation determined by the justices of the supreme judicial court. The *Continental Journal*, 8 March 1781, gives the results of the first valuation which was much lower than the face value of the bills.
18. The two loan acts are in *Acts and Laws*, 17 Feb. 1781, 1:20-22, and 15 May 1781, 1:75-76. These provided for the payment of 6 percent interest in specie, or "current bills of credit," made provision for the retirement of one-fourth of the principal in each of the four years of 1785, 1786, 1787, and 1788, and gave subscribers a 4 percent bonus for subscribing to these new consolidated state securities. Individuals could also loan provisions to the commonwealth in exchange for the new securities. The acts provided for the automatic levying of direct taxes to be used to retire the securities between 1785 and 1788.

winter and spring session of the 1780 General Court had been
quite profitable for the commercial-cosmopolitan interests and
towns. They had modified legal tender and had saddled the commonwealth with a heavy £1.2 million debt that would be retired
rapidly and with specie.

The less commercial interests and towns quickly organized opposition to this legislation. Representatives of the Suffolk County
farming towns met at Dedham and protested what they called the
"infamous" act of 25 January which destroyed the new emission
bills and enriched speculators.[19] A Worcester convention also met,
assailed the speculators, and charged that the January legislation
violated the congressional request of 18 March 1781. A bitter
newspaper debate broke out in the pages of the *Worcester Spy*,
but the editor Isaiah Thomas finally ended the controversy by
pointing out that the dispute had already been "settled by authority."[20] The court refused to swerve from its policies because of a
few conventions. Its response to criticism was an "Address to the
People" which proved to the court's satisfaction that paper money
could not be supported by legislative fiat and concluded that "justice therefore, manifestly dictated a repeal" of an evil system that
deprived creditors of their lawful property. The court also vilified
the opponents of its policies by suggesting that the British and
Tories must be behind the defeatism of those who questioned the
act.[21]

The first session of the 1781 General Court resulted in the complete frustration of the less commercial-cosmopolitan interests. In
a surge of militancy inspired by the conventions, the towns had
elected representatives who opposed the modification of the legal
tender provision of the new emission currency. A motion to repeal
the section modifying the legal tender nature of this currency
passed the house with 62 percent of the vote as the group C and
group B towns cast 76 and 70 percent of their vote in favor and

19. Petition of the Suffolk County Towns, Massachusetts Archives,
142:336-39, and Worcester Petition and Woburn Petition, 16 April 1781, in
ibid., vol. 187.

20. "Centinel" in *Independent Chronicle*, 1 Feb. 1781; "Sydney," *Massachusetts Spy* [Worcester], 1 Mar. 1781. Also notice *Massachusetts Spy*
[Worcester], 22, 29 Mar., 12 Apr. 1781; *Continental Journal*, 5 Apr. 1781;
Independent Chronicle, 12 Apr. 1781; Abner Holden to Caleb Davis, 14 Mar.
1781, Caleb Davis Papers, Massachusetts Historical Society.

21. "The Address to the People," dated 26 Feb. 1781, is in *Acts and Laws*,
1:309-18.

thus overrode the 60 percent of the votes cast by the group A towns opposing repeal.[22] But this decisive victory in the house merely made the defeat in the senate controlled by the commercial-cosmopolitan interests more bitter. The court then ended all legal tender provisions for the new emission bills but permitted their holders to exchange them for state securities.[23] Control of the senate had permitted the most commercial-cosmopolitan interests to triumph in their campaign against legal tender, while rewarding the speculators and merchants who currently held the bills.

These interests then pushed on to continue the consolidation of the state debt and searched for funds with which to pay the interest and principal. Acts passed in October 1781 and March 1782 continued the consolidation, and by the end of 1782 over £1.4 million had been refunded. In order to meet the interest charges the court initiated a state excise system. The excise tax on wines, tea, rum, brandy, and carriages, implemented by a comprehensive administrative system, would not only bring in revenue; as a fringe benefit, it promised to suppress "immorality, luxury, and extravagance."[24] The debate over and the voting on the excise act divided both the commercial-cosmopolitan interests and their opponents. (See table 32.) Many merchants and tradesmen, who either did not hold securities or who had invested in Continental paper, did not favor an excise that would raise prices. At the other extreme, many poorer farmers accepted the excise as a means of avoiding direct taxes on land, property, and polls. When the act first passed in the fall of 1781, all three groups of towns favored it but the group B and C representatives cast a much higher favorable

22. The vote to repeal the clause modifying legal tender is in House Journal, 13 June 1781, pp. 67-68. The senate killed this effort.

23. The legislation is in *Acts and Laws*, 6 July 1781, 1:488-90. See ibid., p. 490, for the specific repeal of the modified legal tender provisions.

24. The act of 20 Oct. 1781, ibid., 1:493-94, permitted the treasurer to receive state securities and value them in accordance with the state's scale of depreciation. (The only exceptions were the soldier's depreciation certificates. For these certificates see Ferguson, *Power of the Purse*, pp. 50-51.) The act of 6 March 1782, *Acts and Laws*, 1:569-70, provided that one-fourth of the principal on these loans was to be paid prior to 1 April during the years 1786, 1787, 1788, and 1789.

The excise act is in ibid., 2 Nov. 1781, 1:536-37. It established duties on rum, brandy, wine, and tea after 10 Dec. 1781. The formal scale of depreciation was provided on 1 Nov. 1781, ibid., 1:533-34. For additional details see Public Papers for ch. 18, 1781, filed in the Office of the Secretary, Boston.

TABLE 32
Vote on the 1781 Excise

| | Percentage of Representatives | |
Towns	For Excise	Against Repeal
Group A	62%	60%
Group B	74	76
Group C	75	66
Total vote	69%	68%
Eastern group A	58%	63%
Western group A	62	56
Western group C	76	60

SOURCES: Based on votes in the House Journal. Vote for the excise, 2 Nov. 1781, pp. 432–33; vote against the repeal, 31 Jan. 1782, pp. 507–08.

vote than did the delegates from the group A towns. Nevertheless, during the winter of 1781-82 residents of both the commercial towns of Ipswich and Worcester and the noncommercial community of Southboro petitioned against the act.[25] Even so the voting lines held in January 1782 when representatives of all three groups of towns voted against repeal, again with the group B and C towns most favorable to the excise. The commercial-cosmopolitan interests soon discovered that this measure did not provide adequate revenue for servicing the debt. In November 1782 the court passed a more comprehensive act that placed a wide range of impost and excise duties on wine, brandy, tobacco, tropical imports, many imported manufactured items, and wrought gold and silver.[26] In March 1783 the court tightened collection procedures and placed a 2½ percent ad valorem duty on all previously untaxed foreign imports.[27]

25. The original vote on the excise is in House Journal, 2 Nov. 1781, pp. 432-33. For the complaints see Southboro Petition, Massachusetts Archives, 187:395; *Independent Chronicle*, 3, 24 Jan. 1782; *Massachusetts Spy* [Worcester], 10, 31 Jan. 1782.

26. The November 1782 Act is in *Acts and Laws*, 8 Nov. 1782, 2:91-105. The court also passed an act explaining the administration of the impost-excise laws; see ibid., 7 March 1782, 1:573-79.

27. The March 1783 law is in ibid., 10 March 1783, 2:128-33. The Public Papers for this legislation in Office of the Secretary, Boston, contain petitions from the Boston sugarmakers, the Bridgewater iron makers, and cider makers. The same file contains an interesting letter from Elijah Hunt (the Hampshire County excise collector) to Henry Gardner (the treasurer), dated 24 Sept. 1782, in which Hunt complains that the opposition of the small shopkeepers, traders, and tavern keepers makes it difficult to enforce the excise legislation.

By the beginning of 1783 the commonwealth's financial program had assumed its basic outlines. Legal tender had been abolished, the state debt had been consolidated at a high value, interest would be paid in specie, and tax sources had been established to fund the debt. The only concession to the less commercial interests was the institution of the excise and impost system which would partially fund and repay the onerous state debt.

For meeting the regular expenses of the commonwealth, the court continued to rely on direct taxes. During its first session the government wasted little time in drawing taxes from the "large resources of the Commonwealth" and levied for 4.6 million pounds of beef.[28] During the winter 1781 session the commercial-cosmopolitan interests secured the right of the senate to consider evaluation acts, previously the sole responsibility of the lower house. This gave the upper house the right to amend each town's proportion of the total tax bill. The house, at first, refused to let the senate amend the valuation. The court, to resolve this impasse, called upon the justices of the supreme judicial court who then gave their opinion that the senate should be involved in drafting the valuation. After this the house capitulated and the senate secured an important victory.[29] After settling the valuation controversy, the court continued to levy heavy direct taxes for state and confederation requirements which totaled over £900,000 by 22 March 1783.[30] These taxes levied in accordance with a valuation system that placed high values on polls and real property and lower assessments on liquid wealth bore hardest on the less commercial-cosmopolitan interests and towns. Only one of the taxes, that of 5 March 1782, could be paid in anything but specie or securities. The court did excuse ministers, Harvard students, and grammar school masters from taxes and gave speculators holding unoccupied land a tax advantage.[31] The less commercial-cosmopolitan towns did on two occasions force the lower house to post-

28. The beef tax is in *Acts and Laws*, 4 Dec. 1780, 1:205.

29. The debate between the two houses is covered in "Opinions of the Judges of the Supreme Judicial Court," in Bacon, ed., *Supplement to Acts and Laws*, pp. 42-49, and in *Acts and Laws*, 9 March 1781, 1:359.

30. All these acts were printed in the *Acts and Laws*, see fn. 3, this chapter, for a complete list.

31. Ibid., since the method of payment and the exemptions are given in each act. For an analysis of requirements see Report of the Committee of Ways and Means, in Massachusetts Archives, 137:387-88. For some support of taxation see "A Recipe for the Easy Payment of Taxes," *Continental Journal*, 30 Apr. 1781, and "Agricola," *Independent Chronicle*, 8 Mar. 1781.

TABLE 33
Voting Against Postponement of Direct Taxes

| | Percentage of Reps in 2 Votes | |
Towns	1	2
Group A	48%	69%
Group B	13	46
Group C	20	34
Total	26%	49%
Eastern group A	58%	78%
Western group A	17	55
Western group C	14	39

SOURCES: The two roll call votes are in House Journal, 14 Feb. 1782, p. 568; and 28 June 1782, pp. 140-41.

pone consideration of a direct tax act. (See table 33.) In February 1782 87 and 80 percent respectively of the voting representatives of the group B and C towns passed a motion preventing the levy of a direct tax and in June 1782 with 54 and 66 percent respectively of their vote they forced the postponement of a direct tax till the next session of the General Court. The fact that in the first instance 48 percent and in the latter 69 percent of the delegates from the group A towns voted against postponement underlines the division over direct taxes that had occurred among the towns by 1782. The commercial-cosmopolitan interests had saddled the commonwealth with a heavy debt and continued a system of valuation and taxation that allowed them to escape paying their full share of the taxes.

During 1783 and 1784 the court tinkered with the system and sought new revenues for funding the debt. An excise act placed a 5 percent ad valorem duty on certain imported manufactured goods and the court tightened administrative procedures by giving the collectors additional power and clamped down on retail liquor sellers.[32] In July 1784 the court placed additional duties on specified manufactured and agricultural imports and established duties, equal to the state's impost, on foreign goods imported into the commonwealth through states with lower tariffs.[33]

32. The new excise act is in *Acts and Laws*, 10 July 1783, 2:506-07. The legislation that tightened up the administration is in ibid., 5 July 1783, 2:504-06.

33. See ibid., 1 July 1784, 2:280-84, and the material in the Public Papers for this legislation.

In 1784 both groups of towns and interests met defeat in their efforts to use impost and excise revenues for general state expenses and to tighten up the collection of direct taxes. The less commercial-cosmopolitan towns and interests, in order to reduce the load of direct taxes, proposed a levy of one shilling per barrel on cider. The proceeds would be used to service the state debt in exchange for the allocation of some of the impost and excise revenues to meet general state expenses. The representatives of the group B and C communities cast 58 and 85 percent of their votes for the new proposal and pushed the measure through the house.[34] But the most commercial-cosmopolitan interests controlling the senate amended several important sections of the bill and bounced it back to the house where it died in disagreement.[35]

While the most commercial-cosmopolitan interests killed this particular reform proposal, they attempted to pass a measure that would increase the yield of direct tax collections. For some time the administration of direct tax collections had been chaotic. The state treasurer, elected by the court, sent out warrants to the collectors and constables of the over three hundred towns, districts, and plantations and these locally elected officers took their time in raising the taxes.[36] Many refused to push their neighbors and friends in bad years, while others speculated and peculated with their collections and were in no hurry to send them into the treasury. The treasurer, when he lost patience, issued executions against these local collectors who had to pay the rates out of their own pockets. Since many of the collectors conveniently disappeared when the sheriff came with the executions, it became more and more difficult to collect back taxes in many of the more isolated communities. The sheriffs after serving the executions also took their time and engaged in the typical speculations, so as a last resort the harried treasurer issued executions against them served by the county coroner. This system, which worked poorly even in good times, simply fell apart under pressure of the heavy tax loads

34. There is an excellent description of the debate on this question in the *Boston Magazine* Mar. 1784, pp. 211-12. The vote is in the House Journal, 3 March 1784, pp. 433-34.

35. *Boston Magazine*, Mar. 1784, p. 212, gives some of the debate.

36. Collection procedures are given in the individual tax acts. One way to follow the administration of the collections of direct taxes is from the Gray-Gardner Ledger, 1774-1782, Treasurer's Papers, Office of the Secretary, Boston (located in the attic of the capitol building in early 1964). Each town occupies a separate page in this ledger and Gardner's decreasing competence is underlined by the lack of entries made after late 1781.

of the early 1780s. In 1782 the death of the treasurer Henry
Gardner resulted in a legislative investigation which found that the
records were so disorganized and incomplete that it would be
impossible to discover the real condition of the treasury.[37] In
order to systematize these collections, the most commercial-
cosmopolitan interests sponsored a measure that permitted the
treasurer to issue his executions against the towns instead of
against the delinquent collectors. (See table 34.) The senate passed
the reform, but the less commercial-cosmopolitan interests am-
bushed it in the lower house where they cast over two-thirds of
their votes against it.[38] Despite the support of three-quarters of

TABLE 34
Voting on Cider Tax and Tax Reform

	Percentage of Reps	
Towns	*Against Cider Tax*	*For Reform*
Group A	58%	72%
Group B	42	24
Group C	15	30
Total	38%	41%
Eastern group A	75%	86%
Western group A	29	38
Western group C	15	18

SOURCES: House Journal, 12 Nov. 1784, pp. 205-07, for reforming the administration of tax collection; 3 Mar. 1784, pp.
433-34, for the cider tax.

37. Details of this confusion may be found in *Acts and Laws*, 22 Oct.
1782, 2:70-73; 25 Oct. 1782, 2:293-94; 1 Nov. 1782, 2:320-21; 9 Nov. 1782,
2:343-44. The committee report is in Report of Joint Comittee to Audit
Gardner's Books, Massachusetts Archives, Office of the Secretary, Boston,
137:440-41. Bacon, ed., *Supplement to Acts and Laws*, 25 June 1782,
pp. 122-23, gives the resolve appointing a joint committee to report a bill for
the better regulation of the treasury. There was a roll call vote on this bill in
House Journal, 6 July 1782, pp. 168-69, but there were only seven negative
votes. The final legislation is in *Acts and Laws*, 3 July 1782, 2:34-36, and
some minor amendments were made in ibid., 27 Sep. 1782, p. 272.
    For some popular criticism see "P.D." in *Independent Chronicle*, 9 May
1782; "Weymouth Instructions," 20 Jan. 1781; *Massachusetts Spy* [Worces-
ter], 10 May 1781. Samuel Cooper to John Adams, 22 July 1782, Adams
Papers, pt. 4, Adams Manuscript Trust, protests that Boston has paid more
than her share of taxes but that the accounts are so badly deranged that these
fail to prove the town's efforts.
    38. Debate on this measure is reported in the *Massachusetts Magazine*,
November 1784, p. 580.

the delegates from the group A communities, the bill failed and the most commercial-cosmopolitan interests could secure only a resolution instructing the sheriffs and collectors to settle their accounts with the treasurer by 1 February 1785.[39]

But the commonwealth still needed more revenue and in an effort to find new tax resources the court passed a stamp act in early 1785. The debate over this question created a furor throughout the state but caused less of a division within the court than had the proposed cider levy or tax reforms. Newspaper editors, threatened by a tax on their papers, attacked the legislation, comparing it to the infamous Stamp Act of 1765, and stirred up a great deal of dissent. Despite their efforts all three groups of towns favored the act with the representatives of the most commercial-cosmopolitan communities casting the highest percentage of affirmative votes.[40] The only serious division occurred when a special committee recommended that additional charges should be levied on certain types of commercial paper. (See table 35.) At that point the delegates from the most commercial-cosmopolitan com-

TABLE 35
Voting on the Stamp Act, 1785

	Percentage of Reps for		
Towns	*Stamp Act*	*Reconsideration*	*Amendment*
Group A	78%	84%	30%
Group B	50	74	65
Group C	53	63	74
Eastern group A	88	84	20
Western group A	56	82	60
Western group C	49	58	76

SOURCES: House Journal, vote one: 10 Mar. 1785, pp. 338–39; vote two: 8 Mar. 1785, pp. 328–29; vote three: 1 July 1785, pp. 181–83.

39. The vote is in House Journal, 12 Nov. 1784, pp. 205-07. The final legislation is in *Acts and Laws*, 12, 13 Nov. 1784, 2:316-18.

40. The final stamp legislation is in *Acts and Laws*, 18 Mar. 1785, 3:186-92. It levied duties on all sorts of legal documents, commercial papers, and on lawyers, newspapers, and almanacs. *Boston Magazine*, Mar. 1785, pp. 115-16, gives the debate on the bill. The protests, especially by editors, may be followed in *Salem Gazette*, 19, 26 Apr., 2, 10, 17 May 1785; *Massachusetts Centinel*, 4, 11, 18, 28, May 1785; *Continental Journal*, 26 Apr., 5 May 1785; *Essex Journal*, 6 Apr., 23 May 1785; *Plymouth Journal*, 25 Apr., 17 May 1785; *Worcester Spy*, 28 Apr., 12, 19 May, 21 June 1785.

munities passed into opposition, but enough of the representatives of the group B and C towns voted for it to secure its passage.

During 1785 and 1786 the entire financial program ran into serious difficulties. Collections from the impost, excise, and stamp act did not meet the interest payments on the debt; the repayment of the principal was scheduled to begin in 1785; the tax collection system remained chaotic; and Continental and state financial requirements made the levying of another direct tax imminent. In addition to these problems writers conjured up others by advocating paper money, scaling down the value of the debt, or suggesting "sponging up" the state debt by calling in the consolidated securities for taxes. James Bowdoin, the new governor who personally held a large share of the debt, made several suggestions for improving the program during the spring and summer of 1785. He hoped to enable all the towns to pay their taxes by establishing potash factories throughout the state and accepting the ashes, which would be sold on domestic and foreign markets, for taxes.[41] The court ignored this scheme, raised the duties on manufactured imports that could be produced in Massachusetts from 10 to 22½ percent ad valorem, bowed to the pressure of the newspaper editors and repealed the tax on newspapers, replacing it with one on advertisements, and permitted local merchants to import molasses on their vessels duty free while foreigners had to pay 5 percent duty.[42]

In October 1785 Bowdoin presented some more suggestions to the court. He pointed out that the consolidated debt had passed £1.5 million, that interest charges amounted to £88,000 per year, and that the time had come to begin payment of the principal.

41. For some examples of the rhetoric see *Massachusetts Centinel*, 23, 27 July, 2 Nov. 1785; 11, 15, 22 Feb., 1 Mar. 1786; *Salem Gazette*, 26 July 1785; *Independent Chronicle*, 3 Nov. 1785; *Hampshire Herald*, 7 Mar. 1786; *Worcester Magazine*, Apr. 1786, pp. 32-33.

A study of the Interest Payment Books, in Treasurer's Papers, Office of the Secretary, Boston, for the period March 1786 through March 1787 shows that Bowdoin received at least £1,000 in interest on his holdings of the consolidated state debt. Bowdoin's address is in *Acts and Laws*, 2 June 1785, 3:711-13. The reply of the court is in ibid. 28 June 1785, 3:664-65.

42. For the additional imposts see ibid., 2 July 1785, 3:452-57, and *Massachusetts Centinel*, 26 Apr., 18 May 1785. For the newspaper tax see *Acts and Laws*, 3 July 1785, 3:658-62; *Boston Magazine*, July 1785, pp. 277-78; *Salem Gazette*, 2, 16, 30 Aug., 20 Sept., 1, 15 Nov. 1785. For the molasses duty see *Acts and Laws*, 2 July 1785, 3:452-57.

The governor proposed that the debt be retired by levying a specie tax of £100,000 a year for fifteen years and that the interest charges be met by improving impost and excise collections. In addition to these taxes, Bowdoin also suggested another tax of £217,000 payable in army notes which had fallen due in 1784 and 1785.[43] These suggestions and the state's financial problems placed the court in a dilemma; the less commercial-cosmopolitan interests would oppose any new direct taxes and would attempt to use the money from the impost for general state expenses, yet these revenues did not even meet the annual interest expenses. The court attempted to escape by letting things drift and wiled away its time constructing a new valuation list.[44]

Critics decried Bowdoin's program as the court drifted. As agitation for paper money broke out in Massachusetts, New Hampshire, and Rhode Island, the supporters of sound money quickly filled the papers with articles proving that paper money "offended heaven, justice, and harmony," that it would rapidly depreciate, and that it would harm the already misused widows and orphans.[45] Other writers advanced the heresy that the state debt could be reduced to its market value and that the interest could be paid in paper indents.[46] These authors pointed out that most holders received almost 18 percent on their original investment in state securities. An "Old Soldier" hit a sore nerve when he charged that he had parted with his securities for 25 percent of their face value and that he would now have to pay heavy direct taxes so the wealthy speculators could redeem at 100 percent.[47] One writer

43. Bowdoin's addresses are in *Acts and Laws*, 20 Oct. 1785, 3:729-31, and 22 Oct. 1785, 3:733-34.

44. For a discussion of the court's efforts to pass a new evaluation see *Boston Magazine*, Dec. 1785, pp. 471-79; *Massachusetts Centinel*, 21, 24 Dec. 1785, 25 Feb. 1786; *Massachusetts Gazette* [Springfield], 26 Dec. 1785.

45. For some comments on the paper money threat see Henry Jackson to Henry Knox, 12 Feb. 1786, Knox Papers, Massachusetts Historical Society; Samuel Dexter to Bowdoin, 21 Jan. 1786, in Bowdoin-Temple Manuscripts, Massachusetts Historical Society. *Massachusetts Centinel*, 2 Nov. 1785. For a debate see "Senex," *Massachusetts Centinel*, 2 Nov. 1785 and "Civis," *Independent Chronicle*, 3 Nov., and 17 Dec. 1785.

46. For the support of this view see: "Publick Faith," *Massachusetts Centinel*, 8 Feb. 1786, and "Objections Against Reducing the Public Debt Examined" in ibid., 1 Mar. 1786. Also note "Plain Truth," 18 Feb. 1786, in ibid.

47. "Old Soldier," *Hampshire Herald*, 7 Mar. 1786.

even pictured vampirelike speculators living in Boston "sucking the state's blood and collecting 20% on their investments."[48]

Faced by this growing opposition, the commercial-cosmopolitan interests, thanks to their control of the senate, beat back efforts to allocate revenue from the impost and excise to meet Continental requisitions which had been previously met by levying direct taxes. After defeating this attempted reform, they then passed a new direct tax act that for the first time allocated some revenues for the payment of interest on the state's debt. In early 1786 the less commercial-cosmopolitan interests introduced a bill permitting the use of impost and excise revenues to meet Continental requisitions. The measure passed the house, but the commercial-cosmopolitan interests throttled it in the senate. In the lower house 84 percent of the delegates from the group A communities voted against using these funds to meet Continental requirements while 68 and 71 percent of the representatives of the group B and C towns respectively voted for it. (See table 36.) The vote on this

TABLE 36
Voting on Use of Impost and Excise Funds to Meet Continental Requirements Compared with Vote on 1781 Consolidation Act

Towns	Vote Against 1786 Reform	Change in Vote from 1781
Group A	84%	+ 4%
Group B	32	-15
Group C	29	- 4
Eastern group A	91	+ 1
Western group A	69	+ 2
Western group C	22	- 5

SOURCES: House Journal, 3 Mar. 1786, pp. 466-68. The vote in 1781 is based on ibid., 24 Jan. 1781, pp. 228-29.

measure when compared with the passage of the consolidation act on 24 January 1781 underlined the increasing polarization that had occurred in the commonwealth over financial questions between 1781 and 1786.[49] After defeating this proposed reform, the commercial-cosmopolitan interests increased political tensions

48. For other similar rhetoric see *Massachusetts Centinel*, 11, 22 Feb., 1 Mar. 1786; *Worcester Magazine*, Apr. 1786, pp. 32-33.

49. There is an excellent discussion of the vote in Robert J. Taylor, *Western Massachusetts in the Revolution* (Providence, 1954), pp. 131-32.

by passing the first direct tax act since 1783. This complex act designed to meet the Continental requisition, the expenses of the state government, and the payment of interest on the state debt allocated £145,000 to the confederation, one-third of which had to be paid in specie, £45,000 for general state expenses, and £29,000 for the payment of interest on the state debt.[50] This legislation signified an important break with the past: for the first time interest on the debt would be partially met through direct taxation. The commercial-cosmopolitan forces had won their greatest victory but in doing so they had further alienated the less commercial-cosmopolitan towns and groups.

In addition to these debates and divisions over the funding program and taxation, the most and less commercial-cosmopolitan groups and towns also split over measures designed to aid debtors. In 1782 when agitation for relief of debtors came to a head, the court in March passed a resolve granting the judges of the supreme judicial court the authority to keep creditors from "unreasonably distressing their debtors" by continuing actions for debt to the next session of the court.[51] Two months later the court passed the so-called declaratory act which permitted justices of the peace to acknowledge the indebtedness of debtors who appeared before them. If the declared debtor did not repay his creditor within the contracted time, the justice could order an execution against the debtor's property without going through the expensive procedure of a trial in the court of common pleas.[52] Some knowledgeable observers claimed that the act actually aided usurers, since under the declaratory procedures it became impossible for the debtor to accuse the creditor of charging usurious interest rates.[53] These acts did little to alleviate conditions or to forestall criticism.

At last, in July 1782, after heavy pressure from western conventions and partially in reaction to Ely's rebellion, the court gave the debtors some real assistance with an act, often incorrectly described as a tender act, which provided that the debtor could use certain types of real and personal property, evaluated by an impartial panel, to pay the execution in favor of his creditor. The debtor

50. Taylor, *Western Massachusetts*, pp. 132-34, has an excellent discussion. The final legislation is in *Acts and Laws*, 23 Mar. 1786, 3:580-605.

51. This legislation is in ibid., 8 March 1782, 1:936.

52. Ibid., 3 May 1782, 1:384-89.

53. See the discussion in the *Salem Gazette*, 8 May 1785, and the letter from Samuel Dexter to William Cushing, 28 Jan. 1785, in Robert Paine Papers, Massachusetts Historical Society.

could not tender his property to the creditor for the debt; he had to wait till his creditor had won his suit and had secured an execution. The protection to the debtor lay in the fact that the panel would give him a higher value for his property than would have been secured at a legal auction. The debtor still had to pay his court fees and costs. Even this act remained in effect for only one year.[54] The most commercial interests opposed even this watered-down measure with 59 percent of their votes, while 60 percent of the group B and 86 percent of the group C delegates voted for it.[55] Thanks to the pressure from conventions and the threat of actual violence in the west, the senate, for once, approved a non-commercially sponsored measure from the lower house.

The financial issue had thus become the central feature of the commonwealth's politics between 1780 and 1786. Although it mainly concerned the payment of the state debt, it also involved creditor-debtor relations, legal tender, the use of tax funds, and the administration of tax collection. Time after time the state was divided on financial measures, with the most commercial-cosmopolitan interests and towns opposing the less commercial ones. This struggle established a basic political pattern that would be the dominant factor in the commonwealth's politics until the late 1780s. In addition to creating a division, the workings of the system frustrated the less commercial-cosmopolitan interests who, despite their frequent control of the lower house, met defeat when the senate ignored their measures. By early 1786 crisis loomed: direct tax revenues had to be used to pay the interest on the debt, and the court still had the problem of finding the funds to pay off the principal.

Although struggles over the financial program resulted in bitter divisions, all three groups of towns agreed on a wide range of issues concerning commerce, protective tariffs, social and institutional structure, the land system, and the legal code, none of which required a roll call vote in the lower house between 1780 and 1786.

The regulation of foreign trade and shipping caused some heated discussion but no outright divisions. Until the end of the war the commonwealth considered all trade with Great Britain illegal and

54. The legislation is in *Acts and Laws*, 2 July 1782, 2:31-32.
55. The vote is in House Journal, 2 July 1782, pp. 150-51. See the discussion in Taylor, *Western Massachusetts*, pp. 117-18.

took steps to prevent it, finally culminating in a comprehensive act in November 1782 that established procedures for seizing illegally imported British goods.[56] After the war the merchants were anxious to reestablish their connections with Great Britain. In March 1783 the court declared that all acts preventing the importation of British goods lapsed with the end of the war and three months later it established regulations for entering and clearing British vessels.[57]

After ratification of the peace treaty, the court attempted to place trade on a regular basis. A comprehensive act established procedures for entering and clearing vessels and changed the regulations controlling the naval officers who had been appointed in all the important ports.[58] Other measures levied light money duties on all shipping, gave Massachusetts vessels an advantage by charging a double duty on foreign tonnage, and placed seamen at the mercy of shipowners by providing that seamen could not be sued for debt till they had completed their contracted voyage and by giving local justices of the peace the authority to return seamen to their masters if the former had deserted their ships or had broken their contracts.[59]

In 1784 and 1785 the commonwealth began to take harsher measures against foreign and especially British shipping and attempted to use state laws and regulations to construct some type of national commercial system. The influx of British goods and factors during 1783 and 1784 stirred a great deal of clamor. By the spring of 1785 the papers were filled with attacks on trade

56. For this early activity see Hancock's address in Bacon, ed., *Supplement to Acts and Laws*, 31 Oct. 1780, p. 24. For legislation see *Acts and Laws*, 12 Feb. 1781, 1:12-14; 9 May 1782, 1:187-90; 8 Nov. 1782, 2:84-91. For agitation see *Boston Gazette*, 3, 13 May, 22 July, 26 Aug., 2 Sept., 2 Dec. 1782; *Independent Chronicle*, 30 Aug. 1782; *Salem Gazette*, 7 Feb. 1783; William V. Wells, *The Life and Public Services of Samuel Adams*, 3 vols. (Boston, 1865), 3:169-72; *Reports of the Records Commissioners of the City of Boston*, 39 vols. (Boston, 1876-1909), vol. 26; 3 Sept. 1782, pp. 270-72; 6 Sept. 1782, pp. 272-75; Petition of Salem, 24 Jan. 1782, in Massachusetts Archives, Office of the Secretary, Boston, 187:370.

57. Legislation is in *Acts and Laws*, 25 Mar. 1783, 2:176-77 and 4 June 1783, 2:674-75.

58. Ibid., 1 July 1784, 3:34-41.

59. For light money see ibid., 22 Oct. 1783, 2:543-45. For agitation for more lighthouses see Petition of the Boston Marine Society in the Public Papers for the act of 2 July 1783, in the Office of the Secretary, Boston. For the regulation of sailors see *Acts and Laws*, 5 July 1784, 3:47-48.

with Britain, the use of British shipping, the evil machinations of British factors, and the moral and economic evils of paying specie for British "geegaws." The Boston merchants, alarmed by the excessive imports of British goods and the use of British ships, also demanded that British imports be limited and that the exportation of American goods in British bottoms be stopped. Agitation brought results. In June 1785 the court passed an act that prohibited all exportation of products in British and foreign ships after 1 August 1785, unless Britain or other foreign nations made commercial treaties with the United States. The act also prevented all foreign vessels from unloading their goods except at the three ports of Boston, Falmouth, and Dartmouth, and provided for increased light and tonnage duties on all foreign shipping. At the same time the court passed a high protective tariff. Some merchants believed this harsh action went too far. Others supported it in the hope that it would lead to foreign concessions or to some type of national commercial policy.[60] The less commercial-cosmopolitan interests apparently took little notice of the problem.

When the commonwealth's attempts to persuade other states to adopt similar harsh commercial regulations were ignored, many in the state protested that the legislation had gone too far. Governor Bowdoin, in a circular letter to the other governors, explained the act and expressed his desire that "Congress may be voted a well *guarded* power to regulate the trade of the United States" upon which the Massachusetts legislation would be discontinued. Bowdoin hoped that the other states in the interim would take similar action so "that no one state may be left to suffer."[61] But

60. For agitation for this type of legislation see *Independent Chronicle*, 12 Aug. 1784; 10, 31 Mar., 8, 14 Apr., 26 May 1785; *Massachusetts Centinel*, 15, 22 Dec. 1784; 12 Jan., 13, 30 Apr., 7, 26 May 1785. For personal views see Mercy Warren to John Adams, 27 Apr. 1785, Warren-Adams Letters, W. C. Ford, ed., 2 vols., Massachusetts Historical Society, *Collections*, vols. 72 and 73 (1917-1925), 72:252; Van Berkel to States General, 27 Apr. 1785, in George Bancroft, *History of the Formation of the Constitution of the United States of America*, 2 vols. (New York, 1882), 1:432; Thomas Russell to Jeremy Belknap, 2 May 1785, Belknap Papers, Massachusetts Historical Society, *Collections*, 5th ser., vols. 2 and 3 (1877), 6th ser., vol. 4 (1891), 5th ser., 3:296. A general view of the discussion is in *Boston Magazine*, July 1785, p. 276. The final legislation is in *Acts and Laws* 23 June 1785, 3:439-44.

61. James Bowdoin to the Governor of Maryland [Circular Letter], 28 July 1785, Massachusetts Historical Society, *Proceedings*, 1st ser., 4:120-22.

Congress took no action, Britain made no treaty, friendly foreign nations protested, and the other states appeared willing to let the commonwealth suffer. Finally in November 1785 the court opened additional ports to foreign shipping and reduced the restrictions on nations that had made commercial treaties with the United States. At the same time it refused to relent against the British in the hope that the Court of Saint James would be forced to make a commercial treaty with the new republic.[62]

Other economic legislation aiding artisans, fishermen, and local shopkeepers also passed without a struggle. The artisans had received some protection from the impost as early as November 1782. In 1785 the court, in response to their demands, gave them better protection than the new national government would after 1789.[63] In the next session the court aided sugar refiners by prohibiting the importation of all foreign loaf sugar after 1 March 1786.[64] Inland traders and shopkeepers also received assistance from the court when an act in 1785 prohibited peddlers and petty chapmen from selling their wares from town to town.[65] Finally fishermen and fishing towns had their taxes abated and in 1786 the court began to provide bounties for whale products.[66]

The only opposition to economic legislation, with the exception

---

62. Bowdoin's address is in *Acts and Laws*, 2 Oct. 1785, 3:727. Discussion of the commonwealth's commercial policies is in John Q. Adams to John Adams, 3 Aug. 1785, in Worthington C. Ford, ed., *Writings of John Quincy Adams*, 7 vols. (New York, 1913-1917), 1:18; Samuel Adams to Elbridge Gerry, 19 Sept. 1785, in Bancroft, *Constitution*, 1:458; Rufus King to John Adams, 2 Nov. 1785, in Charles E. King, *The Life and Correspondance of Rufus King Comprising His Letters; Private and Official. His Public Documents and His Speeches*, 6 vols. (New York, (1894-1900), 1:112-13; Rufus King to Caleb Davis, 3 Nov. 1785 and 17 Oct. 1785, Caleb Davis Papers; James Bowdoin to John Adams, 12 Jan. 1786, Bowdoin-Temple Papers, Massachusetts Historical Society, *Collections*, 6th ser., vol. 9 (1897), 7th ser., vol. 6 (1907), 7th ser., 6:85 86; John Adams to James Bowdoin, 9 May 1786, Adams Papers, pt. 4; *Independent Chronicle*, 15, 22, 29 Sept., 6 Oct. 1785. The legislation is in *Acts and Laws*, 2 Oct. 1785, 3:727.

63. The best secondary account is William Zornow, "Massachusetts Tariff Policies, 1775-1789," Essex Institute, *Historical Collections*, 90:194-215. For the legislation see *Acts and Laws*, 2 July 1785, 3:453-57.

64. Ibid., 30 Nov. 1785, 3:503-05.

65. Ibid., 9 June 1785, 3:430-33.

66. Ibid., 28 Nov. 1785, 3:795-97. The court allocated bounties of £15 per ton for white sperm oil, £3 per ton for yellow or brown sperm oil, and £2 per ton for common whale oil. For examples of abatements see ibid., 31 Jan. 1781, 1:246-47; 9 May 1781, 1:449, and 19 Oct. 1781, 1:756.

of the financial problem, came as a result of the court's efforts to aid Boston by establishing a market in the capital. Boston for years had tried to confine farmers selling their merchandise to a single marketplace in the center of the city. Naturally the farmers would have to pay for space at the market and could no longer sell from door to door. The court supported the Bostonians and passed a market act in 1784 that permitted the capital city to establish and maintain its own markets. This incited the wrath of the farming towns in Middlesex and Suffolk Counties who, with the aid of other farming towns, overwhelmed Boston's resistance and repealed the act one year later.[67]

Despite a vigorous newspaper debate the court also found a consensus when dealing with the complex land problems in the District of Maine. During 1780 and 1781 several writers attacked the large speculative landholdings in the district and advocated higher taxes on unimproved land. One author even advocated an agrarian law that would equalize land holdings throughout the commonwealth, warned that speculators planned to seize large areas of Maine, and urged the court to rescind grants to speculators who had not fulfilled their conditions.[68]

Spurred perhaps by such advice, the court made some feeble efforts to reform the system during 1783 and 1784. It appointed committees to sell land to squatters and to study the land situation in Lincoln County. In March 1784 it established a committee of Boston merchants empowered to investigate huge claims based on dusty charters and patents and instructed it to sell some land to small settlers, lay out townships, limit individual grants to five hundred acres per town, and give one hundred free acres to each family that would settle and clear four acres in four years.[69] But

67. Agitation in Boston for the legislation is in the *Boston Town Records*, 25 Mar. 1783, 31:301. The legislation is in *Acts and Laws*, 18 Feb. 1784, 2:564-66. The local regulations are in *Boston Town Records*, 18 Mar. 1784. The reaction of the farmers is in Petition of the Suffolk Towns, in Public Papers, for the act of 11 Feb. 1785. Boston's reply is in the *Boston Town Records*, 11, 15 Jan. 1785, 31:49. The final legislation is in *Acts and Laws*, 11 Feb. 1785, 3:111-12.

68. Examples of these complaints are in *Continental Journal*, 4 May 1781; *Massachusetts Spy* [Worcester], 17, 24 May, 2 Aug. 1781, 21 Mar. 1782; *Boston Gazette*, 4 Feb., 11 Mar., 29 Apr. 1782.

69. These actions are in *Acts and Laws*, 11 July 1783, 2:729-30; 28 Oct. 1783, 2:799-800; 22 Mar. 1784, 2:895-97.

the court quickly moved to aid the bigger operators as well. In July 1784 it ordered its committee of merchants to lay out townships of thirty-six square miles and sell them to speculators for state securities. In November 1784 it laid down general rules for large grants used to reimburse citizens who had lost land as a result of the New Hampshire–Massachusetts boundary decision of 1740, to pay off holders of certificates drawn on the state treasury, and to reward Nova Scotia refugees who had lost land because of their pro-American activities. By 1785 the court made even larger grants, permitted previous grantees more time to fulfill their conditions, and protected the old grants made to the Waldo and Pepperell families.[70]

Placeholding, the fee system, the legal code, public education, and other social questions also failed to create divisions within the court. In 1781 and 1782 the court copied the colonial pattern in establishing the commonwealth's judicial system. It modeled the supreme judicial court on the colonial superior court, gave the judges the same £300 salaries, and retained the 1773 fee table for court cases and judicial fees.[71] The legislature also continued the courts of common pleas, the probate courts, the court of general sessions, the criminal powers of the justices of the peace, and the registers of deeds. The court did increase the powers of the justices to act in civil causes up to the value of £4 instead of the £2

70. For laying out the townships and for their sale at Boston see ibid., 9 July 1784, 3:282-84. For the sale of land to Nova Scotia refugees and other see ibid., 17 March 1785, 3:400-01; 4 July 1785, 3:662-63. For examples of extending time so that speculators could meet their contracted requirements see 17 Mar. 1785, 3:406-08, 410-11; 21 June 1785, 3:645-47; 13 Mar. 1786, 3:838-39. The Waldo and Pepperell claims are considered in ibid., 9 July 1785, 3:632, and 4 July 1785, 3:699-702.

71. Under the 1780 constitution all former laws remained in force until amended or repealed. See F. N. Thorpe, *Federal and State Constitutions, Colonial Charters, and Other Organic Laws*, 7 vols. (Washington, D.C., 1909), 3:1910. The act establishing the supreme judicial court is in *Acts and Laws*, 20 Feb. 1781, 1:32-33. The new fee schedule is in ibid., 27 June 1782, 2:10-24. In 1773 the first new fee act in fifty years had passed the court. This was supposedly a temporary act that had to be renewed every two years. In 1776 the court drafted a new act that lowered fees below the 1773 level. Additional acts in 1778 and 1780 were based on the 1776 act but increased fees to keep up with inflation. The resolve of 1782 put the fees back at the 1773 level and thus in effect raised them. The sessions for the supreme court were established in ibid., 14 March 1783, 2:141-43.

of the colonial era and eventually made some changes in the 1773 fee table by lowering some fees and raising others.[72] The court took no action to modernize or even codify the commonwealth's antiquated, prolix, and confused laws. It appointed a committee, composed mainly of judges of the supreme court, to review the laws and report a new code based upon the last revision in 1759, but the committee procrastinated and never completed its chore. Sam Adam's dream of a new legal code to complement the new constitution died stillborn.[73] Some critics wrote in favor of simplifying the laws, reducing the fees and court cost, scrapping the courts of common pleas, and paring down the power of attorneys, but such ideas never reached the voting stage.[74]

The court did almost nothing to aid public education during the period. It drafted no legislation to benefit the public primary and grammar schools, but it did charter academies designed to educate the children of socially prominent persons. The legislature gave some assistance to Harvard: it paid the salaries of the professors when the corporation ran into financial difficulties, but the bitter feud between Governor Hancock and the university blocked any further assistance.[75] A few essayists in Boston advocated some

72. For the courts of common pleas see ibid., 3 July 1782, 2:32-34; 10 Mar. 1783, 2:126-28. The courts of general sessions are in ibid., 3 July 1782, 2:39-40. The other courts are in ibid., 11 Mar. 1784, 2:605-09; 17 Mar. 1784, 2:648-51; 12 Mar. 1784, 2:617-19; 16 Mar. 1784, 2:627-31. Increase of the powers of the justices of the peace in ibid., 16 Mar. 1784, 2:627-28 and 629-30.

73. For the appointment of this committee see ibid., 30 Nov. 1780, 1:187-88. For a discussion about how the committee would proceed see Memorandum of Robert Treat Paine, Robert Paine Papers. Also see Samuel Breck to Samuel Adams, 14 Dec. 1781, Henry Alonzo Cushing, *The Writings of Samuel Adams*, 4 vols. (New York, 1908), 4:268-71, especially p. 271. The best secondary account is in John D. Cushing, "A Revolutionary Conservative: The Public Life of William Cushing," (Ph.D. diss. Clark University, 1859), pp. 177-92.

74. *Boston Magazine*, Apr. 1784.

75. Among other relatively minor actions the court chartered the American Academy of Arts and Sciences and passed a copyright law. See Handlin and Handlin, *Commonwealth*, pp. 81 and 104. An example of the court's payment of Harvard salaries is in *Acts and Laws*, 11 July 1783, 2:727-28. Also note James Swan, *National Arithmetick, or Observations on the Finances of Massachusetts* . . . (Boston, 1786), p. 54.

The feud between Harvard and Hancock began over Hancock's poor performance as treasurer of the corporation. See Joseph Willard to Artemas Ward, 25 June 1781, Artemas Ward Papers, Massachusetts Historical Society; John Hancock to Joseph Willard, 20 Oct. 1783, Colonial Society of Massachusetts,

educational reforms including higher salaries for teachers, the education of females, the certification, of teachers, and one demanded that all towns should establish grammar schools—all of which were ignored.[76]

When it came to other social questions, the court almost always followed colonial precedents. In 1782 and 1783 it passed several general acts renewing much of the colonial legislation including the Boston police act of 1761, the acts of 1750 and 1753 regulating ferries and common fields, the 1758 act regulating Indian towns, the vagrancy act of 1756, and the 1757 act that regulated court procedures. The only significant pieces of new social legislation passed by the court permitted the supreme court instead of the council to make the final decisions in divorce suits, created a state penitentiary on Castle Island where criminals could reflect on the rewards of virtue while hammering out nails, and ended the benefit of clergy for literates convicted of capital offenses.[77]

Despite the serious religious differences within the commonwealth and the often heated popular debate over religious questions, the court failed to divide even once over a religious issue during the 1780s. The debate over the religious establishment written into the 1780 constitution continued into the 1780s. Politicians and ministers attacked and defended the establishment and local collectors hauled protesting Baptists away to jail, but the court, instead of listening to the complaints of men like Isaac Backus and Joseph Hawley, excused ministers from paying per-

Publications, 10,320-22. For the academies see *Acts and Laws*, 3 Oct. 1782, 2:49-53; 23 Mar. 1784, 2:557-60; and Thomas Fleet and John Fleet, *Fleet's Pocket Almanack for the Year of Our Lord 1787 . . . to Which Is Annexed the Massachusetts Register* (Boston, 1786), pp. 72-77.

76. For discussions concerning education see Josiah Quincy, *A Municipal History of the Town of Boston During Two Centuries from September 17, 1630 to September 17, 1830* (Boston, 1832), pp. 20-22; *Boston Town Records*, 1-3 May 1785, 31:795, 5 Apr. 1784, 31:16-18; *Massachusetts Centinel*, 2, 5, 9, 23, 30 Mar., 6 Apr., 8, 27 June 1785; *American Herald*, 13 Mar. 1785; *Boston Magazine*, June 1784, pp. 317-18; and *Massachusetts Spy* [Worcester], 12 Jan. 1786.

77. The renewal of the older colonial laws is illustrated in *Acts and Laws*, 7 Feb. 1783, 2:105-08. Changes are made in ibid., 11 Mar. 1785, 3:154-55. *Boston Magazine*, July 1784, gives additional details. For prisons see *Acts and Laws*, 14 Mar. 1785, 3:163-67; 1 Nov. 1785, 3:472-74; 22 Mar. 1786, 3:927-29. The issue is discussed in *Massachusetts Centinel*, 5 Jan. 1785, and in Douglas S. Robertson, ed., *An Englishman in America 1785; Being the Diary of Joseph Hadfield* (Toronto, 1933), 12 Sept. 1785, pp. 184-85.

sonal and property taxes, permitted them to serve in the lower house, and attempted to force speculators to settle them in the Maine towns. It also passed harsh acts against blasphemy, additional acts against cursing and swearing, and after considerable debate, an act to restrict travel on Sunday which forbad needless travel, required all inhabitants to attend services at least once every three months, and gave broad powers to the wardens of the Sabbath who enforced this legislation. This legislation almost created a serious division. Boston and Marblehead petitioned against the act and protested that it gave unconstitutional power to the wardens and infringed on the natural rights of all citizens. The irate citizens of Boston exploded when they learned that Roxbury wardens arrested Boston citizens for their Sunday outings, and after a bitter debate in the press the Roxbury officials prudently withdrew. But the clerical interests did not win all the battles in the court, which rejected temperance and sumptuary legislation aimed at the supposed evils of the coastal cities. [78] Religious issues, despite their vast political potential, did not become important during this period, and not a single roll call vote was taken on a religious question between 1780 and 1791.

78. See especially Joseph Hawley to Massachusetts Senate, 28 Oct. 1780, Massachusetts Historical Society, *Proceedings*, 49:79-81. The legislation is described in *Acts and Laws*, 3 July 1782, 2:27-28; 19 Oct. 1782, 2:59-63; 22 Oct. 1782, 2:63-70. Persons were tried and convicted of blasphemy; see Docket Books, Supreme Judicial Court, Worcester County, Spring 1783 term, available from Suffolk County Court House, Boston, Mass. The act concerning the Sabbath is in *Acts and Laws*, 22 Oct. 1782, 2:63-70. Reaction against it may be found in *General Advertiser*, 31 May 1783; Samuel Roads, Jr., *The History and Traditions of Marblehead* (Boston, 1880), 136; *Boston Town Records*, 13 May 1783, 31:314. The Roxbury affair is covered in *Massachusetts Centinel*, 20 July, 17 Aug. 1785 and *Independent Chronicle*, 25 Aug. 1785.

5

Factions, Tories,
and the Confederation

FACTIONS of ambitious politicians, the return of the Tories, and
the relations of the commonwealth and the confederation all
created political divisions, some of which developed along the
same lines as those underlying the struggle over state financial
policy. During the early 1780s the struggles of the numerous factions for power and place had little relevance to the simultaneous
battle raging over credit and financial measures in the lower house
of the General Court. The popular John Hancock and his follower
Thomas Cushing had little difficulty in winning the annual elections for governor and lieutenant governor, but Hancock's resignation in 1785 created a chance for other factions to attain power.
The gubernatorial election of that year reflected, to some extent,
the divisions throughout the state over fiscal and credit policies.
With James Bowdoin ensconced in office, gubernatorial politics
returned to normal and the 1786 elections had little relevance to
the underlying divisions within the court or society. The returning
loyalists created some serious political divisions in 1783 and 1784
which seemed to reflect the growing polarization within the commonwealth over finances and credit, but popular sentiment shifted
in favor of the former Tories and by 1785 and 1786 the issues had
evaporated. The relationship of the commonwealth to the confederation created three separate categories of issues which resulted in
consensus and conflict throughout the state. All groups of towns
and interests advocated measures designed to bring the commonwealth more benefits from the confederation, ranging from the
national funding of the Penobscot expedition to protection of
New England fisheries. Serious divisions resulted when the court
considered the 1781 impost, the 1783 impost and commutation
proposals, or the granting of supplemental funds to the confedera-

tion. In 1781 the least commercial-cosmopolitan towns backed the national impost, but in 1783 this support evaporated. By 1785 and 1786 the most commercial-cosmopolitan towns backed granting direct tax revenues to the confederation while the less commercial-cosmopolitan communities opposed the scheme. Between 1781 and 1786 the shift of opinion of towns and interests on national fiscal matters brought them closely in line with their votes on state financial questions and by 1786 the less commercial-cosmopolitan towns, stung by heavy direct taxes, opposed levies for both the commonwealth and the confederation. Still this conflict, consensus, and shift on national policy did not yet influence the activities of the Massachusetts delegation in the Confederation Congress which continued to oppose what were called nationalistic solutions throughout the entire period. Even as late as early 1786 these leading spokesmen for the commonwealth believed that the Articles, with certain amendments, would satisfy the economic and commercial requirements of their state. But while the political factions seemed wedded to the confederation, the shifts in support of national programs within the General Court became similar to the polarization of the groups and towns over state fiscal matters. By early 1786 it also became clear that the less commercial-cosmopolitan communities and interests suspected that any efforts to increase the fiscal powers of the confederation would harm them while aiding their more commercial-cosmopolitan opponents.

Elections for governor and lieutenant governor, with the exception of 1785, revolved around the struggle of the various political factions for these two highest offices. The 1780 constitution provided for the annual election of the two highest state officials by direct, popular vote and granted the governor enough power to make the position important.[1] Despite these democratic features, the politicians, grouped into vague and amorphous factions, contested only one campaign for the governorship and one for the lieutenant governorship between 1780 and 1786. This lack of ef-

---

1. F. N. Thorpe, ed., *Federal and State Constitutions, Colonial Charters, and Other Organic Laws*, 7 vols. (Washington D.C., 1909), vol. 3, 1900-1904, gives the method for electing the governor and lieutenant governor. If no candidate secured a majority of the vote the house elected two of the four persons with the largest number of votes and submitted their names to the senate. The senate then chose one of these two candidates. This type of election occurred in 1785 for governor, and in 1787 and 1788 for lieutenant governor.

fective electioneering did not mean that perennial governor John Hancock had been accepted by his former revolutionary associates and political peers. A group of the older Whig revolutionaries that included John and Samuel Adams, James Warren, Elbridge Gerry, James Bowdoin, and their friends and associates despised the popular Hancock as a demagogue and an incompetent and tried to inflame the electors against him.[2] Their efforts failed and between 1780 and 1785 Hancock crushed his constant rival, James Bowdoin, who failed to carry a single county in any of his attempts against the popular governor. Hancock, a lazy but shrewd politician, dodged issues.[3] He failed to take a stand on the 1781 congressional impost, he played the artful dodger during the 1781-1782

2. A good secondary account of the development of this personal feud is found in Neil R. Stout, "The Breakup of the Popular Party in Massachusetts, 1775-1780" (Master's thesis, University of Wisconsin, 1958). For several other examples of anti-Hancock sentiment (especially from the Adams-Bowdoin group) see Samuel to Mrs. Adams, 17 Oct. 1780, in Henry A. Cushing, *The Writings of Samuel Adams*, 4 vols. (New York, 1904-1908), 4:211-12; Samuel Adams to John Lowell, 15 Sept. 1785, in William V. Wells, *The Life and Public Services of Samuel Adams*, 3 vols. (Boston, 1865), 3:107; Theophilus Parsons to Dana, 3 Aug. 1780, Dana Manuscripts, Massachusetts Historical Society; Elbridge Gerry to Samuel Adams, 8 Jan. 1781, Calendar of Samuel Adams Papers, Bancroft Collection, New York Public Library.

For examples in the press see *Continental Journal*, 21 Dec. 1780; *Boston Gazette*, 2 Apr. 1781; *Continental Journal*, 8 Nov., 6 Dec. 1781, 10, 17, Jan. 1782; *Evening Post*, 5, 22 Dec. 1781; *Boston Gazette*, 20 Feb. 1782. For a personal reaction by Gerry see Gerry's Rejection of His Commission, 29 Oct. 1781, Massachusetts Archives, 203:409, and also James T. Austin, *The Life of Elbridge Gerry with Contemporary Letters*, 2 vols. (Boston, 1827-1829), 1:367.

3. Election returns are available in Abstracts of Votes for the Election of Governor and Lieutenant-Governor, Office of the Secretary, Boston, for all the years between 1780 and 1791 with the exception of 1783 and 1784 (cited hereafter as Abstracts-Governor and Abstracts-Lt.-Governor). These returns give the results for every town and for each candidate. The totals from these returns often vary from the official results given in the unpublished Journal of the House of Representatives, available at the Office of the Secretary, Boston, or the unpublished Journal of the Senate, available at the Office of the Secretary, Boston (cited hereafter as House Journal and Senate Journal, respectively), during the first week of the legislative year. However the differences are slight and may be explained by: (1) errors in the original computations by the General Court, or (2) the existence of returns in the abstracts or returns that were received too late to be included in the official totals in the Journals. In no case does the difference between my computations and those of the court amount to over 1 percent of the total vote and in no instance did it change the results of any election.

struggle over the state impost and excise, he declined to commit himself to divisive programs in his enigmatic addresses to the General Court, and he did little to force through the financial programs desired by the most commercial-cosmopolitan interests.[4] To the electors Hancock remained a great revolutionary figure who had given his fortune to the cause and who stood above the swirling, self-interested factions or the divisive struggles over fiscal policy. Before every election the Adams-Warren-Bowdoin axis, in a vain attempt to undercut Hancock's popularity, filled the papers with vicious attacks on his love of luxury, his incompetence, and his foppery. Hancock's associates struck back with accusations of Toryism. Specifically James Sullivan charged that Bowdoin's son-in-law, John Temple, had become a Tory and a British agent. The Bowdoin backers, in return, tried to prevent Sullivan from taking his seat as a Boston representative to the General Court. But the electorate yawned at these political shenanigans and continued to return the patriotic Hancock to the state's highest office.[5]

4. Hancock's dodging on the national impost may be followed in E. M. Bacon, ed., *Supplement to the Acts and Laws of the Commonwealth of Massachusetts* (Boston, 1896), 8 Mar. 1782, pp. 96-97. For his activities on the state impost and excise see ibid., 3 Nov. 1782, p. 145, and 14 Nov. 1782, p. 146. Hancock's more important addresses are listed below. Bacon, ed., *Supplement to the Acts and Laws*, 31 Oct. 1780, pp. 23-25, contains his first and longest address in which he requests the restriction of trade with the British, aid to religion, backs Sabbatarian legislation, and insists on support for defense. In ibid., 1 June 1781, p. 84, he merely points out that the commonwealth faced critical times. In ibid., 13 Sept. 1781, pp. 85-87, he describes the needs of the army. In ibid., 30 Oct. 1781, p. 81 and 24 Apr. 1782, p. 98, he explains his policies during the Temple affair. In ibid., 2 Nov. 1781, he explains his veto of a resolve concerning Sam Adams's rent. In ibid., 2 Jan. 1782, p. 93, and 10 May 1782, p. 100, he explains his veto of a resolve concerning Gerry's seat in the Confederation Congress. For the later period see ibid., 2 June 1783, p. 204; 23 Jan. 1784, p. 212; and 19 Mar. 1784, p. 216.

5. The Temple affair dragged on between the fall of 1781 and September 1783. Sullivan and Hancock accused John Temple, a former member of the British American Board of Customs Commissioners, of being a British spy. Temple defended himself and several influential politicians associated with Bowdoin also assisted him. At last in September 1783 the General Court closed the affair by resolving to cancel Temple's bond but cleared Hancock and Sullivan by deciding that the bond had been justly laid. Samuel Adams to John Adams, 19 Dec. 1781, in Cushing, *Samuel Adams*, 4:267, was probably right when he stated that the affair had embarrassed the efforts of the anti-Hancock group. The affair may be followed, at least superficially, in the following sources: Petition of John Temple, Oct. 1781 in Robert Paine

Hancock's popularity kept him in the governor's chair, but Thomas Cushing's long-term lease on the lieutenant governorship was due to the political fumbles of the Warren-Bowdoin clique. In the 1780 election for lieutenant governor no single candidate had secured the required majority. Bowdoin and James Warren ran first and third; Artemas Ward, the crusty Worcester County general and placeholder, came in second; and Cushing placed a very weak fourth with less than five hundred votes. The election results had no correlation with the serious divisions that would occur in the House during early 1781. Bowdoin, who would later become the leading spokesman for the most commercial-cosmopolitan interests and towns, ran best in the group C communities, and none of the contenders did remarkably well in any of the three groups. Thus the first state-wide election presented no recognizable pattern of voting behavior and certainly failed to indicate the divisions that would occur in the lower house during the 1780s.

After doing well in the popular voting, the Bowdoin-Warren faction blew their chances when actually elected by the General Court. In accordance with the 1780 constitution, the court would select the lieutenant governor if no single candidate secured a majority of the popular vote. In the first round the house nominated Bowdoin and Azor Orne, the Essex senator, to the senate which chose Bowdoin by a vote of 24 to 1. But Bowdoin pleaded his ill health and refused to accept the election. The court then gave the anti-Hancockites another opportunity when the senate elected Warren by a vote of 12 to 7 but Warren claimed that his chores on the Continental Marine Committee absorbed too much of his energy and also declined the position. Finally on the third attempt the house nominated Cushing and Ward to the senate and

Papers, Massachusetts Historical Society; Hancock's address of 31 Oct. 1781, in Bacon, ed., *Supplement to the Acts and Laws*, p. 91; *Acts and Laws of the Commonwealth of Massachusetts, 1780-1797,* 11 vols. (Boston, 1890 1897), 2 Nov. 1781, 1:803-06; Bond for John Temple, 24 Dec. 1781, Bowdoin-Temple Manuscripts, Massachusetts Historical Society. For the newspapers see *Boston Gazette*, 19 Nov., 10 Dec. 1781, 1 Mar. 1782; *Evening Post*, 8 Dec. 1781; *Salem Gazette*, 31 Jan. 1781. Temple's counterattack is in the *Boston Gazette*, 16 Oct. 1782; and the *Evening Post*, 7, 14 Dec. 1782. The dispute was finally ended by the resolve of 22 Oct. 1783; see Bacon, ed., *Supplement to the Acts and Laws*, p. 190.

The efforts to prevent Sullivan from taking his seat as a Boston representative are in *Independent Chronicle*, 26 June, 1 Aug., 5, 12 Dec. 1783; *Evening Post*, 13 Dec. 1783; *Continental Journal*, 13 Nov. 1783.

the upper house chose Cushing by a 14 to 5 margin.[6] Cushing, healthy and not overburdened with work, accepted the position and stepped into a political sinecure that he held until his death in early 1788.

In 1785 the first really contested election for governor permitted the Adams-Warren-Bowdoin faction to move into office. During the winter of 1784 and 1785 the Adams-Bowdoin group had singled out the Tea Assembly established by the young people of Boston for their diversion as evidence of the crumbling morality in a commonwealth led by the immoral or at least amoral Hancock.[7] In the midst of this tempest Hancock stunned everyone by offering his resignation to the General Court. Informed observers believed that he hoped the court would insist upon his retaining office but when the legislature made no such comment Hancock actually resigned and surrendered the governorship to Thomas Cushing in February of 1785. His political rivals, suspicious to the last, believed he intended to elect Cushing in 1785 and step back into the governorship in 1786.[8]

The campaign became excessively nasty as the Adams-Bowdoin group fell behind Bowdoin, other anti-Hancock elements backed Benjamin Lincoln, the former secretary of war for the confederation, and the Hancockites lined up behind the unspectacular

6. The returns are in Abstracts-Lt.-Governor, 1780. The details concerning the election by the General Court are found in Bacon, ed., *Supplement to the Acts and Laws*, 27 Oct., 2, 11, 13, 14 Nov., 1 Dec. 1780, pp. 34, 54, 56. *Massachusetts Spy* [Worcester], 6, 23 Nov. 1780 also gives additional detail. For the actual voting see the Senate Journal, 27 Oct., 7, 11, 12, 13, 29 Nov. 1780. While serving as a lieutenant governor, Cushing was appointed the governor of Castle Island and received a fee of two shillings from all vessels entering and clearing Boston harbor, excepting coasters and fishing vessels.

7. For a continuation of sniping at Hancock see James Warren to Elbridge Gerry, 20 Oct. 1782, Gerry Manuscripts, Massachusetts Historical Society. For the Tea Assembly see *Salem Gazette*, 18, 25 Jan. 1785; *Continental Journal*, 20 Jan. 1785; *American Herald*, 31 Jan., 7, 14 Feb. 1785; *Massachusetts Centinel*, 9, 16 Feb. 1785; *Independent Chronicle*, 17 Feb., 10 Mar. 1785.

8. *Massachusetts Centinel*, 1 Feb., 16 Mar. 1785. Elbridge Gerry to Rufus King, 14 Mar., 7 Apr. 1785, in Charles R. King, *The Life and Correspondence of Rufus King Comprising His Letters; Private and Official. His Public Documents and His Speeches*, 6 vols. (New York, 1894-1900), 1:75-77, 86-87; James Warren to John Adams, 13, 21 Sept. 1785, Warren-Adams Letters, W. C. Ford, ed., 2 vols., Massachusetts Historical Society, *Collections*, vols. 72-73; 72:262; Thomas C. Amory, *Life of James Sullivan With Selections From His Writings*, 2 vols., (Boston, 1859), 1:148.

Thomas Cushing. The pro-Bowdoin propagandists dismissed Cushing as a creature of Hancock and trumpeted Bowdoin's capability and honesty. The Hancock-Cushing writers rebutted by accusing Bowdoin of cowardice during the war and of insulting the electors by rejecting the lieutenant governorship in 1780.[9]

Although none of the candidates received a majority of the popular vote, the election underlined the growing political polarization within the state. (See table 37.) Bowdoin, with 39 percent of

TABLE 37
1785 Election

	Percentage of Votes for				Change in Bowdoin's Vote from 1780 to 1785
	Bowdoin	Cushing	Lincoln	Others	
Towns					
Group A	55%	23%	9%	13%	+33%
Group B	34	41	9	16	+ 8
Group C	21	39	22	18	− 7
Eastern group A	59	24	7	10	+45
Western group A	46	22	13	20	+13
Western group C	23	36	21	21	− 4
State	39	33	13	15	+14

SOURCES: Unpublished Abstracts of Votes for Governor, 1785, available at the Office of the Secretary, Boston. Bowdoin's vote in 1780 is from the unpublished Abstracts of Votes for Lieutenant-Governor, 1780, Office of the Secretary, Boston.

the total vote, received 55 percent of the votes cast in the group A and only 21 percent of the ballots of the group C electors. Bowdoin's direct contacts with the most commercial-cosmopolitan interests enabled him to increase his percentage of the vote in the group A communities by 33 points above his showing in 1780 while he actually lost 7 points in the group C towns. Cushing, on the other hand, received 39 percent of the vote in the least commercial-cosmopolitan towns and about 23 percent in the commercial-cosmopolitan centers, and Lincoln also ran much stronger in the group C towns. The shifts in Bowdoin's vote underline the change in voting patterns which had become much more similar to those in the lower house.

9. For some examples of this propaganda see *Independent Chronicle*, 24, 31 Mar., 8 Apr. 1785; *Massachusetts Centinel*, 26, 30 Mar., 2 Apr. 1785; *Worcester Spy*, 31 March 1785; *Hampshire Herald*, 5 Apr. 1785; *American Herald*, 28 March 1785.

When the failure of any candidate to secure a majority threw the election into the General Court, the campaign became even more bitter. The Bowdoin backers portrayed Cushing as a puppet in the hands of Hancock, a shifty character who had abandoned the patriots in 1771, an incompetent who could not draft a decent address to the court, and a corrupter of morals and believer in luxury.[10] The Cushing-Hancock rebuttal accused Bowdoin of being a lukewarm patriot, now in league with the British, who supported the Massachusetts Tories.[11] The house favored Cushing and gave him 134 votes to Bowdoin's 89 but the senate, controlled by the commercial-cosmopolitan interests, elected Bowdoin as the new governor by a vote of 18 to 10.[12] The 1785 polling showed that for once the gubernatorial election had ceased to be a mere popularity contest. Certain groups made definite choices; the house had favored Cushing and the senate elected Bowdoin. But this pattern did not persist and in 1786 most of the politicians closed ranks around Bowdoin who won easy reelection.[13]

For a time it appeared that the Tory question might produce alignments similar to those produced by state fiscal problems, but by 1785 the issue had almost totally disappeared. Between 1782

10. For some examples of anti-Cushing (and usually anti-Hancock) rhetoric see "Gratitude," 14 May 1785; 18 May 1785; "A Brother Elector," 21 May 1785; and "An Observer," 25 May 1785, all in *Massachusetts Centinel*. Also note the *Falmouth Gazette*, 21 May 1785.

11. For anti-Bowdoin rhetoric see *Independent Chronicle*, 8 Apr. 1785; "A Bowdoinite," in ibid., 21 May 1785; *Massachusetts Centinel*, 16 Apr. 1785; "Brutus" in ibid., 18, 21 May 1785; and a "True Whig" and "A Hancockian," in ibid., 25 May 1785.

12. Elbridge Gerry to Rufus King, 18 May 1785, and ibid., 27 May 1785, in King, *Rufus King*. 1:99, 100-01. House Journal, 26 May 1785, 18-19, gives the figures but no roll call. Senate Journal, 26 May 1785, p. 11, gives the result, but again without a roll call.

13. For discussions of the campaign see *Worcester Spy*, 2 June 1785, where a writer hopes that "scurillity which has disgraced newspapers in the capital may subside." Samuel Osgood to James Bowdoin, 20 June 1785, Bowdoin-Temple Papers, Massachusetts Historical Society, *Collections*, 6th ser., vol. 9 (1897), 7th ser., vol. 6 (1907), 7th ser., 6:55-56; Samuel Adams to John Adams, July 1785, in George Bancroft, *History of the Formation of the Constitution of the United States of America*, 2 vols. (New York, 1882), 1:444.
Bowdoin devoted part of his opening address to the General Court to discussing some of the charges made against him during the campaign; see *Acts and Laws*, 27 May 1785, 3:704-05, and *Worcester Spy*, 9 June 1785, Bowdoin's vote in 1786 is in the Abstracts-Governor, 1786.

and 1785 the lower house voted five times on legislation concerning Tories or absentees. On the first four votes the group A towns favored Tories more than representatives from the other two groups of towns. (See table 38.) The Tory issue divided the towns along much the same commercial-cosmopolitan continuum as the debate over state fiscal policy had.

TABLE 38
Votes on Questions Concerning Loyalists and Absentees

| | Percentage of Votes Favoring Them in | | | |
	Vote 1	*Vote 2*	*Vote 3*	*Vote 4*
Towns				
Group A	73.0%	37%	57%	65.0%
Group B	40.0	15	39	41.0
Group C	39.0	17	39	47.0
Eastern group A	89.0	48	67	65.0
Western group A	45.0	20	44	62.0
Western group C	34.0	14	31	42.0
State	49.5	22	44	50.5

SOURCES: Vote One: "House proceeded to consider the report of a joint committee on the Petition of Thomas Brattle . . . being that he should return to this state upon condition of his not being intitled to any part of his father's estate . . . and question was put if the House would agree with Senate in accepting the report" (Unpublished Journal of the House of Representatives of the Commonwealth of Massachusetts, Office of the Secretary, Boston, 27 Feb. 1783, pp. 524-26 [cited hereafter as House Journal]. Percentage of Yes vote).

Vote Two: Question put on enacting clause of anti-Tory bill, including a provision that no writ of any type could block their ejectment from the commonwealth (Ibid., 25 June 1783, pp. 114-16. Percentage of No vote).

Vote Three: Motion made to reconsider the vote of the morning (vote two), and that the enacting clause be expunged from the proviso (Ibid., 25 June 1783, pp. 121-23. Percentage of Yes vote).

Vote Four: Governor has granted licenses to several returning Tories, resolved that these licenses be approved (Ibid., 2 Nov. 1784, pp. 176-78. Percentage of Yes vote).

Ibid., 25 June 1783, pp. 112-13, gives another roll call on a Tory question, but this passed 140 to 0.

Before 1782 restrictions on Tories, accepted as necessary war measures, caused little political discussion. But as the war drew to a close several politicians attempted to stir up public hatred for returning absentees, among them James Sullivan who demanded the expulsion of John Temple as a British agent.[14] The publica-

14. An example is in *Continental Journal*, 10 Aug. 1780.

tion of the preliminary draft of the treaty of peace catapulted the Tory issue into the midst of politics and led several important merchants and other commercial men to defect from the anti-Tory consensus. They argued that returning Tories would inject additional capital into the commonwealth and would reduce friction with Britain whose merchants had already begun to renew old relationships throughout the state. [15] Although most of these men wanted the Tories to return, they had no intention of permitting them to repurchase or recover their confiscated property as recommended in article five of the treaty. [16] The debate over the return of Thomas Brattle reflected these views. Brattle, the son of a Tory merchant, petitioned the General Court in early 1783 for permission to return to the state. The court considered the request and the senate decided to permit Brattle's return if he surrendered all his claims to his father's confiscated estate. The lower house refused to accept even this compromise and in a close vote, in which 73 percent of the delegates of the group A towns voted for his return, rejected the senate's proposal. [17] The debate over the Brattle petition created a wave of anti-Tory sentiment throughout the entire state that changed the stand of many of the commercial towns and merchants. The Boston artisans, embittered by heavy imports of British manufactured goods, packed a town meeting and sent a circular letter to other communities urging opposition to all measures permitting Tories to return to the commonwealth. Supreme Court Justice William Cushing travelled around the state delivering violent anti-Tory diatribes to grand juries, and news-

15. Rhoda Dorsey, "The Resumption of Anglo-American Commerce" (Ph.D. diss., University of Minnesota, 1956), pp. 345-54 gives some of the background as does the "Notes on Commerce," in Julian P. Boyd et al., eds., *The Papers of Thomas Jefferson* (Princeton 1950-), 7:339. For some newspaper discussion see *Independent Chronicle*, 1, 8, 15, and 22 Aug. 1782.

16. James Warren to John Adams, 1 Nov. 1782, Warren-Adams Letters, 72:183. Also notice the voting patterns of the representatives of the commercial towns on the resolve permitting Brattle to return *without* any claim to his father's property (House Journal, 27 Feb. 1783, pp. 524-26). For the direct interest of many political and commercial leaders in confiscated Tory property see John T. Hassam, "List of Confiscated Estates in Boston," Massachusetts Historical Society, *Proceedings*, 2d ser., 10:162-85.

17. The vote is in the House Journal, 27 Feb. 1783, pp. 524-26. For the debate and reaction see *Independent Chronicle*, 13 Feb. 1783, 6 Mar. 1783; *Salem Gazette*, 6 Mar. 1783.

paper writers urged the electors to select representatives who would be tough on Tories. [18]

This pressure resulted in some changes in the voting patterns of the newly elected 1783 General Court. Tristram Dalton, the new speaker of the house, was converted to anti-Tory policies; the house quickly expelled David Black, a suspected Tory; and in July it passed anti-Tory legislation that modified the 1778 antiloyalist act. This law provided that persons listed in the 1778 legislation who dared to return could be jailed by any two justices of the peace who could then order them transported to any British possession. The law further specified that no legal writ of any kind could be used to delay their expulsion. The representatives from all three groups of towns supported this harsh measure. The group A towns hung back, but even 63 percent of their delegates voted for the law along with 85 percent from the group B and 83 percent from the C towns. [19]

This new law soon ran into difficulty. Politicians and essayists claimed that Tories with political connections remained in the state while justices expelled less important men. Others suggested that decent treatment of the loyalists might influence the British to make a commercial treaty with the United States. [20] This

18. This wave of criticism is covered in *Independent Chronicle*, 3 Apr., 8, 29 May, 5, 12 June 1783; *Boston Town Records*, 7 Apr. 1783, 26:3-6, 3 May 1783, 26:31; Wells, *Samuel Adams*, 3:182. A notation on the Draft of an Address to Grand Juries, Cushing Papers, Massachusetts Historical Society, states that Cushing delivered it to the grand juries of Barnstable, Plymouth, Essex, York, and Cumberland counties between April and June 1783. *Evening Post*, 10 May 1783; *Continental Journal*, 22 May 1783. For some local reactions see D. Hamilton Hurd, ed., *History of Norfolk County Massachusetts, With Biographical Sketches of Many of Its Pioneers and Prominent Men* (Philadelphia, 1884), p. 926; D. Hamilton Hurd, ed., *History of Plymouth County, Massachusetts, With Biographical Sketches of Many of Its Pioneers and Prominent Men*, 2 vols. (Philadelphia, 1889), 1:239; Samuel Sewall, *The History of Woburn, Middlesex County, Massachusetts* (Boston, 1868), pp. 403-05; *Salem Gazette*, 5 June 1783; and *Boston Gazette*, 9 June 1783.

19. *Acts and Laws*, 26 June 1783, 2:697, and 2 July 1783, 2:499-500 for the legislation. The vote is in the House Journal, 25 June 1783, pp. 114-16. For discussion see James Winthrop to Judge Samuel P. Savage, 30 May 1783, Samuel P. Savage Papers, Massachusetts Historical Society.

20. Petition of the Boston Committee of Correspondence and Safety, 15 Oct. 1783, Massachusetts Archives, 188:455; *Independent Chronicle*, 12, 26 Feb. 1784; *American Herald*, 16 Feb., 1 Mar. 1784; Samuel Osgood to Robert Treat Paine, 14 Feb. 1784, Robert Paine Papers.

change of heart even affected the court which passed a new act in March 1784 that allowed most Tories to return when licensed by the governor and council and permitted them to recover lands that had been confiscated but not yet sold by the commonwealth. As a concession to anti-Tories the court promised that the state would defend the title of all those who purchased Tory property.[21]

By the end of 1784 the most commercial towns again warmed towards the returning absentees while the less commercial-cosmopolitan towns remained cool. In November 1784 the house upheld Hancock's licensing of several returnees by a narrow one-vote margin, as the group A towns cast 65 percent of their votes in favor of the returnees while the group B and C towns cast 59 and 53 percent respectively of theirs against them.[22] This roll call reflected the last real contest in the house on the Tory question. After 1784 the Tories, aided by judicial decisions and a decline in popular antipathy, returned to the state.[23] In 1785 efforts to moderate the anti-Tory laws hit an unexpected snag in the senate and final action to remove all disabilities had to wait until the early 1790s.[24] But the absentees returned and in 1790 Barnstable-Plymouth voters elected Sherashrub Bourne, an accused Tory, to the Second Congress of the United States.[25] After 1784 the Tory question was a dead issue.

21. The legislation is in *Acts and Laws*, 24 Mar. 1784, 3:661-64. *Boston Magazine*, Mar. 1784, p. 212, gives the background of the discussion in the house.

22. This vote is in House Journal, 2 Nov. 1784, pp. 76-78.

23. Docket Books, Records of the Supreme Judicial Court, April 1784 term, Hampshire County, pp. 141 and 145, and *Massachusetts Spy* [Worcester], 3 June 1784; *Independent Chronicle*, 9 Sept. 1784. Also see Samuel Phillips, Jr. to Judges of the Supreme Judicial Court, 2 June 1785; Judges of the Supreme Judicial Court to Phillips, 15 June 1785; Order of the Senate, 17 June 1785; and Final Opinion of the Supreme Judicial Court; all in Dana Manuscripts. For some personal comments see David Sewall to William Cushing, 15 Jan. 1785, in ibid., and Theodore Sedgwick to Henry Van Schaack, 15 Apr. 1785, Sedgwick Papers, Massachusetts Historical Society. Richard E. Welch, Jr., *Theodore Sedgwick, Federalist: A Political Portrait* (Middleton, Conn., 1965), pp. 29-31.

24. *Boston Magazine*, Dec. 1785, pp. 476-77. *Massachusetts Centinel*, 19, 26 Nov., 3, 10 Dec. 1785. Vote is in House Journal, 15 Nov. 1785, pp. 295-96. (The vote was 141 to 18.) Rufus King to John Adams, King, *Rufus King*, 1:117. For final action see *Acts and Laws*, 9 June 1792, 7:5.

25. For Bourne's activities see Francis T. Bowles, "The Loyalty of Barnstable in the Revolution," Colonial Society of Massachusetts, *Publications*, 25:263-348.

The commonwealth's reaction to the confederation and its policies was mixed. All interests united to wrest concessions from Congress on the fisheries, the settlement of accounts, and the Penobscot claims. Other issues, especially the congressional impost plans of 1781 and 1783, the commutation of half pay, and the provision of supplementary funds raised through direct taxation, created divisions that as time passed became more and more similar to the conflicts over state financial questions. The reaction of the interests and towns to these national issues resulted in some significant shifts in their nationalistic attitudes. At first the less commercial-cosmopolitan groups and towns supported the strengthening of the confederation and threw their votes behind the national impost of 1781. By 1783 things had begun to change and the less commercial-cosmopolitan groups found themselves opposing the 1783 impost and commutation proposals. By 1785 and 1786 the most commercial-cosmopolitan towns and interests voted for supplemental funds to Congress, while the less commercial-cosmopolitan towns, worried by heavy direct taxes and suspicious of their more commercial cousins, opposed supplemental funds just as bitterly as they did certain sections of the commonwealth's financial program. As the commonwealth divided on national questions, the Massachusetts delegation in Congress hesitated to abandon the confederation in favor of a new national government. They played a leading role in defeating Morris and his programs. As late as 1785 most of them hoped that the confederation would succeed and believed that the commonwealth could function with limited assistance from a central government. Not until 1786 and 1787 did the politicians and the most commercial-cosmopolitan interests rally to the support of those promoting a new national government.

Massachusetts in the early 1780s lost much of her earlier power and influence in Congress. The Lee-Adams junto had fallen apart by the 1780s; Sam Adams returned home to grouse at Hancock and serve as president of the senate; John Adams departed for Europe in 1779 and did not return until 1788, John Hancock, former president of Congress, came home to fill the governor's chair. Elbridge Gerry, one of the few important holdovers from the seventies refused to sit in Congress for two years during the early 1780s because of a fancied insult. In place of these giants the commonwealth sent lesser-known but capable men. Samuel Holten became a regular and hard-working member; Samuel Osgood was appointed a member of the board of treasury; James Lovell and John Lowell played important roles; George Partridge sat often though usually silently; and Rufus King and Theodore Sedgwick, who sat towards the end of the period, began to make national reputations. Competent and hard-working, the Massachusetts delegates quietly observed as the exciting programs and leadership came from other states.

The commonwealth elected eighteen men to Congress between 1780 and 1785. Fifteen of these men resided in the group A towns and the other three sat as local placeholders or had connections with the commercial-cosmopolitan interests. Fifteen of these delegates would openly favor the new Constitution in 1788 and only James Sullivan and Elbridge Gerry actively opposed it. Many would later become Federalist members of the First or Second Congresses and a few would secure important executive positions under Washington.[26] Yet despite their commercial connections and their later careers these men had not become nationalists by the year 1785.

The delegation and practically all the interests in the commonwealth united to fight for measures that would aid the state. Everyone wanted protection of the fisheries, an increase in the quota given to the state for her efforts in retiring the old emission Continental currency, payment from the confederation for bounties given to Revolutionary soldiers, and payment of the expenses of the ill-fated Penobscot expedition.

Massachusetts struggled to protect her vital and vested interest in

26. *The Biographical Directory of the American Congress, 1774-1961*, 85th Cong., 2d sess., House doc. no. 442 (Washington, D.C., 1961) gives details about terms, occupations, and educational background. State positions held by these men may be obtained from the annual lists of senators and representatives in the *Acts and Laws* and from the annual lists of placeholders in Thomas Fleet and John Fleet, *Fleet's Pocket Almanack for the Year of Our Lord [1780-1790] . . . to Which Is Annexed the Massachusetts Register* (Boston, 1779-1789). *Debates and Proceedings in the Convention of the Commonwealth of Massachusetts, Held in the Year 1788, And Which Finally Ratified the Constitution of the United States* (Boston, 1856), 6 Feb. 1788, pp. 87-92, gives the roll call vote on the ratification of the Constitution in 1788. For some information on the Gerry affair see Gerry to the Massachusetts General Court, 9 Feb. 1782, in Edmund C. Burnett, ed., *Letters of Members of the Continental Congress*, 8 vols. (Washington, D.C. 1921-1938), 6:300-01.

the fisheries. In the early 1780s John Adams, the congressional delegation, and the General Court all fought to protect the fisheries from the suspected machinations of Robert Morris and the French. Congress did not give much support to her demands, but John Adams, as one of the peace commissioners, won the right for the state's fishermen to trawl off the coasts of Newfoundland and Nova Scotia and to use the uninhabited shores for drying their fish. In December 1782 Adams could write, "Thanks be to God, my dear Gerry, that our Tom Cod are safe in spite of the malice of enemies, the jealousy of allies, and the mistakes of Congress."[27] The commonwealth echoed these sentiments—the fish were safe with no thanks to Congress, Robert Morris, or the French.

The commonwealth feared that it had been defrauded on refunding the old emission Continental currency. Massachusetts claimed that she had done her duty, had refunded the old bills, and that consequently she had become a dumping ground for speculators who had sent masses of the old money into the commonwealth. The court continually pressed Congress to force the other states to redeem their quotas or to allow Massachusetts to redeem an additional amount—which would naturally be subtracted from her share of the Continental requisitions levied on

27. The fisheries question was related to political questions revolving around the French alliance. See William C. Stinchcombe, *The American Revolution and the French Alliance* (Syracuse, 1969), pp. 62-76, 183-213. See also Samuel Adams to James Warren, 1 Feb. 1781, in Cushing, *Samuel Adams*, 4:243. Instructions to the Massachusetts delegates are in *Acts and Laws*, 29 Oct. 1781, 2:772-73. For the pressure of the coastal towns see *Reports of the Record Commissioners of the City of Boston*, 39 vols. (Boston, 1876-1909) cited hereafter as *Boston Town Records*), 7 Dec. 1781, 26:211; 11 Dec. 1781, 26:213-17; Frederick Freeman, *History of Cape Cod*, 2 vols. (Boston, 1858), 2:128, 401; Joseph Merrill, *History of Amesbury Including the First Seventeen Years of Salisbury, To the Separation in 1654; and Merrimac from Its Incorporation in 1876* (Haverhill, 1880), p. 290; *Records of the Town of Plymouth (1636-1783)*, 3 vols. (Plymouth, 1889-1903), 7, 11 Jan. 1782, 3:438-39. Additional action by the General Court is in *Acts and Laws*, 21 Oct. 1782, 2:319. Also see Arthur Lee to James Warren, 8 Apr. 1782, *Warren-Adams Letters*, 72:171; John Adams to Elbridge Gerry, 14 Dec. 1782; J. T. Austin, *The Life of Elbridge Gerry with Contemporary Letters*, 2 vols. (Boston, 1827-1829), 1:371; John Adams to James Warren, *Warren-Adams Letters*, 71:186; James Lovell to John Adams, 21 June 1781, Burnett, *Letters*, 6:125. Samuel Adams to John Adams, 2 Mar. 1782, Adams Papers, pt. 4, Adams Manuscript Trust, gives the activities in Boston.

the states.[28] In the years 1781, 1783, 1784, the Massachusetts delegation attempted to secure congressional assistance but Congress procrastinated and swept the problem under the legislative rug. This lack of interest intensified the debate between the commonwealth and the confederation and the activities of the Philadelphia speculators did little to increase the popularity of Robert Morris.[29]

Congress's failure to take any action on the bounty problem also raised criticism in the state. Towns throughout the state had raised their quotas for the Continental army by offering large bounties to recruits. These payments added to the financial difficulties of

28. E. James Ferguson, *The Power of the Purse: A History of American Public Finance, 1776-1790* (Chapel Hill, 1961), p. 51 gives the general background. Worthington C. Ford et al., eds., *Journals of the Continental Congress, 1774-1789*, 34 vols. (Washington, D.C., 1904-1937), 30:22, gives the total amount of the old emission currency at about $242 million. *American State Papers: Documents Legislative and Executive.* 38 vols. (Washington, 1832-1861), Finance 1:54, shows that Massachusetts paid in nearly $30 million of this old emission which equalled $747,500 in new emission bills. The commonwealth may have retired even more of the old emission since Ford, ed., *Journals of Congress*, 18 Jan. 1786, 30:22, states that she had retired $37 million worth of the old currency before 18 Sept. 1782. The efforts of Massachusetts to retire this currency raised its value at Boston and it flowed into the city from other states that were making little effort to retire it.

29. For examples of protests see *Boston Town Records*, 13 Mar. 1781, 26:177; *Massachusetts Spy* [Worcester], 10 May 1781; Oliver Phelps to Caleb Davis, 13 May 1781, Caleb Davis Papers, Massachusetts Historical Society; James Lovell to Samuel Holten, 8 Feb. 1781, in Burnett, ed. *Letters*, 5:500. For efforts to influence Congress see E. M. Bacon, ed., *Supplement to the Acts and Laws of the Commonwealth of Massachusetts* (Boston, 1896), 25 June 1781, p. 64; Samuel Osgood to John Lowell, 10 July 1781, in Burnett, *Letters*, 5:141. For action in Congress see *Acts and Laws*, 6 Mar. 1782, 1:889-90; 6 Oct. 1783, 2:744-45; 28 Oct. 1783, 2:793; and 8 Mar. 1785, 3:379-81.

Some discussions of the activities of Congress on this issue are in Connecticut Delegation to Jonathan Trumbull, 2 July 1781, in Burnett, ed. *Letters*, 6:142; Elias Boudinot to the Governor of New Jersey, 23 Oct. 1782, in ibid., 6:525; North Carolina Delegates to Alexander Martin, 25 Oct. 1782, in ibid., 6:525; James Madison to Edmund Randolph, 3 Dec. 1782, in ibid., 6:219-20; Samuel Osgood to James Lovell, 28 Aug. 1781, in ibid., 6:199-200; James Lovell to Samuel Adams, 15 Sept. 1781, in ibid. 7:219-20; Motion of Roger Sherman, 8 Apr. 1784, in ibid., 7:486-87; New Hampshire Delegates to the President of New Hampshire, 5 May 1784, in ibid., 7:514; Tristram Dalton to Elbridge Gerry, 13 Apr. 1784, Gerry Papers, Massachusetts Historical Society. For some newspaper reaction see *Independent Chronicle*, 17 May 1781, and "An American" in *Boston Gazette*, 21 Jan. 1782.

many towns during the 1780s. The towns naturally insisted that Congress should assume the cost. In the fall of 1783 the court collected information about the payment of the bounties and instructed the congressional delegation to press for payment—but as usual nothing was done.[30]

The Penobscot claims represented another sore point between the commonwealth and the confederation. Massachusetts had undertaken this ill-fated expedition in 1779 to clear the British from Maine. It resulted in complete disaster and merchants who had loaned ships and provisions agitated for compensation. The state hoped to shift the expense to the Continent and in 1783 the court instructed its delegates to have Congress assume these charges. The congressmen met a stone wall of resistance from the other states who feared that the assumption of such claims would open a Pandora's box of demands from other states. In 1785 a further attempt to reopen the question also failed.[31]

All these issues involved large and important interests in the commonwealth. The merchant who held worthless old emission Continental currency or claims on the Penobscot expedition, the fisherman who recalled Congress's lack of concern, the farmers who paid heavy taxes in the form of bounties, all had good reason to distrust the confederation. But these issues tended to unify the commonwealth—others would lead to serious political divisions within the state.

By early 1786 divisions within the commonwealth over national financial issues had become almost identical to the splits that had developed on state fiscal policies. Between 1781 and 1786 the most commercial-cosmopolitan interests and the least commercial-cosmopolitan interests practically reversed their positions on Con-

30. Jonathan Smith, "How Massachusetts Raised Her Troops in the Revolution," Massachusetts Historical Society, *Proceedings*, 55:345-79, is the best secondary acount. For other efforts see *Plymouth Town Records*, 19 June 1780, 3:396. Efforts of the state to collect information and secure congressional action are covered in *Acts and Laws*, 6 Oct. 1783, 2:744-45; and in Ford, ed., *Journals of Congress*, 12 Apr. 1785, 28:256-57.

31. The Penobscot issue may be followed in the *Boston Gazette*, 27 Dec. 1779, which contains a report of the committee investigating the disaster. The *Continental Journal*, 17 Aug. 1780, contains the complaints of the merchants who had loaned their ships to the state for the ill-fated expedition. *Acts and Laws*, 6 Oct. 1783, 2:744-45, gives the resolve of the court that requested congressional assistance. Ferguson, *Power of the Purse*, p. 205, estimates that $387,000 was eventually charged to the United States when accounts were finally settled in the 1790s.

tinental finances. The group B and C towns supported the 1781 impost but opposed commutation and the 1783 impost and by 1785 objected violently to the granting of supplemental funds to Congress that would be raised through direct taxes. At the same time the most commercial towns and groups shifted over from opposing the 1781 impost to supporting the voting of supplemental funds by 1786. Table 39 shows this shift over time. The first three votes concerned the passage of the 1781 impost; the next six involved commutation and the passing of the 1783 im-

TABLE 39
Voting of Representatives on National Questions, 1781-1786

Towns	Percentage Favoring Giving Power[a] to Confederation Government on 11 Votes										
	1	2	3	4	5	6	7	8	9	10	11
Group A	44%	39%	42%	46%	53%	41%	68%	76%	61%	39%	59%
Group B	81	74	70	20	24	12	53	52	56	17	29
Group C	67	62	55	11	11	8	50	34	40	22	18
Eastern group A	54	47	40	58	63	50	75	83	66	40	64
Western group A	27	25	50	29	31	17	54	57	53	40	55
Western group C	65	61	60	7	9	7	42	26	31	11	18
Total	58%	57%	55%	26%	28%	21%	56%	54%	52%	25%	34%

Towns	Percentage Voting with Commercial-Cosmopolitan Interests on 3 State Financial Votes		
	A	B	C
Group A	80%	58%	84%
Group B	47	42	32
Group C	33	15	29
Eastern group A	90	75	91
Western group A	67	19	69
Western group C	27	15	21
Total	54%	38%	49%

SOURCES: Vote One: "Whether the impost agreed to be raised shall continue until the debts already undertaken by Congress or that shall be undertaken for carrying on the present war with Great Britain be fully and finally paid. [P]rovided that if Leg. of Mass. can at any future time . . . agree upon any other method of supplying the Treasury of the U.S. for purposes aforesaid . . . to the satisfaction of Congress . . . then this act shall have no effect" (House Journal, 1 May 1782, pp. 715-16. Percentage of Yes vote).

Vote Two: Shall the impost pass to be enacted (Ibid., 1 May 1782, p. 716. Percentage of Yes vote).

Vote Three: That the secretary be directed to forward to Congress immediately an attested copy of the Impost Act (Ibid., 7 June 1782, pp. 67-68. Percentage of Yes vote).

Vote Four: The house considered the 1783 impost. Moved to insert the following: "And provided that no part of the money arising from the duties aforesaid shall be applied to the discharge of the half-pay for life or the commutation thereof." On motion to reconsider this motion after initial passage (Ibid., 8 July 1783, pp. 157-60. Percentage of Yes vote).

Vote Five: Senate amendment limited the impost to twenty-five years and made it effective when Congress notified Massachusetts that all other states had accepted it. Amendment to insert "for the purpose of discharging the interest and principal of the debts contracted on the faith of the United States for supporting the war." (This would have included the debt for commutation.) Question was to concur with the senate and with the amendment (Ibid., 9 July 1783, pp. 165-68. Percentage of Yes vote).

Vote Six: House resumed consideration of the report of the committee of both houses on recommendation of Congress to lay an impost. "The Question of Concurrence with the Proceedings of the Hon. Senate" (Ibid., 8 Oct. 1783, pp. 224-25. Percentage of Yes vote).

Vote Seven: House proceeded to second reading of the impost bill. Vote on the amendment making the impost "irrevocable" (Ibid., 16 Oct. 1783, pp. 252-54. Percentage of Yes vote).

Vote Eight: Motion to add the following provision: "The monies arising from the said impost should not be appropriated to the discharge of the half-pay or commutation thereof promised by Congress to the officers of the Army" (Ibid., 17 Oct. 1783, pp. 258-59. Percentage of No vote).

Vote Nine: Impost Bill. General question then put whether the said bill should pass (Ibid., 17 Oct. 1783, pp. 259-61. Percentage of Yes vote).

Vote Ten: House again considered the bill in addition to an act for the granting of imposts and duties on foreign goods, etc., imported to the United States. Question put on the clause to grant a sum of $224,427 to be levied annually on the polls and estates of the commonwealth to be paid into the treasury of Massachusetts on or before 1 July each year subject only to order of the United States in Congress appropriated only "towards discharging the principal and interest of the national debt contracted during the continuance of the late war" (Ibid., 10 March 1785, pp. 334-36. Percentage of Yes vote).

Vote Eleven: House again proceeded to consider the question whether the house will grant supplementary aids to Congress agreeably to their recommendation of April 1783. Motion made to refer the same to the next session of the General Court (Ibid., 16 March 1786, pp. 518-20. Percentage of No vote).

Vote A: To pass the Consolidation Act (Ibid., 24 Jan. 1781, pp. 246-47).

Vote B: To levy the cider tax (Ibid., 3 March 1784, pp. 433-34).

Vote C: To approve the use of the revenue from the state impost and excise for the payment of part of the national requisition (Ibid., 3 March 1786, pp. 466-68).

The percentage of Yes vote is given on vote A, the percentages of No votes on votes B and C.

a. Taxation and other powers.

post; the last two reflect the response to the voting of supplemental funds to the confederation. For comparative purposes, the vote on three state financial questions is given: (a) the passage of the act modifying legal tender and beginning the consolidation of the state debt in 1781; (b) the vote on passing the cider duty in early 1784; and (c) the vote in early 1786 to use the revenue from the state impost and excise to pay the Continental requisition. Thus by 1786 the towns had switched their positions of the earlier 1780s and the votes on national financial requests by 1786 corresponded rather closely to the reaction of the interest groups and towns to the commonwealth's taxation and debt programs.

In 1781 and 1782 the localistic group B and C towns backed the congressional impost, while the most commercial-cosmopolitan group A communities opposed it. In February 1781 Congress recommended that the state grant it a duty of 5 percent ad valorem on imports, the revenues from which would be used to pay the interest on the Continental debt. The General Court, in the midst of establishing a financial program for the commonwealth, postponed consideration of this impost in the summer of 1781 and requested Congress to change its recommendation to permit the sums collected by the duties to be deducted from the state's payment of requisitions to the confederation. Congress refused to accept this recommendation and the court failed to take any action during its fall session.[32]

During the winter and spring sessions the court, despite a political comedy of errors staged by Hancock, passed the request. In

32. There are some excellent secondary accounts of the relations of the Commonwealth and the Confederation on these financial questions. Jackson T. Main, *The Anti-Federalists: Critics of the Constitution, 1781-1788* (Chicago, 1964), pp. 55-65, 85-88, Robert A. East, "The Massachusetts Conservatives in the Critical Period," in Richard B. Morris, ed., *The Era of the American Revolution* (New York, 1939), pp. 349-91, esp. 349-71. Forrest McDonald, *The Formation of the American Republic, 1776-1790* (Baltimore, 1965), pp. 127-32, gives another view.

Ferguson, *Power of the Purse*, p. 116, gives the background. The response of the court is in *Acts and Laws*, 10 Mar. 1781, 1:373-75. Congressional action is in Ford, ed., *Journals of Congress*, 19 Apr. 1781, 19:420-26. For some opinions of leading politicians see James Lovell to Samuel Holten, 27 Mar. 1781, in Burnett, ed., *Letters*, 6:37; James Lovell to Elbridge Gerry, 27 Mar. 1781, ibid., 6:38; James Lovell to Samuel Holten, 8 May 1781, ibid., 6:83; Robert Morris to the Governor of Massachusetts (circular letter), 27 June 1781, ibid., 6:184. Notice the footnote in ibid., 6:372, for further details.

March the legislature waited till the end of its session to pass the impost and Hancock, claiming that he did not have time to examine the measure, killed it with a pocket veto. The governor assured the court that he favored the impost but he objected to minor provisions in the act and expressed his willingness to continue the legislative session to enable the legislators to either override his veto or draft a new bill. The court adjourned and the measure died, at least temporarily.[33] In May the court accepted an amendment requesting congressional approval for permission for the state to pay its quota by means other than the impost and passed the request by twelve votes. Despite the amendments, the group A towns cast 61 percent of their votes against the bill, while the group B and C communities gave 74 and 62 percent of theirs in favor of the impost and passed the request by a narrow margin of 7 percentage points. The vote of half the Boston delegation and over 90 percent of the delegates from the Essex County group A towns went against the impost and underlined the commercial opposition to the measure.[34] These commercial opponents believed that a Continental impost might hinder the development of commerce and would prevent the commonwealth from using a state impost to fund its own debt.[35] On the other side, the less commercial-cosmopolitan towns had less interest in the state debt and wanted to avoid meeting Continental requisitions with direct taxes.

Hancock again played a few political tricks in order to delay final passage. This time he stated that he intended to veto the impost but a committee of the court notified the governor that he had held the act for five days and that the measure had thus become law without his signature. Hancock fumed and stormed, charged that the irreligious committee had counted the Sabbath as a working day and argued that the bill had not become law. During the first session of the new 1782 General Court, a committee asked the governor if he had delivered official notification of pas-

33. Bacon, ed., *Supplement to Arts and Laws*, 8 Mar. 1782, pp. 96-97. Hancock had warned the court not to approve large quantities of legislation at the end of the session since this would not give him time to analyze it.

34. The votes are in House Journal, 1 May 1782, pp. 715-16 for the amendment and ibid., 1 May 1782, p. 716 for the passage.

35. Ivers to Hancock, 23 Sept. 1783, Massachusetts Archives, 188:469-70, in which the treasurer opposes the national impost because it would reduce the state's impost collections. The court passed a direct tax to meet a national requisition; see *Acts and Laws*, 5 Mar. 1782, 1:547-67.

sage to the Continental Congress. Hancock replied that he had not done this because the "bill you refer to has not been Constitutionally passed."[36] The court then voted on and accepted the report of another joint committee that the bill had been legally passed and hence was in effect. The vote on this resolution, despite the election of a new court, remained almost identical to the division on its original passage. Again the commercial towns cast 58 percent of their votes against the bill while the 70 percent and 55 percent of the votes from the group B and C towns favoring the impost passed it by a narrow margin. Table 40 shows the differences among the three groups of towns in their response to the consolidation of the state debt and to the Continental impost. It substantiates the importance of the support of the group B and C towns for the final passage of the congressional request.

The debate over and the voting on the 1783 impost proposal, linked with commutation, reflected a considerably changed political situation. Partly due to the vigorous anticommutation sentiment in the less commercial-cosmopolitan towns, whose represen-

TABLE 40
Vote on the 1781 Impost

Towns	Delegates Favoring Impost on 3 Votes			Vote 2 Comparison[a]
	1	*2*	*3*	
Group A	44%	39%	42%	−41%
Group B	81	74	70	+27
Group C	67	62	55	+29

SOURCES: The three votes on the impost (all showing the percentage of Yes votes) are from House Journal, 1 May 1782, pp. 715-16, and 7 June 1782, pp. 67-68. The vote on consolidation is from ibid., 24 Jan. 1781, pp. 246-47. The representatives of the future Federalist towns (those who would vote for ratification of the Constitution in 1788) cast 56 percent of their vote for the impost, and the representatives of future Antifederalist towns (those who would vote against ratification in 1788) gave 63 percent of their vote for the impost.

a. Percentages reflect difference between vote two and vote of 24 January 1781 on consolidation.

36. Hancock's message is in Bacon, ed., *Supplement to Acts and Laws*, 10 May 1782, p. 99. For additional information see Samuel Adams to John Lowell, 15 May 1782, in Cushing, *Samuel Adams*, 4:272-74; James Sullivan to Benjamin Lincoln, in Amory, *Sullivan*, 1:387; and Samuel Adams to John Lowell, 4 June 1782, in Cushing, *Samuel Adams*, 4:274-75. For the response of the court see Bacon, ed., *Supplement to Acts and Laws*, 3, 4, 5 June 1782, p. 138.

tatives refused to accept an impost part of which would be used to pay former Continental officers, the position of the towns on this national question indicated an almost complete reversal of their 1781 positions. The commutation question grew out of the difficulties in paying the Continental officers during the Revolution. In the fall of 1780 Congress, by a vote of nine states to three, approved half pay for life for those officers who would continue to serve till the end of the war. The commonwealth opposed the plan and all three Massachusetts delegates present voted against it.[37] The issue then slept for several years and Congress took no action to meet the officers' claims for half pay. In the fall of 1782 the Massachusetts officers, led by General William Heath, protested to the General Court against the lack of attention to their claims and asked the General Court to either pay or commute their pensions. The court procrastinated and Samuel Osgood, a Massachusetts delegate, ascertained that Congress opposed unilateral action by a single state in paying off her officers.[38]

Congress, after complex machinations involving the officers, Robert Morris, and national securities holders, took the matter up in February and March 1783. A grand committee of representatives from all the states reported a proposition to Congress to commute the Continental officers a fixed sum in lieu of their half pay. The Massachusetts delegation tried to water down the proposition but succeeded only in reducing commutation from five and one-half years to five years of full pay.[39] In March and April 1783

37. The early history of commutation is outlined in Ford, ed., *Journals of Congress*, 20 Oct. 1780, 18:956; 21 Oct. 1780, pp. 597, 959-61. The General Court voted half pay to widows and orphans of Continental officers killed in action; see *Acts and Laws*, 5 July 1781, 1:686. The court also attempted to pay the officers their current salaries and tried to make up for depreciation. For examples see ibid., 1 Feb. 1782, 1:831; 11 Feb. 1782, 1:544-45. For some newspaper reaction see "A Friend to Justice," *Independent Chronicle*, 14 Mar. 1782.

38. Merrill Jensen, *The New Nation: A History of the United States During the Confederation, 1781-1789* (New York, 1950), p. 35. Richard H. Kohn, "The Inside History of the Newburgh Conspiracy: America and the Coup d' Etat," *William and Mary Quarterly*, 3d ser., 27:187-220. This gives considerable amount of background about the army and the speculators. See also Samuel Osgood to Henry Knox, 4 Dec. 1782, in Burnett, ed., *Letters*, 6:553. The response of the court is in *Acts and Laws*, 28 Oct. 1782, 2:317. See John Lowell to Benjamin Lincoln, 28 Nov. 1782, Massachusetts Historical Society, *Proceedings*, 1st ser., 24:127-28.

39. Kohn, "America and the Coup," pp. 206-12; Ford, ed., *Journals of Congress*, 25 Feb. 1783, 24:145-48; 26 Feb. 1783, 24:149-50; 10 Mar. 1783, 24:178-79; 22 Mar. 1783, 24:207-10.

Congress interjected the impost issue into the discussion since the 1781 request had been defeated by the lack of state action. In April 1783 Congress requested the states to provide it with a fixed revenue through an impost and the voting of supplemental funds raised by direct taxes. In order to secure the support of the officers Congress decided that the funds collected would be used to pay all claims against the Continent including the commutation of half pay.[40] Thus the debate over the 1783 impost involved an interrelated dispute over three separate provisions: the impost proper, the supplemental funds, and the commutation of half pay.

The general anticommutation sentiment in Massachusetts almost scuttled the entire request. During the summer 1783 session the house of representatives amended a senate resolution accepting the proposal to prevent revenue from the proposed taxes from being used to pay commutation, and later the house rejected a senate amendment permitting the payment of commutation with impost funds. In the two roll calls on these measures the representatives of the group C towns cast 89 percent of their votes against any payment of commutation while the group A towns cast 54 percent and 47 percent of their votes against it, although the eastern group A towns cast 58 percent and 63 percent of their votes in favor of the payments to officers. Thus by July 1783 it had become evident that the less commercial-cosmopolitan towns overwhelmingly opposed any commutation and that despite the support of the eastern group A towns, the lukewarm attitude of the other group A towns made passage impossible.[41] With the impost blocked because of commutation the court protested to Congress that commutation should be separated from the impost proposal.[42]

40. Ford, ed., *Journals of Congress*, 18 Mar. 1783, 24:191-92; 17 Apr. 1783, 24:254-55; 18 Apr. 1783, 24:261.

41. For the rhetoric see *Independent Chronicle*, 5 June 1783, and *Salem Gazette*, 26 June, 3, 10, 17, 24, 31 July 1786. For the voting see the House Journal, 8 July 1783, pp. 157-60, and 9 July 1783, pp. 165-68. Freeman, *Cape Cod*, 2:130, for Sandwich's town meeting vote of 13 Jan. 1783 versus half pay. Hiram A. Tracy and William A. Benedict, *History of the Town of Sutton, Massachusetts; From 1704 to 1876* (Worcester, 1878), p. 120, where Sutton opposed it on 20 Jan. 1783. Hurd, ed., *Norfolk*, p. 927, gives Canton's opposition on 16 May 1783. A good general discussion is in Tristram Dalton to John Adams, 16 July 1783, Adams Papers, pt. 4.

42. Bacon, ed., *Supplement to Acts and Laws*, 11 July 1783, pp. 179-81. Samuel Adams was excused from further service on 25 Oct. 1783 because of ill health. See Richard Cranch to John Adams, 18 July 1783, Adams Papers, pt. 4, for details.

Congress refused to take this advice. It defeated a motion permitting Rhode Island and Massachusetts from settling with their own officers and the commonwealth's delegates then threw in the sponge and informed the court that the state should accept commutation as a less expensive means of paying off a valid debt. In another letter to the court the delegation suggested using the commutation and impost as leverage on Congress for settlement of the Penobscot and old emission currency claims but Nathaniel Appleton, a committee member and supporter of the impost-commutation package, apparently pocketed this letter which did not reach the court until after the passage of the impost during the fall 1783 session.[43]

In addition to the infamous missing letter, several other pressures helped account for the retreat of the court from its anti-impost and commutation position. Newspaper writers vigorously supported the package; Samuel Adams and many other leading politicians who dreaded the military and detested commutation accepted it as the only way of passing the impost; and Robert Morris carefully edited one of John Adam's letters to prove that the author of the 1780 constitution also approved the package plan. The growing realization that Congress would not withdraw commutation and that acceptance of commutation was the only way to secure the impost also swayed some legislators.[44]

During the fall 1783 session the General Court led by the representatives of the group A and B towns did just that and passed the

43. Ford, ed., *Journals of Congress*, 17 Sept. 1783, 25:577-79; 18 Sept. 1783, 25:581-82; 25 Sept. 1783, 25:607-13. Massachusetts delegates to the Committee of the General Court, 1 Oct. 1783, in Burnett, ed., *Letters*, 7:316-17. The infamous missing letter was Massachusetts Delegates to the Committee of the General Court, 11 Sept. 1783, in ibid. 7:294-97. For more discussion about this affair see *Independent Chronicle*, 22 Apr. 1784; Samuel Adams to Elbridge Gerry, 25 Feb. 1784 in Cushing, *Samuel Adams*, 4:292-93; Tristram Dalton to Elbridge Gerry, 4 Feb. 1784 and 11 Feb. 1784, in Gerry Papers. Austin, *Gerry*, pp. 412-16 gives a good secondary account.

44. Samuel Holten to John Kittel, 9 Oct. 1783, in Burnett, ed., *Letters*, 7:324; Stephen Higginson to Theodrick Bland, 6 Oct. 1783, ibid., 7:320-23; Stephen Higginson to Samuel Holten, ibid., 7:325; Robert Morris to the Governor of Massachusetts, 20 Sept. 1783, and Robert Morris to John Adams, 20 Sept. 1783, Adams Papers, pt. 4. Morris extracted sections from Adams's letter that supported the impost. Hancock used this letter in his address to the court on 9 Oct. 1783; see, Bacon, ed., *Supplement to Acts and Laws*, p. 208. Stephen Higginson to Samuel Holten, 14 Oct. 1783, in Burnett, ed., *Letters*, 7:334-35, gives the lineup in the General Court. Tristram Dalton to John Adams, 16 July 1783, Adams Papers, pt. 4, also gives some interesting information.

impost with commutation. At first, on 8 October, in a vote very similar to those in the summer session, the house declined to accept the report of a joint committee which had recommended the approval of both the impost and commutation.[45] But thanks to a variety of pressures the house a week and a half later decided to accept both commutation and the impost. On the three roll call votes that involved the passage of this package, the representatives of the group B, or the smaller commercial towns, gave 52 to 56 percent of their votes for passage and joined by the 61 to 76 percent of the delegates from the group A towns overrode the resistance of 50 to 66 percent of the members from the group C towns who voted against passage. The shift in voting between 8 and 17 October underlined the crucial role of the switch in the voting patterns of the group B and C communities and also indicated the importance of the votes of the justices representing these less commercial-cosmopolitan communities in the final passage of the impost-commutation package. Table 41 shows the changes in voting patterns between 8 and 17 October, the importance of the justices for the final passage of the measure on 17 October, and the differences between the voting patterns on the impost-com-

TABLE 41
The 1783 Impost-Commutation Proposal

Towns	Change in Vote, 8-17 Oct.	Votes for Proposal, 17 Oct., by		Difference in Vote from Cider Tax, 1784
		Justices	Others	
Group A	+20%	59%	63%	+ 3%
Group B	+44	78	41	+14
Group C	+32	58	34	+25
Total	+31%	65%	43%	+14%

SOURCES: House Journal, 8 Oct. 1783, pp. 224-25, and 17 Oct. 1783, pp. 259-61. Justices may be identified with the title Esquire in the House Journal. The cider tax is in House Journal, 3 March 1784, pp. 433-34.

45. The vote is in the House Journal, 8 Oct. 1783, pp. 224-25. There is a discussion about the changes during the fall session in Tristam Dalton to John Adams, 5 Dec. 1783, Adams Papers, pt. 4. Dalton claimed forty representatives had been instructed not to vote money for commutation. Cotton Tufts to John Adams, 5 Nov. 1783, Adams Papers, pt. 4, argued the impost, without commutation, could have been easily approved in May. See also Richard Cranch to John Adams, 1 Oct. 1783, in ibid.

mutation package and the support for the cider tax in March of 1784. The group C towns that had voted heavily for the 1781 impost opposed the 1783 package. The voters of the group A communities also reversed their position and favored the later impost. The group B towns finally supported both the 1781 and 1783 proposals. Compared with their votes against the cider tax in early 1784, the support all groups of communities gave to the impost was much more along the lines of their positions on state fiscal questions. Thus the 1783 impost and commutation struggle marked a midpoint in the overall shift between 1781 and 1786 with the group A and C towns starting to find themselves on opposite sides of both state and national financial questions.

The anticommutation forces, smarting over their defeat, found a new enemy in the Society of the Cincinnati. Several leading politicians, including Samuel Osgood, Samuel Adams, and Stephen Higginson, raised the alarm about a "race of hereditary patricians" and the General Court condemned the society (composed of former Revolutionary officers) as an antirepublican, aristocratic body. Farming towns used the anti-Cincinnati agitation to mobilize support for repeal of the impost-commutation measure. A convention of Suffolk towns, meeting in April 1784, claimed that commutation had never been approved by the people and similar conventions in Worcester, Middlesex, and Hampshire counties echoed these criticisms. This outburst led the society to change many of its original rules including the one by which membership passed only to the oldest male descendant.[46] These changes apparently spiked the anti-Cincinnati criticism and in its summer 1784 session the court took no action except to instruct its delegates to vote

46. Anti-Cincinnati and anticommutation agitation and rhetoric may be found in *Independent Chronicle*, 29 Jan., 5 Feb., 18, 25 Mar., 16 Apr. 1784; *Massachusetts Spy* [Worcester], 25 Mar. 1784; *Massachusetts Gazette* [Springfield], 6 Apr. 1784. For the views of some important politicians see Samuel Osgood to John Adams, 14 Jan. 1784, in Burnett, ed., *Letters*, 7:416; Elbridge Gerry to Sam Adams, 7 May 1784, ibid., 7:516; Gerry to Stephen Higginson, 13 May 1784, ibid., 7:522; Gerry to Samuel Adams, 5 Sept. 1785, ibid., 8:211; Stephen Higginson to Arthur Lee, 27 Jan. 1784, Massachusetts Historical Society, *Proceedings*, 2d ser., 8:178-81; Samuel Adams to Elbridge Gerry, 23 Apr. 1784, in Cushing, *Samuel Adams*, 4:298-300; *Boston Town Records*, 15 Mar. 1784, 31:12. Henry Knox to Samuel L. Parsons, 29 Mar. 1785, Knox Papers, Massachusetts Historical Society, explains the changes made by the Cincinnati the previous year. For a secondary account see Austin, *Gerry*, 1:416-24.

against any peacetime military establishment.[47] After this, the excitement generated by the impost, commutation, and the Cincinnati subsided and politicians settled back to watch other states struggle over the impost.

A third proposal in the congressional request of 1783 created another serious political struggle within the commonwealth. The granting of supplemental funds allowed Congress, upon the approval of the state legislature, to supplement its revenue by levying a direct tax upon polls and estates limited by quotas assigned to the individual states. This proposition again raised the serious political problem of levying direct taxes for the Continental government, a sore point with the less commercial-cosmopolitan towns since the earlier 1780s because the court had already levied heavy direct taxes to pay congressional requisitions. In 1780 and 1781 it had levied two beef taxes payable in meat or money, a clothing tax in June 1781, and two additional taxes payable in specie, certain securities, or new emission money totalling £400,000 by early 1784.[48] These taxes increased the already heavy burden of direct taxes and the less commercial-cosmopolitan towns that had supported the 1781 impost objected violently to any increase in their tax bills from giving Congress additional powers of revenue.

At first none of the groups of towns favored giving such supplemental funds to Congress. During February and March 1785 the court began its considerations of the congressional request and a joint committee reported a bill granting Congress a revenue of $224,000 a year raised by a direct tax on polls and estates. All groups of towns united against this scheme. Even the most commercial-cosmopolitan group A towns cast 61 percent of their votes against it and the group B and C towns overwhelmingly opposed it

47. Samuel Adams to Elbridge Gerry, 19 Apr. 1784, in Cushing, *Samuel Adams*, 4:298-300. See *Acts and Laws*, 9 July 1784, 3:258, for the legislation.

48. Taxes levied to meet Continental requisitions are in *Acts and Laws*, 5 Mar. 1782, 1:547-67; 22 Mar. 1783, 2:153-74; 23 Mar. 1786, 3:580-602. These three taxes amounted to £545,655 or about $1.8 million and do not include the beef and clothing taxes of 1780 and 1781. The first two acts in 1782 and 1783 levied a tax of 10 shillings and 8 pence on each poll. The Continental share of the 1786 tax came to around 12 shillings, 5 pence per poll. Two-thirds of the 1786 Continental taxes could be paid in Continental loan office certificates paid as interest to holders of the Continental debt. The remainder had to be paid in specie.

with 83 percent and 78 percent of their votes.[49] After this defeat the court swept the issue under the carpet until early 1786.

By 1786 a significant political shift had occurred as the group A towns became the chief proponents of granting supplemental funds to Congress. Governor Bowdoin urged the court to complete the financial program outlined by Congress in 1783 and argued that the confederation might collapse unless Congress could secure revenues with which to fund the national debt. Despite Bowdoin's pleas the court voted to postpone consideration of the supplemental funds until the next session of the General Court. The group A towns did cast 59 percent of their votes against the delay but the group B and C communities supported the postponement with 71 percent and 82 percent of theirs.[50]

This vote underlined the significant shift that had taken place in the responses of the three groups of towns to national fiscal questions between 1781 and 1786. During this period the group A towns' proportion of support for Continental fiscal policies had increased by 20 percentage points, while the support by the group B and C towns had declined by 37 points. Relating the votes of the various groups of towns on state financial issues with their votes on these national questions demonstrates a similar shift. In 1781 the group A communities gave 41 percentage points less support to the impost than to the consolidation, but by 1786 this had declined to a 25-point differential. Table 42 shows these various shifts between 1781 and 1786. Thus by early 1786 the shifts among the voting patterns of the groups of towns on these national issues resulted in a much closer correlation with their voting patterns on state fiscal issues. This new relationship would have a tremendous impact upon the responses of the three groups of towns to the new national Constitution during 1787 and 1788.

Abstract conceptions of nationalism or other ideological factors did not cause this shift. Instead it reflected the reaction of the various groups of towns and interests to taxation policies. In 1781

49. *Boston Magazine*, Mar. 1785, p. 115; Samuel Osgood to Elbridge Gerry, 18 Feb. 1785, Gerry Papers. Opposition is found in the *American Herald*, 28 Feb. 1785; *Massachusetts Spy* [*Worcester*], 10, 24, 31 Mar. 1785; *Massachusetts Centinel*, 2 Apr. 1785. The vote is from House Journal, 10 Mar. 1785, pp. 334-36.

50. Bowdoin's message of 25 Feb. 1786 is in *Acts and Laws*, vol. 3. The vote is in House Journal, 16 Mar. 1786, pp. 518-20.

TABLE 42
Voting on National and State Fiscal Issues

Towns	1781 Impost and 1786 Supplemental Funds Vote Change.	1781 Impost Difference in Vote from Consolidation	1786 Supplemental Funds Difference in Vote from 1786 Motion on General Expenses[a]	Change
Group A	+20%	−41%	−25%	+16%
Group B	−45	+27	− 3	−30
Group C	−44	+29	−11	−40
Total	−13%	+ 3%	−15%	−18%

SOURCES: The 1786 vote is in House Journal, 16 Mar. 1786, pp. 518-20; the 1781 impost vote is in ibid., 1 May 1782, p. 716. The vote to use the excise revenue for national and general state expenses is in ibid., 3 March 1786, pp. 466-68.
a. The 1786 motion to use excise and impost for general expenses.
NOTE: The following table shows the shift in voting patterns of the future Federalist and Antifederalist towns during the 1781-1786 period:

	Percentage Favoring			
Towns	1781 Impost	1783 Impost	1786 Supplemental Funds	Difference, 1781-86
Federalist	56%	65%	57%	+ 1%
Antifederalist	63	35	14	−49
Difference between Federalist and Antifederalist	+13	−30	−43	

the commercial-cosmopolitan groups feared an impost while by 1786 the less commercial-cosmopolitan towns had experienced almost six years of heavy direct taxes and they had no intention of adding additional, annually levied, perhaps perpetual, new direct taxes when plagued with executions for overdue state and confederation assessments. These less commercial-cosmopolitan towns proclaimed their willingness to pay congressional requisitions, but they wanted them paid with revenues from the state's impost and excise—a solution that the most commercial-cosmopolitan towns found completely unacceptable.[51] This struggle over and fear of national direct taxes would continue into 1786, would be a major irritant to the westerners before the outbreak of the Regulation, and would lead many of the less commercial-cosmopolitan towns to fear the powers of direct taxation granted to the new national government by the Philadelphia Convention. By 1786 the com-

51. See the vote in House Journal, 3 Mar. 1786, pp. 466-68.

monwealth had begun to split over national questions. Unfortunately the lines of this division complemented those that had existed throughout the earlier 1780s on all sorts of state taxation, credit, and fiscal issues.

As internal divisions over national financial policy widened, the commonwealth's leading politicians gave little support to nationalistic solutions to the problems of the confederation before 1786. Many leaders proposed strengthening the Articles of the Confederation in certain rigidly limited areas, but even these men refused to accept a nationalistic solution which would discard the Articles or give a great deal of power and authority to executive officers under Congress. Indeed they and the most commercial-cosmopolitan interests had little reason to champion such solutions: the state financial program gave them enough revenue to service the state's debt; social and legal reforms posed no threat to any vested interests; the workings of the preparty political system continued to favor the group A towns and the interests controlling those communities; and it seemed that the other states might grant Congress the limited financial and commercial powers that would enable it to take care of the commonwealth's far-flung commercial and financial interests.

Many important Massachusetts politicians played leading roles in the anti-Morris campaign in 1782 and 1783. Even in 1781 many leading politicians suspected Morris, whom they called the Financier, and that spring the Massachusetts delegation in Congress opposed measures that would have increased his power and influence. By the summer and fall other politicians also became suspicious; they feared a sellout to France on the fisheries question or worried that the capable secretary would use his position and inside information to build a Philadelphia interest which could control Congress. But despite these suspicions many other important figures supported at least some of Morris's programs. In March 1782 the General Court chartered his Bank of North America and in 1783 and 1784 important Boston merchants sought his advice when they formed their own Boston bank.[52] But by 1783

52. For an excellent secondary account of the changes in the response of important politicians to the national government, see East, "Massachusetts Conservatives," pp. 367-74. For some early reactions to Morris see Elbridge Gerry to Robert Morris, 2 Sept. 1780, in Burnett, ed., *Letters*, 5:365; James Lovell to Samuel Holten, 5 Sept. 1780, ibid., 5:362; Wells, *Samuel Adams*, 3:128-30; Samuel Adams to Thomas McKean, 9 Aug. 1781, in ibid., 4:260-62; *Acts and Laws*, 8 Mar. 1782, 1:579-81; N. S. B. Gras, *Massachusetts First National Bank of Boston*, (Boston, 1937), p. 131.

many Massachusetts politicos had joined the anti-Morris forces in Congress. Samuel Adams condemned his evil influence, his French connections, his use of the Bank of North America, his connections with Philadelphia speculators, and his method of granting contracts. At a more popular level Congress's refusal to give the commonwealth any relief on the Penobscot claims and the old currency issue made others very suspicious of Morris, Congress, and Philadelphia. In the fall of 1782 Samuel Osgood, a leading Massachusetts politician, joined forces with Arthur Lee, one of Morris's leading opponents, on a congressional committee investigating the activities of the Financier that charged Morris with speculating in congressional funds and claimed that his clerk, Swanwick, had misappropriated Continental monies; Lee concluded that Morris's powers rendered him "a dangerous man to the liberties of his country." [53]

During 1783 the anti-Morris crusade picked up additional support in the commonwealth. In early 1783 hoping to force a showdown Morris submitted his resignation to Congress. The General Court noted this power play and in June 1783 complained to Congress that Morris had permitted the Massachusetts Continental troops to return home without being paid. The Court also objected to the Financier's efforts to pay the discharged soldiers with Morris Notes and suggested that the commonwealth itself pay them with the tax monies collected for the Continental requisitions. [54] The Massachusetts delegation added pressure and backed moves to make Morris account for certain funds and supported motions to pare down his administrative powers. By August, Stephen Higginson, later to become a fervent nationalist, expressed the hope that Morris's enemies might "catch him on the hop and perhaps get rid of him." [55]

During 1783 and 1784 the court and the congressional delegation both worked hard to catch Morris "on the hop." The court

53. Arthur Lee to Samuel Adams, 21 Apr. 1782, in Burnett, ed., *Letters*, 6:331-32; Lee to Francis Dana, ibid., 6:579; Lowell to Samuel Adams, 8 July 1782, ibid., 6:379-80; Lee to James Warren, July 1782, ibid., 6:174.

54. Arthur Lee to Samuel Adams, 5 Mar. 1783, ibid., 7:177-78. Ford, ed., *Journals of Congress*, 5 Sept. 1783, 24:536-37, gives an example of an anti-Morris motion. See also *Boston Evening Post*, 22 Mar. 1783, Bacon, ed., *Supplement to Acts and Laws*, 26 June 1783, pp. 177-78; Arthur Lee to Samuel Holten, 10 Sept. 1783, in Burnett, ed., *Letters*, 6:544-45.

55. Stephen Higginson to Nathaniel Gorham, 5 Aug. 1783, in Burnett, ed., *Letters*, 7:253. For an excellent account of the movement against Morris see Ferguson, *Power of the Purse*, pp. 146-76.

instructed its delegates that Morris's accounts were unsatisfactory, complained of his lack of attention to the Penobscot and old emission claims and told the congressmen to use their "unremitting endeavours to have the office of the Superintendent of Finance abolished," since a single man had far too much power when he controlled the finances of the entire nation. In addition to these injuries, the court insulted the Financier by submitting a detailed examination and criticism of his accounts which included a critique of his estimate of the national debt and the contingency fund which it believed to be much too large.[56] Even when Morris retired, the Massachusetts politicians continued their efforts to destroy his junto. Appleton, one of Morris's few Massachusetts supporters, passed under a cloud because of the misplaced letter affair and other leading politicians supported the formation of a board of treasury which would prevent financial powers from being concentrated in the hands of one man. After some intricate political maneuvering Congress finally replaced the office of secretary with a three-member board on which Arthur Lee, Sam Adams's close friend and associate, and Walter Livingston of New York served together with Samuel Osgood. At last the Massachusetts politicians rejoiced with Francis Dana that they had been "*in on the death* of our political monster."[57]

Although they defeated Morris many Massachusetts politicians and interests did favor the extension of some limited powers to the confederation. The commercial towns shifted over to favor the impost by 1783 and even backed the voting of supplemental funds by early 1786, while a wider group of interests and towns supported the extension of some national controls over commerce. In July 1784 the court without a roll call vote adopted the congres-

56. *Acts and Laws*, 28 Oct. 1783, 2:793. On 18 Oct. 1783, the court appointed a joint committee of five members to examine the accounts that Morris had submitted to the states. With Noah Goodman, Benjamin Goodhue, Thomas Russell, and William Phillips among its members, it submitted an extremely critical report which was incorporated in the above resolve. See the information in the Public Papers, Office of the Secretary, Boston, for the resolve of 28 Oct. 1783. For the complete text see *Acts and Laws*, 28 Oct. 1783, 2:796-98.

57. Details are in Samuel Osgood to Elbridge Gerry, 31 Jan. 1784, Gerry Manuscripts; Stephen Higginson to Arthur Lee, 27 Jan. 1784, Massachusetts Historical Society, *Proceedings*, 2d ser., 8:179-80; Tristram Dalton to Elbridge Gerry, 11 Feb. 1784, Gerry Manuscripts; Dana to John Adams, 12 Dec. 1784, Dana Letterbook, Dana Papers, Massachusetts Historical Society.

sional recommendations of April 1784 that it be granted powers for fifteen years to make certain commercial and navigation laws.[58] At the same time, it also began to use state legislation to keep out foreign shipping and passed harsh legislation against British vessels trading with the commonwealth. In 1785 Bowdoin went even further and suggested that a convention of states be held to consider the commercial problem and the granting of additional powers to Congress. After a brief discussion in the press the court accepted the governor's suggestion, decided that the Articles of the Confederation were "not fully adequate to the great purpose they were originally designed to affect," and also proposed a convention to meet to discuss the commercial situation. The court sent these proposals to their delegates and instructed them to submit a petition to Congress.[59] But many politicians believed Bowdoin and the court had gone too far and the delegates dragged their feet. Samuel Holten, Rufus King, and Elbridge Gerry favored additional congressional powers over commerce, but they feared that a convention might attempt to replace the Articles with a more national or centralized government. For them a convention "would produce throughout the union, an exertion of the friends of Aristocracy" to destroy the decentralized and republican nature of the Articles.[60] Samuel Adams, back in Massachusetts, agreed with the delegates and feared that a convention might replace the Articles with a "Constitution unfavorable to liberty." Adams, like almost everyone in the state, wanted to give Congress additional powers over commerce "without endangering the principles of the confederation by a general revision." A few politicians, such as Nathan Dane, feared that many merchants wanted national commercial powers so much that they might support important amendments to the Articles. The General Court, in reaction to this response, withdrew its support of a convention and instructed the delegates to postpone the presentation of the petition to Congress but it still hoped that Congress would secure additional commer-

58. *Acts and Laws*, 1 July 1784, 3:41.
59. Bowdoin's address of 31 May 1785 is in ibid., 3:709-10. See some of the newspaper criticism in the *Independent Chronicle*, 16, 23 June, 20 Oct. 1785. The response of the court is in *Acts and Laws*, 1 July 1785, 3:666-68.
60. Massachusetts delegates to Bowdoin, 3 Sept. 1785, in King, *Rufus King*, 1:61-64. Rufus King to Nathan Dane, 17 Sept. 1785, in Burnett, ed., *Letters*, 8:218.

cial powers and that other states would coordinate their commercial regulations with those of the commonwealth.[61]

In early 1786 the proponents of a convention secured the appointment of delegates by the General Court, but these men never arrived at Annapolis. In early 1786 Governor Bowdoin submitted a letter to the court from Governor Patrick Henry of Virginia in which Henry announced a proposed convention scheduled for September 1786 at Annapolis. The court responded by selecting four merchant-politicians as delegates, but these men eventually resigned as did those whom the court appointed to replace them and the final appointees left Massachusetts too late to arrive at Annapolis on time. Obviously even in 1786 the most commercial-cosmopolitan interests had still not swung over to a national solution.[62]

Actually the confederation did not seem too bad a deal for the commonwealth. Programs had been passed to service the state debt, regulate commerce and navigation, protect infant industries, and aid the fisheries; the most commercial-cosmopolitan interests apparently had the political situation under control; it seemed that the other states would adopt the congressional financial and commercial programs of 1783 and 1784; and if this occurred, it worked to the benefit of the commonwealth's speculators and commercial men. Naturally some friction had developed. Congress had not acted on all of the commonwealth's requests and bitter internal disputes had split the state over the imposts, commutation, and supplemental funds. Yet overall, most of the interests, politicians, and common citizens of Massachusetts would have agreed with Rufus King's analysis of the situation in December 1785—there was, after all, "no cause of despair."[63]

61. Propaganda for increased powers for the confederation is found in *Boston Magazine*, Dec. 1785, pp. 474-75; *Massachusetts Centinel*, 3 Aug. 1785; *Independent Chronicle*, 1 Sept. 1785. For politicians see Samuel Adams, to Elbridge Gerry, 19 Sept. 1785, in Bancroft, *Constitution*, 1:457; Gerry to Samuel Adams, 30 Sept. 1785, in Burnett, ed., *Letters*, 8:224; Nathan Dane to Rufus King, 6 Oct. 1785, in King, *Rufus King*, 1:67-70; *Acts and Laws*, 25 Nov. 1785, 3:789, and the Public Papers for the act. Also see *Acts and Laws*, 8 Dec. 1785, 3:817-19; Rufus King to Caleb Davis, 3 Nov. 1785, Caleb Davis Papers.

62. Bowdoin's message of 27 Mar. 1786 is in *Acts and Laws*, 3:915. The appointments are in ibid., 24 Mar. 1786, 3:947-48. Chapter 8 discusses the failure of this group to attend the convention.

63. Rufus King to John Adams, 4 Dec. 1785, in King, *Rufus King*, 1:116.

6

The Frustration of the Less Commercial-Cosmopolitan Interests

PRE-PARTY politics had brought frustration and despair to the less commercial-cosmopolitan interests and communities. The commonwealth had expelled the British, had established her own constitution, and had based her new government on the principles of republicanism and morality. The Hutchinson-Oliver clique had departed. Governor, lieutenant governor, senators, councillors, and representatives to the lower house were popularly elected. Yet despite all these changes and reforms the hopes and needs of the more local and less commercial interests and towns continued to be ignored. The most commercial-cosmopolitan interests, although poorly organized in comparison with modern political parties or pressure groups, had refunded and consolidated the state debt at an extremely high value, killed legal tender, continued the levying of heavy direct taxes, smothered most efforts to reform the credit system or tax structure, and in early 1786 succeeded in using direct taxes to pay the interest on the state debt and to meet the Continental requisition. The less commercial-cosmopolitan towns had unsuccessfully opposed every one of these programs and the senate strangled any reform measures that might sneak through the lower house. Thus to many residents of the less commercial-cosmopolitan communities it seemed that the new commonwealth was even less responsive to their demands than the colonial government had been. Yet these towns and interests continued their attempts to influence the political system. The towns sent instructions to their representatives and petitioned the General Court. County and local conventions, composed of town delegates, met to formulate policies and increase the pressure on the court, but since the court ignored these protests, many citizens turned to violence to prevent the seizure of property for debts and taxes.

The frustration of the more locally oriented communities grew when they saw other groups successful in their protests. The court acknowledged protests about high taxes by relieving the tax burdens of eastern fishing centers, Maine shipbuilding centers, and eastern and western commercial centers, but it did little to aid the subsistence farming communities in the east and west. The Boston artisans used their control of the town meeting to defeat efforts by the merchants and professionals to replace the meeting with a better organized mayor-council form of government, but they had little interest in the problems of their country cousins. Nantucket, by threatening secession, blackmailed the court into granting a bounty on whale oil, and in Maine many district towns met to mobilize sentiment for a new state which the court attempted to halt by incorporating new communities, increasing the district's representation in the house of representatives and by establishing new counties in the frontier areas. But the court continued to ignore the petitions from towns and conventions that advocated basic changes and reacted only when violence broke out in Hampshire County in 1782.

By 1785 and 1786 political polarization and commercial recession had brought the frustration and fears of the less commercial-cosmopolitan interests to a head. In the court the less commercial-cosmopolitan towns now opposed the most commercial-cosmopolitan communities on a broad political front that ranged from the payment of supplemental funds to the confederation government to the use of the state impost and excise for general expenses. While the conflicting interests snarled at each other in the court, a commercial recession, beginning in 1784, made it even more difficult for the less commercial farmers to pay their debts or meet their taxes. The courts filled with suits and towns fell further and further behind in their payments to the state treasury. By 1786 only a series of compromises by the most commercial-cosmopolitan interests could have prevented an explosion. But, instead of modifying the fiscal program, these interests used the summer 1786 session of the court to defeat reforms and pushed through the grant of supplemental funds to the confederation government.

How could the westerners respond? Their representatives in the court could not outvote the delegates of the commercial towns and their placeholding allies. The senate had become virtually a club composed of leading politicians and judges. The court ignored their petitions. Their county conventions were ineffectual. A shadowy conspiracy appeared to be enveloping them and they feared that the future would bring even harsher policies that would swallow up their property and their freedom. Many westerners, remembering the court's reaction to the Ely rebellion in 1782, opted for Regulation. Since the political system offered no relief of their burdens of debts and taxes, they would "regulate" the courts in the western counties and prevent the judges from taking action against farmers who owed private debts and back taxes. They had no intention of destroying the social or political structure of the commonwealth. They merely desired certain reforms and, if the court could not be prevailed upon to give them justice, they would achieve it through Regulation and violence. Between 1781 and 1786 these communities repeatedly tried to influence the court. They petitioned, they held conventions, they instructed their representatives, and a few individuals even attacked constables and tax collectors, but by early 1786 it seemed that all these efforts had failed and the less commercial-cosmopolitan towns and interests seethed with political frustration.

The less commercial-cosmopolitan towns of the west and Bristol County sent representatives to the General Court who voted against the programs of the most commercial-cosmopolitan interests. Despite these efforts several factors reduced the effectiveness of these delegates. The representatives from the group A towns in the west and Bristol County voted with the most commercial-cosmopolitan interests on most of the crucial roll calls, preventing a unified western interest from developing that might have been able to force some concessions. In addition to the defection of the group A towns, many of the western communities sent to the lower house justices of the peace who tended to favor the commercial-cosmopolitan programs to a much greater extent than did the nonplaceholding delegates from these western towns. Finally the western counties continued to elect well-known placeholders and professionals to the state senate and these men tended to strengthen the power of the most commercial-cosmopolitan interest in the upper house. Table 43 shows the voting patterns of the three groups of towns in the four western and Bristol counties on two important roll calls during the early 1780s and compares the voting patterns of the justices with the votes of other delegates.

Meanwhile the western and Bristol group B and C towns stood

TABLE 43
Western Voting Patterns

Towns	Representatives Against Commercial-Cosmopolitan Programs		Voting in the 2 Roll Calls of			
	Consolidation, Jan. 1781	Excise, Mar. 1785	Justices		All Others	
			1	2	1	2
Western group A	33%	31%	50%	25%	22%	50%
Western group B	59	77	56	67	69	83
Western group C	73	78	50	70	78	82
Total	61%	69%	52%	56%	64%	78%

SOURCES: Unpublished Journal of the House of Representatives, Office of the Secretary, Boston, 24 Jan. 1781, pp. 246-47 (cited hereafter as House Journal). Use of the income from impost and excise to meet national requisition is from ibid., 16 Mar. 1786, pp. 466-68.

by as the General Court aided a number of other towns and counties in meeting their tax problems. Towns in all sections of the state protested their assessments but the court, by a resolution of November 1781, gave most of the assistance to the eastern and Maine maritime and fishing towns that had been hard hit by the war. In addition to this general resolve, the court also abated the taxes on all of the Barnstable County towns on 5 March 1785. Thus the westerners had to bear their heavy taxes and smile as the court aided the maritime communities in solving their financial problems.[1]

1. For a convenient list of petitions requesting the abatement of taxes see the tables in Robert A. Feer, "Shays' Rebellion" (Ph.D. diss., Harvard University, 1957-1958), pp. 531-39. For the most important and wide-ranging abatement resolve, see: *Acts and Laws of the Commonwealth of Massachusetts*, 11 vols. (Boston, 1890-1897), 2 Nov. 1781, 1:802-04. This abated the taxes of 112 towns. These were located as follows:

Towns	Towns with Taxes Abated	Towns	Towns with Taxes Abated
Eastern group A	48%	Western group A	20%
Eastern group B	60	Western group B	24
Eastern group C	47	Western group C	24
Total eastern	52%	Total western	24%
Total Maine	31%	Total state	33%

Towns also sent in a wide range of petitions that requested boundary changes, additional powers, the division of counties, and charters as districts or as incorporated communities. The court considered these and often acceded to the towns' requests.[2] The farming towns in Suffolk County forced the repeal of the Boston Marketing Act, the court incorporated new towns, and all sorts of local legislation aided numerous communities.[3] When the citizens of Nantucket, both a town and a county, petitioned to secede in 1785, the court mollified the irate islanders by providing bounties on whale oil.[4] The Bristol and western towns also sent in at least twenty-one petitions for changes in basic state policies from 1781 to 1785.[5] But these petitions for the reductions of salaries, attack-

2. For examples of this type of legislation for a part of 1785 only, see *Acts and Laws*, 14 June 1785, 3:432-33, for "An Act to Prevent Damage being done by Neat Cattle and Horses on Pocha Beach, in the Town of Eastham and Meadows thereunto Adjoining"; 14 June 1785, 3:434, for an "Act for Annexing a Gore of Land Lying Between the Towns of Worcester and Sutton, to the Town of Worcester"; 17 June 1785, 3:436-39, "An Act for Incorporating a Certain Tract of Land Lying in the County of Hampshire . . . into a District By the Name of East Hampton"; 21 June 1785, 3:443-44, for "An Act for Erecting . . . [certain parts of various towns] into a Town by the Name of Gardner"; 30 Nov. 1785, 3:498-500, for "An Act for Incorporating Certain Lands in West Springfield, in the County of Hampshire, into a Common Field."

3. The legislation repealing the Boston Market Act is in ibid. 11 Feb. 1785, 3:114.

4. Ibid., 28 Nov. 1785, 3:795-97. Alexander Starbuck, *The History of Nantucket County* (Boston, 1924), pp. 386-87." Bellisarious," *Massachusetts Centinel*, 2 April 1785.

5. These petitions have been tabulated from the table in Feer, "Shays' Rebellion," pp. 540-41. The following proportion of the twenty-one listed petitions favored the listed reforms:

	Petitions		
			Total,
Reform	1782	1783-1785	1782-1785
Reduction of salaries	71%	27%	41%
Publication of information	57	33	41
Passage of tender law	43	20	29
Reduction of taxes	29	27	29
Reorganize the courts	71	0	21
Heavier luxury taxes	0	20	14
Move capitol from Boston	14	13	14
Establish local registrars and judges of probate	29	0	0

ing communication and the Society of the Cincinnati, or requesting the issuance of legal tender paper money usually suffered the
same neglect as those for tax or debt relief.

The Boston artisans added insult to injury when they success-
fully used their local political power to protect their position in
Boston politics. The artisans and laborers almost always selected
placeholders, merchants, and professionals as their representatives,
their selectmen, and their overseers of the poor, but they intended
to retain the turbulent town meeting which made most of the
important decisions.[6] Boston citizens voted much more heavily
than those of other towns and when interested in local questions
they packed the town meeting and controlled policy.[7] Many merchants and professionals naturally preferred a mayor-council form
of government which would give them almost complete control
over the city and in the spring of 1784 several respectable gentlemen began agitating for a reformed city government. Samuel
Adams, always on the alert for antirepublicanism, warned his artisan followers that the new system would introduce an "aristocracy, a government, of all others . . . the worst." Mobilized by
Adams and other leaders, the artisans blocked the original attempt
to push the changes through and the reformers had to be satisfied
with a committee that would consider and suggest changes in the
city's constitution. On 4 June 1784 this committee reported two

6. A study of the *Reports of the Record Commissioners of the City of
Boston*, 39 vols. (Boston, 1876-1909) (cited hereafter as *Boston Town Records*), vols. 26 and 31; the lists of representatives in the *Acts and Laws;* the
occupations in John Norman, ed, *The Boston Directory, Containing a List of
the Merchants, Traders and Others of the Town of Boston* (Boston, 1789),
and "Assessor's Taking Books of the Town of Boston" [1780] in Bostonian
Society, *Publications*, 9:9-59, gave the following results. Nine of the eleven
men who served as selectmen between 1780 and 1784 were either merchants
or retired merchants, one was a justice of the peace, and one was a notary
public. Twelve of the fifteen representatives to the lower house were merchants or retired merchants, one was the Continental loan officer for Massachusetts, one was an insurance broker, and one was an attorney. Ten of the
fourteen men who served as overseers of the poor were either active or retired
merchants.

7. According to the unpublished Abstracts of Votes for Governor and Lieutenant-Governor, Office of the Secretary, Boston, for the entire period
1780-1791, the voting rate in Boston was almost double that of the remainder of the commonwealth. See ch. 3 for additional information.

proposals both of which discarded the town meeting in favor of a mayor and council.[8]

The artisans soundly defeated these new proposals. They turned out, packed Faneuil Hall, and shouted down speakers attempting to support the plans with cries of "No! No!" Jeremy Belknap, an associate of some of the reformers, sourly observed from the gallery that the majority that defeated change paid less than 2 percent of the city's taxes.[9] The "better people" still didn't give up. They mounted a propaganda campaign against the town government and attempted to convince the artisans that a mayor-council government could keep the streets lighted and eject Negroes, prostitutes, and other undesirables. The artisan propagandists responded with tales of aristocratic plotters out to get the "low folks."[10] During the fall of 1785 the artisans again defeated any basic changes in the structure of government. In October a committee of inhabitants petitioned the town meeting to appoint another committee to consider the feasibility of drafting a new constitution for the town. In November the meeting appointed a

8. Josiah Quincy, *A Municipal History of the Town and City of Boston During Two Centuries from September 17, 1630 to September 17, 1830* (Boston, 1832), pp. 23-24. For the agitation see *Massachusetts Centinel*, 28 Apr., 1 May 1784. A record of the town meetings is in *Boston Town Records*, vol. 31, 11 May 1784, p. 25, and *Massachusetts Centinel*, 12, 15 May 1784. Samuel Adams's statement is in ibid., 15 May 1784. The committee and its reports are covered in *Boston Town Records*, vol. 31, 11 May 1784, p 25; 21 May 1784, p. 37; 28 May 1784, p. 40; and 4 June 1784, p. 42. For some debate see *American Herald*, 10 May 1784, 14 June 1784; *Massachusetts Centinel*, 19, 26 May 1784. The committee was composed of six merchants, the attorney general, two insurance brokers, three attorneys, a physician, and Samuel Adams. Both plans proposed by the committee were also published as pamphlets. Both established a mayor-council government, limited the number of town meetings to three per year for election purposes only, and vested the power of the meeting in an elected group of councilmen and aldermen. The first proposal permitted the voters to choose one alderman and two councilmen from each of the twelve wards; the second provided for an eighteen-member council with six members elected at large and the other twelve selected from each of the twelve wards.

9. There is an excellent description of this meeting in Jeremy Belknap to Hazard, 19 June 1784, Belknap Papers, Massachusetts Historical Society, *Collections*, 5th ser., vols. 2, 3 (1877), 6th ser., vol. 4 (1891), 5th ser., 3:358-61. See also *Boston Town Records*, 17 June 1784, 31:92; *Independent Chronicle*, 3, 17 June 1784; and *Massachusetts Centinel*, 5, 16 June 1784.

10. Examples of propaganda for change: *Massachusetts Centinel*, 10 July, 18 Dec. 1784, 4 June 1785; *Independent Chronicle*, 10 Feb. 1785. Opposition in: *Massachusetts Centinel*, 19 Oct. 1785.

committee, chaired by Sam Adams and packed with his supporters, which decided that the constitution needed no revision.[11] The meeting accepted this report and limited reform to a recodification of town laws and orders. After several weeks of meetings and discussions the Suffolk County Court of General Sessions approved the new code in early 1786.[12] The artisans had won their two-year struggle to prevent changes in the town meeting form of government and demonstrated their strength, their leadership, and their willingness to smear their opponents as aristocratic enemies of the Republic.

In another effort to increase their political power, western and other groups fell back on the revolutionary Massachusetts tradition of the convention. These bodies, composed of delegates elected by the various towns, met to discuss programs and drafted petitions and instructions which could be backed by a bloc of citizens and delegates. Towns throughout the commonwealth met in these conventions, but their chief strength lay in the west, where they frequently mobilized sentiment against state policies, and in the District of Maine, where they advocated separation from the commonwealth. Just as the westerners had seen the successes of the Boston artisans and the eastern towns, they watched as the development of the secession movement in Maine led the General Court into making all sorts of concessions to the district.

Maine's citizens had supported the commercial-cosmopolitan programs during the early 1780s, but many had complained about their subordination to Massachusetts for some time. Maine towns begrudged the expense of sending representatives all the way to Boston, criticized the state for its niggardly expenditures for defense during the Revolution, rankled at the lack of interest in land reform, wanted more incorporated towns that could send delegates to the court. In 1784 and 1785 some merchants were irritated by the new commercial policies that interfered with their

11. Continued agitation and action in: *Massachusetts Centinel*, 19, 29 Oct., 9, 19, 20, 23 Nov. 1785. *Boston Town Records*, vol. 31, 16 Sept., p. 88; 26 Oct., p. 91; 9 Nov., p. 91, 30 Nov. 1785, pp. 92-93.

12. Details about the eventual passage of the new by laws are in: *Boston Town Records*, vol. 31, 6, 7, 8 Dec. 1785, 25, 27 Jan. 1786, pp. 93-96. *Massachusetts Centinel*, 7, 14 Dec. 1785. The new rules were published as *The By-Laws and Town Orders of the Town of Boston, Made and Passed at Several Meetings in 1785 and 1786, and Duly Approved by the Court of Sessions* (Boston, 1786).

trade with Britain and Nova Scotia. Behind these criticisms lay the fact that Maine differed ethnically and religiously from old Massachusetts and faced completely different problems.[13] In early 1785 the founding of Maine's first newspaper, the *Falmouth Gazette*, gave the secessionists a forum. Throughout the summer they filled its pages with essays proving that Maine would fare better as a separate state. By the end of the summer some writers were urging a district-wide convention to discuss secession and in September several leaders called for an October convention at Falmouth. The thirty citizens who attended this first meeting requested all the district towns to send delegates to a larger Falmouth convention to be held in January 1786.[14] This open agitation alarmed Gover-

13. The following table is based on United States Bureau of the Census, *Historical Statistics of the United States: Colonial Times to 1957* (Washington, D.C., 1960), p. 756, which gives ethnic data.

Percentage of the Population

Section	*English*	*Scotch*	*Ulster Irish*	*Southern Irish*	*German*	*French*	*Unassigned*
Maine	60.0%	4.5%	8.0%	3.7%	1.3%	1.3%	21.1%
Massachusetts	82.0	4.4	2.6	1.3	0.3	0.8	8.4

The following religious data is based upon Thomas Fleet and John Fleet, *Fleet's Pocket Almanack for the Year of Our Lord 1787...to Which Is Annexed the Massachusetts Register* (Boston, 1786) (cited hereafter as Fleet, *Register*), pp. 51-58.

Polls per
Congregational Minister

Towns	*Maine*	*Massachusetts*
Group A	232	238
Group B	262	221
Group C	465	201
Total	305	215

For examples of friction with Massachusetts see William Lithgow to Caleb Davis, 12 May 1781, Caleb Davis Papers, Massachusetts Historical Society; "A Friend to the Rights of Mankind" and "Impartialis," both in *Falmouth Gazette*, 4 June and 12 Nov. 1785; Col. J. Brooks to Henry Knox, 25 Dec. 1785, Knox Papers, Massachusetts Historical Society.

14. For examples of the rhetoric see *Falmouth Gazette*, 5 Mar., 16 Apr., 7, 14, 21 May, 4, 11, 18, 25 June, 9, 16, 23 July, 6, 13, 20, 27 Aug., 3, 10 Sept. 1785. The call for the convention is in ibid., 17 Sept. 1785. *Massachusetts Centinel* noted this on 22 June 1785. See also *Independent Chronicle*, 12, 26 May 1785. For agitation against the timber law see *Falmouth Gazette*, 22 Jan., 5, 19 Feb., 12 Mar. 1785.

nor Bowdoin and other Massachusetts politicians and also excited a leading Maine placeholder, Judge Sewall of York County, who cryptically noted that "one Revolution in an age is quite sufficient."[15]

The placeholders and the group A Maine towns attempted to block any such revolution. Sewall used his personal influence to prevent the town of York from sending delegates and Falmouth, the only group A town that sent representatives, reconsidered its action and recalled them. Only two of the district's judges of the common pleas court and one senator in office between 1780 and 1786 attended the convention.[16]

The membership of the conventions held in January and September 1786 showed the movement to be strongest in the group C towns and especially, when compared with their record of attendance in the General Court, in the least cosmopolitan-commercial settlements that had no shipping industry. Table 44 compares the membership of these two conventions with the representation of the district in the lower house of the General Court between 1780 and 1785. Yet, despite the fact that few placeholders were among the delegates who came from the poorer and less commercial towns, the January 1786 convention took no radical action. It seated the five Falmouth delegates, in spite of their recall, elected as president one of the placeholders, Judge William Gorham of Cumberland County, and appointed a committee on grievances that promptly presented ten complaints including the lack of representation of frontier towns, the method of taxing polls and estates, and the expense of government and justice. The session

15. Bowdoin's message is in *Acts and Laws*, 20 Oct. 1785, 3:731-32. David Sewall to George Thatcher, 25 Nov. 1785, Massachusetts Historical Society, *Proceedings*, 58:194-95. Tristram Dalton to John Adams, 23 Jan. 1786, Adams Papers, pt. 4, Adams Manuscript Trust. Also notice the *Falmouth Gazette*, 15, 22, 20 Oct. 1785.

16. The lists of delegates to the two conventions are given in "Proceedings" [of Maine Convention], in Massachusetts Historical Society, *Collections*, 4:28-30. The delegates who held elective or judicial offices between 1780 and 1785 and 1786 and 1791 may be determined from the lists in *Acts and Laws*, and in Fleet, *Register*. For additional information see David Sewall to George Thatcher, 25 Nov. 1785, Massachusetts Historical Society, *Proceedings*, 58:194-95; Sewall to William Cushing, 22 Dec. 1785, Cushing Papers, Massachusetts Historical Society; J. Thaxter to John Adams, 22 Jan. 1786, Adams Papers, pt. 4. Joseph Avery to Caleb Davis, 14 Nov. 1786, Caleb Davis Papers. *Massachusetts Centinel*, 8 Feb. 1786, shows opposition.

TABLE 44
Maine Secession Conventions and Senate Membership

| | Representatives at | | | |
| | General Court (1780–85) | January Convention | September Convention | Senators (1780-85) |
Towns				
Group A	16%	13%	16%	33%
Group B	35	16	10	61
Group C	49	71	74	6

SOURCES: "Proceedings," Massachusetts Historical Society, *Collections*, 4:28-30. See *Acts and Laws of the Commonwealth of Massachusetts, 1780-1797*, 11 vols. (Boston, 1890-1897) (cited hereafter as *Acts and Laws)*, and Thomas Fleet and John Fleet, *Fleet's Pocket Almanack for the Year of Our Lord [1780-1790] . . . to Which Is Annexed the Massachusetts Register* (Boston, 1779-1789) (cited hereafter as Fleet, *Register*, with the year and date of publication) for lists of representatives and placeholders.

adjourned after calling for another convention at Falmouth for September 1786.[17]

While the towns pondered and sent their representatives to Boston, an even more moderate movement, based in Lincoln County, agitated for the establishment of a new county government to serve the frontier area between the Penobscot River and the Canadian border. A committee at Machias argued that Massachusetts could retain the allegiance of the region by creating a new county and William Lithgow, a Lincoln County judge and member of the January convention, joined by ten justices of the peace submitted a petition to the General Court asking for a new county.[18] The court, worried by the secession movement, appointed a committee chaired by General Benjamin Lincoln to treat with the Indians and to investigate the situation in eastern Maine.[19] During the fall of 1786 the governor and the court moved to meet some of these more moderate requests. Governor Bowdoin proposed the creation of two new counties in the district, the recognition of marriages performed by town clerks as well as clergy, and the distribution of the published session laws to

17. "Proceedings," Massachusetts Historical Society, *Collections*, 4:38-39.
18. These actions are covered in Committee of Machias to Caleb Davis and Benjamin Hitchborn, 22 May 1786; Petition of Justices at Pownalborough, 8 June 1786, and James Avery to Caleb Davis, 9 June 1786, all in Caleb Davis Papers.
19. Legislative actions are in *Acts and Laws*, 16 Nov. 1786, 4:394-96, and in the Public Papers for this act, Office of the Secretary, Boston.

the Maine towns. Lincoln's committee also recommended the establishment of two new counties and the construction of a road from the Penobscot River to Passamaquaddy Bay, and the court began to investigate the possibilities of creating the new counties.[20]

These concessions and the outbreak of the Regulation in Massachusetts divided the secession forces. Maine had not been affected by the political disputes of the 1780s in the same manner as the west. Between 1780 and 1786 the district towns that sent delegates supported the programs of the most commercial-cosmopolitan interests as did most of the towns with legislative voting records at the two secession conventions. York County, the hardest hit by debts and taxes, had less secessionist sentiment than did the other two counties which had lower than the average number of debt suits per thousand polls or back taxes per poll.[21] Some of the secessionists wanted the district to support the Regulators and the western conventions, but the September 1786 convention at Portland concentrated on the secession issue drafting a petition to the General Court and publishing an address to the people of Maine which urged them to send representatives to a third convention at Portland in January 1787 and requested the towns to take a vote on whether to secede from Massachusetts.[22] The voting and

20. Bowdoin's message is in *Acts and Laws*, 4 Oct. 1786, 4:940. The committee report is in ibid., 16 Nov. 1786, 4:894-96, and in the Public Papers, Office of the Secretary, Boston, concerning this resolve.

21. See ch. 4 for the problems of taxation and the voting records of the Maine towns. New legislation in 1786 raised the taxes in Lincoln County. A comparison of the taxes levied in Maine for the tax act of 31 Oct. 1781 for £303,000 for the entire state and the one of 23 Mar. 1786 for £300,489 shows the following differences:

County	Levied in 1781	Levied in 1786
York	£ 9,224	£10,609
Cumberland	12,120	14,095
Lincoln	6,967	12,994

There were at least twenty-four towns, districts, and plantations in Lincoln County that had never been assessed for a state tax until the 1784/86 valuation and the 1786 tax act. See *Acts and Laws*, 31 Oct. 1781, 1:503-19; 23 March 1786, 4:580-600.

22. *Massachusetts Gazette*, 1, 12, 15 Sept. 1786; "Proceedings," Massachusetts Historical Society, *Collections*, 4:30-39; Stephen Jones and James Avery to Caleb Davis, 24 Nov. 1786; Stephen Jones, George Stillman, James Avery to Caleb Davis, 23 Dec. 1786, all in Caleb Davis Papers. See *Independent Chronicle*, 26 Apr. 1787 for anti-Regulator speech by William Lithgow.

the January 1787 convention gave little comfort to the more radical secessionists. Only about one-third of the Maine towns bothered to vote on the secession question and the moderates who wanted to petition the General Court defeated the radicals who sponsored paper money and the abolition of the senate.[23] The Maine representatives at the court did not present this petition until March 1787 and the General Court further cooled down the situation by chartering towns and creating new counties during the summer of 1787.[24] In addition to these direct benefits the court aided other district citizens by suspending suits for debt and by refusing to levy new direct taxes. In September 1787 a small convention met at Portland and again recommended a vote on secession, but the towns never made any returns and the issue remained dormant until the early 1790s.[25]

Despite its collapse, the movement for separate statehood for Maine had some important effects on the commonwealth's politics. The movement worried many influential Massachusetts politicians and together with the problems of Regulators, national commerce and finance, and the collapse of the state's financial system, it helped bring some of them to a more nationalistic position. In 1786 the larger-than-usual Maine delegation to the General Court increased the political tensions in the commonwealth by voting, generally, for the programs of the most commercial-cosmopolitan interests. Some of the leaders of the Maine secession movement, then relatively unknown, would become Antifederalists during the convention of 1788 and eventually join the Democratic-Republicans in the 1790s, but they were not close friends of the western farmers in 1786.[26]

23. "Proceedings," Massachusetts Historical Society, *Collections*, 4:32-34, 40. Letter of Samuel Thompson in *Cumberland Gazette* 23 Mar. 1787. Also notice "Scribble-Scrabble" in *Cumberland Gazette*, 16, 23 Mar. 1787.

24. *Worcester Magazine*, Sept. 1787, pp. 305, 341.

25. T. B. Wait to George Thatcher, 29 Feb. 1788, Thatcher Papers, Boston Public Library. Daniel Cony to George Thatcher, 15 Mar. 1788, ibid., in which Cony suggests waiting for the establishment of the new national government. Cony declared that the vote was 852 to 22 in favor of separation. See also *Worcester Magazine*, Mar. 1788, p. 324; William Widgery to George Thatcher, 14 Sept. 1788, Thatcher Papers; *Independent Chronicle*, 15 Jan. 1789; Stephen Hall to George Thatcher, 21 Mar. 1789, Thatcher Papers; *Massachusetts Magazine*, Mar. 1791, p. 190; July 1791, p. 45 and August 1791, p. 51. Also see ibid., Feb. 1792, p. 130.

26. A comparison of the towns attending the Maine separation conventions with their voting patterns in the 1788 convention shows that 10 of the 18 towns that voted against the Constitution sent delegates to Portland while only 5 of the 21 towns favoring the Constitution had sent representatives.

The Massachusetts convention movement achieved its greatest strength in Worcester and Hampshire counties between 1780 and 1785. During this period the state experienced three waves of convention activity. The first, engendered by the debate over the 1781 financial legislation, included towns in Worcester and Suffolk counties that protested the passage of the January 1781 law modifying legal tender currency and consolidating the state debt. In late 1781 and early 1782 the next wave, in response to high taxes and the new impost-excise system, spread over the entire western section of the state and included demands for constitutional and credit reforms. This series of conventions ended during the fall of 1782 after the passage of legislation relieving debtors in the summer 1782 session of the court. The last wave, beginning in early 1783, cresting in 1784, and receding by 1785, considered a wide range of questions but concentrated on opposition to the military, commutation, and the Society of the Cincinnati. In addition to these major outbreaks, small groups of towns located throughout the state held conventions to mobilize sentiment on local issues including reduction of taxes, the creation of new counties, and the establishment of new probate districts.[27]

The convention movement, unfortunately, was singularly ineffectual. The court did not repeal the 1781 legislation concerning legal tender and the state debt; the assistance to debtors passed in 1782 lapsed after only one year; the commonwealth eventually voted the impost with commutation in 1783; the anti-Cincinnati drive evaporated after 1784. Several factors accounted for this lack of success. In the first place, the varied interests of the different classes of towns within the same convention often created internal conflicts that the delegates found difficult to resolve. In the Hampshire County convention that met at Hatfield on the first Tuesday of April 1782 the various towns disagreed over a motion to request the judges of the supreme judicial court to forbear giving judgments except where the creditor could lose his debt. Table 45 shows that differences among the three groups of towns within a particular convention could often result in serious divisions. The towns represented at these conventions sometimes did not follow the recommendations of the joint body. In early 1781

---

27. Several excellent modern studies give the background of the convention movement. See Robert J. Taylor, *Western Massachusetts in the Revolution* (Providence, 1954), pp. 96-98, 109-23.   Feer, "Shays' Rebellion," pp. 88-96, and his list of petitions and conventions on pp. 540-46. J. R. Pole, *Political Representation in England and the Origins of the American Republic* (New York, 1966), pp. 226-44, also has some excellent insights.

TABLE 45
Vote in Hatfield Convention, 1781

Vote	Group A	Group B	Group C	Total Towns
Yes	25%	0%	48%	42%
No	75	100	52	58

SOURCES: James R. Trumbull, *History of Northhampton Massachusetts from Its Settlement in 1654* (Northhampton, 1902), p. 454. See the Rev. John Lockwood, *Westfield and Its Historic Influences, 1669–1919*, 2 vols. (Springfield, 1922), 2:48, for a list of towns and delegates. Robert J. Taylor, *Western Massachusetts in the Revolution* (Providence, 1954), p. 112, also gives an analysis of the vote.

six Suffolk towns held a convention at Dedham that recorded its opposition to the January 1781 financial legislation. A few months later only 50 percent of these towns voted in favor of a motion to repeal the modification of the legal tender nature of the new emission bills while 33 percent voted against repeal and 17 percent neglected to vote.[28] Placeholders and influential politicians often attempted to prevent their communities from sending delegates to these conventions and, after the enthusiasm passed, the town often neglected to follow the recommendations even if it had sent delegates.[29] In addition to these problems the convention forces found that even if they mobilized a majority in the lower house, the commercial-cosmopolitan control of the senate blocked their programs and reforms. Finally the opponents of the conventions consistently and constantly attacked them throughout the 1780s as breeding grounds for faction and party spirit that would undermine the republican nature of government because of their "immorality."[30] Although towns electing delegates to these

28. Petition of the Suffolk Towns, 9 Apr. 1781, Massachusetts Archives, 142:338-40 in Office of the Secretary, Boston; compare this with the vote in the unpublished Journal of the House of Representatives, available at the Office of the Secretary, Boston (cited hereafter as House Journal), 13 June 1781, pp. 67-68.

29. Abner Holden to Caleb Davis, 14 Mar. 1781, Caleb Davis Papers.

30. For reaction against conventions see Pole, *Political Representation*, pp. 235-36; Taylor, *Western Massachusetts*, pp. 141-42; Feer, "Shays' Rebellion," pp. 90-93. "Aminadab" in *Massachusetts Spy* [Worcester], 22 Mar. 1781, is an excellent early example of anticonvention rhetoric. As Samuel Adams put it in a letter to Noah Webster, 30 Apr. 1784, Calendar of Samuel Adams Papers, Bancroft Collection, New York Public Library, "under the present Constitutional government county conventions and popular committees no longer serve a useful purpose. . . " For satiric instructions for a convention see "Paskalos" in *Massachusetts Spy* [Worcester] , 28 June 1781.

conventions did not accept such charges, they had to expend much energy, which could have been put to better use, answering them.[31]

The failure of the first round of conventions called in early 1781 to protest the infamous financial legislation of 25 January reflected these various weaknesses. In Worcester County, Sutton, the home of Amos Singletary, a leading opponent of the 1781 financial legislation, called a county convention to consider the situation. It met in April and condemned the court for modifying legal tender and mobilized the Worcester County group B and C towns to cast 94 percent of their votes for a motion repealing the modification of legal tender in June 1781.[32] Despite this local success the senate killed reform and the movement failed to accomplish its objective. In Suffolk County a smaller convention failed even to mobilize sentiment from its participating towns as only 60 percent of those voting supported the repeal of the legal tender modification during the first session of the 1781 General Court.[33]

The second round of conventions represented a wider geographical distribution and a broader interest in reform than did the first round which had reacted to the new fiscal legislation. Town meetings in Bristol, Hampshire, and Worcester counties first objected to tax relief for land speculators, heavy direct taxes, evaluation procedures, and local grievances including the problems of registering deeds in Hampshire County.[34] The county conventions advocated even broader reforms. The Worcester meeting in April 1782 demanded the settlement of accounts with all state officers,

---

31. *Salem Gazette.* 2 May 1782, for an example of a western convention, in this instance the Worcester convention of 18 Apr. 1782, replying to these charges.

32. *Massachusetts Spy* [Worcester], 22 Mar. 1781; Petition of the Worcester Convention, 24 Apr. 1781, Massachusetts Archives, 142:357. The roll call vote is in the House Journal, 13 June 1781, pp. 67-68. Also see Taylor, *Western Massachusetts*, pp. 109-10.

33. "Petition of the Suffolk Towns," 9 Apr. 1781, Massachusetts Archives, 142:338-40; *Boston Town Records*, 13 Mar. 1781, 26:177-78; House Journal, 13 June 1781, pp. 67-68.

34. Some examples of these petitions are Spencer Petition, 11 Feb. 1782, Massachusetts Archives, 187:412-13; West Springfield Petition, 16 Jan. 1782, ibid., 187:339; Norton Petition, 7 Jan. 1782, ibid., 187:327. See Rev. John Lockwood, *Westfield and Its Historic Influences, 1669-1919*, 2 vols. (Springfield, 1922), 31 Dec. 1781, 2:53; *Records of the Town of Plymouth (1636-1738)*, 3 vols. (Plymouth, 1889-1903), 3 Dec. 1781, 3:437, and 24 Dec. 1781, 3:438; *Taylor, Western Massachusetts*, p. 109.

the enlargement of the civil jurisdiction of the justices of the peace, the payment of direct taxes in provisions and farm produce, and an immediate settlement of the accounts of the commonwealth with the confederation.[35] In May a later Worcester convention petitioned to remove the capital from Boston, to create an annual state budget, to investigate the court of common pleas, and to reform the Maine land system.[36] The Hampshire convention showed its radicalism by recommending the abolition of the court of common pleas and the reduction of the authority of the court of general sessions.[37] A few months later another smaller convention met and recommended the repeal of the excise, the reduction of judicial fees, and the passage of legislation making real and personal property a legal tender for debts.[38] Thus the 1782 conventions, unlike those of 1781, did not stop at recommending changes in the fiscal system. Several wanted radical changes in the judicial and political institutions.

These widespread conventions and the incidence of violence in the west helped convince many members of the court of the need for at least some reforms. The lower house, thanks to the overwhelming support of the less commercial-cosmopolitan western towns, passed a temporary act permitting the impartial valuation of certain real and personal property seized by executions for debts. The senate, for once, knuckled under to pressure and the measure, limited to one year, became law.[39] In addition to this reform, the court appointed a committee composed of Samuel Adams, Nathaniel Gorham, and Artemas Ward that travelled to Hampshire County, investigated the causes of dissatisfaction, explained the financial situation to the citizens, and met with a large county convention at Hatfield from August 7 through 10. With the committee looking on, the delegates urged tax reductions, lower salaries, and an indemnity for all those, with the exception

35. *Salem Gazette*, 2 May 1782.

36. William Lincoln, *History of Worcester, Massachusetts* (Worcester, 1837), p. 132.

37. James R. Trumbull, *History of Northampton Massachusetts From Its Settlement in 1654*, 2 vols. (Northampton, 1898-1902), 2:454; Lockwood, *Westfield*, 2:48; Taylor, *Western Massachusetts*, pp. 111-12.

38. Lockwood, *Westfield*, 2:53.

39. The roll call vote is in the House Journal, 2 July 1782, pp. 150-51. See also William V. Wells, *The Life and Public Service of Samuel Adams*, 3 vols. (Boston, 1865), 3:161-63; James Sullivan to John Adams, 24 July 1782, Adams Papers, pt. 4.

of Samuel Ely, who had engaged in the 1782 riots.[40] The court took the convention's recommendation, pardoned all those involved but Ely, and in March 1783 closed the affair by releasing Ely on condition that he leave the state.[41]

After the passage of these conciliatory measures, the conventions became less radical and by 1783 and 1784 began to interest themselves in commutation and the threat of the military. In Hampshire County twenty-seven towns attended a moderate convention in October 1782 that suggested prompt repayment of personal debts and discussed the location of a county seat.[42] Another smaller convention met at Hatfield early in 1783, criticized the court for its suspension of the habeas corpus law in 1782, and suggested that the towns refuse to pay certain taxes.[43] Later conventions held at Deerfield in September and Hatfield in October of 1783 complained of commutation and proposed a reduction in taxes.[44] In Worcester and Middlesex counties conventions in 1783 recommended the settlement of public accounts and the use of state securities as legal tender for the payment of executions.[45] During 1784 this moderate trend continued with conventions considering local and Continental problems instead of agitating for basic reforms. A convention of Suffolk County farm towns attacked commutation and later another Suffolk convention tried

40. *Acts and Laws*, 2 July 1782, 3 July 1782, 2:240-41, 5 July 1782, 2:248; Trumbull, *Northhampton*, p. 466; Lockwood, *Westfield*, 2:58; John Eliot to Jeremy Belknap, 14 Aug. 1782, Belknap Papers, 3:277; Jonathan Judd's diary entry for 7 Aug. 1782, in Lockwood, *Westfield* 2:158; *Massachusetts Gazette*, 13 Oct. 1782; *Independent Chronicle*, 29 Aug. 1782; *Salem Gazette* 20 Aug. 1782; Taylor, *Western Massachusetts*, pp. 119-20.

41. *Acts and Laws*, 2 Oct. 1782, 2:278-79; 4 Nov. 1782, 2:81-82; 17 Mar. 1783, 2:449-50.

42. James M. Crafts, *History of the Town of Whately, Massachusetts, 1661-1899* (Orange, Mass., 1899), p. 234.

43. Summons to a Convention, 4 Mar. 1783, Robert Paine Papers, Massachusetts Historical Society; Trumbull, *Northampton*, p. 468; Taylor, *Western Massachusetts*, pp. 121-22.

44. Trumbull, *Northampton*, p. 468; Joseph G. Holland, *History of Western Massachusetts, the Counties of Hampden, Hampshire, Franklin, and Berkshire*, 2 vols. (Springfield, 1855), 1:233; James M. Crafts, *History of the Town of Whately, Massachusetts, 1661-1899* (Orange, 1899), p. 235.

45. D. Hamilton Hurd, ed., *History of Worcester County, Massachusetts with Biographical Sketches of Many of its Prominent Men.* (Philadelphia, 1889), pp. 348-49; Alexander Shepard to the Selectmen of Cambridge, 18 Dec. 1783, Miscellaneous Papers, Massachusetts Historical Society.

to start a movement for the creation of a new county that would separate the farm towns from Boston.[46] In the fall of 1784 the Suffolk towns met again, this time to protest against the Boston Market Act, and in spite of the vigorous protests of the capital city the court repealed the act. In Worcester a convention in March 1784 complained of the lack of money, the failure of the treasurer to publish the state financial accounts, the location of the capital in Boston, commutation, the 1783 impost, and Congress's failure to redeem the oustanding old emission currency.[47] In Plymouth and Hampshire counties conventions met that opposed commutation and agitated for the division of the county.[48] During 1785 the Massachusetts counties remained calm despite the rising fever for conventions and secession in the District of Maine.

Generally these conventions reflected direct responses to political actions or the lack of specific reforms by the General Court. The conventions reacted against the 1781 financial program, the destruction of legal tender currency, high taxes, and the 1783 impost-commutation proposal. At the same time they advocated reforms that would ease the payment of debts, reduce taxes, publicize the expenditure of state funds, and pare down the powers of the court of common pleas. By 1786 all sections of the state had long experience in holding these extralegal political gatherings, an experience that would enable the western counties and Bristol to react quickly to the legislation of the 1786 session of the General Court.

Violence became in the preparty commonwealth, as in many more complex societies, the final political resort of interests who failed to gain their political goals through regular channels. Minor

46. *Independent Chronicle*, 25 Mar., 8 Apr., 14 May 1784. *Boston Town Records*, vol. 31, 8 Mar. 1784, p. 3; 15 Mar. 1784, p. 12; 12 Apr. 1784, p. 49; 14 May 1784, p. 26; 18 Jan. 1785, p. 49. Watertown Historical Society, *Watertown Records* (1634-1829), 8 vols. (Watertown, 1894-1939), vol. 5, 8 Sept. 1784, p. 314.

47. William A. Benedict and Hiram A. Tracy, *History of the Town of Sutton, Massachusetts; From 1704 to 1876* (Worcester, 1876), p. 122. Lincoln, *Worcester*, p. 133.

48. John S. Barry, *A Historical Sketch of the Town of Hanover, Massachusetts, With Family Genealogies* (Boston, 1853), pp. 129-30; Taylor, *Western Massachusetts*, p. 123; Rev. John Hubbard, "An Account of the Town of Northfield," in Massachusetts Historical Society, *Collections*, 1st ser., 2:232-33; George Sheldon, *A History of Deerfield, Massachusetts*, 2 vols. (Deerfield, 1896), 2:761.

outbreaks appear to have been endemic in the western and Bristol counties between 1781 and 1786 but rioting peaked in 1782 and then declined during 1783 and 1784. Two very different types of violence broke out between 1781 and 1786 in these counties. The first, locally oriented, consisted of a few irate farmers mobbing a tax collector or preventing the sale of a neighbor's estate for debts. The second included at least partially organized rioters from a large number of towns who mobilized and attempted to close the courts or to rescue their leaders from jail. These actions became politically significant only when the local authorities confessed their inability to deal with them. During the early 1780s the local constables, sheriffs, and militia handled the riots as the bulk of the population remained loyal to the government and controlled the rioters. Yet at least in one instance some westerners learned that violence could pay some political dividends. Ely's rebellion and the violent outbreaks in Hampshire County during the summer of 1782 increased the pressure on the court and gained a consideration of western demands.

An analysis of the indictments in seven of these incidents shows that the occupations and residential patterns of those indicted represented a skewered cross section of the western population. (See table 46.) The juries indicted no placeholders or important politicians but gentlemen or residents of group A towns accounted for 15 percent of the individuals on their bills. Less than 2 percent were professionals or traders while over 84 percent and 80 percent lived in the future Antifederalist towns or engaged in agriculture as yeomen, husbandmen, or laborers. Naturally the juries indicted the best-known ringleaders which would have increased the proportion of gentlemen and residents of the group A towns, but the exclusion of the gentlemen would leave only 2 percent of these rioters engaged in professional or commercial activities that would have related them to the most commercial-cosmopolitan interests. In other words this scattered violence reflected the response of the less commercial-cosmopolitan groups of the population.

The local incidents usually involved small mobs against constables and tax collectors. In October 1781 Job Shattuck led a mob of Groton men against tax collector William Nutting. In the same year a Bristol County mob attempted to prevent the sale of oxen by a constable. In Berkshire County Reuben Munn and seven others seized a constable collecting debts and liberated the oxen he had taken. In Worcester County a crowd of Sturbridge laborers and yeomen found some amusement in attacking the home of

TABLE 46
Violence in the West

Breakdown of Rebels by	Rebels Indicted
Towns	
Group A	30%
Group B	18
Group C	51
Politics (by town)	
Federalist	16%
Antifederalist	84
Social groups	
Gentlemen	15%
Professionals	1
Traders	1
Artisans	1
Yeomen	27
Husbandmen	36
Laborers	17
Juveniles	2

SOURCES: The following incidents are all recorded in the Docket
Books of the Supreme Judicial Court, Clerk's Office, Suffolk County
Court House:
Commonwealth vs. Hobbs et al., Worcester, October term, 1782,
p. 285. Incident dated 10 Sept. 1781.
Commonwealth vs. Coleman et al., Hampshire, April term, 1784,
p. 146. Incident dated 8 Feb. 1783.
Commonwealth vs. Chamberlain et al., Worcester, April term,
1784, p. 178. Incident dated 19 Feb. 1783.
Commonwealth vs. Silas Fowler et al., Hampshire, Spring term,
1786, p. 207. Incident dated 10 Mar. 1783.
Commonwealth vs. Job Shattuck, et al., Middlesex, April term,
1784, pp. 85-86. Incident dated 8 Oct. 1783.
Commonwealth vs. Nash et al., Hampshire, April term, 1784, pp.
146-47. Incident dated 9 Dec. 1783.
Commonwealth vs. John Kent et al., Hampshire, September term,
1785, pp. 181-83. Incident dated 20 May 1783.

Justice Timothy Newall and in demanding the release of Nathan
Cutler, detained by the justice.[49] In 1783 a rash of these incidents
broke out in Worcester County. A mob at Douglas attacked a tax
collector, a crowd at Sutton attempted to prevent an execution
sale, and a group at Ward milled around for forty-eight hours

49. Docket Books of the Supreme Judicial Court, Suffolk County Court
House, Commonwealth vs. Shattuck et al., Middlesex, April term, 1782,
pp. 161-62; Commonwealth vs. Hobbes et al., Worcester, October term, 1782,
p. 285. See also Seth Paddelford to Robert T. Paine, 22 July 1782, Robert
Paine Papers.

without beginning a riot. Colonel Nathan Tyler of Uxbridge became so alarmed that he wrote Hancock for assistance and the governor forwarded his letter to the General Court which promptly suspended the writ of habeas corpus for four months.[50] This action calmed the situation and after a brief scare in March the county became quiet.[51] But the contagion spread into Hampshire County where Nathaniel Coleman and his associates celebrated the coming of 1783 by imprisoning a deputy sheriff at Deerfield. In March a Westfield mob attempted to riot and in May rioters swarmed into Springfield in an effort to block the court. The local militia turned out, protected the court, and drove off the mob.[52] In August a mob of twenty men tried to break into Northampton jail and another attempt on the same jail in November also failed.[53] Violence continued in Middlesex where the perennial troublemaker Job Shattuck mobilized a mob and fell upon a couple of hapless local tax collectors. In Bristol County Joseph Daggett and his friends attacked a deputy sheriff out serving civil executions.[54]

But while this local violence added to tension, it had little political result. The scattered assaults made by yeomen and husbandmen led by down-at-the-heels gentlemen could never become serious so long as the "good people" turned out and supported the law. Without the neutrality of the militia and the tacit support of the population, the feeble violence of the Shattucks and the Daggetts was doomed to fail.

Like almost all other activities, violence must be organized in order to have political results. Large numbers of persons must

50. Benedict, *Sutton*, p. 121; E. M. Bacon, ed., *Supplement to the Acts and Laws of the Commonwealth of Massachusetts* (Boston, 1896), 3 Feb. 1783, p. 148.

51. Worcester Committee of Correspondence to the Governor, 26 Feb. 1783, Robert Paine Papers; Bacon, ed., *Supplement to Acts and Laws*, 24 Feb. 1783, p. 154, 25 Feb. 1783, p. 154.

52. Taylor, *Western Massachusetts*, p. 121; Holland, *Western Massachusetts*, 1:232; *Salem Gazette*, 12 June 1783; Commonwealth vs. Fowler et al., Docket Books, Supreme Judicial Court, Hampshire County, May term, 1786, pp. 206-07.

53. Taylor, *Western Massachusetts*, p. 121; *Independent Chronicle*, 28 Aug. 1783; Commonwealth vs. Nash et al., Docket Books, Supreme Judicial Court, Hampshire County, April term, 1784, pp. 146-47.

54. Commonwealth vs. Shattuck et al., Docket Books, Supreme Judicial Court, Middlesex County, April term, 1784, pp. 85-86; Commonwealth vs. Daggett et al., Bristol County, April term, 1784.

assemble to prevent courts from meeting or to free prisoners and the mob must be strong enough to overawe the local supporters of government. Between 1780 and 1786 only the Ely rebellion mobilized this kind of support and although the local Hampshire militia handled the incident, Ely's activities helped the westerners get a few reforms through the General Court.

The Ely affair began in early 1782 when Samuel Ely, a former Congregational minister, travelled through Hampshire County urging his listeners to revoke the 1780 constitution and replace it with a better document that he claimed to have in his pocket. These statements brought him into difficulty and Justice Joseph Hawley gave the exminister a warning and released him. Then on 12 April 1782 a mob of laborers and husbandmen led by David Wells poured into the valley from the hill towns and petitioned the supreme judicial court to cease civil hearings since "the present proceedings of this court in the trial of civil causes will unavoidably convulse the nervous system of this state." But mob action did not lead to rebellion; the Northampton militia turned out and forced the rioters to return home. The authorities then arrested Ely for fomenting the riot. After his contrite confession, the judges jailed him for six months and fined him £250.[55]

While this original riot attracted little attention, an effort by a mob to release Ely from jail created consternation throughout the commonwealth. On 12 June 1782 an armed mob marched into Springfield, broke open the jail, and freed Ely. The local supporters of government turned out, pursued the rioters, and after a complicated series of scuffles and negotiations secured three hostages for Ely's return whom they lodged in Northampton jail. A few days later the rioters reappeared at Hatfield and marched on Northampton to free the hostages. Twelve hundred local militia men turned out and dispersed the rioters after the hostages refused to leave jail. These incidents frightened both the governor and the court. Hancock informed the legislature of the disturbances and the court permitted him to move the hostages from Northampton to a safer jail and paid the militia and deputies who had fought the mob. Finally on 27 June the court suspended the writ of habeas corpus for six months and permitted the governor and council to "apprehend and secure in any gaol . . . any person or persons

55. There are excellent secondary accounts of Ely's rebellion; see Taylor, *Western Massachusetts*, pp. 112-20; Robert E. Moody, "Samuel Ely: Forerunner of Shays," *New England Quarterly*, 5:105-34.

whose being at large may be judged by his Excellency and the Council, to be dangerous to the people and well being of this or any of the United States."[56] Because of these actions and the loyalty of the Hampshire militia, the county quieted down and supporters of the government remained in control of the Connecticut valley. But many westerners saw that violence could pay political dividends. Under pressure from rioters and conventions the senate accepted a measure relieving debtors and the court sent a committee to examine conditions in Hampshire County.

The presence of violence in the commonwealth during the early 1780s underlined the inability of the state's preparty political structure to alleviate economic, financial, and political conditions that drove at least some westerners to riot. When divisive issues arose, it was almost impossible, without parties or even lobbying organizations, to find outlets for resistance to certain policies in constitutional channels. The influence of years of revolutionary activity and war tended to legitimatize the use of violence and extralegal political activities. As soon as conditions became critical in the west or the General Court failed to act on western demands, rounds of conventions, designed to mobilize political sentiment, and incidents of violence broke out.

During 1785 and 1786 two developments created a critical condition in the western counties. Commercial recession resulted in a rapid increase in debt cases and many towns fell even further behind on their tax payments. At the same time political polarization between the more and less commercial-cosmopolitan towns increased and covered a much wider range of issues. By the spring and summer of 1786 the political tinder was dry; the summer session of the 1786 General Court ignited it; and the commercial-cosmopolitan interests and the state's leading politicians gasped in terror as their perfect republic went up in flames.

56. Hancock's message of 17 June 1782 is in Bacon, ed., *Supplement to Acts and Laws*, p. 141. The action of the general Court is in *Acts and Laws*, 27 June 1782, 2:6-7.

7

The Regulation

POLITICAL polarization, the growing frustration of the less commercial-cosmopolitan towns and interests with the workings of the
preparty system, the continued pressure from debts and new and
back taxes in the western counties, and the actions of the summer
session of the 1786 General Court combined to set off a political
explosion that almost destroyed the commonwealth. By early
1786 the most and the least commercial-cosmopolitan interests
faced each other on a broad political front on both national and
state financial and credit issues. The most commercial-cosmopolitan towns continued their drive to set the commonwealth's and
confederation's finances in order even if this meant granting supplemental funds to the confederation that would have to be collected through additional direct taxes. They also opposed any effort to use the impost and excise revenues for general state
expenses. Some of them looked forward to the eventual repayment of the state debt in specie. When the court ignored their
appeals for tax reductions, credit reforms, and paper currency, the
subsistence farmers became convinced that a conspiracy led by
wealthy speculators intended to seize control of the commonwealth and oppress the "little people." As their representatives
fought a losing battle in the General Court, the rural towns continued to petition for reform and organized county conventions to
hammer out programs and gather support. When these efforts
failed, violent men in the west and Bristol County mobilized farmers and laborers, who had lost confidence in the ability of their
government, to block or regulate the courts. They had no intention
of overthrowing the commonwealth and were seldom violent even
when confronting the crustiest placeholder or judge, but by bar-
ring the courts from sitting they effectively prevented the fulfill-
ment of contracts and the collection of back taxes. When the

"good people" in the west demonstrated a loss of faith by refusing to turn out against the Regulators, it became obvious that only reforms or military action would soothe or overawe the dissenting westerners.

The disagreement over the best course of action divided the commonwealth into four warring factions. At one extreme, a small but highly influential group of merchants, placeholders, and unemployed military men urged Bowdoin to crush the Regulation with military force, arguing that reforms would be interpreted as signs of weakness. They saw no reason for the western violence since everyone had an opportunity to use the constitutional channels of political protest. Many of them blamed Tories or dangerous anarchists for the western protests. A far larger and more broadly based group, also strongest in the commercial towns and among the more dynamic interests, shied away from a military response preferring to solve the problem by giving the westerners some minor reforms that would not harm the financial and fiscal programs and interests. The largest single group, spoken for by the representatives from the less commercial-cosmopolitan towns, deplored the violence of the Regulators while pushing for as many reforms as possible. Finally the Regulators and their allies, at the radical extreme, intended to agitate until the commonwealth granted their demands and gave them amnesty.

The choice of response to the Regulators was as divisive an issue as the financial program had been between 1780 and 1786. The fall 1786 session of the court passed some minor reforms that satisfied neither the Regulators nor those who wanted them crushed by force. In December and January of 1786 and 1787 the militants around Bowdoin finally prevailed upon him to send the militia into the western counties. Despite the objections of the western moderates, Lincoln marched, the Regulation collapsed, and it seemed that commercial-cosmopolitan militants had won a victory that would ensure the survival of the commonwealth's financial program and prevent even minor reforms. But they had won a battle only to lose a political war when the new General Court elected in 1787 scuttled the financial program so carefully constructed during the earlier 1780s. At that point the impact of both the Regulation and the spring 1787 election forced many of the commercial-cosmopolitan militants and moderates into the rapidly growing nationalist camp that pinned its hopes on the results of the Philadelphia Convention.

The spring of 1786 brought little relief for citizens and towns plagued with personal debts and back taxes. Both of these problems had serious political repercussions during the two years between 1786 and 1788. The consistently high numbers of suits brought for the repayment of debts led to agitation for stay legislation, the passage of a tender act, or some legislation that might suspend suits for debt for a particular period. The judicial system, now overburdened with debt suits, was exposed to attacks on the income and privileges of lawyers and the high fees charged by the court of common pleas which seldom settled suits. Publicists advocated wholesale reorganization that would make justice quicker and cheaper. As back taxes mounted, the court continued to vote additional levies which more and more communities and taxpayers found it difficult to pay. This resulted in the development of programs designed to reduce direct taxes, made the less commercial-cosmopolitan interests unreceptive to any sort of direct taxation for the national government, and intensified the appeal for some sort of legal tender which could be used to retire present and past taxes. During its summer 1786 session the court ignored the mounting debts and tax problem and instead continued the existing fiscal and taxation program, even voting supplemental funds for the use of the confederation.

Suits for the repayment of private debts had increased substantially in 1782 and had remained on a high level since 1784. During the three years of 1784 through 1786 the supreme judicial court handled 3,800 cases for the recognizance of debts that had been upheld by the courts of common pleas. State-wide this amounted to over 40 such cases for every 1,000 polls for the entire period. The rate in Worcester County, however, ran to over 100 cases per 1,000 polls and this, of course, did not include the many cases which never reached the supreme judicial court.[1] The December

1. Docket Books, Supreme Judicial Court, Worcester County, County Court House, Boston, Office of the Clerk, Suffolk, April term, 1785, pp. 111-81 and September term, 1785, pp. 87-156. Recognizance cases were those in which the defendent appealed a decision of the court of common pleas to the supreme court and then failed to continue his case in the higher court. This forced the plaintiff (creditor) to file a recognizance so that the supreme court could affirm the judgment of the court of common pleas.

The form ran as follows: "_____ of _____ in _____, _____, complained that at a Court of Common Pleas, held at _____ in and for the county of _____ on the _____ _____ he received judgment against _____, of said _____ for the sum of _____ Damages and costs, from which judgment the said _____ appealed to this

term of the court of the common pleas heard over 600 suits for debt per year between 1783 and 1786 in Worcester County and over 800 in Hampshire County in 1785 alone.[2] Worcester County had the most suits but in 1785, Bristol, Middlesex, and Suffolk counties all had much higher rates of recognizances per 1,000 polls than did the state as a whole.[3] The constantly high rate after 1783 naturally created all sorts of economic and political pressures, especially in Worcester County. The court system, almost overwhelmed by cases, seemed to need reform and agitators advocated restriction on fees, increasing the speed and decreasing the expense of trials, the regulation of lawyers, and the abolition of the courts of common pleas since all its cases could be appealed to the supreme judicial court. Strangely enough the situation improved slightly in 1786.[4] The number of recognizances increased only in Suffolk and Barnstable counties and, although the Worcester ratio remained at over 30 cases per 1,000 polls, this reflected a slight decline from 1785. During 1786 the number of suits decreased substantially in all the other counties led by Bristol which had a decline of almost 40 percent.[5] Although the decline alleviated the problem, it did not solve it. The rate had been extremely

---

court, and recognized to present his final appeal with effect but has failed to do so. Wherefore the complainant pray'd for affirmation of the said Judgement, with additional Damages; and costs of _____."

The data also include a handful of other types of debt suits brought to the supreme judicial court on appeal from the common pleas. The following table shows the coverage, by term, of the docket books for the period 1781-1786:

Volume	Terms Covered
1781–1782	Feb. 1781–Dec. 1782
1783	Feb. 1783–Dec. 1783
1784	Feb. 1784–Nov. 1784
1785	Feb. 1785–Nov. 1785
1786	Feb. 1786–Nov. 1786

2. Robert J. Taylor, *Western Massachusetts in the Revolution* (Providence, 1954), p. 127, and Robert A. Feer, "Shays' Rebellion" (Ph. D. diss., Harvard University, 1957-1958), pp. 60-61.

3. Notice the citation to the Docket Books, Supreme Judicial Court, for citations for 1785, fn. 1, this chapter.

4. See L. Kinvan Wroth and Hiller B. Zobel, eds., *Legal Papers of John Adams*, 3 vols. (Cambridge, Mass., 1965), 1:xxxviii-lii.

5. Notice the citation to the Docket Books, Supreme Judicial Court, for citations for 1786, fn. 1, this chapter.

high since 1783 and by 1786 many citizens, especially in Worcester County, wanted some major credit and judicial reforms.

As the burden of personal debts eased in 1786, the pressure of new and old taxes became even more unbearable. Worcester, Hampshire, Berkshire, and Bristol counties all had a higher than average rate of overdue taxes. By 1787 Bristol, Worcester, and Hampshire counties had a higher rate of back taxes actually out on execution than did any of the other counties. Bristol, Worcester, and Hampshire counties contained four-fifths of the towns with twice the state average per poll of taxes out on execution and over two-thirds of their towns had a higher than average amount of back taxes out on execution.[6] Newly levied taxes added pressure especially since the March 1786 act actually levied a higher than average tax per poll on the citizens of Worcester County.[7] Not only had Worcester, Hampshire, and Bristol been overwhelmed with their old taxes, but their citizens found also that almost two-thirds of the total bill for back taxes would have to be paid in specie which relatively few citizens possessed.[8] Table 47 gives a picture of the taxation and debt problems faced by these counties.

These heavy debts and high taxes naturally increased the political frustration of the less commercial-cosmopolitan western communities. Between October 1785 and March 1786 eighteen towns petitioned the General Court for reforms. The least commercial-cosmopolitan western group C communities accounted for over four-fifths of these petitions and all but one of the towns requested the issuance of paper currency.[9] Yet these efforts, like those of the earlier 1780s, had little impact. The court passed a

6. Taxes Out on Execution at the Death of Treasurer Ivers [1787], and Taxes Outstanding at the Death of Treasurer Ivers [1787], in Treasurer's Papers, Office of the Secretary, Boston (located in the attic of the capitol building in early 1964), list the total back taxes for every town in the state as of early 1787.

7. The 1786 tax act is in *Acts and Laws of the Commonwealth of Massachusetts, 1780-1797*, 11 vols. (Boston, 1890-1897), 23 Mar. 1786, 3:580-605.

8. Taxes out on Execution at the Death of Treasurer Ivers [1787], in Treasurer's Papers, Office of the Secretary, Boston, lists the various taxes, due in specie, for every one of the towns.

9. These petitions are listed in Feer, "Shays' Rebellion," pp. 541-42. The percentage of the petitions, between Oct. 1785 and Feb. 1786 that requested specific reforms were 94 percent to issue paper money, 28 percent in favor of a tender law, 6 percent to postpone courts, 6 percent to tax luxuries, and 6 percent to reorganize the courts.

TABLE 47
Debts and Taxes, 1783–1787

County	Per-Poll Amount of Various Taxes			Percentage of Towns with		Recognizances Per 1,000 Polls					
	On Execution (1787)	Overdue (1787)	Levied (1786)	Executions Against Them	Over £3.4 Due Per Poll	'82	'83	'84	'85	'86	Total, 1783-85
Bristol	£2.74	£7.26	£2.98	75%	25%	9	14	16	16	9	46
Middlesex	0.84	4.88	3.57	15	3	18	21	17	20	17	58
Worcester	3.73	7.66	3.27	67	52	17	16	34	32	30	81
Hampshire	2.65	6.64	2.70	67	29	8	5	8	6	2	19
Berkshire	1.14	8.01	2.87	32	4	1	4	15	13	15[a]	32
State average	£1.64	£5.94	£3.17	43%	22%	10	11	15	14	12	39

SOURCES: Polls from the Evaluation, 1784/86, in vol. 163 of the Massachusetts Archives, Office of the Secretary, Boston (cited hereafter as Evaluation, 1784/86). The polls, per county, are based on the extrapolations computed as described in ch. 3. Taxes on execution are from Taxes Out on Execution [1787], and overdue taxes are from Taxes Outstanding, Treasurer's Papers [1787]. The taxes levied in 1786 are from Acts and Laws of the Commonwealth of Massachusetts, 1780-1792, 11 vols. (Boston, 1890-1897), 3:580-605 (cited hereafter as Acts and Laws). Suits for debt are based on the Docket Books, Supreme Judicial Court, Clerk's Office, Suffolk County Court House, Boston.
a. Figure is for 1787.

new direct tax act that allocated revenues from the direct levies for the payment of interest on the state debt. It seemed that nothing would be done.

While these western towns worried, Benjamin Austin, a Boston merchant-manufacturer and son of an influential local politician, attacked lawyers and the legal profession. Attorneys, whose number had increased rapidly during the early 1780s, had never been popular and many citizens complained of their fees, their control over the profession through bar associations, their preference for intricate laws, and their growing political power. [10] In March 1786, Austin, writing as "Honestus," presented a program designed to check the power of this legal order by reducing fees and reforming the code. [11] Other publicists defended the lawyers and when Austin finally suggested the abolition of the profession, the debate assumed a scurrility unusual even for the 1780s. [12] Austin's crusade inspired newspaper essays on both sides and some towns adopted resolutions calling for lower fees, the recodification of the laws, and more control over attorneys. [13] Austin had only ex-

10. For some of the earlier pre-"Honestus" assults see *Massachusetts Centinel*, 16, 19 Nov. 1785, 18 Jan. 1786; Taylor, *Western Massachusetts*, pp. 134-35.

11. Thomas C. Amory, *Life of James Sullivan with Selections from His Writings*, 2 vols. (Boston, 1859), 1:188-89 gives identification. *Independent Chronicle*, 9, 13, 30 March 1786 gives the earlier numbers. See also Allen Johnson and Dumas Malone, eds., *Dictionary of American Biography*, 22 vols. (New York, 1928-1944) for Samuel Eliot Morison, "Jonathan L. Austin," 1:435.

The entire collection was later published as a pamphlet. There was also a spate of essays for other reforms. For usury see *Massachusetts Centinel*, 4 Jan. 1786. For a tender act see William A. Benedict and Hirman A. Tracy, *History of the Town of Sutton, Massachusetts; from 1704 to 1876* (Worcester, 1878), 9 Jan. 1786, p. 124; Rev. Abijah P. Marvin, *History of the Town of Lancaster, Massachusetts: From the First Settlement to the Present Time, 1643-1879* (Lancaster, 1879), pp. 108-09. For private debts see *Independent Chronicle*, 9 Mar. 1786. For paper money see fn. 9, this chapter.

12. *Independent Chronicle*, 27, 30 Mar., 13, 27 Apr. 1786; *American Herald*, 27 Mar., 17, 24 Apr., 8, 15 May 1786; *American Recorder*, 28 Apr. 1786; *Essex Journal*, 5 Apr. 1786; and *Massachusetts Centinel* 12 Apr. 1786.

13. *Worcester Magazine*, May 1786, p. 71; D. Hamilton Hurd, ed., *History of Norfolk County, Massachusetts, with Biographical Sketches of Many of Its Pioneers and Prominent Men* (Philadelphia, 1884), p. 347; Rufus King to Elbridge Gerry, 14 May 1786, in Charles R. King, *The Life and Correspondance of Rufus King Comprising His Letters; Private and Official. His Public Documents and His Speeches*, 6 vols. (New York, 1894-1900), 1:136.

pressed the debt-ridden yeoman's concern over high fees, the mystery of the law, and the superfluous court of common pleas.

Nevertheless, worsening conditions, petitions for paper money, and Austin's campaign were not enough to bring out the masses for the 1786 elections in which the commercial-cosmopolitan interests increased their strength in the General Court. John Hancock, Bowdoin's only possible competition, remained ill and James Sullivan, Hancock's hatchet man in the Bowdoin-Temple affair, made his peace with John Temple who had reappeared as a British consul in New York City. [14] Friends of Sam Adams sent up a trial balloon to test his political strength against Lieutenant Governor Cushing, but they quickly retracted it when Cushing's allies accused Adams of being an embezzler of public funds and an enemy of George Washington. [15] Turnout declined and Bowdoin secured 73 percent of the total vote, carrying every county but two—Bristol, where paper money agitation had seeped across the Rhode Island border, and Lincoln, at that time a center of strength for the Maine secessionists. He secured over 65 percent of the vote in Worcester, Hampshire, and Middlesex counties and failed to carry only 6 percent of the group A, 26 percent of the group B, and 17 percent of the group C towns. [16] Cushing ran ahead of the governor with 76 percent of the vote and carried every county. Thus the election for the highest offices substantiated James Warren's observation that "indeed when a man is once in, it is for life." [17]

Warren's adage also applies to the senatorial elections as the voters elected 32 of the 40 senators of whom 18 had served at least three years in the upper house. The court selected four new men when it filled the eight vacancies but in only one case did it replace an incumbent with a newcomer. The combination of judges of the common pleas and residents of the group A towns

14. *Massachusetts Centinel*, 7 Jan. 1786. James Sullivan to Rufus King, 29 Jan. 1786, a copy in the Sullivan Papers, Massachusetts Historical Society.

15. *Worcester Spy*, 9, 16 Mar. 1786; *Massachusetts Centinel*, 18 Mar. 1786; *American Herald*, 20, 27 Mar. 1786; *American Recorder*, 24, 28 Mar. 1786; and *Continental Journal*, 30 Mar. 1786.

16. Voting data is from the unpublished Abstracts of Votes for Governor and Lieutenant-Governor, Office of the Secretary, Boston, for 1786 (cited hereafter as Abstracts-Governor and Abstracts-Lt.-Governor, respectively).

17. Ibid., and James Warren to John Adams, 30 Apr. 1786, Warren-Adams Letters. W. C. Ford, ed., Massachusetts Historical Society, *Collections*, vols. 72-73 (1917-1925), 72:272-73.

sitting in the senate fell slightly from 68 percent in 1785 to
65 percent but the group A towns picked up strength on the council and their slight loss in the senate had little political effect.[18]
In the lower house the most commercial-cosmopolitan towns and
the placeholding justices did quite well in May 1786. The group A
towns sent 34 percent of the representatives, compared with
30 percent in 1785 and 33 percent for the entire 1780-1791 period. The combined strength of the justices and delegates from
these most commercial-cosmopolitan towns accounted for 56 percent of the total representation. The group A towns did not increase their actual numbers over 1785, but many group C towns
failed to send representatives and the proportion from the western
group C towns, for example, fell from 26 percent to 19 percent of
the total membership.[19] The proportion of representatives from
the future Federalist communities also increased slightly. In 1785
towns that would vote for the national Constitution sent 50 percent of the delegates to the lower house; in 1786 they sent 53 percent of the total.[20] The Maine towns which increased their representation at the urging of the Falmouth convention also added to
the strength of the most commercial-cosmopolitan interests in the

18. For lists of senators and results of the senatorial elections see *Acts and
Laws*, 3:623-24, for 1785; 4:267-68, for 1786. Unpublished Journals of the
Senate, Office of the Secretary, Boston (cited hereafter as Senate Journal),
25, 26, 27, 28 May 1785, pp. 3ff, and 31 May, 1, 2, 3, 6, 7 June 1786,
pp. 3ff. Judges are listed in Thomas Fleet and John Fleet, *Fleet's Pocket
Almanack for the Year of Our Lord 1786 . . . to Which Is Annexed the Massachusetts Register* (Boston, 1785) (cited hereafter as Fleet, *Register*) and ibid.,
1787 (Boston, 1786). Members of the council are in *Acts and Laws*, 3:623, for
1785 and 4:267 for 1786. The election of the council is in the Senate Journal, 27 May 1785, and 1, 2, 6, 7 June 1786.

19. For lists of representatives see the Unpublished Journal of the House of
Representatives available at the Office of the Secretary, Boston (cited hereafter as House Journal), 1785 and 1786, and *Acts and Laws* 3:622-26, for
1785 and 4:266-70, for 1786.

20. *Debates and Proceedings in the Convention of the Commonwealth of
Massachusetts, Held in the Year 1788, and Which Finally Ratified the Constitution of the United States* (Boston, 1856), (cited hereafter as *Proceedings in
the Convention*), 6 Feb. 1788, pp. 87-92, gives the final vote on ratification.
Towns whose representatives voted for the Constitution are listed as Federalist; communities whose delegates voted against it are listed as Antifederalist.
Several communities sent no delegates; these are listed as not voting and in a
few cases representatives from the same town divided over ratification; these
towns are listed as divided.

house, so, over all, those interests exercised a greater relative control of the 1786 court. [21]

The record of the summer session of the 1786 court reflected its composition. It further alienated the westerners by voting supplemental funds and defeating the use of the revenues from the state's impost and excise for paying general state expenses. During the session the voting lines looked almost like carbon copies of the earlier divisions on financial questions with the least commercial-

21. These Maine towns and representatives voted consistently in favor of programs backed by the most commercial-cosmopolitan towns. The following list gives the percentage of their votes that favored these programs on important roll calls between July and November 1786:

Vote One: 75 percent
Vote Two: 72 percent
Vote Three: 74 percent
Vote Four: 69 percent
Vote Five: 54 percent
Vote Six: 54 percent
Vote Seven: 86 percent

These votes were as follows:

Vote One: Whether the house will grant to the United States the supplementary funds agreeable to requisitions of Congress of 18 April 1783 and 16 Feb. 1786. (House Journal, 9 June 1786, pp. 69-70. Percentage of Yes vote)

Vote Two: Should the above pass to be engrossed? (Ibid., 30 June 1786, pp. 150-52. Percentage of Yes vote)

Vote Three: Should the above as amended pass to be engrossed? (Ibid., 30 June 1786, pp. 152-55. Percentage of Yes vote)

Vote Four: The house rejected the report of a committee recommending the use of revenue from the impost and excise for use only to pay the interest on the state debt. After this motion [based on the report] was defeated, a vote was taken on the motion to reconsider this vote [the rejection] and thus to accept the original report. (Ibid., 5 July 1786, pp. 167-69. Percentage of Yes vote)

Vote Five: Should the Governor's salary be reduced? [Was it constitutional to reduce his salary?] (Ibid., 19 Oct. 1786, pp. 274-75. Percentage of No vote)

Vote Six: Should the bill suspending the laws for the collection of private debts be passed. [This would suspend suits for private debts.] (Ibid., 26 Oct. 1786, pp. 294-95. Percentage of No vote)

Vote Seven: On motion to reconsider the previous affirmative vote to give the Supreme Judicial Court the authority to try certain offenders outside the county of their residence. (Ibid., 8 Nov. 1786, pp. 328-29. Percentage of No vote)

For representatives see Acts and Laws, 3:622-26; 4:266-70; House and Senate Journals for 1785 and 1786; Fleet, Register, 1786 (1785), and 1787 (1786), and Proceedings in the Convention, pp. 87-92.

cosmopolitan towns failing to prevent the passage of supplemental funds and having their efforts to use the impost and excise revenues for general expenses blocked by the senate.

The division over supplemental funds became the central issue during the session. In 1783 Congress requested the states to allow it to levy a 5 percent impost on imported goods and in addition to grant supplemental funds levied by an annual direct tax for a given number of years which would place the annual requisition on a permanent basis and give the Congress some control over direct taxation. [22] Since at least part of these revenues would be used to pay the interest and principal on the national debt, Bowdoin and the most commercial-cosmopolitan interests and towns supported passage of this plan. Naturally the less commercial-cosmopolitan interests opposed it since it would increase their direct taxes in order to pay off security holders who lived in other communities. A few opponents insisted that the grant should not be approved until Congress decided to pay off the debt at its market value instead of its face value—a solution completely unacceptable to the speculators and to the other most commercial-cosmopolitan interests. [23]

The potent combination of representatives from the most commercial-cosmopolitan towns, communities that would later vote for the national Constitution, and the District of Maine pushed supplemental funds through the court. (See table 48.) On 9 June, 57 percent of the representatives tentatively approved the granting of funds but on 30 June the measure hit an unexpected snag and 53 percent of the delegates voted against engrossing the bill. This unfavorable decision resulted from the defection of many delegates from the group B communities whose support for the proposal dropped by 17 percentage points. The proponents of the grant quickly passed a reconsideration of the vote to permit amendment, whereupon the house agreed to permit the harried taxpayers to pay supplemental direct taxes with indents issued for interest on the confederation's debt by the Continental loan of-

22. The best background is in E. James Ferguson, *The Power of the Purse: A History of American Public Finance, 1776-1790* (Chapel Hill, 1961), p. 166.

23. Bowdoin's message is in *Acts and Laws*, 2 June 1786, 4:902-09; and *Independent Chronicle*, 22, 29 June, and especially 17 Aug. 1786, that gives an account of the important debates for the entire session. For early agitation see "Lucius," *Independent Chronicle*, 1 Dec. 1785; John Adams to James Warren, 4 July 1786, in Warren-Adams Letters, 72:277, for the importance of the debt to Adams.

TABLE 48
Vote on Supplemental Funds, 1786

	Votes for			Changes in Vote from	
	Original Approval	Engrossing	Final Approval	Original Approval to Engrossing	Original to Final Approval
Towns					
Group A	76%	75%	82%	− 1%	+6%
Group B	51	37	47	−14	− 4
Group C	29	20	30	− 9	+1
Federalist	76	68	77	− 8	+1
Antifederalist	37	12	31	−25	−6
Maine	75	72	74	− 3	−1
Eastern group A	81	81	86	0	+5
Western group C	31	19	23	−12	−8
Justices	77	69	80	− 8	+3
Total vote	57%	47%	57%	−10%	0%

SOURCES: "Original Approval" in the unpublished Journals of the House of Representatives of the Commonwealth of Massachusetts, Office of the Secretary, Boston, 9 June 1786, pp. 69–70 (cited hereafter as House Journal). "Engrossing" in ibid., 30 June 1786, pp. 150–52. "Final Approval" in ibid., 30 June 1786, pp. 152–55. See also note 21.

ficers. The delegates from the group A towns, Maine, and the future Federalist communities and the justices sitting in the house threw their support behind the amended version and passed it with 57 percent of the total vote. With this solid base of support, the most commercial-cosmopolitan interests had forced another proposition upon the less commercial-cosmopolitan communities and the senate passed the measure with little debate. [24] Before the bill became law on 5 July 1786 the court, realizing that the act would be bitterly resented by the less commercial-cosmopolitan interests, added a lengthy apology for its passage. After all, the national debt had to be paid, the grant would not take effect until other states ratified the agreement, and part of the taxes could be paid in indents. [25] But this failed to convince the less commercial-cos-

24. See the votes in House Journal, 9 June 1786, pp. 69-70, and 30 June 1786, pp. 150-52 and 152-53. Also note fn. 20, this chapter.
25. *Independent Chronicle*, 17 Aug. 1786. The final legislation is in *Acts and Laws*, 5 July 1786, 4:37-53; also note James Bowdoin to Nathaniel Gorham, 24 June 1786, in Bowdoin-Temple Papers, Massachusetts Historical Society, *Collections*, 7th ser. 6:103-05.

mopolitan interests who now feared the specter of a Continental direct tax collected by national officials whom the towns could not control. After the passage of this act, a more powerful national government meant heavier and more efficient direct taxes to many citizens from the less commercial-cosmopolitan communities which explains much of the opposition to the new national Constitution in 1788. In their view the weak and controllable government of the commonwealth had levied exorbitant taxes and it would be even less likely that a powerful national government dominated by unknown aristocratic interests and controlling an army and a corps of tax collectors would be very responsive to their problems or demands.

The commercial-cosmopolitan interests also throttled all efforts at change and reform. (See table 49.) The less commercial-cosmo-

TABLE 49
Impost and Excise Reform, 1786

	Final Vote for Supplemental Funds	Vote Against Impost Reform	Change Between Two Votes
Towns			
Group A	82%	79%	− 3%
Group B	47	32	−15
Group C	30	19	−11
Federalist	77	74	− 3
Antifederalist	31	14	−17
Maine	74	69	− 5
Eastern group A	86	87	+ 1
Western group C	23	11	−12
Justices	80	67	−13
Total vote	57%	48%	− 9%

SOURCES: "Final Vote for Supplemental Funds" in House Journal, 30 June 1786, pp. 152–55. "Vote Against Impost Reform" in ibid., 5 July 1786, pp. 167–69. See also note 21.

politan interests proposed once again that at least part of the revenue from the impost and the excise be used for general state expenses. With some support from the justices and the group B and future Antifederalist towns, this bill passed in the house with 52 percent of the vote.[26] But the commercial-cosmopolitan inter-

26. House Journal, 5 July 1786, pp. 167-69. See fn. 20, this chapter. See *Independent Chronicle*, 29 June 1786, for criticism of a speech advocating a reduction in value of the consolidated securities to their market price.

est rejected the measure in the senate and after some complicated parliamentary maneuvering the court passed instead an act that extended the operation of the impost system until July of 1789 with the revenue being used only to meet the interest charges on the state debt.

Other efforts at reform failed even more dismally. The court, in two unrecorded roll call votes, overwhelmed a bill for paper money by 100 to 18 and defeated a bill permitting the evaluation of property seized for debt, similar to the 1782 act, by a vote of 89 to 35. The antilawyer agitation led the court to replace attorney Theodore Sedgwick with Samuel Holten in the state's delegation to the Continental Congress but the senate killed a bill regulating lawyers.[27] Nevertheless the court avoided completely alienating the least commercial-cosmopolitan interest by quietly interring a proposal made by Governor Bowdoin that the state should levy direct taxes amounting to over £380,000 per year in 1787, 1788, and 1789 in order to retire the state debt.[28] After passing supplemental funds, saving the speculators' income from the state impost, and defeating all efforts for change the Court gave up two crumbs of reform: (1) an act permitting Massachusetts citizens to pay debts owed in other states in the paper currency of that state—a measure aimed at the paper currency issued

27. *Independent Chronicle*, 17 Aug. 1786; Christopher Gore to Rufus King, 25 June 1786, in King, *Rufus King*, 1:138; Richard E. Welch, *Theodore Sedgwick, Federalist: A Political Portrait* (Middletown, Conn., 1965), pp. 40-41. For action in towns see *Plymouth Journal*, 6 June 1786, for Bridgewater; *Independent Chronicle*, 15 June 1786, for Stoughton; *Worcester Magazine*, June 1786, p. 129, for opposition of Newburyport to paper money; Ibid., June 1786, p. 134, for Dedham; *American Recorder*, 9 June 1786, for New Braintree; Hurd, ed., *Norfolk*, p. 347, for Braintree.

28. Bowdoin's message is in *Acts and Laws*, 2 June 1786, 4:910-13. The various acts that consolidated the state debt had also provided for the automatic levying of taxes for the repayment of the principal. These were supposed to become effective between 1785 and 1789. Under the terms of the legislation the treasurer had been ordered to issue his warrants for these taxes unless the court specifically ordered him not to carry out this action. The best brief description is in James Swan, *National Arithmetick, or Observations on the Finances of Massachusetts . . .* (Boston, 1786), p. 53. According to Swan the debt would become payable as follows (the amounts are rounded to the nearest £10,000): 1785: £110,000; 1786: £340,000; 1787: £360,000; 1788: £340,000; and 1789: £240,000. Swan proposed a complex plan involving a sinking fund which he claimed would repay the debt by 1803. Also see the Public Papers, Office of the Secretary, Boston, for the resolve of 7 July 1786, when the senate wished to levy an additional tax to pay off part of the principal. This was rejected by the lower house.

by Rhode Island; and (2) a decision to ascertain the amount of fees being collected by the various clerks of the courts of common pleas. [29] Then to add insult to injury the court decided, for the first time since the Revolution, not to hold a fall session at which additional grievances could be presented. [30]

This session aggravated an already tense situation. The court had passed supplemental funds, the senate had defeated at least two important reforms, and the house, much more influenced by the most commercial-cosmopolitan interests than usual, had opposed others. The most commercial-cosmopolitan towns had not packed the court; they had merely taken advantage of the apathy of the less commercial-cosmopolitan interests. With no pressure groups or lobbies to warn them, with the convention movement quiet in the west in 1785 and early 1786, with light turnouts for the 1786 election, it is not surprising that the court should have been unaware of the crisis it was creating. Indeed many observers believed that a tough attitude in the face of petitions and criticism would restore peace to the commonwealth. Few politicians could have answered the question "Z" posed in the *Independent Chronicle* of 20 July 1786: If the state was so quiet, why did so many people continue to complain?

The western and Bristol County towns reacted vigorously to the failure of the court to consider a redress of their grievances and their flood of complaints ran in the three channels well worn in the earlier 1780s. Western towns sent petitions to the court, instructed their representatives, and watched as their delegates haplessly opposed supplemental funds and supported the use of impost and excise revenues for general expenses. County conventions met, discussed grievances, petitioned the General Court, and attempted to formulate programs and mobilize political support. Finally rioters, encouraged by the growing distaste for the government among the "good people," assembled and used force to prevent the sessions of the court of common pleas.

In the western counties four vaguely defined attitudes toward these protests emerged. At one extreme, a small group of western placeholders and commercial-cosmopolitan towns opposed the

29. The legislation is in *Acts and Laws*, 8 July 1786, 4:68-69, and 28 June 1786, 4:301-02.

30. A study of the *Acts and Laws* for the period 1780-1786 shows that the court had always held a fall session (at least since 1780).

Regulation, frowned on the convention movement, and continued to support many of the programs of the most commercial-cosmopolitan interests in the General Court. During the summer session of the General Court these western group A communities cast 50 to 64 percent of their votes for supplemental funds. During both the summer and fall sessions they cast a much higher proportion of their votes with the most commercial-cosmopolitan interests than did the western group C towns. Several of these more commercial-cosmopolitan western communities refused to send delegates to local conventions and a number of leading placeholders stood resolutely against conventions or violence. Few Regulators lived in these communities and their militia often fought against the rioters. [31]

Moderate westerners who wanted political reform but deprecated violence involved themselves in legislative and convention

31. The following table gives the voting records of the western group A towns on the seven divisions between July and November 1786. See fn. 20, this chapter. Sources: House Journal, 9 June 1786, pp. 69-70, 30 June 1786, pp. 150-52; 30 June 1786, pp. 152-55; 5 July 1786, pp. 167-69; 19 Oct. 1786, pp. 274-75; 26 Oct. 1786, pp. 294-95; 8 Nov. 1786, pp. 328-29. The percentages show the votes cast with the commercial towns and interests.

For the refusal of some of these towns to send delegates to conventions and for the reaction of several western placeholders to the movement, see Taylor, *Western Massachusetts*, pp. 140-41, for Springfield, Cambridge, and other towns. See D. Hamilton Hurd, ed., *History of Worcester County, Massachusetts, with Biographical Sketches of Many of Its Prominent Men* (Philadelphia, 1889), p. 30, for Lancaster. See also Rev. John H. Lockwood, *Westfield and Its Historic Influences, 1669-1919*, 2 vols. (Springfield, 1922), 2:64; Seth Paddelford to Robert T. Paine, 8 Aug. 1786, Robert Paine Papers, Massachusetts Historical Society; Joseph Allen to William Cushing, 2 Sept. 1786, Cush-

| | Votes | | | | | | |
Towns	1	2	3	4	5	6	7
Western group A	55%	50%	64%	38%	40%	30%	55%
Western group C	31	9	23	13	17	17	17

ing Papers, Massachusetts Historical Society; Circular letter of Concord in *Massachusetts Gazette*, 12 Sept. 1786, signed by Joseph Hosmer; Theodore Sedgwick to [William] Whiting, 14 Sept. 1786, Massachusetts Archives, Office of the Secretary, Boston, 189:174-75; Sedgwick to Bowdoin, ibid., 190:284-86; Cotton Tufts to Abigail Adams, 14 Oct. 1786, Adams Papers, pt. 4, Adams Manuscript Trust; David Cobb to Bowdoin, 22 Oct. 1786, Massachusetts Historical Society, *Proceedings*, 2d ser., 1:76-77; Charles Storer to John Adams, 19 Aug. 1786, Adams Papers, gives the background on the town of Worcester's refusal to send a delegate.

activities. The less commercial-cosmopolitan interests whose representatives opposed the most commercial-cosmopolitan interests in
the General Court formed the nucleus of support for the convention movement. Many of the convention men who attended local
and county meetings had served in the General Court or had won
election to local militia commands, but although a few had commissions as justices of the peace almost none of them had served as
senators or common pleas judges. [32] These politicians hoped to use
the conventions to pressure the General Court into passing reforms, but the erosion of western popular support for the government played into the hands of a more radical group.

The more militant and radical westerners joined the Regulators.
Strongest in the poorer and more isolated group C communities,
they incorporated farm laborers, yeomen, and husbandmen into
ranks led by lower grade militia officers, discontented former Revolutionary War officers, a few justices, and, at most, one judge.

32. Several of the leading convention men held political office and would
later play an important role in state politics. The letter of Seth Paddelford to
Robert T. Paine, 8 Aug. 1786, Robert Paine Papers, lists several of these men
for Bristol County. Phanuel [Phenual] Bishop served in the state senate in
1788 and 1789 and ran for Congress in 1788-1789 and 1790-1792. Nathaniel
Leonard of Taunton had served in the lower house in 1780, would serve there
again in 1787 and 1788, and voted against ratification at the convention in
Feb. 1788. John Pratt sat for Mansfield in 1782 and 1784, would serve again
in 1787-1788, and also sat in the ratification convention.

Other sources list additional convention men. See especially William Lincoln, *History of Worcester, Massachusetts* (Worcester, 1837), p. 133; Hurd,
ed., *Worcester County*, 1:755; and Harold R. Phelan, *History of the Town of
Acton* (Cambridge, Mass., 1954) for the following leaders: Deacon Willis Hall
of Sutton, chairman of the Worcester County convention who represented
Sutton in 1782; Amos Singletary, of the same town, who served in the house
during 1781-1782 and 1783-1784, and who was to sit in the senate between
1787 and 1790. He became a leading Antifederalist speaker at the ratification
convention in 1788. John Fessenden of Rutland, who would attempt to
prevent Lincoln's march against the Regulators in early 1787, would serve in
the senate between 1787 and 1790. He had represented his town in the house
in 1780-1781, and 1784-1785. John Nutting, the chairman of a small Middlesex convention (see *Worcester Magazine*, Aug. 1786, p. 211), had been the
representative for Pepperill in 1781. Caleb Ammidown and Caleb Curtis of
Charlotte, Worcester County, had both served in the house and Curtis would
be the town's delegate to the ratification convention in 1788. Francis Faulk-
ner of Acton represented Acton-Carlisle in the house from 1782 through
1785, Samuel Reed of Littleton, Middlesex County, served as chairman of the
Middlesex convention and would serve in the house in 1787 and represent the
town at the ratification convention of 1788.

The Regulators expressed demands very similar to those of the conventions. They asked for stay legislation that would suspend the hearing of suits for debt, they wanted court sessions postponed, but they made no effort to overthrow the government. Indeed their violence was highly selective. With only one exception they refrained from attacking local placeholders or unpopular politicians. With few exceptions they assembled only to prevent the sessions of the court of common pleas. [33] In their own minds they were "regulating" the courts by postponing sessions, but they were not rebels out to change the social, economic, or political institutions of the commonwealth. They differed from the moderates only in their use of highly selective violence to achieve their political goals.

The westerners who remained apathetic composed the last and, perhaps even in 1786 and 1787, the largest single group. A large majority of westerners neglected to vote in 1786 and even after the Regulation about one-half of the qualified voters failed to appear at the polls. Many towns still sent no representatives to the court, housed no Regulators, and refused to send delegates to conventions. These communities, usually poor and relatively iso-

33. See Feer, "Shays' Rebellion," pp. 432-33, for a list of local officials indicted or convicted for supporting the Regulators. William Whiting was the only major placeholder indicted for his cooperation with the Regulators. Theodore Sedgwick, his accuser, was the only placeholder who was physically attacked by the rioters. Welch, *Sedgwick*, pp. 45-55, gives a secondary account. Also see Theodore Sedgwick to William Whiting, 14 Sept. 1786, Massachusetts Archives, 189:174-76; and Whiting to Sedgwick, 13 Sept. 1786, Robert Paine Papers. For the assault see Feer, "Shays' Rebellion," pp. 237-38. For an example of a Regulator (as compared to a convention's) petition, see Address to the People [Regulators], 7 Dec. 1786, Massachusetts Archives, 190:297. For persons involved in the regulation see the Black List or Rebels Gone from . . . in the Robert Treat Paine Papers which gives the names of suspected Regulators, by town, for the counties of Hampshire and Worcester. The list also gives the names of all the local militia officers who were suspected of cooperating with the Regulators. For Berkshire county see the Docket Books, Supreme Judicial Court, Berkshire county, March 1787 term, in Clerk's Office, Suffolk County Court House, Boston, p. 58, which lists indictments by town and social position. On 14 Dec. 1786, General Shepard, commander of the Hampshire district militia, estimated the number of "insurgents" by town for Hampshire county. His list is in Bowdoin-Temple Papers, Massachusetts Historical Society, *Collections*, 6th ser., vol. 9 (1897), 7th ser., vol. 6 (1907); 7th ser. 6:116-17, and contains around 970 names. Federalist and Antifederalist towns are determined by their vote on ratification in Feb. 1788.

lated, apparently possessed no local leaders willing or able to organize support for conventions, the Regulation, or the government. [34] So the three active groups fought for control of the west
while a large group of apathetic farmers looked on.

The goals and methods of the three active groups changed over
time and in response to conditions. The western placeholders and
commercial towns that had supported the commercial-cosmopolitan programs during the earlier 1780s shifted to a more moderate
position during the fall of 1786. Many leading western placeholders, while opposed to rioters and conventions, advised Bowdoin and his council to be lenient with the westerners and their
demands. Many argued that the riots had been blown up out of all
proportion to their danger by the eastern militants. The few western leaders who remained as bitterly opposed to riots and conventions as their eastern counterparts lost some of their influence
since the western commercial communities and interests generally
backed minor reforms in an effort to prevent further disturbances. [35]

The westerners who worked for reform through political action
in town meetings, county conventions, and the General Court petitioned the court both as individual towns and as conventions. In
the fall 1786 session of the General Court they introduced and
supported legislation that would ease the burden on debtors, reduce the load of direct taxes, eliminate the courts of common
pleas, move the capital from Boston, and reduce the salaries of
state officials. They opposed the harsh anti-Regulator legislation
proposed by the more militant commercial-cosmopolitan interests
and made constant appeals for leniency to Bowdoin and his council. These efforts resulted in some notable legislative successes during the fall session, but reform came too late to satisfy the Regu-

34. Voting analysis is based on the Abstracts-Governor, 1785, 1786, and
1787.

35. For the changed position of some westerners about the Regulators see
Thomas Dwight to John Lowell, 13 Dec. 1786, Massachusetts Historical Society, *Proceedings*, 1st ser., 5:15-16; William Shepard to James Bowdoin,
17 Dec. 1786, Bowdoin-Temple Papers, 7th ser., 6:119-20; Samuel Lyman to
Samuel Breck, 27 Dec. 1786, ibid., pp. 122-24; Shepard to Bowdoin, 30 Dec.
1786, ibid., pp. 126-27. The change in voting by representatives from the
western group A towns is shown in fn. 31, this chapter and in House Journal,
30 June 1786, pp. 152-55, for the passage of supplemental funds; ibid.,
19 Oct. 1786, pp. 274-75, for the governor's salary; and ibid., 26 Oct. 1786,
pp. 294-95, for the measure suspending suits for debt.

lators although it antagonized the commercial-cosmopolitan militants.

While the legislators worked, the western towns kept up a constant stream of petitions to the court. Between August 1786 and February 1787 twenty-six western and Bristol towns submitted twenty-seven petitions requesting the General Court to initiate various reforms. Over one-half of these petitions requested a reduction in the salaries of governmental officials and a reorganization of the courts, while over one-fourth asked for the postponement of court sessions, moving the capital from Boston, the reduction of taxes, and the regulation of lawyers. Nevertheless the upheaval of 1786 still had not unified the various groups of western communities. For example, over three-fourths of the group C towns but only one of the fifteen petitioning A and B towns requested the immediate postponement of court sessions. Differences also appeared along the lines of future divisions over the national Constitution as the Antifederalist towns petitioned for the postponement of court sessions and the reduction of taxes, while the future Federalist communities had much greater interest in the regulation of lawyers and the taxation of luxuries. [36]

The convention movement faced similar divisions. At least eight county conventions that had met between July 1786 and February 1787 petitioned for reforms different from those advocated by the individual towns and varying from convention to convention. One-half or more petitioned for a tender law, moving the capital from Boston, reducing the salaries of state officers, regulating lawyers, taxing luxuries, and the complete reorganization of the judicial system. [37] The convention movement had difficulty establishing a political power base. Several conventions attempted to coordinate their activities by sending special delegates to other conventions, and some established committees of correspondence, but little came from these efforts. The court at least discussed the varied demands, passed a law suspending suits for debt, established a committee to consider moving the capital, and published the detailed "Address to the People" explaining its policies. But the measures reducing Bowdoin's salary and using the impost and excise revenue for general state expenses, passed by the house, died in the senate, and the legislature took no action on

36. See Feer, "Shays' Rebellion," tables between pp. 543-46.
37. Ibid., which gives grievances presented by the more important conventions.

the other demands. Thus the moderates in the conventions got squeezed between the more conservative commercial-cosmopolitan groups and the radical westerners. While the court failed to implement much of their program, the Regulators continued to postpone the sessions of the courts.

Yet these Regulators who blocked the courts had no intention of destroying the social and political institutions of their commonwealth. A Regulator convention that met in Worcester in December 1786 presented a list of grievances much less sweeping than many listed by earlier conventions but they demanded the immediate postponement of the court sessions and amnesty for themselves.[38] Much of the Regulators' success depended on the large number of westerners who had become so dissatisfied with the government that they would not turn out to defend the unpopular courts. In 1782 the Hampshire militia had handled Ely and his followers, but in August and September 1786 the Worcester County militia commander informed the governor that "there did appear universally that reluctance in the people to turn out for the support of Government; as amounted in many instances to a flat denial; in others to an evasion or delay which amounted to the same thing."[39] The ineffectiveness of their representatives in the court and the spotty successes of the conventions convinced many westerners that only force might bring political results. So the "good people" stood aside and let the Regulators have their way.

But many influential placeholders and politicians in both the east and west failed to recognize the differences among the westerners or to perceive how highly selective the Regulators were in choosing their targets. They saw only that a serious conflagration had broken out, fanned by the conventions. Therefore, many lumped the Regulators and convention men together as dangerous rebels. The conventions and the outbreak of the Regulation in August and September raised a storm of criticism in the eastern press and among the commercial-cosmopolitan leaders. Even before the rioting began, the eastern press charged that "designing men" led the illegal and unconstitutional conventions that intended to overthrow the government. Once the riots started many easterners saw the west in open rebellion. Then writers accused the

38. See the Address to the People [Regulators], 7 Dec. 1786, Massachusetts Archives, 190:297.

39. Jonathan Warner to James Bowdoin, 3 Sept. 1786, Massachusetts Archives, 190:230.

conventions of aiding the rioters and accused both the conventions and the Regulators of Toryism, treason, and anarchy. They urged harsh action against the rebels in order to protect the commonwealth.[40] Rumors flew about the state and increased the tension. The people of Newburyport, miles from any disturbance, shivered and expected a nocturnal visit from the rebels.[41] Thomas Clarke informed Bowdoin that the rebels had petitioned the British Parliament and Artemas Ward warned the council that British emissaries galloped through the west attempting to stir up a civil war.[42] In response, George Brock, one of the few convention supporters in the eastern press, charged that only aristocrats opposed the conventions and urged the "little people" to "cut to the root of aristocratical privilege . . . which begins to manifest itself among the wealthy order of men in this state."[43] For many the struggle was between good and evil, between Tory-influenced rebels and aristocratic juntos. No wonder that it became more and more difficult for the various factions and groups in the state to even communicate, much less understand each others' goals and grievances.

The government, although warned as early as June 1786 that violence might occur in Bristol County, had been taken by surprise by the speed and effectiveness of the Regulation. County conventions met in Bristol and the western counties during July and August and in late August the Regulators began to block the sessions of the court of common pleas. By the second week in September the rioters had prevented the sessions of the common pleas in five counties as the local militia failed to defend these unpopular bodies.[44] The Regulators and other westerners be-

40. For some examples of this rhetoric see *Worcester Magazine*, Aug. 1786, p. 246; *Massachusetts Gazette* [Springfield], 22, 25 Aug. 1786; *American Herald*, 28 Aug. 1786; *Hampshire Herald*, 29 Aug. 1786; *Independent Chronicle*, 31 Aug. 1786; John Q. Adams, diary entry, 9 Sept. 1786, Adams Papers, pt. 1.

41. *Massachusetts Gazette* [Springfield], 22, 29 Sept. 1786.

42. Thomas Clarke to Bowdoin, 8 Sept. 1786, Massachusetts Archives, 190:238-40. Governor Bowdoin to Moses Gill, 8 Sept. 1786, in which Bowdoin requests Gill to investigate Clarke's fears, and Moses Gill to Bowdoin, 9 Sept. 1786, in ibid. Artemas Ward to Bowdoin, 12 Sept. 1786, ibid., p. 252, gives Ward's suspicions.

43. Brock's articles were printed under the name of "Attleborough" in the *Independent Chronicle*, 10, 31, Aug. 1786.

44. For the first warnings see Seth Paddelford to Robert T. Paine, 19 June 1786, and Zeph. Leonard to Paine, 1 Sept. 1786, both in Robert Paine

haved differently to the supreme judicial court which on its western circuit sat without incident at Worcester during the week of 19 September. A week later eight hundred militia turned out to protect this court at Springfield from some Regulators, but the judges adjourned the session because they could not impanel the required number of grand jurors. The judges themselves made the decision not to continue into Berkshire County.[45]

Bowdoin, his council, and important politicians who advised him found it difficult to take action against the rioters. At first on 2 September the governor and council decided to instruct the Worcester sheriff to defend the common pleas court and called on the militia commanders in the western and Bristol counties to help the sheriffs. When the militia refused to turn out, the Regulators were able to block the Worcester court.[46] At that point a special council urged the use of eastern militia to protect the Middlesex court at Concord, but Bowdoin, despite the arguments of Paine and the judges, decided that it would be illegal to march the Suffolk militia into Middlesex without a declaration of rebellion by the General Court. With no eastern militia available, the Regulators then blocked the Middlesex court.[47]

Papers. For the chronology and description of the early regulation see Taylor, *Western Massachusetts*, pp. 143-48; Feer, "Shays' Rebellion," pp. 180-82, 186-90, 197-99, 216-17. George R. Minot, *The History of the Insurrections in Massachusetts, in the Year 1786, and the Rebellion Consequent Thereon* (Worcester, 1788), is still a good account of the outlines of the regulation.

45. The supreme judicial court held a full session at Worcester. See Docket Books, Supreme Judicial Court, Worcester county, September 1786 term, pp. 354-404. During this term the court handled over 200 cases of "recognizances" of debts. For the activities at Springfield see Taylor, *Western Massachusetts*, pp. 143-46; *Worcester Magazine*, Sept. 1786, p. 303; and *Massachusetts Gazette* [Springfield], 29 Sept. 1786. For Berkshire see Taylor, *Western Massachusetts*, p. 146, and Theodore Sedgwick to Bowdoin, 5 Oct. 1786, Massachusetts Archives, 190:277-78 in which Sedgwick recommends the cancellation of the Berkshire session. The term *Regulator* will be used to describe those who blocked the courts for two reasons: (1) this is the term they used to describe themselves and (2) they never considered themselves in rebellion; they merely intended to "regulate" the court sessions.

46. Unpublished Records of the Council, available in the Office of the Secretary, Boston, 2 Sept. 1786, 29:481. The proclamation is on pp. 484-85. Letters to the militia major-generals are on p. 458. See also *Massachusetts Gazette* [Springfield], 5 Sept. 1786; Jonathan Warner to James Bowdoin, 3 Sept. 1786, Massachusetts Archives, 190-230; and Taylor, *Western Massachusetts*, p. 144.

47. Records of the Council, 7 Sept. 1786, 29:486. This special council was composed of Samuel Adams, Robert T. Paine, the judges of the supreme

Bowdoin's apparent moderation did not include any concessions to the rioters during the fall session of the 1786 general court which had originally been called by the governor to discuss the latest congressional requisition. In his opening address Bowdoin declared that there had been "no sufficient or justifiable reason" for the riots and urged the court to vindicate the injured dignity of the commonwealth.[48] The next day he rubbed salt in some old western wounds by recommending that the court levy $324,000 in specie taxes and $200,000 collected in indents so that the state could pay its share of the congressional requisition by July 1787.[49] Bowdoin's proposals received the support of the commercial militants who wanted to crush the rebellion with military force. "Civis," an essayist, summed up their program: a declaration of rebellion and martial law and only then a discussion of grievances.[50]

---

judicial court, Benjamin Lincoln, Samuel Phillips, and all the council members available in Boston. The Hancockites, i.e., Thomas Cushing, Hancock, and James Sullivan were not present and neither were any representatives from any of the conventions in Bristol or the western counties. For the activities of this special council see ibid., 8 Sept. 1786, 29:491; 12 Sept. 1786, 29:488; 10 Sept. 1786, 29:489; 11 Sept. 1786, 29:491; 12 Sept. 1786, 29:492-96; *Massachusetts Gazette*, 12, 15 Sept. 1786; and Feer, "Shays' Rebellion," pp. 197-99, 203-07.

For the response of the Bowdoin administration see Feer, pp. 201-02, where he argues that the governor behaved legally and backed civilian authority but also shows that he had no advisors outside of a very narrow interest group. For the legal suggestions of a leading attorney, see "Observations" of Theophilus Parsons [August 1786], Bowdoin-Temple Papers, 6:108-11, in which he argues that a mob assembling under arms was an illegal assembly that could be dispersed with force. Parsons claimed that he had shown his suggestion to the judges who had not disapproved it.

48. The special fall session of the General Court was originally called to consider the congressional requisition for 1786. *Massachusetts Gazette*, 29 Aug. 1786, and Records of the Council, 24 Aug. 1786, 29:479. Ferguson, *Power of the Purse*, pp. 225-226, gives the background for this requisition. Bowdoin's opening address is in *Acts and Laws*, 29 Sept. 1786, 4:927-33.

49. Bowdoin's financial message is in ibid., 29 Sept. 1786, 4:933-36.

50. "Civis" in *Massachusetts Gazette*, 6 Oct. 1786; Henry Jackson to Henry Knox, 28 Sept. 1786, Knox Papers, Massachusetts Historical Society; and Samuel Dexter to James Bowdoin, 3 Oct. 1786, Bowdoin-Temple Manuscripts, Massachusetts Historical Society. Dexter believed that the court should show as much energy as "can consist with a constitution which, though excellently calculated for good christians [*sic*] and philosophers, is by far too democratical for the ignorant and unprincipled multitude. . . ." For some examples or earlier suggestions and actions see Peter Thatcher to

The court rejected Bowdoin's advice and, plagued by the same divisions that had developed during the earlier 1780s, attempted to hammer out a compromise program. The delegates from the most commercial-cosmopolitan interests and towns voted against fiscal and political reforms, the senate played its customary pro-commercial-cosmopolitan role, and the representatives from the less commercial-cosmopolitan towns voted for change and against a harsh reaction to the Regulation. These conflicting forces pieced together a program that attempted to stop the riots by force while conciliating more moderate westerners with some financial and credit reforms. The house quickly and unanimously expressed its abhorrence of "certain unwarranted and outrageous proceedings" in the west and approved Bowdoin's conduct during the September crisis.[51] It later passed an act that authorized any magistrate or justice to warn disorderly or armed crowds to disperse and gave these officials the authority to call on the sheriff or local militia for assistance in dispersing mobs. The senate strengthened the measure by increasing the fines on individuals who refused to aid the sheriff or militia in dispersing crowds and the act eventually passed without a roll call vote.[52] A harsher punitive measure, the suspension of habeas corpus, ran into more difficulties. After some complicated parliamentary maneuvering, an act, very similar to the one passed in July 1782, emerged from the court which gave the governor and the council the authority to jail all "persons whatsoever" who in their opinion would be dangerous to the "safety of the Commonwealth" and denied such individuals the right to habeas corpus procedures until 1 July 1787.[53] Toward the end of

---

Thomas Cushing, 15 Sept. 1786, Cushing Papers, where Thatcher accused Bowdoin and the council of vacillation and argued that this lack of action would advance Cushing's career. The town of Boston took a firm stand against the Regulators. See *Reports of the Record Commissioners of the City of Boston*, 39 vols. (Boston, 1876-1909), 8 Sept. 1786, 31:125ff., and *Massachusetts Gazette*, 15 Sept. 1786, which gives Bowdoin's reply to Boston's circular letter. The already cited letter from Thatcher to Cushing gives information about the divisions in the town meeting that approved the circular letter.

51. House Journal, 4 Oct. 1786, pp. 228-30; 5 Oct. 1786, pp. 235-36.

52. The legislation is in *Acts and Laws*, 28 Oct. 1786, 4:87-90. Senate action is in Senate Journal, 25, 26, 27, 28 Oct. 1786.

53. *Acts and Laws*, 10 Nov. 1786, 4:102-03; *Massachusetts Gazette*, 20 Oct., 3 Nov. 1786; Senate Journal, 12, 13, 14, 30 Oct., 9, 10 Nov. 1786.

the session the court passed its harshest and most bitterly debated repressive legislation, an act that gave the Regulators until 1 January 1787 to surrender and take the oath of allegiance to the government. (See table 50.) All who took the oath would be in-

TABLE 50
Voting on Supplemental Funds and Reconsideration on Trials

Towns	Votes for Supplemental Funds	Votes Against Reconsideration
Group A	82%	79%
Group B	47	44
Group C	30	30
Total	57%	54%
Eastern group A	86%	89%
Western group C	23	17
Western group A	64	55
Maine	74	86
Federalist	77	73
Antifederalist	31	29

SOURCES: "Voting for Supplemental Funds" in House Journal, 30 June 1786, pp. 153–55. "Voting Against Reconsideration," in ibid., 8 Nov. 1786, pp. 328–29.

demnified from prosecution but those who refused would be tried in any county "where law and Justice may be administered" instead of their county of residence.[54] The group B and C towns attempted to have the house reconsider the section providing for trial outside the county of residence, but despite the fact that they cast 56 percent and 70 percent respectively of their votes for reconsideration the group A towns cast 79 percent and the Maine towns 86 percent of their votes against it and carried the day. The vote on this measure was almost identical to the lineup on the final vote approving supplemental funds during the summer session and reflected the continuation of the former political divisions even in a period of crisis. But the court refused to go further in repression; it passed no declaration of rebellion and declined to declare martial law in the west, although both measures had been

54. *Acts and Laws*, 15 Nov. 1786, 4:111-13. Vote is in House Journal, 8 Nov. 1786, pp. 328-29.

TABLE 51
Shift of Support: Passage of Supplemental Funds
and Suspension of Suits for Debt

Towns	Votes for Supplemental Funds	Votes Against Suspension	Change
Group A	82%	68%	-14%
Group B	47	26	-21
Group C	30	31	+ 1
Total	57%	42%	-15%
Eastern group A	86%	80%	- 6%
Western group C	23	17	- 6
Western group A	64	30	-34
Maine	74	71	- 3
Federalist	77	55	-22
Antifederalist	31	26	- 5

SOURCES: "Voting for Supplemental Funds" in House Journal, 30 June 1786, pp. 152–55. "Voting Against Suspension" in ibid., 26 Oct. 1786, pp. 294–95.

urged by more militant members of the commercial-cosmopolitan interests.[55]

The court balanced these repressive measures with several reforms that reduced the load of taxes and the pressures of private debts on the western and less commercial-cosmopolitan interests and towns. The court rejected Bowdoin's scheme to levy new and heavier direct taxes; it established a mint in order to pump some additional specie into the economy; and it reduced the load of overdue back taxes by permitting the payment of specie taxes levied prior to 1784 in certain specified types of provisions.[56] In

55. For examples of this pressure see James Sullivan to John Adams, 12 Oct. 1786, in Amory, *Sullivan*, 1:128-29; Cotton Tufts to John Adams, 14 Oct. 1786, Adams Papers, pt. 4; James Swan to Henry Knox, 26 Oct. 1786, Knox Papers. The absence of a declaration of rebellion was significant and important; significant because it proved that the militants did not have absolute control over the court, and important because it led to later criticism of Bowdoin and his council when they took military action against the Regulators without the actual authority of the General Court.

56. *Acts and Laws*, 11 Nov. 1786, 4:387, and 8 Nov. 1786, 4:90-97. Also see the Public Papers in the Office of the Secretary, Boston, for the act of 8 Nov. 1786. Swan, *National Arithmetick*, pp. 70-72, described a plan similar to that approved by the court that envisioned the payment of provision taxes into a sinking fund which could be used to retire the principal of the state debt by the early 1800s. Another resolve of 17 Nov. 1786, *Acts and Laws*, 4:400, added potashes as a commodity that could be received for back taxes.

order to reduce the financial strain it established a gigantic land lottery for eighteen thousand square miles of Maine land in the hope of collecting £163,000 in specie and state-consolidated securities. It finally decided to use part of the impost and excise revenues for the payment of general state expenses.[57] The house passed a measure that allocated 50 percent of these revenues to general expenses, but the senate, as usual, rejected this and the two houses eventually accepted a compromise that allocated one-third of the revenue for current state expenses.[58] The extension of assistance to debtors resulted in a division within the house and a bitter dispute with the senate. When a joint committee reported a bill suspending suits for the collection of debts for a brief period, the senate declared that such a suspension would violate the 1780 constitution and the 1783 peace treaty. The house refused to accept the senate's arguments, insisted on reform, and joined with the senate in appointing another joint committee.[59] This new committee again recommended the passage of legislation suspending the collection of debts for a limited period. In the house a significant number of representatives from the group A and B towns swung over to support the suspension, and the bill passed despite the fact that 68 percent of the group A and 71 percent of the Maine representatives voted against it.[60] (See table 51.) The senate refused to accept this measure and forced the appointment of a third joint committee which recommended suspension of suits for debt. The senate finally, after reducing the term of the measure to eight months, capitulated and passed it.[61] The final act

57. *Acts and Laws*, 9 Nov. 1786, 4:97-102. The legislation provided for the sale of 2,720 tickets at £60 each. Prizes varied from 320 acres to an entire township.

58. Ibid., 17 Nov. 1786, 4:116-17. This new procedure was to become effective on 1 Jan. 1787. Also see the *Worcester Magazine*, Oct. 1786, p. 362, and *Massachusetts Gazette*, 10 Nov. 1786.

59. See the comments in the *Independent Chronicle*, 19 Oct. 1786; *Worcester Magazine*, Oct. 1786, p. 362. Action in the house and senate may be followed in Senate Journal, 4 Oct. 1786, for the appointment of the joint committee; 10 Oct. 1786, for the senate's order for the committee to report; and 17 Oct. 1786, for the senate's action in regard to the treaty and the 1780 constitution.

60. The new joint committee is covered in Senate Journal, 18 Oct. 1786. The roll call is in the House Journal, 26 Oct. 1786, pp. 294-95.

61. The struggle between the house and senate is covered in Senate Journal, 4 Nov. 1786, 5 Nov. 1786, 9 Nov. 1786, 10, 11, 13, and 15 Nov. 1786. Additional information is in *Massachusetts Gazette*, 15 Nov. 1786; and *Independent Chronicle*, 2 Nov. 1786.

suspended all actions for the collection of debts for eight months unless the creditor agreed to accept the tender of impartially valued real or personal property. Although the senate exempted all debts due to the Massachusetts Bank and to British creditors, and retained the payment of specie interest on personal debts, the act did provide considerable relief for westerners. The blocking of the courts in 1786 and the extension of the suspension act meant that few new debt cases would be filed until the summer of 1788.[62]

While the court, led by the house, passed some fiscal and credit reforms, the senate blocked all efforts at any basic institutional changes. A joint committee recommended the abolition of the court of common pleas, but the senate refused to accept the report. Both houses recommitted it, and it died in committee.[63] The senate also blocked efforts by the house to reduce fees and defeated a bill that would have prohibited collectors of impost and excise from sitting in the General Court.[64] It refused to reduce Bowdoin's salary. The cut backed by 61 percent of the lower house and supported by 76 and 73 percent respectively of the delegates from the group B and C towns failed to pass the upper house.[65] The senate did pass an act permitting debtors to confess their debts before justices of the peace who could then issue attachments against them without the creditors going through the costly procedures of the common pleas. With the house, the senate appointed a committee to consider a new location for the capital, but these measures were the limited extent of judicial and institutional reform.[66]

62. The final legislation is in *Acts and Laws*, Nov. 1786, 4:113-16. Table 66 shows the tremendous decline in debt cases brought before the supreme judicial court after the passage of this law (and its extension in 1787).

63. The discussion between the two houses is covered in Senate Journal, 4 Oct. 1786 and 20 Oct. 1786.

64. Senate Journal, 11 Nov. 1786.

65. House Journal, 19 Oct. 1786, pp. 274-75; *Massachusetts Gazette*, 27 Oct. 1785.

66. The legislation is in *Acts and Laws*, 15 Nov. 1786, 4:105-11. There is a discussion in *Massachusetts Gazette*, 27 Oct., 3 Nov. 1786. Under the provisions of this act a debtor could confess his debt to a justice of the peace after his creditor had brought suit. This would, in effect, save the debtor the fees of the common pleas court. If the debtor refused to confess the debt the case would be sent to referees and only if their decisions was not acceptable to either of the parties would the creditor be permitted to institute a suit before the common pleas.

The court completed its session by publicizing its repression-reform program to the electors in the lengthy "Address to the People." In this document the court analyzed the condition of the state, urged the payment of both the state and national debts, claimed that state expenses had been light and that governmental officials had not been overpaid, and justified its financial program of the earlier 1780s. It assailed paper money, upheld the morality of paying private debts, condemned the evils of luxurious living, vilified the Regulators, and called upon the westerners to support the commonwealth. In brief, the court, despite some reforms, defended its program of the earlier 1780s and held out little hope for additional changes. [67]

Considering the internal divisions within the court, the over-representation of the commercial-cosmopolitan interests, and the state of emergency within the commonwealth, the delegates did a relatively effective job. They provided important financial and credit reforms that, if they had been implemented during the summer session, would probably have prevented the Regulation, and they refused to be overly harsh against the westerners. At first glance it seemed that the moderates had won, and that conditions, after a brief period, might return to normal. But unfortunately these policies had failed to mollify the extremists; the Regulators wanted complete amnesty, while the commercial militants itched to use military force against the rebels to prove the strength of the new republican government.

The more moderate westerners in the convention movement accepted the policies of the court. After October the movement began to die down. On 11 November a Hampshire County convention met, declared the court of probate to be a grievance, appointed a committee to correspond with other conventions, and adjourned till January. In late November the Worcester convention held another session, deplored the activities of the Regulators, reaffirmed the constitutional rights of the conventions, and entreated the western towns to send full delegations to the lower house to push for further reforms. [68] But none of these conven-

---

67. The Address to the People [Regulators] is in *Acts and Laws*, 14 Nov. 1786, 4:142-64. Debts are covered on pp. 142-46, taxes on 147-53.

68. These activities are covered in *Hampshire Gazette*, 15, 29 Nov. 1786; *Massachusetts Gazette*, 3, 28 Nov., 13 Dec. 1786. *Worcester Magazine*, Nov. 1786, pp. 404-06; and Rev. Abijah P. Marvin, *History of the Town of Winchendon* (Winchendon, 1868), p. 189.

tions suggested any really new or more radical proposals and, indeed, all failed to reiterate their broader demands of August and September.

Despite the fading of the convention movement, the commercial militants pushed for harsher action. Henry Jackson, Henry Knox, Jeremy Belknap, Samuel Adams, Cotton Tufts, Christopher Gore, James Sullivan, and many other leaders agreed that the government must uphold its dignity against the Regulators.[69] Knox spread reports of the rebellion throughout the nation, and, thanks to his efforts, Congress authorized the recruiting of troops, purportedly against the western Indians, but actually for use against the Massachusetts rebels.[70] Henry Jackson, an unemployed military associate of Knox, received command of the Massachusetts contingent which he wanted to use against the Regulators.[71] As time passed, the social, judicial, and intellectual institutions of the state threw their weight against conventions and Regulators and the militant spirit grew rapidly. The Society of the Cincinnati pledged its support to the government as long as it upheld the sacred nature of public faith and credit. An association of Christian ministers charged that the rioters prevented the state and nation from doing justice "on the payment of *national* and *personal* debts."[72] Judges harangued grand juries about the evils of conventions and paper money, and warned their hearers that the Regulators wanted to divide all property equally among their supporters.[73] Journalists harried the conventions and the Regulators

69. James Sullivan to John Adams, 12 Oct. 1786, in Amory, *Sullivan*, 1:128-29; Jeremy Belknap to Hazard, 25 Oct. 1786, Belknap Papers, 6th ser., 4:446; Christopher Gore to Rufus King, 7 Nov. 1786, in King, *Rufus King*, 1:193-96; Richard Cranch to John Adams, 3 Oct. 1786, Adams Papers pt. 4; Stephen Higginson to Henry Knox, 23 Nov. 1786, Knox Papers; Rufus King to Elbridge Gerry, 5 Nov. 1786, King, *Rufus King*, 1:192-93; James Swan to Henry Knox, 26 Oct. 1786, Knox Papers; Cotton Tufts to John Adams, 14 Oct. 1786, Adams Papers, pt. 4.

70. There are two excellent secondary accounts of Knox's efforts. See Joseph P. Warren, "The Confederation and Shays' Rebellion," *American Historical Review*, 11:42-67, and Robert A. East, "The Massachusetts Conservatives in the Critical Period," in Richard B. Morris, ed., *The Era of the American Revolution* (New York, 1939), pp. 380-86.

71. Henry Jackson to Henry Knox, 11 Dec. 1786, Knox Papers; and East, "Massachusetts Conservatives," 382-86.

72. *Massachusetts Gazette*, 13, 24 Oct. 1786, 10 Nov. 1786; and *Salem Mercury*, 4 Nov. 1786.

73. *Worcester Magazine*, Nov. 1786, pp. 406-09; *Massachusetts Gazette*, 14 Nov. 1786; *Salem Mercury*, 18 Nov. 1786.

in the press. The authorities made the situation even more one-sided by arresting George Brock, a defender of conventions, for sedition.[74]

The continued activities of the Regulators added to these calls for their repression by force. In October, Regulators attempted to steal cannon from Dorchester Neck, freed a prisoner from the Worcester jail, almost mobbed Theodore Sedgwick in Berkshire County, and about 130 turned out to block the Bristol County Court of Common Pleas.[75] This latter effort failed as General David Cobb with 375 militia faced down the rioters, and the court met as scheduled.[76] Bowdoin, cheered by this development, ordered out 2,000 eastern militia to defend the unthreatened supreme judicial court at Cambridge and the council then decided to defend the common pleas courts scheduled for 28 November and 6 December at Cambridge, Salem, Worcester, and Barnstable.[77] When the Middlesex court met without interruption, the governor decided to crush the weakened Regulators in that county by arresting certain leaders. Some Suffolk militia, led by Colonel Benjamin Hitchborn, marched to Groton and arrested four important rebels.[78] But the council decided to make no effort to protect the

74. For examples of the rhetoric see *Worcester Magazine*, Sept. 1786, pp. 295-98, Oct. 1786, p. 358; *Massachusetts Gazette*, 17, 24, 30 Oct., 7 Nov. 1786; *Hampshire Gazette*, 20 Sept., 4, 11 Oct., 1, 15, 22 Nov. 1786; *American Herald*, 3 Oct. 1786; *Independent Chronicle*, 5, 12, 19 Oct., 2 Nov. 1786; *American Museum*, Oct. 1786, pp. 315-20; *Salem Mercury*, 14, 21 Oct., 4 Nov. 1786. The Brock affair is covered in Leonard W. Levy, *Freedom of Speech and Press in Early American History* (New York, 1963), p. 207, and *Massachusetts Gazette*, 3 Nov. 1786. Petition of George Brock to Governor Bowdoin, 1786, and George Brock to Robert T. Paine, both in Robert Paine Papers, give further details.

75. *Massachusetts Gazette*, 13, 20 Oct. 1786; *Worcester Magazine*, Oct. 1786, p. 342; Sedgwick to Governor Bowdoin, 5 Oct. 1786, Massachusetts Archives, 190:277-78. The best secondary account of the brawl in Berkshire county is in Stephen T. Riley, "Dr. William Whiting and Shays' Rebellion," American Antiquarian Society, *Proceedings*, n.s. 66:119-66.

76. The affair in Bristol County is in Records of the Council, 21 Oct. 1786, 32:15-16; Governor Bowdoin to David Cobb, 21 Oct. 1786, in ibid. Cobb's report is in David Cobb to Governor Bowdoin, 22 Oct. 1786, Massachusetts Historical Society, *Proceedings*, 2d ser., 1:76-77.

77. *Massachusetts Gazette*, 3 Nov. 1786.

78. The background for this decision is in "Draft of an Opinion by Judge Lowell, 1786," Massachusetts Historical Society, *Proceedings*, 1st ser., 13:129-30. See Records of the Council, 27 Nov. 1786, 30:38-40; 28, 30 Nov., pp. 40-41, 44-46; *Massachusetts Gazette*, 28 Nov. 1786; Feer, "Shays' Rebellion," pp. 318-22, and especially p. 322 for the rumors of atrocities that spread after the raid.

Worcester court on 6 December when General Warner informed it that his local militia remained unreliable.[79] When Regulators led by Shays at Worcester on 5 December were faced by a body of local militia mobilized without orders, it seemed that violence might occur but a severe blizzard cooled everyone off. On 8 December the judges arrived to find 350 Regulators assembled and adjourned the court until 23 January. The snowbound Regulators wiled away their time in their own convention protesting against the expensive methods of collecting debts, the suspension of the writ of habeas corpus, and the tax exemptions given to government securities.[80] As they returned home, William Hartley became the rebellion's first fatality when he stumbled into a snow drift and froze to death. Thomas Dwight, an important Springfield merchant, wrote that the Regulators were "chopfallen" by their experience and informed his friend John Lowell that "there would not be the least danger in returning to Boston by this road [Springfield]" since the Regulators had lost all interest in "offering injury to anybody."[81]

The weakness shown by the Regulators encouraged the militants around Bowdoin to completely crush them by military force. The capture of Shattuck by the militia and the retreat from Worcester emboldened the militants and by 2 December the council had apparently begun to plan some form of operation against the Regulators.[82] While the council laid the groundwork, Bowdoin gave Benjamin Lincoln a commission as justice of the peace throughout the commonwealth, and Henry Knox, Jackson, and others worked to persuade the monied men of Boston to put up the cash to finance a state or Continental expedition into the west.[83]

79. Records of the Council, 1, 2 Dec. 1786, 30:47-51.

80. A good secondary account is in Feer, "Shays' Rebellion," pp. 324-29. Feer then notes that little was heard from the Regulators for the next three weeks in December (see esp. p. 330).

81. Thomas Dwight to John Lowell, 13 Dec. 1786, Massachusetts Historical Society, *Proceedings*, 1st ser., 5:15-16; Artemas Ward to Bowdoin, 7 Dec. 1786, Shays' Rebellion Manuscripts, Massachusetts Historical Society. *Massachusetts Gazette*, 8 Dec. 1786.

82. Nathaniel Gorham to Henry Knox, 13 Dec. 1786, Knox Papers; Records of the Council, 2 Dec. 1786, 30:49-50.

83. Henry Knox to Henry Jackson, 3 Dec. 1786, Knox Papers, and the excellent secondary account in East, "Massachusetts Conservatives," pp. 384-86, for the failure of Jackson's efforts to raise money when the merchants decided to finance the Lincoln expedition.

Bowdoin and the council decided to make the 23 January 1787 meeting of the Worcester court the showdown between the commonwealth and the Regulators. When General Shepard, the militia commander in Hampshire, assured Bowdoin that he could mobilize 2,000 militia to join Lincoln's easterners at Worcester, the governor and his advisors saw that they had the means to destroy the Regulation and arrest its leaders. They paid almost no attention to the rumor that the rebels wanted to seize the arsenal at Springfield. Indeed, General Knox, who had been spreading the rumor, informed Shepard that his militia would not be permitted to use the weapons for, as he assured Nathaniel Gorham, it was unlikely that the rebels would bother the arsenal if the militia also left it alone.[84] Knox was right. On 26 December 300 Regulators moved into Springfield to block the session of the common pleas and the judges, after having a drink with the Regulator leaders in a nearby tavern, adjourned the court. The Regulators offered no insult to any judge or placeholder, and although they had the run of the town for two days, they made no effort to seize the arsenal.[85]

During the first week in January, Bowdoin, the council, and the militants perfected their plans. The council authorized Shepard and the sheriff of Hampshire to issue warrants for the arrest of the leading Regulators about 23 January and to transport these prisoners to Boston.[86] The Boston merchants backed these militant efforts by subscribing over £5,000 to pay for the expedition with twenty-five men alone contributing £2,500.[87] With money available the council decided to call out a total of 5,200 militia, 2,000 from the eastern counties, 1,200 from Worcester, and 2,000 from

84. Feer, "Shays' Rebellion," pp. 333-37, has a different interpretation of the council's actions. For the preparations see James Bowdoin to William Shepard, 14 Dec. 1786, Knox Papers. William Shepard to Knox, 17 Dec. 1786, in ibid.; "Shepard's Memorandum Concerning the Number of Regulators in Hampshire County," in Bowdoin-Temple Papers, 6:116; Henry Knox to Nathaniel Gorham, 24 Dec. 1786, Knox Papers.

85. Eleazer Parker to Governor Bowdoin, 26 Dec. 1786, Bowdoin-Temple Papers, 6:121-22; Samuel Lyman to Samuel Breck. 27 Dec. 1786, ibid., pp. 122-24; Hampshire Gazette, 3 Jan. 1787; Henry Jackson to Henry Knox, 31 Dec. 1786, Knox Papers; Levi Shepard to James Bowdoin, 28 Dec. 1786, Bowdoin-Temple Papers, 6:125-26.

86. Records of the Council, 4 Jan. 1787, 30:62.

87. The subscription list for this loan is in Massachusetts Archives, 189:66-67.

Hampshire to converge on Worcester to protect the court and remain in service for one month after 23 January. Benjamin Lincoln, the commander, stated he intended to hound the Regulators out of the state even if they gave no cause.[88]

Many individuals and towns throughout the state objected to this new militancy. General Shepard, in Hampshire County, suggested that the governor call the General Court into special session to declare a rebellion since such an action would "remove all occasion for scruple in the most nice."[89] Rufus Putnam, officer and speculator, informed Bowdoin that Shays had talked with him and that "he [Shays] may be bought off."[90] A few Worcester towns met in convention in early January charged the government with brutality in arresting Shattuck and the other Middlesex leaders and requested the adjournment of the common pleas courts in the west until after the May session of the newly elected General Court.[91] John Fessenden, a Worcester County convention leader, presented the petition to the council and informed it that the Regulator leaders had agreed not to obstruct the courts. The council considered the petition an insult and refused to receive it.[92] The town of Sutton, a Hampshire convention, and the towns of Barre and New Salem also informed the council that the Regulators would not close the courts, all of which gave the council an excellent opportunity to test the Regulators.[93] If they did not appear at Worcester on the 23 January, the trouble would be ended; if they blocked the court, the governor could ask, within one week, for a declaration of rebellion from the General Court. Much to the joy of Higginson, Parsons, Lowell, and other mili-

88. Records of the Council, 4 Jan. 1787, 30:63-64; Henry Jackson to Henry Knox, 7 Jan. 1787, Knox Papers.

89. William Shepard to James Bowdoin, 30 Dec. 1786, Bowdoin-Temple Papers, 6:126.

90. Rufus Putnam to James Bowdoin, 8 Jan. 1787, ibid., pp. 250-54.

91. "Petition of the Committee," 11 Jan. 1787, Massachusetts Archives, 190:301-02; Records of the Council, 19 Jan. 1787, 30:73. See Feer, "Shays' Rebellion," pp. 342-43, for a list of towns petitioning against the proposed expedition.

92. Records of the Council, 19 Jan. 1787, 30:73.

93. "Petition of Sutton," 17 Jan. 1787, Massachusetts Archives, 190:305; "Petition of Hampshire Committee," 17 Jan. 1787, ibid., 190:304; "Petition of Barre," 18 Jan. 1787, ibid., 190:308-09; "Petition of New Salem," 18 Jan. 1787, ibid., 190:306.

tants, the council continued its preparations since they feared that the winter session of the General Court, unimpressed by the power of government, might attempt additional reforms and that in the spring elections the Regulators and convention men could join forces and gain even more power in the court. A smashing victory would overawe the court and cut down the political power of the conventions and the Regulators. [94]

The militia under Lincoln's command marched for Worcester on 20 January as the council issued warrants for the arrest of fifteen Regulator leaders in Worcester County and nineteen in Hampshire County. In a last desperate attempt to avoid this confrontation, Amos Singletary and Fessenden, Worcester convention leaders who would both become state senators, appealed personally to the council to recall the militia and gave additional assurances that the court would not be blocked. The council refused and Lincoln arrived in Worcester on 22 January. [95] In Hampshire, Shepard assembled 1,000 militia at Springfield on 18 January and on 19 January the Regulators began to assemble at West Springfield. [96] The rest of the story is well known. Shays assembled his contingent east of Springfield where they found themselves cut off from the Regulators west of the Connecticut River by Shepard's forces in the town. When Lincoln arrived at Worcester and continued his march into Hampshire, Shays, caught between the two forces, decided to march through Shepard's men and join with Luke Day west of the river. Shepard, claiming that Shays intended to seize the arsenal, borrowed some cannon and when Shays's men tried to march through, Shepard's men fired into them and killed four Regulators. Shays then retreated up the Connecticut River pursued by Shepard and Lincoln who, after an arduous night march, caught up with the Regulators at Petersham and completely dispersed them. [97]

The militants had won their victory. Minor incidents of violence continued in the west for several months but the commonwealth

94. Col. Hitchborn to John Adams, 16 Jan. 1787, Adams Papers, pt. 4; Stephen Higginson to Henry Knox, 20 Jan. 1787, Knox Papers; Orderly Book, entry 19 Jan. 1787, Sedgwick Papers, Massachusetts Historical Society.

95. Henry Jackson to Henry Knox, 21 Jan. 1787, Knox Papers.

96. Taylor, *Western Massachusetts*, pp. 159-60.

97. Ibid., pp. 116-63, and an excellent account in Feer, "Shays' Rebellion," pp. 366-400.

had crushed the Regulators. They did not yet realize that their victory merely confirmed the suspicions of many members of the less commercial-cosmopolitan interests of the existence of sinister, aristocratic, antirepublican, militaristic juntos and that these suspicions would lead to a serious political defeat of their candidates in April and May 1787. Conservatives had won a military encounter but were unwittingly about to lose a political war.

8

The Revolution of 1787

LINCOLN'S victory and the fading of the Regulation led to staggering political reverses for the most commercial-cosmopolitan interests and to new political patterns within the commonwealth. Even during the winter the court refused to levy any additional taxes to meet the mounting public debt created by the expedition, made no effort to use the impost-excise revenues solely for paying the interest on the state debt, and even attempted to cut Bowdoin's salary. The 1787 elections confirmed this trend. The voters turned out in record numbers in April, replaced Bowdoin with Hancock, and defeated several long-term placeholding members of the state senate. In May scores of less commercial-cosmopolitan communities that had failed to send representatives in 1786 sent delegates to the court and the most commercial-cosmopolitan interests found their strength in the lower house proportionately diminished. Several members of the commercial-cosmopolitan interests feared a revolution and charged that the people had filled the court with rebels and Shaysites. But the 1787 court was actually controlled by moderates who did little to forward the programs of the most commercial-cosmopolitan interests. It passed legislation modifying the repressive legislation against the Regulators; it continued the law suspending suits for debts; and it did absolutely nothing to find new revenue sources for the payment of the state debt or of congressional requisitions.

Throughout this period between January and August 1787 the divisions within the court and among the electorate continued to resemble the former splits within the house and to predict the future divisions over the national Constitution. Towns that supported moderate anti-Regulator policies and the suspension of debt suits tended to be the same ones that opposed the state's financial program during the 1780s and that would vote against ratification of the national Constitution in February 1788. On the

other side, the most commercial-cosmopolitan interests and towns
advocated harsher measures against the Regulators, opposed the
suspension of debt suits, and would eventually support the national Constitution.

Yet, despite this continuing pattern, the politics of the commonwealth began to change during the year 1787. In the first place the
Regulation and the government's response to it had aroused the
electors into voting and sending delegates to the lower house. The
concern aroused by the Regulation continued to be fed during the
summer of 1787 by accounts of aristocratic plots and juntos that
planned to crush the "little people" and by the debate over the
Constitution in the fall. The electorate was not only more involved
in politics; it also began to support political factions because of
their positions on issues rather than because of the popularity of
the candidates. In the 1787 election both Hancock and Cushing
ran best in counties with high turnouts, the less commercial-
cosmopolitan towns, and in communities that would vote against
the new national Constitution in 1788. This correlation is not
accidental. The rhetoric of Hancock's supporters pictured him as a
moderate, in contrast to Bowdoin who had violated the constitution to destroy the Regulators. As the summer progressed, the
Hancockites, under severe attack from the commercial militants
for their softness toward the Regulators, struck back by accusing
their opponents of forming juntos and cliques that planned to
destroy the Republic. Thus by the fall of 1787 it seemed that for
the first time the lineup of political factions had begun to be
consistent with the underlying political differences within the
commonwealth.

Yet paradoxically, just as this began to occur, the moderate
measures of the General Court began to remove the reasons for
such political divisions. Private debt became less of a problem
when suits had been suspended and people did not complain when
the courts of common pleas handled few cases. Taxation ceased to
be a divisive issue since the court refused to levy heavy taxes and
with part of the funds from the impost and excise going to pay
state expenses the less commercial-cosmopolitan interests had little complaint to make. Indeed the most commercial-cosmopolitan
interests now began to object. It seemed that the debt would not
be repaid; the court had little interest in taxes; even the impost
had been seized and used for general expenses; and the future
looked blacker yet since the voters had defeated Bowdoin and

pared down their control of the court. Journalists even accused them of forming anti-Republican organizations. It was enough to make any old commonwealth man into a new nationalist and by the fall of 1787 the commercial-cosmopolitan interests and towns had joined ranks behind the new national Constitution which might not give them everything they wanted but certainly offered more than Hancock and a moderate General Court. When the less commercial-cosmopolitan forces observed this support for the Constitution by their old enemies, they quickly swung over into opposition and, despite the changes that had been occurring in 1787, the divisions over the national Constitution in 1788 would be almost identical with those of the earlier 1780s over state and national financial policy.

Made confident by Lincoln's success, the General Court in its winter session again bared the claws of repression. The members expressed their satisfaction with Bowdoin and his council and the Lincoln expedition, passed a declaration of rebellion, and approved the special loan of £40,000 to meet the costs of Lincoln's campaign and to repay the merchants for their "patriotic subscription" for its expenses.[1] The court then moved to root out violence and cripple the political strength of the Regulators. It authorized the enlistment of 1,500 militia to serve for four months in the west, offered rewards for the capture of Regulator leaders, disqualified former Regulators from voting or serving on juries or as town officers until after 1 May 1788, accepted the charges against William Whiting, a judge of common pleas for Berkshire, and requested his removal by the governor, expelled Moses Harvey from the house of representatives because he had been charged with sedition, and requested the governor to revoke the commissions of

1. This legislation is in *Acts and Laws of the Commonwealth of Massachusetts, 1780-1797*, 11 vols. (Boston, 1890-1897), 4 Feb. 1787, 4:423-28; 5 Feb. 1787, 4:430; and 6 Feb. 1787, 4:165-68. This £40,000 loan should not be confused with the earlier private patriotic subscription by the Boston merchants to finance Lincoln's expedition. A special journal [for the loan of 1787] in the Treasurer's Papers, Office of the Secretary, Boston, gives the list of subscribers to the Feb. loans. These included: James Bowdoin subscribed for £1,763; William Phillips for £2,235; and Samuel Breck for over £365. Others included: E. H. Derby, the Salem merchant, for £100; Thomas Russell for £198; Moses Gill for £68; Oliver Wendell for £60; David Sears for £60; and Jonathan Mason, Jr., for £180.

two justices who appeared to have aided the Regulators.[2] In addition to striking at the Regulators and their leaders, the court established machinery to carry out repressive policies. It established a special commission to tour the western counties to examine the loyalty of citizens and schedule special sessions of the supreme judicial court to bring offenders to speedy trial.[3] It also attempted to guarantee the loyalty of town and militia officers by requiring the former to take a loyalty oath and provided punishments for militia officers who failed to mobilize their local units against the rebels.[4]

The reaction to this program of repression depended upon the position of the observer. The militants and the more commercial-cosmopolitan interests were jubilant. The Boston merchants who had financed the expedition reached deeper into their pockets and subscribed to the £40,000 loan and the Massachusetts Bank rushed to the assistance of the treasurer and advanced short-term credits to permit the payment of the militia mobilized in the west.[5] Cotton Tufts senator, and Henry Jackson, military man, praised the action of the court. Reverend Jeremy Belknap hoped the commonwealth would follow Cromwell's advice to "pay well and hang well," and John Q. Adams, still at Harvard, rejoiced that the government had finally acted with dignity.[6] Some politicians wanted to push even further. Stephen Higginson feared a recurrence of the Regulation unless the government took harsh action since "the people of the interior parts of this state have by far too

2. This legislation is in *Acts and Laws*, 8 Feb. 1787, 4:431-35; 16 Feb. 1787, 4:177-80; 8 Mar. 1787, 4:479; and 26 Feb. 1787, 4:554. For good secondary accounts see Robert A. Feer, "Shays' Rebellion," (Ph.D. diss., Harvard University, 1957-1958), pp. 432-33; Stephen T. Riley, "Dr. William Whiting and Shays' Rebellion," American Antiquarian Society, *Proceedings*, n.s. 66:119-66, for the story of the Sedgwick-Whiting dispute.

3. *Acts and Laws*, 10 Mar. 1787, 4:515-16. The commissioners were given power to pardon certain types of offenders in accordance with the provisions of the disqualification act.

4. Ibid., 2 Mar. 1787, 4:244-47.

5. Ibid., 20 Feb. 1787, 4:445-46.

6. Henry Jackson to Henry Knox, 3 Feb. 1787, Knox Papers, Massachusetts Historical Society; Cotton Tufts to John Adams, 6 Feb. 1787, Adams Papers, Adams Manuscript Trust; Jeremy Belknap to Hazard, 7 Feb. 1787, Jeremy Belknap Papers, Massachusetts Historical Society, *Collections*, 5th ser., vols. 2 and 3 (1877), 6th ser. vol. 4 (1891), 5th ser., 2:460; John Q. Adams, diary entry of 8 Feb. 1787, p. 152, Adams Papers, pt. 1. Also note Jeremy Belknap to Hazard, 27 Feb. 1787, Belknap Papers, 5th ser., 2:464.

much political knowledge and too strong a relish for instructed freedom, to be governed by our feeble system, and too little acquaintance with real sound policy or rational freedom and too little virtue to govern themselves. They have become too well acquainted with their own weight in the political scale, under such governments as ours and have too high a taste for luxury and dissipation, to sit down contented in their proper line, when they see others possessed of much more property than themselves." Higginson concluded that these people would have to be "compelled by force to submit to their proper stations and mode of living."[7] Benjamin Lincoln, publicly an apostle of moderation, in his private correspondence suggested hanging a few Regulators as examples, and Rufus King hoped that the court would give "minute attention . . . to the eradication of every seed of insurgency."[8] Writers in the eastern papers supported the activities of the court and attempted to find scapegoats for the rebellion. In Boston several writers pounced on Benjamin Austin, the author of the "Honestus" essays, as the cause, and one suggested that the execution of Samuel Ely in 1782 might have prevented the rebellion.[9]

Not all the important politicians supported such repression. John Hancock, in mourning for the death of his only son, made no public statement and did not contribute to the loans supporting the expedition.[10] James Warren believed that the court had gone

7. Stephen Higginson to Nathan Dane, 3 Mar. 1787, in Thomas W. Higginson, *The Life and Times of Stephen Higginson* (Boston, 1907), pp. 106-08.

8. Benjamin Lincoln to Henry Knox, 17 Feb. 1787, Knox Papers; Rufus King to Gerry, 11 Feb. 1787, in Charles R. King, *The Life and Correspondence of Rufus King Comprising His Letters; Private and Official. His Public Documents and His Speeches*, 6 vols. (New York, 1894-1900), 1:201. By 1 Mar. 1787 Lincoln had apparently become more moderate. See his letter to Henry Knox, 1 Mar. 1787, Knox Papers.

9. *Independent Chronicle*, for "Tully," 1 Feb. 1787; "Mentor," 22 Feb. 1787, and 1 Mar. 1787. See also *Massachusetts Centinel*, 3 Mar. 1787; and *Worcester Magazine*, Feb. 1787, pp. 585-87. For an anti-Regulator writer in the west, see "Ploughman, No. 2," in *Hampshire Gazette*, 7 Feb. 1787.

10. Jeremy Belknap to Hazard, 10 Mar. 1787, Belknap Papers, 2:466. Belknap noted that several of the judges of the supreme judicial court wanted to hang the Regulators by court martial. Hancock's name is not listed among the subscribers to the Feb. 1787 loans; see Special Journal [Loan of 1787], Treasurer's Papers, Office of the Secretary, Boston. Henry Jackson to Henry Knox, 3 Feb. 1787, gives Hancock's grief, and Knox to Hancock, 11 Feb. 1787, and Hancock to Knox, 14 Mar. 1787, is the interchange; all in Knox Papers.

too far and James Sullivan, who had favored militancy in the fall, complained that the "people in this state are exceedingly soured" by the harsh measures of the court and charged the militants with creating a reign of terror in Boston that accused a man of rebellion "if he does not loudly approve every measure as prudent, necessary, wise and *constitutional*." [11] The former Hancockites had begun a metamorphosis into the moderates of 1787.

In Sullivan's words the people had been "soured" by the repressive policies of the court. Individuals charged Bowdoin and his council with violating the constitution in sending the troops into the west and claimed that the court had itself violated the 1780 charter by suspending the writ of habeas corpus, in depriving former Regulators of their civil rights and liberties, and by providing for the trial of rioters outside the counties of their residence. [12] In addition the underground grapevine spread stories of atrocities committed by the militia and told of the formation of an aristocratic, anti-Republican junto which planned to seize power. [13] The combination of repression, dissension, and rumors about the future led many persons who had opposed the Regulation to dislike as well the administration that had crushed it. Unlike the disenfranchised Regulators many electors had no intention of taking violent action but they intended to use the vote to express their dissatisfaction.

The court, however, did not revoke the reforms passed in the fall session and in fact did little to reestablish the state's financial system. It refused to repeal the law suspending suits for debts, declined to authorize any new direct taxes, and even passed a new fee act that reduced some fees from the 1783 levels and provided for the removal of officials who overcharged. [14] The court did

11. James Sullivan to Rufus King, 25 Feb. 1787, in King, *Rufus King*, 1:214-15.

12. Feer, "Shays' Rebellion," p. 322, gives some information about the spread of these rumors. For a specific instance see Nathaniel Ames, diary entry for 30 Jan. 1787, in Ames Papers, Dedham Historical Society, Dedham, Mass.

13. For the use of this type of rhetoric see *Hampshire Gazette*, 14, 28 Feb., 7, 14 Mar. 1787. "A Citizen" defended "Honestus" in the *Independent Chronicle*, 29 Mar. 1787. The *Essex Journal*, 21 Mar. 1787, criticized the suspension of habeus corpus proceedings during the regulation.

14. *Acts and Laws*, 5 Mar. 1787, 4:479-80; 1 Mar. 1787, 4:220-22; 28 Feb. 1787, 4:226-27.

nothing to remedy the state's financial situation. Tax revenues declined, the debt had been increased, part of the impost continued to be used for general expenses, and the legislature, in order to mollify the merchants, permitted them to pay only one-third of their import duties in specie. By April 1787 it had become evident that only heroic action and the levying of heavy direct taxes could prevent the collapse of state securities. [15]

The issue that divided the court along the lines of both past differences and those yet to develop was the reduction of Bowdoin's salary. The court, as a concession to the moderates and westerners, cut the governor's salary by £300. Bowdoin claimed that the court did not possess the constitutional authority to reduce his salary and vetoed the bill. The house, by less than a majority, upheld the governor's veto, an action which tended to further diminish Bowdoin's popularity. The vote reflected older divisions over fiscal measures and foreshadowed newer ones over the ratification of the Constitution. The most commercial-cosmopolitan towns cast 50 percent of their vote against the original bill and 64 percent against overriding the governor's veto, while the group B and C towns cast over 63 percent of their vote for the act and favored passage over the veto. [16] Looking to the future, over 60 percent of the delegates from towns that would eventually support the new Constitution voted against the bill and opposed passage over the veto while over 75 percent of the representatives of future Antifederalist communities favored the bill and overriding the veto. [17]

As violence gradually died down in the west, political activity

15. Ibid., 6 Feb. 1787, 4:165-68; 5 Mar. 1787, 4:479-80. George R. Minot to Nathan Dane, 3 Mar. 1787, Massachusetts Historical Society, *Proceedings*, 48:429-30, noted the end of heavy direct taxes.

16. Unpublished Journals of the House of Representatives, available at the Office of the Secretary, Boston (cited hereafter as House Journals), 6 Mar. 1787, pp. 483-84, gives the vote on the bill and 10 Mar. 1787, pp. 499-500, for its passage over Bowdoin's veto. His veto message is in *Acts and Laws*, 9 Mar. 1787, 4:976-77.

17. House Journals, 6, 10 Mar. 1787, and *Debates and Proceedings in the Convention of the Commonwealth of Massachusetts, Held in the Year 1788, and Which Finally Ratified the Constitution of the United States* (Boston, 1856), 6 Feb. 1788, pp. 87-92 (cited hereafter as *Proceedings in the Convention*), for the vote on ratification. Also note Nathaniel Gorham to Henry Knox, 11 Mar. 1787, Knox Papers.

increased throughout the commonwealth. Some of the Regulator leaders fled to Vermont, New Hampshire, or New York and led raids back across the border, but by the end of February even these ceased to be a menace. General Warner in Worcester County informed the governor that additional militia would not be required and on 21 February Lincoln released the militia who had been mustered in January.[18] The last major incident occurred in late February when the Berkshire militia exchanged fire with some raiders from New York.[19] This decline in violence did not bring political peace to the state. Many persons such as Nathaniel Ames, Fisher's stay-at-home brother, noted that the government had violated the constitution and had expended energy and money needlessly in order to stamp out a rebellion that was already dead.[20] In commercial Essex County, the inhabitants of agrarian Rowley chose a committee to investigate the conduct of the militia who had arrested Shattuck back in November 1786, and in Worcester County, Leominster and Lancaster dredged up their old complaints about heavy taxes, the existence of the common pleas courts, and the location of the capital in Boston.[21] Even the moribund convention movement began to stir again as the citizens of Lunenberg in Worcester County sent out a circular letter call for a county convention to select a ticket of candidates for the state senate.[22] Several newspaper writers caught the contagion as "A Friend" defended the conventions, "Amicus" urged leniency,

18. John Sullivan [Governor of New Hampshire] to Bowdoin, 13 Feb. 1787, Bowdoin-Temple Papers, Massachusetts Historical Society, *Collections*, 7th ser., 6:134-35; Benjamin Lincoln to Bowdoin, 14 Feb. 1787, ibid., pp. 136-37; William Greenleaf [sheriff of Worcester County] to Bowdoin, 17 Feb. 1787, ibid., pp. 138-40; General Shepard to Bowdoin, 20 Feb. 1787, ibid., pp. 141-43; Jonathan Warner to Bowdoin, 20 Feb. 1787, ibid., pp. 148-49; *Massachusetts Centinel*, 3 Mar. 1787.

19. Col. Ashley to Gen. Lincoln, *Worcester Magazine*, Mar. 1787, p. 619.

20. Nathaniel Ames, diary entry of 20 Jan. 1787, Ames Papers, Dedham Historical Society. Much of the evidence for popular discontent comes from the letters of leading politicians: see Benjamin Hitchborn to Henry Knox, 25 Mar. 1787, Knox Papers, who sees Bowdoin as doomed. Henry Jackson to Knox, 31 Mar. 1787, ibid., saw a hot election. Stephen Higginson to Nathan Dane, 3 Mar. 1787, in Higginson, *Higginson*, p. 108, feared that the governor and General Court had gone too far and had alienated many citizens.

21. *Salem Mercury*, 10 Feb. 1787; *Worcester Magazine*, Feb. 1787, pp. 532-33.

22. *Massachusetts Centinel*, quoted in *Worcester Magazine*, Mar. 1787, pp. 629-31.

and others attacked the role of the Society of the Cincinnati and the military men who had played leading roles in crushing the rebellion. [23]

This agitation both reflected and stimulated the interest that made the 1787 elections a new departure in Massachusetts pre-party politics. Large numbers of voters, angered or confused by the conduct of the government, turned out to cast their ballots replacing incumbents apparently well entrenched in office with several new men who had been involved in the convention movement. The surge of voters resulted in a smashing defeat for Bowdoin and his militant supporters as the electors for the first time unseated an incumbent governor, an important shift in the membership of the senate, and finally in May a significant change in the composition of the lower house as the less commercial-cosmopolitan towns overcame their previous apathy and sent as many delegates as possible. Both the surge and its results frightened many prominent political, social, and economic leaders who saw in it a continuation of the rebellion and feared what the new men might do. Some were appalled when they discovered that the voters had failed to select their former leaders and began to fear for the existence of society and for the future of republican institutions. Others became frustrated by the degree of popular influence allowed by the supposedly conservative 1780 constitution and the commercial-cosmopolitan interests worried about the future of their dearly purchased financial system.

Most of the militants who had wanted to crush the rebellion stood squarely behind Governor Bowdoin's campaign for reelection and the group A towns gave the governor his greatest voting support. The Bowdoin backers pointed with pride to the governor's campaign against the Regulators, to his efforts to uphold the dignity and honor of the state government, and to his efforts to support both the national and state debts. [24] Several claimed that only rebels could vote against such a distinguished, intelligent, and capable governor and accused Hancock, his rival, of being stupid

23. *Hampshire Gazette*, 14, 28 Feb., 7, 14 Mar. 1787; *Worcester Magazine*, Feb. 1787, pp. 545-46; *Massachusetts Centinel*, 14 Mar. 1787.

24. For some examples of this see *Independent Chronicle*, 15, 29 Mar. 1787. The anti-"Honestus" campaign continued in "Tully," 1, 5, 29 Mar. in ibid. Also see *Massachusetts Centinel*, 24 Mar. 1787. *Essex Journal*, 28 Mar. 1787, in supporting Bowdoin claimed that a vote against Bowdoin was a vote against the government's policies in 1786 and 1787.

and soft on the rebels. [25] On the other side stood the moderates, the people disenchanted by the activities of Bowdoin and the court, and the old Hancock faction of the earlier 1780s. United by a detestation of Bowdoin, they rallied behind the popular ex-governor and played on the distrust of Bowdoin and the militants. The Hancock writers accused the militants of being an aristocratic junto that had destroyed the constitution, run roughshod over civil and political rights, and planned to drive old patriots like Hancock and Cushing from public life for the benefit of Tories. [26] This election rhetoric reinforced the conviction of many electors that a vote for Bowdoin would be a vote for repression and aristocracy while a vote for Hancock would promote leniency and republicanism.

The campaign for lieutenant governor created more confusion due to the proliferation of candidates. The Bowdoin backers hoped to dump Cushing and replace him with their newly minted military hero Benjamin Lincoln, fresh from his triumphs in the west. Lincoln could be presented to the public as a moderate because of his official statements although he took a much harsher promilitant tone in his private correspondence. [27] In order to increase his appeal, the Lincoln supporters trotted out the usual charges against the placeholding Cushing family. [28] Cushing, on the other hand, tied himself to Hancock's coattails and thus won the approval of many moderates. His propagandists accused Lincoln of being repressive and harped on the dangers of the general's membership in the evil Society of the Cincinnati. [29] Other moderates, suspicious of Cushing, who after all had been on the council dur-

25. Samuel Dexter to James Bowdoin, 20 Mar. 1787, Bowdoin-Temple Manuscripts, Massachusetts Historical Society, believed that "such as for H. are the insurgents and their friends ＿＿ Rascals to a man!" For other examples see *Independent Chronicle*, 29 Mar. 1787; *Massachusetts Centinel*, 24, 28, 31 Mar. 1787; *Essex Journal*, 28 Mar. 1787. *Massachusetts Centinel*, 24 Mar. 1787, trotted out the old tale of Hancock's extravagance.

26. For examples of this see *Massachusetts Centinel*, 28, 31 Mar. 1787; *Independent Chronicle*, 28 Mar. 1787. *Essex Journal*, 21 Mar. 1787, the suspension of habeas corpus in 1786.

27. *Cumberland Gazette*, 16, 30 Mar. 1787; *Massachusetts Centinel*, 28 Mar. 1787; *American Herald*, 2 Apr. 1787; *Hampshire Gazette*, 28 Mar. 1787; *American Recorder*, 30 Mar. 1787; *Salem Mercury*, 31 Mar. 1787.

28. Especially in the *Cumberland Gazette*, 30 Mar. 1787; and *Massachusetts Centinel*, 24 Mar. 1787.

29. *American Herald*, 2 Apr. 1787; *Massachusetts Centinel*, 14, 21 Mar. 1787.

ing the period of repression, balked at the Lincoln-Cushing choice and sought other candidates such as William Heath, a non-Cincinnati general from Suffolk County, Samuel Holten, the antinationalist congressman, Nathaniel Gorham, a merchant politician, or James Warren who had opposed repressive measures. Samuel Adams also had his backers but he still opposed Hancock and had the reputation in early 1787 of being as militant and as repressive as Bowdoin himself. [30]

The 1787 campaign also brought, for the first time, some public discussion of the senatorial elections. A Worcester convention met in March to mobilize support for an opposition ticket, the Bristol opposition became active, but the defenders of the old order used the papers to assail the horrible practice of voting for an entire ticket and urged the electors to stand firm for the honorable senators who had guided the commonwealth through its most difficult period. [31] By election day several leading figures commented that it had become the hottest election in their memories. [32]

On election day the voters came to the polls in great numbers. (See table 52.) Throughout the state almost 200 percent more electors voted for governor and around 175 percent more cast ballots for their county senators than in 1786. [33] This increase varied significantly from county to county with the greatest in-

30. *Massachusetts Centinel*, 31 Mar. 1787; William V. Wells, *The Life and Public Services of Samuel Adams*, 3 vols. (Boston, 1865), 3:243; "Laco," in *Massachusetts Centinel*, 28 Mar. 1787.

31. *Worcester Magazine*, Mar. 1787, p. 637, mentions members of a convention at Lunenberg and Sutton, ibid., p. 639, gives a circular letter from this convention. *Massachusetts Centinel*, 31 Mar. 1787; *Independent Chronicle*, 29 Mar. 1787; *Essex Journal*, 28 Mar. 1787.

32. Jeremy Belknap to Hazard, 10 Mar. 1787, Belknap Papers, 2:466, was so discouraged that he criticized holding the election. See also Benjamin Hitchborn to Henry Knox, 25 Mar. 1787, Knox Papers; Henry Jackson to Henry Knox, 31 Mar. 1787, ibid.; Major North to Henry Knox, 31 Mar. 1787, ibid.; Nathaniel Gorham to Henry Knox, 1 Apr. 1787, ibid. Elbridge Gerry to Samuel R. Gerry, 6 Apr. 1787, Gerry Manuscripts, Massachusetts Historical Society, in which Gerry expressed the fear that the bitter political feud would "terminate into a civil war and ruin to the Country must be the consequence."

33. Several electors even wrote Hancock's name in gold on their ballots, see *Essex Journal*, 4 Apr. 1787. Election statistics are from the unpublished Abstracts of Votes for Governor, Lieutenant-Governor, and Senators, available at the Office of the Secretary, Boston, all for 1787 (cited hereafter as Abstracts-Governor; Abstracts-Lt.-Governor; and Abstracts-Senators, respectively).

TABLE 52
Increase in Percentage of Votes from 1786 to 1787

			Increase in Percentage Points of Votes for	
County	For Governor	For Senate	Governor	Senate
Bristol	515%	582%	33%	31%
Plymouth	429	547	36	19
Cumberland	259	107	10	6
Essex	252	224	20	15
Middlesex	221	216	30	20
Worcester	200	245	23	21
York	190	171	9	7
Suffolk	169	145	28	22
Lincoln	153	197	5	6
Hampshire	111	41	10	3
Barnstable	83	57	7	6
Islands	65	54	8	8
Berkshire	75	52	8	5
State average	199%	179%	18%	15%

SOURCES: Unpublished Abstracts of Votes for Governor, Lieutenant-Governor, and Senators, available at the Office of the Secretary, Boston, for 1786 and 1787 (cited hereafter as Abstracts-Governor, Abstracts-Lt.-Governor, and Abstracts-Senators). The number of males over twenty-one per county is computed as described in ch. 3.

creases of 582% and 547% occurring in Bristol (582 percent) and Plymouth (547 percent) counties while Hampshire and Berkshire counties, due to the disfranchisement of former Regulators, rose only 41 percent and 52 percent respectively. The increased turnout resulted in an increase of 20 percentage points in the number of adult males voting for governor and 14 points in the number casting ballots for senators. The greatest increase of 33 and 31 points occurred in Bristol while Hampshire with an increase of only 10 and 3 points brought up the rear.

This new wave of votes completely submerged Bowdoin in his race for the governorship. (See table 53.) Hancock polled 75 percent of the vote and ran best in the counties with the largest increase in turnout, as 87 percent of the Bristol, 82 percent of the Plymouth, 81 percent of the Cumberland, 83 percent of the Middlesex, and 84 percent of the Worcester electors voted for the popular exgovernor.[34] In addition to carrying these counties by a

34. Returns in Abstracts-Governor, 1787.

TABLE 53
Election for Governor, 1787

Towns	Vote for		Bowdoin Vote				Vote as Percentage of Their Total Vote		
	Bowdoin	Hancock	1780	1785	1787	Change .1785-87	Bowdoin	Hancock	All Candidates
Group A	33%	66%	22%	55%	33%	– 22%	54%	32%	36%
Group B	17	81	26	34	17	– 17	27	37	35
Group C	15	80	28	21	15	– 6	19	31	29
Total			25%	39%	22%	– 17%			
Eastern group A	33	66							
Western group C	19	76							
Federalist	29	68							
Antifederalist	14	84							
State total	22%	75%							

SOURCES: Abstracts-Governor, 1785, 1787, and Abstracts-Lt.-Governor, 1780. *Debates and Proceedings in the Convention of the Commonwealth of Massachusetts, Held in the Year 1788, and Which Finally Ratified the Constitution of the United States* (Boston, 1856), pp. 87–92 (cited hereafter as *Proceedings in the Convention*) gives the Federalist and Antifederalist towns.

larger margin than his state average, Hancock ran very well in the group B and C towns where he picked up 81 and 80 percent of the vote respectively and in the communities that would later oppose the federal Constitution where he received 84 percent of the ballots. Although he carried every one of the three groups of towns, he ran poorest in the commercial-cosmopolitan group A towns, and in Hampshire and Berkshire counties he received 58 percent of the vote in the group C towns but only 39 percent in the more commercial-cosmopolitan group A and B communities.[35] Hancock with his aura of moderation received about one-third of his total vote from each of the three groups of towns, but on the whole ran strongest in the towns that had tended to oppose repressive policies and had fought against the financial program of the earlier 1780s. Bowdoin, on the other hand, ran best in the group A towns where he secured more than double the proportion of votes that he received in the group B and C towns. The governor's strength concentrated in these most commercial-cosmopolitan communities accounted for 54 percent of his total vote, resembled his support in the 1785 election, and differed completely from his showing in 1780 when the group C towns gave him the largest proportion of any of the three groups.[36] Thus the election for governor demonstrated the tendency for the old political factions to become attached to certain social and economic groups of towns within the commonwealth.

Much the same pattern developed in the election for lieutenant governor although the much greater number of candidates made the results more complex. (See table 54.) Cushing secured a decisive plurality with 46 percent of the votes but his failure to win an absolute majority threw the election into the General Court. Cushing, although he did not run as well as Hancock did in the counties with the largest increase in vote, ran strongest in the group B and C and the future Antifederalist towns where he secured 56 percent, 46 percent, and 55 percent of the total vote. Two minor candidates supported by many moderates, William Heath and Nathaniel Gorham, between them received over 21 percent of the vote in the group C towns, so Cushing's relative failure in those communities does not mean that the vote went to more repressive

35. Sources are in Abstracts-Governor, 1787.
36. Based on sources in Abstracts-Governor, 1785, 1787; and Abstracts-Lt.-Governor, 1785.

TABLE 54
Election for Lieutenant-Governor, 1787

Towns	Vote for			Lincoln Vote			Cushing Vote		
	Cushing	Lincoln	Others	1785	1787	Change, 1785-87	1785	1787	Change, 1785-87
Group A	38%	37%	25%	9%	37%	+28%	23%	38%	+15%
Group B	57	26	18	9	26	+17	41	56	+15
Group C	43	30-	27	22	30	+ 8	39	46	+ 7
Total				13%	32%	+19%	33%	46%	+13%
Boston	59	29	12						
Other Eastern group A	42	31	27						
Western group C	41	35	23						
Federalist	41	38	11						
Antifederalist	54	23	23						
State total	46%	32%	22%						

SOURCES: Abstracts-Lt.-Governor, 1785, 1787, for the voting returns. *Debates and Proceedings in the Convention of the Commonwealth of Massachusetts, Held in the Year 1788, and Which Finally Ratified the Constitution of the United States* (Boston, 1856), pp. 87–92 (cited hereafter as *Proceedings in the Convention*) gives the Federalist and Anti-federalist towns.

candidates. Benjamin Lincoln, who had run best in the group C towns in 1785, ran poorer in these same communities in 1787; he acquired his largest proportion of the votes in the group A communities where Samuel Adams, also considered favorable to repression, secured 6 percent of the vote.[37] Lincoln, like Bowdoin, also ran better in the future Federalist towns and almost 45 percent of his total vote came from the most commercial-cosmopolitan communities. Thus, even in the confused race for the lieutenant governorship, the voting patterns had begun to resemble the divisions within the General Court and the future differences over the national Constitution.

The new voters had an even more devastating effect on the senatorial elections. Before 1787 the voters had chosen 29 to 33 of their 40 senators and councillors, usually placeholders or incumbents, by majority vote in the April election. In 1787 the new voters cast their ballots for so many candidates that they selected only 23 senators and they elected a greater percentage of newcomers to these offices than at any other time during the 1780s, thereby turning several long-established senator-placeholders out of office.[38]

In four of the five counties with the largest increase in the vote for senator, counties that had also gone heavily for Hancock, the electors returned only three of the sixteen sitting senators. In Plymouth County Nathan Cushing and Charles Turner had been continually reelected by large margins since 1782, and in 1785 and 1786 Hugh Orr had won his seat with over 70 percent of the vote. In 1787 the voters cast only 24 to 29 percent of their votes for the three long-term, previously popular incumbents and elected only one man, Nahum Mitchell, a political newcomer to the upper

37. Abstracts-Lt.-Governor, 1787, gives the returns by county. The following table based on ibid. gives the percentage of vote of the minor candidates by group of towns.

Candidate	Group A	Group B	Group C	Total
Adams	6%	1%	2%	3%
Heath	4	8	8	6
Gorham	4	5	14	7

38. Based on the annual list of senators in *Acts and Laws*. The unpublished Journal of the Senate, available at the Office of the Secretary, Boston (cited hereafter as Senate Journal), also gives the returns for the senators chosen by popular vote and the votes for those chosen in a joint session of the General Court. The *Acts and Laws* gives the final list of senators.

house. Half of Mitchell's support came from three towns that would either oppose the national Constitution or divide over it. Charles Turner, the incumbent receiving the most votes, got only 10 percent of his votes from these communities and only 7 percent of his total in the three group C towns, while Mitchell secured 13 percent of his vote from the least commercial-cosmopolitan communities. [39] In Plymouth the combination of new voters and strong support of new men in the group C and future Antifederalist towns proved too much for the long termers.

In Bristol County the new voters turned out all three incumbents and elected a whole new slate of senators. The Bristol voters had returned Walter Spooner and Thomas Durfee since the early 1780s and in 1785 and 1786 had elected Elisha May with over 64 percent of their votes. But in 1787 none of these men received over 27 percent of the vote. Abraham White, who led the new ticket, received 70 percent of his total vote from towns that would later oppose the national Constitution, while Thomas Durfee, the most popular of the incumbents, received only 45 percent of his total from these six communities. [40] The higher turnout did not result in such complete changes in Worcester and Middlesex counties where the voters returned three incumbents, two of whom had held office only in 1786, to the senate. The Middlesex voters selected one newcomer and the Worcester voters elected two new men to the upper house. [41] Important changes also occurred in counties with lesser increases in turnout. In Maine the electors selected one incumbent, but in Lincoln County they chose a new man, Samuel Thompson, a leading secessionist and a future Antifederalist. [42] In York County the incumbents received only 20 percent of the vote while new men, although not elected, got 41 percent and 48 percent of the total. In Suffolk County four of the six incumbents won election but the other two failed to receive enough votes to be nominated to the General Court for the un-

---

39. Analysis is based on the Abstracts-Senators, 1787, for Plymouth County. The figures are the percentages of the candidate's total vote that he received from the various groups of towns. Since each voter could vote for more than one senator, it was impossible to analyze each candidate's proportion of the total vote, but I was able to determine what proportion of a candidate's vote came from specific types of towns.

40. Ibid., for Bristol County.

41. Ibid., for Worcester and Middlesex counties.

42. Ibid., for Lincoln County.

filled vacancies. [43] Even in Barnstable County the voters turned Solomon Freeman, judge and senator since 1780, out of office and replaced him with Thomas Smith, a political unknown. [44] Incumbents did far better in Hampshire and Berkshire counties where the disfranchisement of the Regulators lowered the increase in turnout. In Berkshire County the electors returned both of their seated senators by larger margins than in 1786 and in Hampshire County the voters elected only one incumbent but selected no new men for the senate. [45] After the returns had been counted, many of the social and political leaders of the commonwealth were horrified to discover that the voters had reelected only twelve of the forty incumbents while choosing eleven newcomers for the upper house. Only the fact that the General Court would select the remaining seventeen senators kept them from despair. [46]

The results of the election dismayed those who had urged repression and had backed Bowdoin. Henry Jackson summed up these feelings when he wrote that "the senators formally chosen are a miserable set and the good people are much alarmed at the completion of them." Cotton Tufts, senator and friend and correspondent of John Adams, feared that the upper house had been packed with too many democratic members but hoped that the "best people" could keep such newcomers at bay until the people could be enlightened. [47] After meeting disaster in April the militants and Bowdoin backers looked forward with both dread and anticipation to the house elections held during the month of May.

The rhetoric for this election centered around the question of moderation or repression in dealing with the Regulators. The militants accused the moderates of being soft on the rebels or of being disguised Regulators, while the moderates replied with more stories of aristocratic juntos planning to crush both the Regulators and the "little people." The supreme judicial court, on its special western circuit, condemned to death fourteen former Regulators and fined several others. [48] As soon as news of the condemnations

43. Ibid., for Suffolk County.
44. Ibid., for Barnstable County.
45. Ibid., for Hampshire and Berkshire counties.
46. Senate Journal, 30, 31 May, gives the names and votes of the elected senators and of the leading candidates.
47. Cotton Tufts to John Adams, 21 May 1787, Adams Papers, pt. 4; Henry Jackson to Henry Knox, 8 Apr. 1787, Knox Papers; Cotton Tufts to John Adams, 15 May 1787, Adams Papers, pt. 4.
48. For a good secondary account see Feer, "Shays' Rebellion," pp. 410-12. For the original records see Docket Books, Supreme Judicial Court,

reached the towns, petitions flowed in to the governor and council requesting pardons for the convicted men. On 12 April, after Hancock's victory had become known, the council ordered the postponement of the execution of Regulators condemned in Berkshire County and eighteen days later pardoned eight of the condemned in Hampshire and Berkshire counties but decided to execute four men from the same counties on 24 May.[49] These efforts satisfied few. The moderates wanted pardons for all, while the militants wanted to uphold the honor of the state by hanging as many as possible.[50] As the house election approached, the militants blamed the rebellion on the people's misconception of the mysteries of government and their love of luxury and urged the execution of Regulators and the repeal of the law suspending debts.[51] Many important men subscribed to these views which, as General Shepard put it, represented the ideas of the "men of sense and importance in this part of the state."[52] In order to make some political headway, militant writers created some stir in the papers by accusing the moderates of being in league with the rebels.[53] In reply moderate spokesmen like "Old Rock" warned the "smaller

Berkshire County, March term, 1787, pp. 59-66; Hampshire County, April term, 1787, pp. 77-82; Worcester County, April term, 1787, pp. 101-03; Middlesex County, April term, 1787, pp. 122-26; *Worcester Magazine*, Apr. 1787, pp. 37, 51, 62; May 1787, p. 76. See especially "Judge Cushing's Charge to the Middlesex Grand Jury," 9 May 1787, ibid., June 1787, pp. 107-10.

49. There are a large number of petitions for the convicted Regulators in Massachusetts Archives, vol. 189, dated 2-28 Apr. 1787, pp. 224-70. Also see unpublished Records of the Council, available at the Office of the Secretary, Boston (cited hereafter as Records of the Council), 12, 27, 28, 30 Apr. 1787, 30:147-48, 153-55. The death of Ivers forced Bowdoin and the council to call a special session of the General Court; see Records of the Council, 12 Apr. 1787, 30:137; and *Massachusetts Centinel*, 14 Apr. 1787.

50. "Honestus," in *Independent Chronicle*, 19 Apr. 1787; "A Citizen," in ibid.; Wells, *Samuel Adams*, 3:245-47; Benjamin Tupper to Henry Knox, 30 Apr. 1787, Knox Papers; "Tobias," *Hampshire Gazette*, 9 May 1787.

51. *Worcester Magazine*, Apr. 1787, pp. 7, 8, 46; *Independent Chronicle*, 3, 10 May 1787; *Hampshire Gazette*, 9 May 1787; Richard Cranch to John Adams, 29 May 1787, Adams Papers, pt. 4.

52. William Shepard to James Bowdoin, 12 May 1787, Bowdoin-Temple Manuscripts. Jeremy Belknap to Hazard, Belknap Papers, 2:466, John Pickering to Timothy Pickering, 28 Apr. 1787, Pickering Papers, Massachusetts Historical Society.

53. *Massachusetts Centinel*, 2 May 1787, for an example. Cotton Tufts to John Adams, 15 May 1787, Adams Papers, in which Tufts accused Warren of backing the Regulators.

sort of folk" to attend to their own town meetings and elect representatives or the "better *sort will be able to carry their schemes of policy into effect.*" "Probus" charged that "*overgrown* rich individuals" wished to continue the "abominable system of enormous taxation, which is crushing the poor to death," claimed that the holders of the state securities planned to pack the court, and warned the people to be on guard against those who wished to "aggrandize the few, to the destruction of the many." [54] "A Real Republican" urged the voters to turn out and charged that the penmen who attacked the qualifications of the new senators were agents of "*a formidable combination of Aristocracy*" which wished to seize complete power. [55]

This combination of popular interest, charges of aristocratic plots, and the general bitterness of the electors toward the government resulted in house elections that gave another shock to the commercial-cosmopolitan interests. (See table 55.) The voters failed to return 50 men who had served for three or more years prior to 1787 and reelected only 77 of the 203 members of the 1786 General Court who would account for only 29 percent of the membership of the new house. [56] But this turnover did not have as great an effect as two other surprising developments in the 1787 elections. First, the less commercial-cosmopolitan towns increased their total membership dramatically as town after town in western Massachusetts sent delegates to the court, and, second, these group B and C towns developed a sudden aversion to electing justices to the lower house. These two changes significantly altered the composition of the 1787 court compared to either the 1786 or the typical membership throughout the 1780s. In 1787 the group C towns accounted for 36 percent of the total membership, an increase of six points over 1786 and one or two points in comparison with the entire period between 1780 and 1790. The western group C towns alone sent 30 percent of the delegates, an increase of eleven points over 1786 and of four points for the

54. *Independent Chronicle*, 10 Apr. 1787; "Old Rock," in *Massachusetts Centinel*, 5 May 1787; James Warren to John Adams, 18 May 1787, Adams Papers, pt. 4. Warren claimed that the government had violated the constitution of 1780.

55. *Massachusetts Centinel*, 12 May 1787.

56. This analysis of the house is based upon the lists in *Acts and Laws*, 1784, 3:184-85; 1785, 3:622-26; 1786, 4:266-70; 1787, 4:664-67, supplemented by the lists in the House Journals.

TABLE 55
House Membership in the 1780s

	Membership in				Change, 1786-87	Change, [1780–90] to 1787
	1780-90	1785	1786	1787		
Towns						
Group A	33%	30%	34%	30%	− 4%	−3
Group B	34	32	36	34	− 2	0
Group C	33	37	30	36	+ 6	+3
Eastern group A	20	21	23	19	− 4	−1
Western group C	25	26	19	30	+11	+5
Maine	10	11	15	8	− 7	−2
Federalist	n.a.	50	53	45	− 8	n.a.
Antifederalist	n.a.	43	40	49	+ 9	n.a.
Justices + group A	52	55	56	42	−14	−10

SOURCES: *Acts and Laws of the Commonwealth of Massachusetts, 1780-1797*, 11 vols. (Boston, 1890–1897), 1784, 3:184–85; 1785, 3:622–26; 1786; 4:266–70; 1787, 4:664–67, supplemented by the lists in the unpub-lished Journal of the House of Representatives of the Commonwealth of Massachusetts, Office of the Secretary, Boston (cited hereafter as House Journal). Chapter 3 gives the distribution of membership between 1780 and 1790; and *Proceedings in the Convention*, pp. 87–92, gives the vote in the ratification convention.

n.a. = not applicable.

entire period 1780 through 1790. Not only did the representation of these least commercial-cosmopolitan towns increase, but their reluctance to send justices as representatives also decreased the voting power of the group A towns-placeholder combination from 56 percent of the members in 1786 to 42 percent in 1787. The proportionate strength of the future Federalist towns also declined from 53 percent of the members in 1786 to 45 percent in 1787. The political upheaval of 1787 had unseated an incumbent governor and changed the composition of both the senate and the house.

Despite these important changes the new General Court was not a radical body by any definition. It selected representatives of the more commercial-cosmopolitan interests as its officers, filled up the vacancies in the senate with placeholders and incumbents, and refused to seat some of the newly elected men. It passed no more major reforms although it moderated the repressive measures re-stricting the Regulators. But the militants wanted repression not moderation and the commercial-cosmopolitan interests rankled at the governor and the court's reluctance to reconstruct the shattered financial program of the earlier 1780s. By the end of the summer the rhetoric on both sides had become more strident and as the most commercial-cosmopolitan groups looked to the Philadelphia Convention for a solution to their difficulties, political lines drew tighter in and outside the General Court.

The new court chose important politicians for its officers and filled up the senate with placeholders. The senate elected Sam Adams, no friend of the Regulators, as its president and the house selected James Warren, one of the few leading politicians who had criticized repressive measures, as its speaker.[57] The two houses then met in joint sessions and filled the seventeen vacancies in the senate with eleven men who had previously served in the upper house and only six newcomers.[58] Not only did the court elect incumbents; it reduced the number of new senators by refusing to seat Phanuel Bishop of Bristol and Jonathan Grout of Worcester County, and Samuel Curtis, another new man, resigned from the senate.[59] Despite their regard for established politicians, the court did give the westerners more positions on the council, an important consideration since that body had the power to pardon

57. Senate Journal, 30 May 1787; House Journal, 30 May 1787.

58. It took the court a considerable amount of time to fill the vacancies in the senate. See Senate Journal, 30 May, 31 May, 1, 8 June 1787. The six newcomers were: Elijah Dunbar (Suffolk), Walter McFarland, (Middlesex), Amos Singletary (Worcester), David Smead (Hampshire), Tristram Jordan (York), and Mathew Mayhew (Islands). The eleven former senators were: Benjamin Austin (Suffolk), Jonathan Greenleaf (Essex), Stephen Choate (Essex), Tristram Dalton (Essex), Nathan Cushing (Plymouth), Charles Turner (Plymouth), Joseph Hosmer (Middlesex), Seth Washburn (Worcester), John Hastings (Hampshire), Oliver Phelps (Hampshire), and Edward Cutts (York).

59. Thomas Durfee was elected in place of Bishop. See Senate Journal, 8 June 1787. The voters, like many historians, had difficulties in spelling Bishop's first name. Ballots were deposited for Fanuel, Fannel, Phannuel, etc. Bishop and the senate decided that these had been cast for different candidates.

The Curtis resignation is in Senate Journal, 18 June 1787. Curtis retained his seat as the representative for the town of Worcester in the house and John Fessenden replaced him in the senate.

The Grout affair is in Senate Journal, 14 June 1787. Grout had been returned to the Senate and the house and took his seat in the house before appearing in the senate. The senate decided by a vote of 13 to 11 that he had no right to his senate seat and the next day voted 12 to 12 not to reconsider its vote of the previous day. Samuel Adams, as president of the senate, cast the tying (and defeating) vote. See Senate Journal, 15 June 1787. For the

convicted Regulators. [60] The court's rejection of new men did not mean that it had gone over to the militants. James Warren and Samuel Adams joined forces to prevent the house from recommending Benjamin Lincoln to the senate as a candidate for lieutenant governor. The house, controlled by the moderates, nominated Cushing and Gorham instead, and the senate elected Cushing by a unanimous vote. [61] The moderates controlled the house for the rest of the summer session. The house refused to annul the anti-Regulator legislation but took no new harsh measures against the so-called rebels. It also refused to reconstruct the financial program of the earlier 1780s while at the same time rejecting reforms such as paper money, complete pardon for the Regulators, moving the capital from Boston, or abolishing the court of common pleas.

The court took little new action against the Regulators. It resolved to retain five hundred to eight hundred militia on duty in the west, gave the treasurer permission to borrow £3,000 to pay these troops, and requested Hancock to remove two justices who had fled to New York when indicted for sedition. [62] In addition to taking no repressive action, the court relieved some of the pressure in the west by repealing the hated disqualifying act and refusing to repeal the law suspending suits for debt. The militants and the most commercial interests had attempted to make repeal of the disqualifying act as partial as possible while the less commercial-cosmopolitan interests supported complete repeal. In a vote of 155 to 45 the court instructed the committee drafting a new bill to retain some former disqualifications. [63] After lengthy parliamentary maneuvering the senate proposed a measure that pardoned everyone who had supported the riots against the com-

---

selection of Fessenden and Joseph Stone, see Senate Journal, 19 June 1787. Grout and Bishop became leading Antifederalists and Curtis voted against ratification on 3 Feb. 1788. There was bad blood between Grout and Artemas Ward; see Grout's petition, 6, 12 June 1787, for an incident that occurred on 7 Mar. 1787 in Ward Manuscripts, Massachusetts Historical Society.

60. For the election of the council, see Senate Journal, 1 June 1787.

61. Senate Journal, 1 June 1787; Henry Knox to Rufus King, 8 June 1787, in King, *Rufus King*, 1:222; John Q. Adams to John Adams, 30 June 1787, in Worthington C. Ford, ed., *Writings of John Quincy Adams*, 7 vols. (New York, 1913-1917), 1:33.

62. *Acts and Laws*, 15 June 1787, 4:677-79; 21 June 1787, 4:691; 6 July 1787, 4:715-17.

63. House Journal, 8 June 1787.

TABLE 56
The Disqualification Act, 1787

| | Percentage of Votes for | | |
Towns	Supplemental Funds	Disqualification	Change
Group A	82%	68%	−14%
Group B	47	46	− 1
Group C	30	45	+15
Eastern group A	86	69	−17
Western group C	23	45	+22
Federalist	77	80	+ 3
Antifederalist	31	27	− 4
Total state	57%	52%	− 5%

SOURCES: Vote on "Disqualification" is in House Journal, 13 June 1787, pp. 60–61; vote on "Supplemental Funds" is in ibid., 30 June 1786, pp. 152–56.

monwealth since 1 June 1786, restored all their political and civil rights, and returned their firearms. This proposal exempted only nine named persons, those who refused to take an oath of allegiance by 12 September 1787 and those convicted of treason. The acts further provided that civil suits could be brought against former Regulators for damages caused by riots or other incidents. [64] When the measure reached the house many western and less commercial-cosmopolitan members worked to liberalize it even further. They failed, by a vote of 72 to 38, to delete the names of all the excepted individuals and by a vote of 147 to 67 to delete the names of 4. [65] (See table 56.) When these amendments failed, they voted against the final passage of the bill which passed by a narrow 8-vote margin. The vote on this bill showed several interesting political shifts. The group A towns supported it with 68 percent of their votes but the group C towns cast only 55 percent of theirs against the measure. The most vigorous resistance to the measure came from the Worcester group C towns which cast 92 percent of their votes against the bill, but the group C towns outside Worcester went along with this moderate proposal. A divi-

64. Ibid., 13 June 1787; Senate Journal, 12, 13 June 1787. *Worcester Magazine*, June 1787, p. 212, gives some of the debate.
65. The votes, but no roll calls, are in the House Journal, 13 June 1787. See also Nathan Dane to Nathaniel Gorham, 22 June 1787, Massachusetts Historical Society, *Proceedings*, 59:95.

sion indicative of future differences appeared when the towns that were to become Federalist cast 80 percent of their votes for passage while the Antifederalist towns gave 73 percent of theirs to the opposition. [66] By the summer of 1787 the battle lines that would be so strong in the January-February 1788 convention had already formed!

In addition to this legislation the court later passed a resolution ending all prosecutions for seditious activities committed between 1 June 1786 and 15 June 1787. [67] The court also extended the law suspending suits for debt. For a time it appeared that the senate might reject extension since the upper house by one vote rejected the report of a joint committee recommending continuation. At this point the house showed its overwhelming support of extension by suspending the rules, giving the measure three readings, and passing it in a single day. Faced with such overwhelming sentiment in the house, the senate gave way and extended the suspension till 1 January 1788. [68]

Despite its moderation the court paid little attention to more radical demands for reform. The house rejected a report by one of its committees recommending the location of the capital at Concord and the house and senate referred the report of a joint committee considering the abolition of the court of common pleas to the placeholder-dominated and practically dormant committee for the revision of the laws. [69] The house by a vote of 103 to 47 declined to appoint a committee to investigate the possibilities of issuing paper money and Hancock sidetracked the efforts to cut the governor's salary by making a public gift of £300 to the treasury with a proviso that this grant would not serve as a constitutional precedent. The court accepted the grant by the wily governor and waived the thorny constitutional question that had plagued the court in 1786. [70]

Despite its lack of effort at reform the court refused to reimple-

66. The roll call vote is in House Journal, 13 June 1787, pp. 60-61.

67. *Acts and Laws*, 7 July 1787, 4:733.

68. Senate Journal, 6, 22, 29 June 1787; *Worcester Magazine*, June 1787 p. 167; *Acts and Laws*, 30 June 1787, 4:560.

69. House Journal, 15, 27 June, 6 July 1787; *Worcester Magazine*, June 1787, pp. 153, 167; John Q. Adams, 30 June 1787, in Ford, ed., *John Q. Adams*, 1:31-32.

70. House Journal, 23 June 1787; *Acts and Laws*, 21 June 1787, 4:991. *Worcester Magazine*, June 1787, p. 167; *Massachusetts Centinel*, 30 June 1787.

ment the financial program of the earlier 1780s. The death of Treasurer Ivers in April gave another shock to the state's financial structure already undermined by the expenses of the campaign against the Regulators. Bowdoin called a special April session of the court to consider the financial situation, but the court merely selected Alexander Hogdon as the new treasurer and declined to take further action. [71] By the summer of 1787 it was apparent that the costs of the Regulation, the use of impost funds for general expenses, and the permitting of merchants to pay part of their duties in securities had rendered the payment of specie interest on consolidated securities difficult if not impossible. During the summer the court appointed several committees to examine the situation, but none of them could suggest a program that would fund either the interest or principal on the state debt without levying direct taxes and the moderate court refused to vote direct taxes. [72] By the end of the session it was obvious that the moderates joined by the old Hancockites had emerged victorious over both the former Regulators and extreme convention men and the commercial militants behind Bowdoin. Yet this victory paradoxically increased political tension as the Bowdoin backers and the militants continued their vituperative campaign against the moderates who answered with smears of their own.

While the court proceeded with its moderate programs, the moderates applauded and the militants jeered the handling of the condemned Regulators by the governor and council. Bowdoin and his council dropped the problem into Hancock's lap by staying the executions of the six condemned Regulators until 21 June 1787.[73] The new governor and council, after poring over a flood of petitions praying for pardons, decided to reprieve five of the six men until 2 August and later reprieved Job Shattuck, the sixth man, till 26 July. [74] In order to impress the former Regulators the government staged a mock execution at Northampton at which

71. *Acts and Laws*, 27 Apr. 1787, 4:521-22; 30 Apr. 1787, 4:525-27; 2 May 1787, 4:527.

72. For some of these efforts see House Journal, 14, 19, 20 June, and 8 July 1787.

73. Records of the Council, 12 May 1787, 30:174; 16 May 1787, 30:181; 17 May 1787, 30:185-86; 28 May 1787, 30:191.

74. Ibid., 13 June 1787, 30:198; 14 June 1787, 30:200, 15 June 1787, 30:202, 16 June 1787, 30:203; 26 June 1787, 30:217. Petitions may be found in the Massachusetts Archives, 189:297-313, 318-40, 451-60.

two of the already-reprieved rioters guarded by 400 militia men marched to the gallows only to be informed of their reprieve two minutes before their scheduled execution. [75] The government planned to stage a similar exhibition in Berkshire County but the two principals frustrated the scheme by breaking jail and fleeing to New York. After these incidents the council extended the reprieves of the four remaining men (including the two reprieved earlier) until 20 September and as petitions continued to pour into the council it pardoned two of them on 31 August. [76] The last two men, Shattuck and Parmenter, became the focus of bitter debate within the council. Sullivan argued that Parmenter, who had murdered a man during a fracas, had been convicted of treason and not of homicide and so should be pardoned with the others. Eventually the council pardoned both men and the commonwealth hanged not a single one of the convicted Regulators. [77] The combination of moderation in the court and pardon by the council helped to quiet the west. In August Hancock toured the western counties, reviewed the militia, and found everything quiet. [78] A great deal of local bitterness remained as several persons brought suits against individual Regulators for damages caused during the riots. Dr. David Young secured a verdict of £900 against a number of rioters who had injured his knee and in October 1789 someone fired at General Shepard as he reviewed the Hampshire militia but no one ever uncovered his potential assassin.[79] This bitterness remained local, and after 1787 all groups and factions made a decided effort to forget the Regulation and the riots.

But during the summer of 1787 the militants had no desire to support a government that pardoned the condemned and passed a few reforms. Cotton Tufts spoke for many others when he fumed about setting "the gallows despairing fellows at liberty" and many newspaper writers such as "Vicar O'Bray" and "Observer" de-

75. *Worcester Magazine*, July 1787, p. 180.

76. Ibid., June 1787, p. 156; Records of the Council, 29 July 1787, 30:235.

77. *Independent Chronicle*, 9 Aug. 1787. Thomas C. Amory, *Life of James Sullivan, with Selections from His Writings*, 2 vols. (Boston, 1859), 1:203-06; and Records of the Council, 31 Aug. 1787, 30:244; 12 Sept. 1787, 30:246. See also *Worcester Magazine*, Sept. 1787, pp. 333, 338-40, 347.

78. *Worcester Magazine*, Aug. 1787, p. 237.

79. *Massachusetts Magazine*, July 1789, p. 391; J. Q. Adams, diary entry of 5 Aug. 1788, Adams Papers, pt. 1; *Salem Mercury*, 20 Oct. 1789.

manded executions.[80] Others assaulted the mild reforms of the
court. Sedgwick charged that the extension of the law suspending
suits for debt was "precisely the worst measure which could have
been devised," laid it to the door of the "natural effects of pure
democracy" and dismissed its backers as the "dregs and scum of
mankind."[81] Tufts accused the moderates of being "levellers"
who would take no action to pay the commonwealth's debt and
who were "characters that in sober times would have been hissed
off the stage and been expelled as members unfit to grace the seats
of legislators."[82] As the summer progressed Sedgwick's outlook
became even gloomier and he concluded that "the end of government security cannot be attained by the exercise of principle
founded upon democratic equality" since "war is now actually
levied on virtue, property and distinctions in the Community."
Against this background newspaper writers cried out for the rees-
tablishment of state credit and the repeal of the law suspending
suits for debt. Some of the nastier militants even stooped to the
level of printing purported letters from Daniel Shays expressing his
satisfaction with the activities of the court and of Hancock.[83]

The moderates and Hancockites responded to these charges by
dredging up new evidence of aristocratic plots. In August someone
stole a copy of a letter signed "S.H.," which everybody took to be
Stephen Higginson, that had been mailed to Lincoln during the
winter of 1787. In the letter S.H. claimed that he and his cohorts
planned to manage the General Court as Lincoln had managed the
Regulators. The moderates and Hancockites naturally claimed that
the letter proved the existence of a military-commercial-political
junto that had intended to destroy republicanism and crush the

80. Cotton Tufts to John Adams, 30 June 1787, Adams Papers; *Hampshire
Gazette*, 4, 11 July 1787; *Massachusetts Centinel*, 21 July 1787.

81. Theodore Sedgwick to Nathan Dane, 5 July 1787, Sedgwick Papers.
The tender act was assaulted in *Massachusetts Centinel*, 11 July 1787, 1 Sept.
1787, and in the *Worcester Magazine*, Aug. 1787, p. 265.

82. Cotton Tufts to John Adams, 30 June 1787, Adams Papers, pt. 4.
Other examples included Mrs. Sedgwick to Theodore Sedgwick, 17 June
1787, Sedgwick Papers; Nathan Dane to Nathaniel Gorham, 22 June 1787,
Massachusetts Historical Society, *Proceedings*, 59:95; Christopher Gore to
Rufus King, 28 June 1787, in King, *Rufus King*, 1:226-28.

83. Sedgwick to King, 18 June 1787, in King, *Rufus King*, 1:224; *Massachusetts Centinel*, 18, 21, 25 July 1787, 25 Aug. 1787; *Hampshire Gazette*, 4,
18 July 1787; *Hampshire Chronicle*, 7 Aug. 1787; *Independent Chronicle*,
16 Aug. 1787; *Worcester Magazine*, Aug. 1787, p. 287.

"little folks."[84] Writer after writer appeared to defend or attack Higginson, argue for or against a plot by an aristocratic junto, and urge or oppose an investigation by the General Court.[85] The whole affair fitted neatly into the moderate propaganda campaign which had been playing on the bitterness of the electors since early 1787 with claims of plots and juntos. They could now provide proof of a real plot to counter the militants' charges of treachery against the court and the governor.

By September 1787 the militants and the commercial-cosmopolitan interests who had hoped for victory in February had been pushed onto the defensive. The moderates and Hancock had taken control of the government, had compromised with the west and least commercial-cosmopolitan interests in playing down repression and had extended minor reforms and refused to reestablish funds for paying the interest and principal on the state debt. In addition they had developed a highly effective propaganda campaign that had smeared the militants and the leaders of the most commercial-cosmopolitan interests as evil aristocrats scheming to control the state. Finally, and perhaps the worst insult of all, the people who poured out to vote in April and May had ignored their natural leaders and had elected the very "dregs and scum of mankind" to high political office. To many persons in the commercial-cosmopolitan camp it seemed that salvation could come only from the deliberations of the Philadelphia Convention.

84. *Massachusetts Centinel*, 1 Aug. 1787; Amory, *James Sullivan*, 1:207.
85. *Massachusetts Centinel*, 4, 8, 11, 15, 18 Aug. 1787; *Independent Chronicle*, 2 Aug. 1787.

9

The Constitution

DIVISIONS over the new national Constitution among the political factions and the socioeconomic interests and groups were almost identical to those over state and Continental financial policies during the earlier 1780s and over the response to the Regulation in 1786 and 1787. The towns and interests that had voted against the fiscal programs of the 1780-1786 period and had sponsored reforms and opposed repression in 1786 and 1787 threw their weight against the new charter. The most commercial-cosmopolitan towns and interests that supported the state's credit, debt, and financial measures during the earlier 1780s and had opposed reform and sponsored repression during the Regulation and its aftermath lined up in favor of the new nationalist document. The factions of important politicians also tended to respond to the Constitution as they had supported moderation or repression as the correct reply to the Regulation. The moderates and Hancockites, composed of such men as Hancock, Cushing, Sullivan, and Warren, tended to oppose or were lukewarm toward the new Constitution, some of them suspecting the motives of its most ardent supporters, those same commercial militants who had accused them of weakness and treason during the summer of 1787. In addition to these divisions the fears of the ideological Antifederalists such as Gerry and Samuel Adams aroused by the national and possibly antirepublican character of the Constitution led them to cooperate with their old enemies, Hancock and Sullivan.

Adams and Gerry, unlike other groups and individuals who supported or opposed the charter, at least were consistent. During the earlier 1780s many of the politicians and the most commercial-cosmopolitan groups had opposed Morris's efforts to strengthen the confederation, had voted against the 1781 impost, and had worried about the antirepublican and aristocratic dangers involved

in the proposed convention of 1785. Thus the support of the
Constitution by these groups and towns reflected a complete
change in their response to a more powerful national government,
a change that was the result of three distinct developments between 1785 and 1788. First, the weakness of the confederation
under the Articles of the Confederation was the apparent cause of
the refusal of foreign nations to make commercial treaties and
Congress's failure to secure funds and regulate commerce. Second,
the Regulation exposed the weakness of the commonwealth since
it was at first unable to repress the rioters. Third, and most important, the 1787 election and the political developments of that
summer had shown that popular, organized groups could use the
framework of the 1780 constitution to influence political decisions, and the failure of the court to show any sympathy for the
financial programs of the earlier 1780s gave the most commercial-
cosmopolitan interests the unique experience of being shut out of
control of the commonwealth's policies. Between the summer of
1786 and the fall of 1787 leaders of the most commercial-cosmopolitan interests became more and more convinced that only a
new Constitution could save their situation in Massachusetts.
These men and groups did not become ideological nationalists;
they simply came to believe that a new Constitution would both
assist the commonwealth and strengthen their position in state and
national government. Like the less commercial-cosmopolitan interests during the 1780s they turned to a convention to short-circuit
the regular political channels!

On the other side the less commercial-cosmopolitan interests
also shifted their ground during the 1780s. In 1781 they voted for
the impost but by 1788 they voted against the Constitution. They
changed because of their response to heavy debts and high taxes,
their dislike of the militants, and their suspicion that a powerful
government could be used to thwart their own interests. They had
good reason for suspecting a government they could not control.
Such a government had levied heavy taxes during the earlier
1780s, had refunded and consolidated a heavy state debt, had
brushed aside all efforts at reform, and had eventually used military force to put down the Regulators. Even after they had secured some leverage over the government in the 1787 elections,
newspaper writers kept informing them of aristocratic plots and
plotters who hoped to end republican government and crush the
"little people." Thus the new Constitution frightened many of

these more locally oriented people who believed, based on their own past experience, that such a powerful government could and would levy direct taxes, stamp out any resistance with a national army, and enforce its policies through the national courts. They also saw that this government would be even harder to influence than that of the commonwealth. The popular House of Representatives would be elected from districts as large as those for the Massachusetts senate, and the senate had consistently supported the programs of the most commercial-cosmopolitan interests throughout the 1780s. These vast powers, virtually unchecked by local influences, apparently had little constitutional limitation since the new document, unlike the Massachusetts constitution of 1780, provided for no bill of rights. The less commercial-cosmopolitan groups then saw that their old enemies in the towns and cities overwhelmingly supported the new Constitution and this intensified their fears of aristocratic plots and their suspicion that the entire document was a job sponsored by these most commercial-cosmopolitan interests to undermine their local power. But most of these less commercial-cosmopolitan towns did not become ideological Antifederalists. They had little objection to a powerful government if it didn't violate their particular interests and when in the 1790s the new national administration failed to levy direct taxes and lifted the burden of the state debt from their shoulders many of these anti-Constitutional towns became strongly Federalist. Unlike many of the ideological Antifederalists who later became Republicans or some of the anti-Constitutional towns in the east and Maine that eventually supported Jefferson, most of the less commercial-cosmopolitan towns only wanted a guarantee that the new national government would not legislate a program like the one the commonwealth had developed in the earlier 1780s.

Thus the debate over the Constitution, instead of raising the curtain on new divisions that would exist in a new political era, actually climaxed the political struggles of the earlier period. After ratification the old issues would begin to dissipate and with no organized parties to retain the old divisions the bitter struggles of the 1780s would soon become only a memory for most Massachusetts citizens.

The defeat of proposals designed to strengthen the confederation government and the failure of the United States to give more assistance to American commerce disturbed many important Massachusetts politicians by the fall of 1786. During the spring and summer of that year New York balked on the 1783 impost, the Barbary nations insisted on presents, several states declined to give commercial powers, requested in 1784, to Congress, the British government refused to negotiate a commercial treaty, and efforts to ratify the commercially profitable Jay-Gardoqui Treaty foundered on southern refusal to close the Mississippi River. New York, the last state to act on the 1783 impost request, passed an act on 4 May 1786 that granted a revenue to Congress but provided that customs duties could be paid in New York paper currency and that the New York legislature could remove Continental collectors.[1] Congress, on 27 July, declined to accept this offer and Governor George Clinton refused to call the legislature into special session to reconsider the grant. By the fall of 1786 it became evident that the confederation would not secure its needed revenue from customs.[2] At the same time a congressional committee reported that only six states had passed laws in accordance with the 1784 request for additional commercial powers and it seemed that the movement to strengthen the confederation had collapsed.[3] Foreign nations made no effort to aid either the commonwealth's or the nation's commerce. John Adams informed several important Massachusetts politicians that a treaty with the Barbary powers would cost more than Congress would provide and as early as May Rufus King had accepted the fact that Britain would make no commercial treaty with her former colonies.[4] Even when for-

---

1. E. James Ferguson, *The Power of the Purse: A History of American Public Finance, 1776-1790* (Chapel Hill, 1961), pp. 238-41. Pennsylvania had also attached conditions to her grant. For further details see W. C. Ford et al., eds., *Journals of the Continental Congress, 1774-1789,* 34 vols. (Washington, D.C., 1904-37), 27 July 1786, 31:332; 11 Aug. 1786, 31:557; 23 Aug. 1786, 31:557-58.

2. Ferguson, *Power of the Purse*, pp. 241-43. Rufus King to Elbridge Gerry, 19 July 1786, in Charles R. King, *The Life and Correspondence of Rufus King Comprising His Letters; Private and Official. His Public Documents and His Speeches,* 6 vols. (New York, 1894-1900), 1:187.

3. *Journals of Congress* 23 Oct. 1786, 31:907-09.

4. Rufus King to John Adams, 4 May 1786, Adams Papers, Adams Manuscript Trust; John Adams to Thomas Jefferson, 23 May 1786, in Julian P. Boyd et al., eds., *The Papers of Thomas Jefferson* (Princeton, 1950-), 9:564-65; John Adams to Rufus King, 14 June 1786, in King, *Rufus King,* 1:182-83; Nathan Dane to King, 11 Aug. 1786, in Edmund C. Burnett, ed, *Letters of Members of the Continental Congress,* 8 vols. (Washington, D.C., 1921-38), 8:419-20.

eign nations seemed agreeable, as when Cabot's associate, Gardoqui of Spain, drafted a treaty with John Jay which would have opened some Spanish ports to Massachusetts shipping, Congress declined to pay the price of closing the Mississippi for twenty-five years and the commonwealth's merchants and politicians watched as another potential aid to their commerce went up in smoke.[5]

These developments irritated many in the commonwealth but did not transform them into nationalists. Many politicians, for example, had doubts about the Annapolis Convention. Rufus King at first suspected fraud since he knew that Virginia had little interest in a national commercial system and might use the convention instead to organize support for an effort to change the Articles.[6] Theodore Sedgwick, even more suspicious, concluded that the convention was intended to sabotage the plan for enlarging the commercial powers of the confederation.[7] Many of the commercially oriented delegates appointed by the court to the convention resigned their commissions and the court, the governor, and council found it difficult to fill these vacancies. The finally appointed replacements tarried at home for so long that the Annapolis meeting had adjourned before they arrived.[8]

5. For background see Rufus King to Elbridge Gerry, 4 June 1786, Massachusetts Historical Society, *Proceedings*, 1st ser., 9:9-12; Otto to Vergennes, 10 Sept. 1786, in George Bancroft, *History of the Formation of the Constitution of the United States of America*, 2 vols. (New York, 1882), 2:389-92. For Cabot's connections with Gardoqui see John and Andrew Cabot to Gardoqui, 16 July 1785, Dana Papers, Massachusetts Historical Society. For congressional action see *Journals of Congress*, 10 Aug. 1786, 31:510; 28 Aug. 1786, pp. 569-70; 30 Aug. 1786, pp. 600-03. Also see Thomson's notes for 16, 18, 21 Aug. in Burnett, ed., *Letters*, 8:429, 439. King was also worried about the relative rate of western growth; see King to Elbridge Gerry, 4 June 1786, Massachusetts Historical Society, *Proceedings*, 1st ser., 9:9-12.
6. Rufus King to Jonathan Jackson, 11 June 1786, Massachusetts Historical Society, *Proceedings*, 49:85-87.
7. Theodore Sedgwick to Caleb Strong, 6 Aug. 1786, in Burnett, ed., *Letters*, 8:415-16. Stephen Higginson shared these suspicions in his letter to John Adams, ? July 1786, Adams Papers.
8. Action is covered in *Acts and Laws of the Commonwealth of Massachusetts*, 1780-1797, 11 vols. (Boston, 1890-1897), 17 June 1786, 4:286-87; Elbridge Gerry to the General Court, 23 June 1786, Gerry Papers, Massachusetts Historical Society; and unpublished Records of the Council, available at the Office of the Secretary, Boston (cited hereafter as Records of the Council), 8 Aug. 1786, 29:459; 9 Aug., p. 465; 11 Aug., p. 464; 24 Aug., p. 489. King felt the meeting did little good; see Rufus King to John Adams, 20 Oct. 1786, Adams Papers, pt. 4.

These disappointments did embitter several leaders toward the confederation and the Articles. Reverend John Lathrop wrote that "if the states do not vest Congress with more power it will be impossible to support the Confederacy: some other form of government will take its place" and advocated amendment of the Articles.[9] Later in the summer "a Bostonian" advocated drastic amendments that would increase the executive, legislative and judicial powers of the Articles.[10] Others, instead of looking to a more powerful national government suggested, as did Theodore Sedgwick, that "no other substitute can be deemed than that of contracting the limits of the confederacy to such as are natural and reasonable and within these limits instead of a nominal to institute a real and efficient government."[11]

The General Court's reaction to the Regulation had the significant effect of speeding up the drift of many toward favoring a stronger national government. It had frightened many Massachusetts politicians who believed they had lost control of the situation and irritated others who opposed any reforms that might alleviate conditions in the west.[12]

General Knox, the commonwealth's highest confederation official and a nationalist prior to the fall of 1786, used the rebellion to propagandize an increase of national powers. The general constantly called the Regulation a rebellion and frightened Congress with the threat that the rebels would seize the national arsenal at Springfield. In October he informed that body that "it is doubtful in the present convulsed state of the government whether any effectual measures can be adopted for the protection of stores in their present situation, unless powerfully assisted by the United

9. John Lathrop to John Temple, 20 March 1786, Bowdoin-Temple Papers, Massachusetts Historical Society, *Collections*, 6th ser., vol. 9 (1897), 7th ser., vol. 6 (1907), 7th scr., 6:93-95; and Rufus King to Jackson, 3 Sept. 1786, in Burnett, ed., *Letters*, 8:458-60.

10. *Independent Chronicle*, 3, 10 Aug., 7 Sept. 1786. *Worcester Magazine*, July 1786, p. 206.

11. Theodore Sedgwick to Caleb Strong, 6 Aug. 1786, in Burnett, ed., *Letters*, 8:415-16.

12. There are two excellent secondary accounts concerning the impact: Joseph P. Warren, "The Confederation and Shays' Rebellion," *American Historical Review*, 11:42-67; and Robert A. East, "The Massachusetts Conservatives in the Critical Period," in Richard B. Morris, ed., *The Era of the American Revolution*, (New York, 1939), pp. 336, 380-88.

States."[13] Knox then campaigned to raise 1,340 troops, purportedly to fight the western Indians, who would actually be used to protect the arsenal and crush the Regulation.[14] Congress followed the suggestion of its secretary of war, authorized the troops, and approved a loan of $150,000 to pay and supply the new army.[15] Since the General Court steadfastly refused to declare a rebellion much less request federal troops, Knox was playing into the hands of the commercial militants in the state who were in a frenzy for repressive measures.[16] Ebenezer Wales, Stephen Higginson, Samuel Osgood, and Samuel Lyman all claimed that the disturbances had led many to favor a more powerful national government and James Sullivan, urging militant action against the Regulators, warned Adams that many of the old Whigs proposed to limit the power of the states. In the words of Knox, "The commotions of Massachusetts have wrought prodigious changes in the minds of men in that state respecting the power of government, everybody says that they [sic] must be strengthened and unless this is effected there is no hope for liberty and property."[17]

Knox, however, was wrong; "everybody" did not feel that way. The less commercial-cosmopolitan towns indicated no interest in strengthening the national government and several important politicians apparently shared their views. Sullivan and Benjamin Hitchborn, who had arrested Shattuck, worried about the increasing

13. Knox's reports may be found in the *Journals of Congress*, 20 Sept. 1786, 31:675-76; 28 Sept. 1786, pp. 698-700; 6 Oct. 1786, pp. 751-53; and 13 Oct. 1786, p. 875. Also note 4 Oct. 1786, pp. 739-40.

14. Ibid., 18 Oct., 1786, 31:886-88; 20 Oct. 1786, pp. 891-92. He also wrote to George Washington; see Knox to Washington, 23 Oct. 1786, Knox Papers, Massachusetts Historical Society.

15. *Journals of Congress*, 21 Oct. 1786, 31:892, 895-96.

16. East, "Massachusetts Conservatives," pp. 381-83. This is one of the more curious developments in the entire regulation. Since the General Court had approved no declaration of rebellion and since neither Bowdoin, the governor, or Shepard, the militia major-general for Hampshire County, had officially or unofficially requested national troops Knox's reports can be interpreted either as (1) a hysterical reaction to the regulation or (2) a program designed to increase national power by using an army to put down a local rebellion.

17. Henry Knox to George Washington, 21 Dec. 1786, Knox Papers; Ebenezer Wales to Caleb Davis, 4 Nov. 1786, Caleb Davis Papers, Massachusetts Historical Society; Stephen Higginson to Knox, 25 Nov. 1786, Knox Papers; Samuel Osgood to John Adams, 14 Nov. 1786, Adams Papers; *Massachusetts Gazette*, 27 Oct. 1786.

support of a national solution and in a message to the General Court Rufus King opposed calling a national convention in May 1787 to revise the confederation since he believed it could be changed only as specified in the Articles. [18] The court, not excited by the proposal, postponed consideration until its winter 1787 session and even Nathan Dane, who wanted to strengthen the confederation, opposed calling a convention that might replace the Articles. [19]

The conversion of the commercial-cosmopolitan interests and their leaders to nationalism had not really been completed by early 1787. During March 1787 the court considered sending delegates to the Philadelphia Convention. A joint committee chaired by Samuel Adams drafted instructions which recommended the creation of a national commercial system, certain specific changes, and other alterations "consistent with the true republican spirit and genius of the present Articles of the Confederation," but specifically forbad the delegates to change the annual election of congressmen. [20] The court then appointed a delegation composed entirely of important members of the commercial-cosmopolitan interests who had not yet become fervent nationalists. Caleb Strong, an important Hampshire County attorney, handled cases for local and eastern merchants and had served in the state senate; Rufus King did legal work for Newburyport merchants; and Elbridge Gerry and Nathaniel Gorham engaged in both mercantile and speculative operations. [21] The four men had accumulated al-

18. Benjamin Hitchborn to John Adams, 26 Oct. 1786, Adams Papers; James Sullivan to John Adams, 16 Dec. 1786, in ibid. Address by Rufus King, 11 Oct. 1786, in Burnett, ed., *Letters*, 8:478-80. Dane's address is in *Massachusetts Gazette*, 17 Nov. 1786.

19. *Acts and Laws*, 20 Oct. 1786, 4:936-37. John Adams to Thomas Jefferson, 30 Nov. 1786, in Boyd, ed., *Papers of Jefferson*, 10:6. *Massachusetts Gazette*, 17 Nov. 1786, for Dane's statement. Adams in his letter to Jefferson noted, "Don't be alarmed at the late Turbulence in New England. The Massachusetts Assembly had, in its zeal to get the better of their Debt, laid on a tax, rather heavier than the people could bear; but all will be well, and this Commotion will terminate in additional strength to the government."

20. *Acts and Laws*, 19 Feb. 1787, 4:973-74; 22 Feb. 1787, 4:447-49; 10 Mar. 1787, 4:517. James Sullivan to Rufus King, 25 Feb. 1787, in King, *Rufus King*, 1:213,

21. Information about all the delegates may be found in the *Biographical Congressional Directory*, since all had served in Congress. Sketches may be found in the *Dictionary of American Biography*. There is a biography of

most all their political experience at the national level. None had
served as governor or as lieutenant governor and only Strong had
sat for more than one term in the state senate.[22] Despite their
involvement in continental politics, none had been especially nationalistic during the earlier 1780s. Gerry and King had opposed
Morris's schemes for centralization, Gorham had the reputation of
being a political trimmer, and Strong had remained outside the
nationalist movements. Although not nationalistic the delegation
did not represent the balance of political forces in the commonwealth. Not one of the delegates had any sympathy for the convention movement, much less the Regulation, and all had supported the commercial-cosmopolitan programs of the earlier
1780s.[23] In a real sense the delegates represented not the commonwealth but the most commercial-cosmopolitan interests within the state.

Caleb Strong in Massachusetts Historical Society, *Proceedings*, 1st ser.,
1:289-99. There is another sketch of Dana in D. Hamilton Hurd, ed., *History
of Middlesex County, Massachusetts, with Biographies of Many of Its Prominent Men* (Philadelphia, 1890), p. xxx. All these men lived in group A communities: Gorham in Charlestown, Strong in Northampton, Dana in Cambridge, Gerry in Marblehead and Cambridge, and King in Newburyport.

22. See the lists of state senators in the *Acts and Laws*, 1780-1787. Strong
had served seven years in the senate prior to 1787.

23. According to the Interest Payment Books, in Treasurer's Records,
Office of the Secretary, Boston, for March 1786 through April 1787,
Gorham, Gerry, and Strong all received interest payments on their holdings of
consolidated securities. Gorham received £227, Gerry £447, and Strong only
£28. Gerry represented Marblehead in the 1786 General Court. On 9 June
1786 according to the unpublished Journals of the House of Representatives,
available at the Office of the Secretary, Boston, pp. 67-70 (cited hereafter as
House Journal), he voted in favor of granting supplemental funds to the
confederation. On 30 June 1786, ibid., pp. 150-51 and 152-53 he continued
to vote for this measure. On 19 Oct. 1786 ibid., pp. 274-75, he voted that it
was unconstitutional to reduce Bowdoin's salary and on 8 Nov, 1786, ibid.,
pp. 328-29, he voted to permit the trial of accused rioters outside of the
county of their residence. Thus on every single vote Gerry opposed the least
commercial-cosmopolitan interests that would later form the backbone of the
opposition to the Constitution. Nathaniel Gorham represented Charlestown
between 1781 and 1785. On 8 July 1783, ibid., pp. 157-60, he voted to grant
an impost with the commutation proposal attached. On 10 Mar. 1785, ibid.,
pp. 334-36, he voted to grant supplemental funds to Congress. On 6 Mar.
1787, ibid., pp. 483-84, and 10 Mar. 1787, ibid., pp. 499-500 he voted
against cutting Bowdoin's salary and opposed overriding the governor's veto
of the salary-cut bill.

The shift of three of these delegates into the nationalist camp during the spring and summer of 1787 reflected the changed outlook of their associates and constituents at home. The heavy turnout of voters and the defeat of Bowdoin and many senators worried Gorham who concluded that the nation needed a new constitution since "the present phantom of a government must soon expire."[24] In Philadelphia the delegates received more disturbing news from the commonwealth as the court extended the law suspending debt suits, struck down anti-Regulator legislation, refused to provide for the state's bond holders, and Hancock and his council refused to hang any of the convicted Regulators.[25] As the summer progressed the security holders, militants, Bowdoin backers, and many other members of the most commercial-cosmopolitan interests launched a bitter propaganda offensive against Hancock and the court, an offensive not without its influence on the delegates who were not allied with Hancock and had no sympathy for Regulators or convention men.[26] Thus it appears that the final shift of most of the delegates and the interests they represented into a nationalistic position occurred only after the successful repression of the rebellion and the disaster of the spring 1787 elections.

The positions taken by the Massachusetts delegation during the Philadelphia Convention reflected the political realities within the commonwealth and foreshadowed bitter political divisions. All the delegates supported provisions that would assist all groups and interests within the commonwealth; all of them supported policies that would favor the most commercial-cosmopolitan interests within the state, even those that conflicted with the legislation passed by the court; but they differed among themselves over

24. Nathaniel Gorham to Caleb Davis, 22 May 1787, Caleb Davis Papers. For other shifts toward a nationalist position see: Benjamin Lincoln to Henry Knox, 1 Mar. 1787, Knox Papers; Stephen Higginson to Henry Knox, 8 and 13 Feb. 1787, Knox Papers; Nathaniel Gorham to Henry Knox, 18 Feb. 1787, Knox Papers.
25. See ch. 8 for the activities of the court, the council, and Hancock during the summer of 1787.
26. See ch. 8 for the reaction of many groups and leaders to the political situation in Massachusetts. See Gerry's remarks in Max Farrand, ed., *The Records of the Federal Convention of 1787*, 4 vols. (New Haven, 1911-1937), 31 May 1787, 1:48-50.

questions dealing with the division of power between the national and state governments.

All of them spoke for and supported policies that would aid commerce and security holders within the commonwealth. King urged the national assumption of state debts on two occasions and claimed that the state creditors would not support the new constitution without such a guarantee. Gerry went even further and urged a specific constitutional provision for repaying the national creditors whom he at least considered to be the unsung heroes of the Revolution. [27] Gorham championed national commercial powers and in speaking against a provision requiring a two-thirds majority for the passage of navigation and commercial legislation bluntly warned that Massachusetts would have little reason to join a union that would not assist her commerce. [28] King spoke against any state power to tax exports and Gorham proposed that the states not even be allowed to levy inspection and packing charges on their exports. Gerry opposed all taxes of any kind on exports and Gorham hoped that the new government would not levy duties on the coastal trade. [29] The delegation could depend on the support of all sections and interests in the state on these questions since even the least commercial-cosmopolitan groups raised few objections to all sorts of tariff, impost, and navigation legislation passed by the court during the 1780s to favor the commonwealth's commerce.

However, not all the interests would have supported the delegates in their struggles against the evils of paper money and stay legislation. A minority in the court favored paper currency in both the summers of 1786 and 1787 and a majority had passed two acts suspending suits for debt since the fall of 1786. Gerry and King both supported prohibiting states from issuing currency and all the delegates backed the provision that forbad states from interfering with the rights of contract—a provision that might have made the acts for suspending suits for debt unconstitutional in the new national courts. [30] On these questions the delegates spoke and

27. For Gerry and King, see Farrand, ed., *Records of Convention*, 18 Aug., 2:326; 22 Aug., 2:327; 25 Aug., 2:377.
28. Farrand, ed., *Records of Convention*, 22 Aug., 2:307; 21 Aug. 2:362; 31 Aug., 2:480.
29. Ibid., 16 Aug., 2:307; 21 Aug., 2:362; 31 Aug., 2:480.
30. Ibid., 28 Aug., 2:439, 14 Sept., 2:619. See chs. 7 and 8 for the divisions in the General Court on this type of legislation.

voted for their particular interests and not for the entire commonwealth.

The delegation split wide open over the division of power between the state and national governments. Gerry, throughout the convention, favored what he termed a federal government in which the states, through their legislatures, would play an important role by electing the legislative and executive branches of the new government. In addition to a federalist structure, Gerry also championed a bill of rights designed to limit the powers of the new national government in its relations with the states and with individual citizens. Gorham and King consistently supported a more nationalistic solution in which the national government would not be controlled by or through the states and opposed any bill of rights. Strong, although eventually supporting the Constitution, remained silent but often voted with Gerry on important questions. This division had little to do with either economics or democracy. Gerry, a holder of national securities, wanted them funded and he showed little appreciation for the 1787 General Court or for the convention men. [31] He had ideological objections to a centralized government that might destroy the power of the states and result in a harsh oligarchical autocracy. Like many of Samuel Adams's associates he "stumbled at the threshold" of the new national system. Gerry, of course, possessed the virtue of consistency and really adhered to his position of the earlier 1780s when he opposed Morris's schemes for centralization while at the same time he favored granting limited commercial and fiscal powers to the confederation. [32] On the other side King and Gorham had started from much the same position but became convinced during 1787 that the national government needed greater authority to control the activities of the states. They felt a powerful national government would protect certain commercial-cosmopolitan interests with stay laws and prohibitions on paper money; it would open up new vistas of political activity beyond the reach of county conventions and Regulators; and it could develop programs that could not be dismantled by the disaster of a single election.

Gerry, throughout the convention, reiterated his support for a

31. According to the Interest Payment Books, Treasurer's Papers, March 1786 through April 1787, Gerry had collected at least £447 in interest from his state securities. His views are in Farrand, ed., *Records of Convention*, 31 May 1787, 1:48-50, 57.

32. For Gerry's earlier activities see ch. 5.

federalist structure. He suggested that the president be elected by the governors and rejected election by popular vote as destructive of state authority. [33] He objected to national control over the state's militia, the admission of national officials into its territories without its consent, and the popular election of members of the lower house which he believed would reduce the power of the state legislature. [34] He urged that these legislatures be granted the authority to instruct their congressmen and be permitted to remove them at any time. [35] Gerry's federalism played a significant role in the adoption of the senatorial compromise since he realized that a popularly elected House and a legislatively elected Senate would be the most federal option that could pass the convention. Thanks to Strong's support on this question the Massachusetts delegation split and permitted the adoption of the famous federal solution for the Senate. [36]

In addition to advocating a federal structure of government, Gerry also advocated the limitation of national power through other devices including a bill of rights   Gerry and Strong favored annual election of representatives from comparatively small districts, while Gorham and King appealed for longer terms and larger

33. Farrand, ed., *Records of Convention*, 7, 8, 9, June 1787, 1:149, 163, 174, 175, 181; 24 July, 2:94, 100, 102, 105.

34. Ibid., 17 Aug. 1787, 2:317; 23 Aug., 2:385, 388.

35. Ibid., 31 May 1787, 1:48-50.

36. The Massachusetts delegation was badly divided over the famous senatorial compromise. As early as 31 May, King had sponsored an upper house based on population of the states; ibid., 1:51, 52, 58, 59. Gerry on 7 June favored the election of senators by state legislatures; ibid., 7 June, 1:152, 154-55. Gorham on 25 June advocated a Senate based on the relative populations of the states; ibid., 1:404-05, 412-13. On 29 and 30 June, King, Gerry, and Gorham all defended their positions; ibid.,1:462-63, 467, 470, 474, 489, 492, 499, 502. On 2 July, Strong spoke in favor of committing the question to a special committee and was supported by Gerry who became a member of the committee; ibid., 1:515, 519. On 5 July Gerry delivered the report of the committee and engaged in a debate with Gorham; ibid., 1:526, 527, 532, 535. The next day King sided with Gorham and the debate continued in ibid., 1:540, 541, 545, 550, 551, 553. On 14 July Strong gave his rationale for supporting the committee's compromise; ibid., 2:7. On 16 July the final vote on the question to agree with the committee's report found the convention divided five states in favor and four opposed with Massachusetts evenly divided. Gerry and Strong voted for the compromise while Gorham and King opposed it. Without this division of the Massachusetts delegation the vote would have been five to five and the famous senatorial compromise would have been defeated, or at least postponed; ibid., 16 July 1787, 2:14.

districts. [37] Gerry opposed permitting the seating of national office holders in Congress to the dismay of Gorham and King who
believed these persons would support the manufacturing and commercial interests. [38] Gerry's most dynamic and original contribution was his insistence on adding a bill of rights to the Constitution. In early September he proposed a whole bundle of
limitations including jury trials in civil cases, the prohibition of ex
post facto laws and bills of attainder, the publication of the House
journals, freedom of the press, and the publication of all governmental expenditures, and urged the appointment of a committee
to prepare a bill of rights. [39] Gorham and King joined the majority
in opposing his motions and the original Constitution contained
no bill of rights.

King and Gorham, unlike Gerry, favored more nationalistic solutions to the various problems before the convention. King believed
that "a Union of the states is a union of the men composing them,
from whence a *national* character adheres to the whole" and believed that "much of their power ought to be taken from" the
states. [40] King and Gorham opposed any state interference in the
election of either branch of the national Congress, supported national control over the militia, and hoped that placeholders, government contractors, and other directly interested men would be
allowed to sit in Congress. [41]

Gerry's refusal to sign the finished Constitution had serious political repercussions within the commonwealth. Although he had
never been allied with Hancock and the moderates or the less
commercial-cosmopolitan interests, these groups used his objections as propaganda. Gerry's refusal to sign also underlined the
fact that several other major politicians including Hancock, Samuel Adams, and James Warren might be unfavorably disposed to

37. Ibid., 12 June 1787, 1:214-15, 220, 221; 21 June, 1:359, 361, 365,
368. Gorham and King eventually accepted the ratio of one representative to
every 30,000 of population; see ibid., 17 Sept. 1787, 2:643.
38. The debate on this issue came on 23 June 1787, in ibid., 1:387, 388,
392-94. Gerry raised the issue again on 14 August; see ibid., 2:285.
39. Gerry's support of a bill of rights may be found in ibid., 22 Aug. 1787,
2:375; 12 Sept., 2:588; 14 Sept., 2:613, 617-18; 15 Sept., 2:632-33.
40. King's philosophy is best expressed in his lengthy speech of 19 June
1787, ibid., 1:323, 327-28, 331-32.
41. For their opposition to antiplaceholding legislation see ibid., 22 June
1787, 1:375-76, 379, 391.

the new charter.[42] Instead of a rerun of the old most commercial-cosmopolitan versus the less commercial-cosmopolitan struggles of the earlier 1780s the opponents of the new Constitution had to deal with opposition from men who had been their political allies in the earlier campaigns.

The Constitution dropped right into the midst of a serious political struggle in the fall of 1787. The moderates and Hancockites had the militants on the run with their handling of the "S.H." letter affair. The fall session of the General Court, with a majority of its membership from towns that would oppose the Constitution in February 1788, overcame the opposition of the most commercial-cosmopolitan groups to continue its summer program of moderate reform. Indeed, members of these more commercial interests such as Sedgwick and Gore hoped that the new constitution would save them from the "wreck" of the current government and prevent a descent into "anarchy and disgrace."[43]

The fall session continued to descend into disgrace if not anarchy by passing a further extension of the law suspending suits for debt, giving no aid to the securities holders, and by making no effort to pass a direct tax. In his opening address the usually reticent Hancock, perhaps stung by the personal attacks on him during the summer, recommended the use of the impost and excise for general state expenses and he and his council continued to pardon the Regulators.[44] The main struggle during the session came over the extension of the law suspending suits for debt. (See table 57.) As usual the group A towns opposed extension with 58 percent of their votes but the group B and C towns overcame their resistance by casting 64 and 74 percent of theirs in favor. The same type of division separated the future Federalist towns from the Antifederalist communities; the former cast 69 percent of their votes against the measure while the latter cast 80 percent of theirs for the extension. Two important differences between the vote in the fall of 1786 and November 1787 reflected significant changes in voting patterns. The differences among the three socioeconomic groups of towns still remained although diminished by the passage of time, but the divisions between the future Feder-

42. Ibid., 15 Sept. 1787, 2:632-33.
43. Theodore Sedgwick to Rufus King, 18 June 1787, in King, *King*, 1:224. Christopher Gore to Rufus King, 28 June 1787, ibid., 1:226.
44. Governor's address in *Acts and Laws*, 18 Oct. 1787, 4:993-94.

TABLE 57
Suspension of Debts, 1786 and 1787

	Votes Against Extension		
Towns	*1786*	*1787*	*Change*
Group A	68%	58%	−10%
Group B	26	36	+10
Group C	31	26	− 5
Federalist	55	69	+14
Antifederalist	26	20	− 6
Total vote	42%	39%	− 3%

SOURCES: *Debates and Proceedings in the Convention of the Commonwealth of Massachusetts, Held in the Year 1788, and Which Finally Ratified the Constitution of the United States* (Boston, 1856), 6 Feb. 1788, pp. 87–92 (cited hereafter as *Proceedings in the Convention*). Vote of 1786 is in the unpublished Journal of the House of Representatives, available at the Office of the Secretary, Boston, 26 Oct. 1786, pp. 294–95 (cited hereafter as House Journal). The vote from 1787 is from ibid., 13 Nov. 1787, p. 367.

alist and Antifederalist towns had widened, a change which foreshadowed the bitter opposition over the new constitution.

In addition to passing the extension the court proceeded with more minor reforms. It granted a longer period for the collection of the March 1786 direct tax, ordered the treasurer to use the specie collected to pay the congressional requisition for general state expenses, and made absolutely no effort to bail out the sinking securities holders.[45] As usual the senate attempted to apply the brakes and blocked motions passed by the house to replace all the impost and excise collectors and to pardon all the Regulators.[46]

The General Court, plagued by its old and developing divisions, next had to consider how the Constitution would be ratified in Massachusetts. The problem of adoption had worried the members of the Philadelphia Convention. Gerry had taken the logical but politically impossible position that it would have to be accepted by all thirteen states since he could discover no other way to set

45. *Acts and Laws*, 8 Nov. 1787, 4:761; 19 Nov. 1787, 4:590-93. *Massachusetts Centinel*, 14 Nov. 1787.

46. Cotton Tufts to John Adams, 28 Nov. 1787, Adams Papers, pt. 4, explains the actions of the senate.

aside the unanimously adopted Articles of the Confederation. [47]
Gorham and King naturally opposed such a solution and the convention finally agreed on a ratification effected by nine states. [48]
Everyone blanched at the thought of submitting it to a direct
popular vote even though the commonwealth had voted on her
own 1780 charter. Gerry opposed submission to the people since
"the people in that quarter [Massachusetts] have at this time the
wildest idea of government in the world" and proved his point by
stating that they had tried to abolish the state senate. [49] At last
the convention decided to submit the document to specially
elected conventions where it would not be bottled up by legislative maneuvering and for which the people, according to Gorham,
would choose "better men" who would naturally favor the new
charter. [50] After a brief flush of enthusiasm in September 1787
the pro-Constitutional forces realized that they could have a long
and bitter struggle ahead of them. First they had to convince the
court to hold a ratification convention, and since over 55 percent
of the delegates came from towns that would oppose the Constitution in February 1788, this was difficult. [51] Elbridge Gerry made
their task even more difficult when he submitted a letter to the
court that outlined his objections to the Constitution and thus
provided propaganda for its opponents. [52] Despite these obstacles
the pro-Constitutionalists made a few concessions and carried the
call for a convention through the court. At first they hoped to
have a quickly organized convention in December at which the
state would not pay the members' salaries. But the anti-Constitutionalists were strong enough to force them to compromise when

47. *Records of the Convention*, 10 Sept. 1787, 2:561.

48. Ibid., 10 Sept. 1787, 2:560-63.

49. Ibid., 5 June 1787, 1:123, 127-29; 23 July 1787, 2:89-92.

50. Ibid., 23 July 1787, 2:90. Gorham was correct, at least for Massachusetts, and the importance of the large number of placeholders elected to the
Massachusetts convention will be discussed later in this chapter.

51. Unpublished Journals of the House of Representatives, available at the
Office of the Secretary, Boston, 13 Nov. 1787, p. 367 and compare with
the *Debates and Proceedings in the Convention of the Commonwealth of
Massachusetts, Held in the Year 1788, and Which Finally Ratified the Constitution of the United States* (Boston, 1856), 6 Feb. 1788, pp. 87-92 (cited
hereafter as *Proceedings in the Convention*). This differential reflects the fact
that the Federalists realized that a special convention would increase their
power.

52. *Records of the Convention*, 3:128-29.

William Widgery of Maine sponsored a motion to have the Constitution voted on by the people and the court. Although they defeated this move they had to agree to hold the convention in
January and have the state pay the salaries and expenses of the
delegates. The Constitutionalists also succeeded in ruling out of order a motion by Daniel Kilham declaring the new Constitution illegal and beat off efforts to hold the convention outside of Boston.[53] The Constitutionalists had their convention, but the later
date and the payment of salaries and expenses meant that
the smaller towns, more interested in politics since early 1787,
would be there in force.

With the preliminaries completed, the Constitutionalists began a
massive campaign for ratification that included the use of pamphlets and the press, personal efforts by politicians and placeholders, and careful organization and campaigning in important
towns. The newspaper and pamphlet barrage supporting ratification developed the themes that the new Constitution would aid
the commonwealth, that the powers of the new government had
been so limited that no one could possibly be threatened by them,
and that anyone opposing such an excellent plan must be either a
fool or a traitor. Writers urged that ratification would result in
more jobs, more protection for artisans, more commerce for everyone, and a much healthier economic future. Other propagandists
promised the farmer reductions in direct taxes and wider markets
for his produce if he would only vote for the new system.[54] Some

53. *Worcester Magazine*, Oct. 1787, pp. 62-65; *Massachusetts Centinel*, 24,
27 Oct. 1787; Public Papers for the Resolve of 25 Oct. 1787, in *Acts and
Laws*, 25 Oct. 1787, 4:740-42. The delegates were to be paid from state taxes
and the towns were to send as many representatives as they could to the
lower house of the General Court.

54. The Massachusetts papers during the months of November and December 1787 were filled with these arguments. One of the best samplers of the
rhetoric of the campaign is still Paul L. Ford, ed., *Essays on the Constitution
of the United States, Published During Its Discussion by the People,
1786-1788* (Brooklyn, 1892). For some other local materials see *Massachusetts Centinel*, 26 Sept. 1787, which printed the text of the Constitution. For
other essays in the various papers see "A True American," 29 Sept. 1787;
"Convention," 13 Oct. 1787; "One of the People," 17 Oct. 1787; "Truth,"
24 Nov. 1787, all in *Massachusetts Centinel*. "The Interests of This State,"
20 Nov. 1787, and "An American Citizen," 23 Oct. 1787, appeared in the
Salem Mercury. Others appeared in the *Independent Chronicle* on 11,
18 Oct., 25 Oct., 6 Dec. 1787.

claimed that the new Constitution would save the nation from anarchy and followed James Wilson's reasoning that the government would be so limited in nature that no bill of rights would be required, while other enlisted Washington's popularity to win dubious supporters.[55] In addition to praising the new Constitution, the writers smeared its opponents. They pilloried the anti-Constitutionalists as debtors, Regulators, or, at best, placeholders with a vested interest in the current system.[56] These assaults became so strident that one anti-Constitutionalist parodied their argument as follows: "Look ye, brother Martin and Jack if you do not believe this crust of bread to be as good as a shoulder of mutton as was sold in Leden Hall market, I pronounce you both a couple of blind, positive conceited sons of bitches, and may the d——l blast you to all eternity."[57]

Under cover of the newspaper barrage, leading Constitutionalists worked to convert their enemies or prevent their election. Rufus King attempted to influence his former cronies in Maine, and Theodore Sedgwick toured the west and debated with John Bacon. According to Sedgwick, never one to underestimate his importance, Bacon became convinced by his logical arguments and de-

55. Wilson's speech appeared in the *Massachusetts Centinel*, 24 Oct. 1787. This was an important Federalist argument against the need for a bill of rights. Notice also "Valerius" ibid., 28 Nov. 1787. "Medium" appeared in *Worcester Magazine*, Dec. 1787, p. 135, and in the *Hampshire Gazette*, 25 Dec. 1787, where he suggested the adoption of a bill of rights through amendments. Also note *Salem Mercury*, 30 Oct. 1787; *Massachusetts Centinel*, 17 Oct., 3, 10, 21, 24 Nov., 8 Dec. 1787; *Independent Chronicle*, 3 Jan. 1788; *Essex Journal*, 21 Nov. 1787; *Massachusetts Gazette*, 12, 23, 30 Nov. 1787.

56. Notice "Cato," *Essex Journal*, 28 Nov. 1787; "A.B." in *Massachusetts Centinel*, 14 Nov. 1787, and "One of the People," in ibid., 17 Nov. 1787. Also see *Massachusetts Centinel*, 17, 24, 31 Oct., 3, 10, 17, 24, 28 Nov., 8 Dec. 1787; *Essex Journal*, 21 Nov. 1787; *Independent Chronicle*, 3 Jan. 1788; *Massachusetts Gazette*, 16, 23, 30 Nov. 1787.

57. *Hampshire Chronicle*, 13 Nov. 1788. Also see "Protest of Minority in Pennsylvania," *Independent Chronicle*, 8 Nov. 1787; Gerry's objections are in ibid., 8 Nov. 1787; "An Officer of the Continental Army," *Massachusetts Centinel*, 21 Nov. 1787; "Agrippa," *Massachusetts Gazette*, 11, 14, 18, 25 Dec. 1787, and in Ford, ed., *Essays*, pp. 66-78; "A Republican Federalist," 29 Dec. 1787, 2 Jan. 1788; *Massachusetts Centinel*. "Agrippa" was James Winthrop; see Ford, ed., *Essays*, pp. 53-66. James Sullivan was "Cassius," *Massachusetts Gazette*, 18 Sept., 20 Oct., 16, 23 Nov. 1787. See also James Sullivan to Rufus King, 28 Sept. 1787, in King, *Rufus King*, 1:259-60.

cided not to vote against the Constitution. [58] Congregational ministers urged ratification upon their parishioners and the Federalists enlisted leading Baptists, such as Samuel Stillman and Isaac Backus, in their campaign. [59] The Federalists also took care that commercial towns would not send secret or open enemies of the Constitution to the convention. In Newburyport they defeated Dr. Kilham; at Milton they purged James Warren; and at Cambridge they kept Elbridge Gerry and James Winthrop, two of the leading anti-Constitutional writers, out of the convention. The ideological Antifederalists were badly beaten in these elections. Men like Gerry, Sullivan, Winthrop, and Warren lived in commercial towns and were seldom chosen as delegates to the convention. This meant that the most articulate or establishment Antifederalists were shut out and the Antifederalist arguments had to be carried by the former convention leaders like Bishop and Singletary, or by Maine separatists like Thompson and Widgery. [60] But in many towns the tide ran too strongly against the Federalists and

58. At first some thought ratification would be simple. See Christopher Gore to Rufus King, 7 Oct. 1787, in King, *Rufus King*, 1:261. But Cotton Tufts foresaw a close struggle; see Cotton Tufts to John Adams, 31 Oct.1787, Adams Papers; also Rufus King to Henry Knox, 28 Oct. 1787, Knox Papers, Massachusetts Historical Society. The Berkshire activities are in John Bacon to Sedgwick, n.d., and Theodore Sedgwick to ?, 28 Oct. 1787, Sedgwick Papers, Massachusetts Historical Society. See also Jeremiah Wadsworth to Rufus King, 16 Dec. 1787, Knox Papers; *Worcester Magazine*, Dec. 1787, p. 139.

59. See *Worcester Magazine*, Oct. 1787, p. 64; Henry Jackson to Henry Knox, 11 Nov. 1787, Knox Papers; Nathaniel Gorham to Henry Knox, 30 Oct. 1787, Knox Papers.

60. Samuel A. Otis to Dana, 12 Nov. 1787, Caleb Davis Papers, gives the efforts to prevent the inland towns from instructing their delegates. The Federalists feared, with good reason, that most of the less commercial-cosmopolitan communities would attempt to force their delegates to oppose ratification. *Worcester Magazine*, Nov. 1787, p. 113, shows how Northampton advised selecting "uninstructed" (and hence pro-Constitutional) delegates.

For activities in York county see Jeremiah Hill to George Thatcher, 12 Dec. 1787, Thatcher Papers, Boston Public Library; Hill to Thatcher, 1 Jan. 1788, ibid., where he sees the Shaysites as supporting the Antifederalists. Sedgwick to Henry Van Schaack, 13 Dec. 1787, Sedgwick Papers, gives the activities at Sheffield, one of the western group B towns. Nathaniel Gorham to Knox, 16 Dec. 1787, Knox Papers, sees a solid Federalist delegation from the coastal towns. Henry Jackson to Henry Knox, 25 Nov. 1787, Knox Papers; John Q. Adams, diary entry of 13 Oct., 29 Oct., 25 Nov. 1787, Adams Papers.

many placeholders who had played important roles in the earlier 1780s discovered that they would not represent their communities.

Even the results of the Boston election worried the Federalists. Despite their efforts the twelve elected delegates included Samuel Adams, John Hancock, and Thomas Dawes, all ideological Antifederalists considered neutral toward the Constitution. In an effort to boost the delegation all the Boston delegates but Hancock and John Winthrop dined with Bowdoin on the night of 5 January, but Samuel Adams spoiled their appetites by informing them of his opposition to certain sections of the Constitution, especially those dealing with representation and direct taxation. [61] Gore believed Adams would oppose the Constitution unless it was amended in such a fashion as would "totally destroy it" and the nationalists, fearing more defections, decided to put pressure on the Boston members. Two days later a meeting of artisans headed by Paul Revere and Benjamin Russell declared their support of the Constitution and proclaimed that they would give no political support to the enemies of ratification. [62] This pressure did not immediately change Adams's mind, but he kept his doubts to himself and thus let the Boston group appear united behind the Constitution.

Despite all these efforts the election of delegates did not result in a Federalist victory. Many Baptist towns in Bristol County refused to follow the lead of Stillman and Backus and sent Antifederalists to the convention. [63] The Nantucket Quakers also dis-

---

61. Christopher Gore to Rufus King, 6 Jan. 1788, in King, *Rufus King*, 1:311-12; Nathaniel Gorham to Henry Knox, 6 Jan. 1788, Knox Papers. See Samuel Adams to Richard Henry Lee, 3 Dec. 1787, in William V. Wells,*The Life and Public Services of Samuel Adams*, 3 vols. (Boston, 1865), 3:251-53, for the famous letter expressing Adam's fears.

62. *Massachusetts Centinel*, 9 Jan. 1788. This still remains a rather confusing event. Russell was a leading merchant and speculator and Revere, though described as an artisan, was deeply involved in commercial and manufacturing activities. Other well-known artisan leaders (who were also not artisans by occupation) such as Charles Jarvis and the Austins apparently took no part in putting pressure on Adams. In summary the rank and file artisans and laborers may have favored the Constitution but their "betters" provided the leadership.

63. The following information is based on Thomas Fleet and John Fleet, *Fleet's Pocket Almanack for the Year of Our Lord 1787 . . . to Which Is Annexed the Massachusetts Register* (Boston, 1786), pp. 51-58 and the vote in *Proceedings in Convention*, pp. 87-92. In the voting patterns of towns, by group, that had only Baptist ministers, group B towns gave 3 Yes votes for

appointed the Federalists; the island, whose delegates had voted with the most commercial-cosmopolitan interests in the 1780s, neglected to send delegates to the convention.[64] But the black cloud of delegates from the west most frightened Gorham and Dane who believed that the "state would divide on the question [the Constitution] as it has on all questions for several years past."[65] In January 1788 the Federalists knew that they still had their work cut out for them.

The composition of the convention verified the opinions of those who foretold a close decision. The Federalists convinced the eastern group A towns to send full delegations, but despite their efforts the commercial-cosmopolitan interests and their placeholding allies did not achieve the usual degree of control that they had held over the General Court during the earlier 1780s. (See table 58.) The political combination of delegates from the group A towns and placeholders from the two other groups accounted for 47 percent of the total representatives instead of the over 55 percent these interests had sent to the 1785 and 1786 Courts or the 52.1 percent of the membership that they sent to the lower house

---

ratification of the Constitution, and 2 No votes, while group C towns of the same type gave 2 Yes votes and 5 No votes. Again it seems that the Federalists were most successful in winning over leaders rather than rank and file voters and that they had their greatest success in communities whose commercial contacts inclined them to favor the Constitution.

64. Nathaniel Gorham to Henry Knox, 6 Jan. 1788, Knox Papers. Some historians have speculated that the Quakers on Nantucket refused to send delegates because of what they termed the militaristic nature of the new Constitution, but in 1783 the representatives from the island voted for the impost and commutation on all four of the roll call votes. See House Journal, 8 July 1783, pp. 157-60; 9 July, 165-68; 8 Oct., pp. 224-25; and 16 Oct., pp. 252-54. Nantucket had failed to send representatives to the 1787 General Court and would also neglect to send any to the 1788 sessions. The islanders may have intended to increase the fears of their secession in order to frighten the commonwealth into aiding the whaling industry. Two of the towns in Duke's County (Martha's Vineyard) sent delegates to the convention who voted for ratification.

65. Several towns did instruct their delegates; for an example see D. Hamilton Hurd, ed., *History of Worcester County, with Biographical Sketches of Many of Its Prominent Men* (Philadelphia, 1889), p. 31, for Lancaster; also Nathaniel Gorham to Henry Knox, 6 Jan. 1788, Knox Papers. For other information see Nathaniel Gorham to Rufus King, 12, 29 Dec. 1787, in King, *Rufus King*, 1:263, 265; Nathan Dane to Henry Knox, 27 Dec. 1787, 30 Dec. 1787, Knox Papers.

TABLE 58
Representation at the Ratification Convention

Towns	Percentage of Representatives					Change in Strength, 1780-91		
	At Convention	In Lower House				1787 to Convention	1786 to Convention	Total Compared with Convention
		1785	1786	1787	1780-91			
Group A	33.0%	30.4%	34.3%	29.8%	32.5%	+3.2%	-1.3%	+0.5
Group B	30.8	32.4	35.8	34.4	34.0	-3.6	-5.0	-3.2
Group C	36.3	37.2	29.9	35.9	33.5	+0.4	+6.4	+2.8
Group A + placeholders from B & C	47.0	55.3	56.4	42.4	52.1	+4.6	-9.4	-5.1

SOURCES: Representation for the 1780-91 period from ch. 3. Membership in the house in 1785, 1786, 1787, from the lists in *Acts and Laws of the Commonwealth of Massachusetts, 1780-1791*, 11 vols. (Boston, 1890-1897), and House Journals. Membership at the convention from *Proceedings in the Convention*, pp. 31-43.

between 1780 and 1791. The commercial-cosmopolitan-placehold-
ing interests had increased their strength when compared with the
1787 General Court, but they had not attained their typical
strength. If the interests voted on the Constitution as they had on
past issues it would indeed be a close decision.

The recognition of both sides that the composition of the convention could bring about a close vote prevented early divisions
and led the Federalists and Antifederalists to attempt to win over
the small but very important group of undecided or moderate
delegates. The Federalists counted on the support of the influential politicians, judges, and ministers at the convention to bring
moderate or even Antifederalist delegates into line. They also realized that they had better speakers and they devised tactics to
delay any divisive votes until they controlled the convention. The
Antifederalists probably should have pushed for a quick decision
but they were never sure at any given time that they had enough
strength to defeat the Constitution. Thus both sides agreed not to
quarrel over organization or the seating of disputed delegates and
the convention selected Hancock as president and Thomas Cushing
as vice president without any debate or division. The convention
then appointed a committee to investigate disputed elections
which took no action to eject any of the representatives elected by
the towns. Another committee reported that six Antifederalist and
four Federalist towns had sent more delegates than their due but
the convention took no action and these representatives also remained at the session. The hesitation to purge any representatives
resulted from the even balance of power, the important position
of the undecided or moderate group, and the unwillingness of
both the Federalists and Antifederalists to risk a division. Despite
the efforts of the Federalists to pack the convention, it was to be a
very close vote, and the pressures applied within the convention
and the influence of the proposed amendments gave the Federalists their narrow margin of victory. [66] The Federalists won an

66. There are several excellent secondary accounts about the convention.
The best for solid, old-fashioned narrative is still Samuel B. Harding, *The Con-
test Over the Ratification of the Federal Constitution in the State of Massa-
chusetts* (New York, 1896). Excellent modern studies include Jackson T.
Main, *The Anti-Federalists: Critics of the Constitution, 1781-1788* (Chapel
Hill, 1961), pp. 201-10, and Forrest McDonald, *We the People: The Eco-
nomic Origins of the Constitution*, (Chicago, 1958), pp. 182-202. Also see
E. A. Bernhard, *Fisher Ames, Federalist and Statesman, 1758-1808* (Chapel

important victory when they convinced the convention to discuss
the Constitution paragraph by paragraph before any final vote.
Backed by the moderates on this particular issue, they hoped that
oratory and pressure would win over enough delegates to give
them the victory. In exchange for stalling final action, the Federalists permitted Elbridge Gerry, the leading and most vocal ideological Antifederalist, a seat on the floor. [67]

During the next three weeks the opposing forces debated on the
floor and brought all sorts of pressures to bear on the uncom-
mitted or wavering delegates. The Federalists possessed a great
advantage in their heavy support from ministers, politicians,
judges, and other opinion leaders who had been elected to the
convention. Senators, judges, justices, and ministers accounted for
almost two-fifths of the total seats and over four-fifths of these
important people would vote for the new Constitution. [68] The
overwhelming support by the influential citizens enabled the Federalists to increase their pressure on undecided delegates and permitted them to dominate the debates. Henry Jackson summed up
the situation when he wrote: "to see the weight of respectability,
integrity, property and ability on the side of the proposed Constitution and on the other side the — — characters that oppose it.
My God what a contrast." [69]

In debate the Federalists attempted to prove that the Constitution would aid the commonwealth and that it would create a

---

Hill, 1965), pp. 55-66, and Richard E. Welch, Jr., *Theodore Sedgwick, Federalist: A Political Portrait* (Middleton, Conn., 1965), pp. 56-65. For the begin-
nings of the sessions see *Proceedings in the Convention*, 11 Jan. 1788,
pp. 48-49; 12 Jan., pp. 50-54; 14 Jan., p. 55; Belknap's Notes 9, 11, 12 Jan.
1788 in Belknap Papers, 2:296-97; Belknap to Hazard, ibid., 3:5.

67. *Proceedings in the Convention*, 14 Jan. 1788, 55-56.

68. Rufus King to Madison, 27 Jan. 1788, in King, *Rufus King*, 1:316-17,
argues that the weight of intelligence and property was so favorable to ratification that this in itself made the opposition suspicious and reinforced their
fears of the rich and powerful using the new government to achieve their
goals. For contemporary popular belief in a plot to corrupt the convention
see *Proceedings in the Convention*, 21 Jan. 1788, pp. 64-65. Also notice
John Q. Adams, diary entry for 11 Feb. 1788, Adams Papers, in which he
details his disgust at Parsons's reports of Federalist machinations during the
convention. For the domination of Federalist speakers see Jeremy Belknap to
Hazard, 20 Jan. 1788, Belknap Papers, 3:6, and Nathaniel Freeman to
John Q. Adams, 27 Jan. 1788, Adams Papers. For a good secondary discussion see Main, *Anti-Federalists*, pp. 202-05.

69. Henry Jackson to Henry Knox, 20 Jan. 1788, Knox Papers.

limited and popularly controlled federated government. Ames, Bowdoin, and other speakers continued to emphasize the points that the Constitution provided a government with strictly limited powers that could not be used in a tyrannical fashion. They urged delegates to approve the new charter in order to create a limited federal government that could foster the commonwealth's commerce and the economy of all sections of the state. [70] Several observers and many historians have commented on the effectiveness of the Federalist oratory, but it swayed few delegates and after three weeks of steady speaking the Federalists ruefully admitted that the decision remained doubtful. [71]

The Antifederalist speakers quite openly suspected the supporters of the new Constitution of wanting a more powerful national government that could overwhelm popular resistance to its programs and policies. They had opposed the commonwealth's financial programs of the earlier 1780s, they had voted against repressive legislation in the 1786 and 1787 General Courts, and they had passed some reform legislation after the Regulation. They realized the amount of time and effort it had taken to change the policies of the commonwealth, and they feared that a national government, controlled by the nation's leaders, would be even less responsive to popular demands than their own commonwealth. They did not object to the anti- or undemocratic nature of the new charter; they feared it because they believed a new, uncontrolled, powerful national government would levy heavy direct

70. For examples of rhetoric see especially (town and its group are given in brackets for each speaker): Fisher Ames [Dedham-A], 15 Jan. 1788, *Proceedings in the Convention*, pp. 104-08; Christopher Gore [Boston-A], 15 Jan., ibid., p. 114; Theophilus Parsons [Newburyport-A], 16 Jan., ibid., p. 124; Judge Dana [Cambridge-A], 17 Jan., ibid., p. 135-37; Thomas Dawes [Boston-A], 18 Jan., ibid., pp. 139-41; and Dawes [Boston-A], 21 Jan., ibid., pp. 157-59.

Federalist speakers also played down the need for a bill of rights. Most of them followed James Wilson's argument in Pennsylvania and claimed that the new government was already controlled by internal checks. See Joseph B. Varnum [Justice from Dracut-C], 23 Jan., ibid., pp. 178-79; James Bowdoin [Boston-A], 23 Jan., ibid., pp. 178-79; Parsons [Newburyport-A] and Dawes [Boston-A], 24 Jan., ibid., pp. 197-99; Nathaniel Gorham [Charlestown-A], 25 Jan. ibid., p. 207.

71. Henry Jackson to Henry Knox, 20 Jan. 1788, Knox Papers; Samuel Nasson to George Thatcher, 22 Jan. 1788, Thatcher Papers; Rufus King to Madison, 27 Jan. 1788, in King, *Rufus King*, 1:316-17, still expected a majority of eight or twelve against ratification.

taxes to pay off the national debt, would collect these taxes through its own administrative and judicial systems, and could use military force to put down any resistance. This powerful government would hardly be influenced by isolated farming communities in western Massachusetts. The president, elected by a college of aristocratic electors, would be less responsive than the governor of the commonwealth. The senators selected by the General Court would be similar to the men who served in the Confederation Congress and the representatives would be elected from districts even larger than those established for the state senate. Everything indicated the establishment of a government with enormous powers that could not be controlled by town instructions or through county conventions.

The growing belief in aristocratic juntos and plots intensified this distrust of the new government. The same men who had backed the financial programs of the 1780s, who had urged repression in 1786, and who had been implicated in the shadowy "S.H." letter affair backed the new Constitution and the less commercial-cosmopolitan interests naturally assumed that their old enemies planned to give them a gold brick. The Antifederalist speakers used this logic in criticizing the new Constitution and often used examples from the political history of the commonwealth to reinforce their points. Samuel Thompson, in opposing the biennial election of members of the House, pointed out that "had the last administration continued one year longer, our liberties would have been lost, and the country involved in blood; not so much, Sir, from their bad conduct, but from the suspicions of the people of them." [72] William Widgery argued that the commercial interests would control Congress and would saddle the farmers with heavy direct taxes for paying the interest on the national debt while keeping the imposts as low as possible. Abraham White pointed out that the new government could not only levy these taxes but could collect them with the assistance of a standing army. But it was Amos Singletary who dramatized all these fears when he pictured the "little people" being swallowed up by a new Leviathan.

Other Antifederalists attacked congressional power over elections and the large size of the congressional districts. They suspected that Congress would change the election laws to aid certain

72. Samuel Thompson [Justice-Topsham-C]. His speech is in *Proceedings in the Convention*, 15 Jan. 1788, pp. 112-13.

interests and they realized that the large districts would foster the candidacy of placeholders and professionals. Others denounced the absence of a bill of rights pointing out that the new government would be at least as repressive as the commonwealth and would be bound by no restrictions of any kind. [73] These Antifederalists raised neither stupid nor irrational objections to the new Constitution. They merely postulated that a future national government controlled by commercial-cosmopolitan interests would certainly use its taxation and funding powers as effectively as the commonwealth. They thus foresaw heavy direct taxes, the stifling of popular response, and a tendency toward tyranny or at least aristocracy. That these fears failed to materialize does not reflect on their intelligence; it merely illustrates that past experience is not an infallible guide to future developments.

On many other issues the Antifederalists disagreed among themselves or found themselves in accord with the Federalists. Neither side seemed enthusiastic about the three-fifths clause which gave the South representation for slaves, and spokesmen on both sides condemned the slave trade. [74] Singletary made a violent speech against the lack of a religious test for national officers but other Antifederalists did not follow his lead. They also debated among themselves over the lack of a property requirement for officehold-

73. For additional fears about taxation see William Bodman [Williamsburgh-C], ibid., 21 Jan. 1788, pp. 159-60; Amos Singletary [Justice-Sutton-B], ibid., pp. 160 and 371-72; Abraham White [Justice-Norton-B], ibid., p. 156; William Widgery [New Gloucester-C], ibid., pp. 156, 371. Also see Proceedings in the Convention, 25 Jan. 1788, p. 203; 22 Jan. 1788, pp. 169-75, for the long speech of William Symmes [Andover-A], and 23 Jan. 1788, ibid., pp. 176 and 312, for Ebenezer Pierce [Justice-Partridgefield-C].

The fourth of the proposed amendments provided that Congress should levy no direct taxes except when revenue from the impost and excise were insufficient to meet expenses. See ibid., 31 Jan. 1788, p. 80. This was later amended by a special committee to provide for Congressional requisitions on the states in lieu of a direct collection of taxes. See ibid., 4 Jan. 1788, p. 82.

For more of the Antifederalist rhetoric see ibid., 16 Jan. 1788, p. 121; 17 Jan., pp. 134 and 298-99; 22 Jan., p. 168, for Dr. Samuel Willard [Uxbridge-B]; 22 Jan. 1788, pp. 169-75, for William Symmes [Andover-A]; 23 Jan., ibid., pp. 180-81, for Samuel Thompson [Justice-Topsham-C]; 24 Jan., ibid., pp. 201-02, for Amos Singletary [Justice-Sutton-B] and Thompson; 25 Jan., ibid., pp. 202-03, for Singletary's long speech; 25 Jan., ibid., p. 267, for William Widgery [New Gloucester-C]; 26 Jan., ibid., p. 209, for Thompson and John Taylor [Justice-Douglas-C]; 1 Feb. 1788, ibid., pp. 236-40, for Samuel Nasson [Sandford-C].

74. Notice ibid., 25 Jan., pp. 319-20, and 17 Jan., pp. 300-01.

ing and voting. [75] Thus the main thrust of the Antifederalist arguments rested upon their experience with the political system in their own commonwealth and their fears for the future.

The Federalists drove Gerry from the sessions but they found by the end of January that they still could not control the convention. On 19 January Gerry rose to reply to a question put to him the previous day. The Federalists made acid comments about Gerry's presence on the floor and when he tried to defend himself they argued that he could only reply to specific questions. Judge Dana then launched into a virulent personal assault on Gerry; the two men almost came to blows and Gerry, in a huff, withdrew from the proceedings and refused to return unless permitted to defend himself against such personal abuse. Since the convention declined to act on his request, the Antifederalists lost an effective supporter. [76] Even after Gerry's departure the Federalists feared for the outcome but fortunately for them the Antifederalists had also failed to secure a majority. The latter group, annoyed at the unending debate on the Constitution, moved to discuss the document as a whole; Widgery urged the convention to take an immediate vote and on 29 January, Nasson made a similar motion, but Samuel Adams, speaking for the moderates who still held the balance of power, informed the convention that he had not made up his mind and that he wanted his doubts eased by a continued discussion. [77]

By the end of the month the convention appeared to be stalemated. The Antifederalists lacked the votes to shut off discussion and the Federalists feared that a vote on passage would result in defeat. Since so much depended on the moderates, the Federalists

75. Singletary made his objection on 19 Jan., ibid., p. 143, and reiterated it on 21 Jan., ibid., p. 311. None of the other Antifederalist speakers followed his lead. Thompson spoke for a property qualification for federal representatives in ibid., 17 Jan., p. 133. But according to Parsons's notes in ibid., p. 298, it was Abraham White, another Antifederalist [Justice-Norton-B] who objected to the absence of qualifications while Thompson supported their absence. In any event the division among the Antifederalists was underlined when Gilbert Dench [Hopkinton-B], 17 Jan., ibid., p. 299, opposed these requirements.

76. Rufus King to James Madison, 20 Jan. 1788, in King, *Rufus King*, 1:314. Henry Jackson to Henry Knox, 20 Jan. 1788, Knox Papers; Jeremy Belknap to Hazard, 20 Jan. 1788, Belknap Papers, 2:6; *Proceedings in the Convention*, 22 Jan. 1788, pp. 65, 173.

77. Ibid., 23 Jan. 1788, pp. 180-81, 195-96; 24 Jan., pp. 75, 196-97.

devised a strategem to win this group over to ratification by proposing amendments. This idea had been around since the appearance of the "Medium" articles in mid-December, and Benjamin Lincoln noted that amendments had been discussed as early as the second week in January. [78] By the third week the Federalists accepted Gorham's premise that "we cannot gain the question without some amendments" and began to search for a method to introduce them. [79] After some nebulous negotiations with Hancock and Adams, the Federalists won them both over by permitting Hancock to submit the recommended amendments. Some writers have postulated a political deal between the Federalists and Hancock, but in any event the two men backed them and won many moderates over to the side of the Constitution. [80]

The amendments presented by Hancock on 31 January had been tailored to meet several objections raised in the convention. They limited congressional power to levy direct taxes, provided for a larger House of Representatives, proposed jury trial in civil cases, reserved more power to the states, and limited the jurisdiction of the national courts. [81] Adams then rose, stated that these proposals had his approval, and seconded the amendments. [82] Two days later the convention appointed a committee of two members from each county, one Federalist and one Antifederalist, to con-

78. *Worcester Magazine*, Dec. 1787, p. 135; *Hampshire Chronicle*, 25 Dec. 1787; William Cranch to John Q. Adams, 22 Jan. 1788, Adams Papers; Rufus King to James Madison, 27 Jan. 1788, in King, *Rufus King*, 1:316-17; Henry Jackson to Henry Knox, 23 Jan. 1788, Knox Papers; Benjamin Lincoln to George Washington, 27 Jan. 1788, *Proceedings in the Convention*, p. 402.

79. Nathaniel Gorham to Henry Knox, 30 Jan. 1788, Knox Papers.

80. Rufus King to Henry Knox, 27 Jan. 1788, Knox Papers. King wrote that the *Centinel* of 26 January contained propositions for conditional ratification and that Hancock appeared to favor the new Constitution but didn't "care to resque [sic] anything in its favor." The idea of a Federalist deal with Hancock (and perhaps with Samuel Adams) is discussed in Main, *Anti-Federalists*, pp. 205-06. Whether a deal existed or not (and the Federalists made no effort to challenge Hancock in 1788 for the governorship), the honeymoon ended in the summer of 1788 when Hancock prevented Lincoln, the newly elected lieutenant-governor from becoming governor of Castle Island (a well-paying sinecure that had been held by Thomas Cushing, as lieutenant governor, since 1780). The convention also was the first step in bringing Hancock and Samuel Adams together as a political team that would dominate the two highest state offices after 1789. (See chs. 10 and 11 for more details.)

81. *Proceedings in the Convention*, 31 Jan. 1788, pp. 224-25, 80-81.

82. Ibid., pp. 225-27.

sider the amendments and on 4 February it recommended only one major change, a proposal that Congress could impose direct taxes only when the states failed to pay other types. [83] The success of the proposed amendments raised the spirits of the Federalists and Lincoln, Belknap, and Gorham all agreed that the Constitution would now be ratified. [84] The following week the effect became noticeable when Barrell of York, a previous opponent, stated that he would now vote for ratification since he had been assured that the proposed amendments would be accepted and in the next few days Turner of Scituate and Symmes of Andover both announced their support. [85] With their support slipping the Antifederalists, in a last ditch effort to prevent ratification, moved to adjourn but were defeated by a vote of 329 to 115. Adams almost spoiled the plot when he proposed a list of additional amendments on 6 February, but the Federalists convinced him to withdraw these proposals the next day. [86]

In spite of the fact that the Federalists had the ablest speakers, the most prestigious delegates, and the ultimate support of the moderates, the very close final vote on ratification closely followed the voting patterns of the earlier 1780s and continued to reflect the older political divisions within the commonwealth. (See table 59.) Six significant divisions appeared in the vote, all of them related to the earlier political responses of the various groups and towns. The first division, arising from the splits over financial questions that dated back into the earlier 1780s, reflected the fact that the Antifederalists believed that the new national government would institute the type of policies they had fought so bitterly in the commonwealth. The group A towns voted heavily for the Constitution, the group C towns opposed it, and the group B towns split on the question. In many respects political divisions had remained almost stationary since 1781 when the vote on the Consolidation Act resulted in almost identical divisions. When we

83. Ibid., 2 Feb. 1788, p. 82; 4 Feb. 1788, pp. 82-85. The committee of 25 members included 15 men who would vote for ratification. 16 of the 25 members came from group A towns, 5 from group B and 4 from group C communities. See Main, *Anti-Federalists*, p. 206, fn. 54, for a list of potential shifters.

84. Benjamin Lincoln to George Washington, 3 Feb. 1788, in *Proceedings in the Convention*, p. 404; Jeremy Belknap to Hazard, 3 Feb. 1788, Belknap Papers, 3:15; Rufus King to James Madison, 3 Feb. 1788, in King, *Rufus King*, 1:318.

85. *Proceedings in the Convention*, 5 Feb. 1788, pp. 264-65, 274-77.

86. Ibid., 5 Feb. 1788, pp. 265-66; 6 Feb. 1788, pp. 86, 226.

TABLE 59
Vote on Ratification Compared with Vote on Consolidation Act of 1781

Towns	For Constitution	For Consolidation Act
Group A	82%	80%
Group B	51	47
Group C	29	33
Eastern group A	89	90
Western group A	58	67
Western group C	20	27
Total vote	53%	54%

SOURCES: *Proceedings in the Convention*, 6 Feb. 1788, pp. 87–92, for the Constitution and House Journal, 24 Jan. 1781, pp. 246-47.

examine the response to the commonwealth's entire financial program we see that the roughly one-third of the communities represented at the convention who had favored it cast 81 percent of their vote for ratification, while those who opposed the program cast 69 percent of theirs against the Constitution.[87] The struggle over the Constitution was thus directly related to splits over the financial program of the earlier 1780s.

The amount of back taxes outstanding in a town, another legacy from the earlier 1780s, also influenced its vote. About three-fifths of the voting delegates at the convention represented towns that had a below-average amount of back taxes out on execution in early 1787; these towns cast 64 percent of their votes for ratification. On the other side stood around one-third of the delegates representing communities relatively hard hit by executions by 1787 who gave 71 percent of their votes against ratification of the new charter.[88]

87. See *Proceedings in the Convention*, 6 Feb. 1788, pp. 87-92, for percentage for ratification. The four groups of towns are based on the following votes: final vote on act modifying legal tender and beginning the consolidation of the state debt in House Journal, 24 Jan. 1781, pp. 246-47; vote on the so-called tender act, ibid., 2 July 1782, pp. 150-51; vote on the cider tax, ibid., 3 Mar. 1784, pp. 433-34; vote on bill to tighten up administration of tax collections, ibid., 12 Nov. 1784, pp. 205-07; vote on bill to use revenue from state impost and excise to pay general expenses, ibid., 16 Mar. 1786, pp. 518-20. These votes are discussed in detail in ch. 4.

88. This information is based on the figures from Taxes out on Execution at the Death of Ivers [1787], in Treasurer's Papers, Office of the Secretary, Boston. The totals are divided by the number of 1784 polls for each town to get the per poll averages.

TABLE 60
*Vote on Ratification: Response of Towns to Repressive and Reform
Legislation, 1786–1787*

Type of Town	Voting Delegates for Ratification
Opposed to reform, for repression	78%
Not voting on these issues	58
Divided over these issues	52
Supported reform, opposed to repression	28

SOURCES: *Proceedings in the Convention*, pp. 87–92, for percentage of representatives for ratification. The four groups of towns are based on an analysis of the following votes:

Vote One: To pass the bill providing supplemental funds to the confederation (House Journal, 30 June 1786, pp. 150–52).

Vote Two: To pass the above after amendment (Ibid., 30 June 1786, pp. 152–55).

Vote Three: To engross the act providing for the suspension of suits for debt (Ibid., 26 Oct. 1786, pp. 294–95).

Vote Four: To concur with the senate to accept its report on modifying the Disqualification Act (Ibid., 13 June 1787, pp. 60–65).

Vote Five: To extend the law suspending the collection of private debts (Ibid., 13 Nov. 1787, p. 367).

NOTE: Towns that voted with the most commercial-cosmopolitan interests over two-thirds of the time are included in the category "Opposed to reform, for repression." Towns opposed to these same policies for more than two-thirds of the time are listed in the "Supported reform, opposed to repression" category. Towns whose representatives stood between these two extremes are listed in the "Divided over these issues" category, and towns whose delegates either failed to vote or took no part in the session are listed in the "Not voting on these issues" category.

Since the Regulation episode was the culmination of the popular response to the financial program, the towns also divided over the Constitution as they had in their attitudes toward the Regulators in 1786 and 1787. (See table 60). The towns that voted for repressing the Regulators and opposed reforms cast 78 percent of their votes for the new Constitution while the communities that took the opposite position voted by a three-to-one margin against ratification. When we look at the response to both the financial programs of the 1780s and to the Regulation of 1786 and 1787, we see that over nine-tenths of the delegates from those towns that voted for the financial programs, against reforms, and for repressive policies favored the Constitution. (See table 61.) On the other side almost three-fourths of the representatives from the communities that opposed the financial programs, favored reforms, and voted against repression opposed ratification. Thus the strug-

TABLE 61

*Vote on Ratification: Response of Towns to Financial Program
and to Repressive and Reform Legislation, 1781-1787*

Type of Town	Voting Delegates for Ratification
Favored fiscal program, opposed reform	96%
Not voting on these questions	62
Divided over these questions	46
Opposed fiscal program, favored reform	26

SOURCES: Based on the combination of votes listed in table 60.
See fn. 87 for vote on financial program in the 1780s.

NOTE: Towns in the "Favored fiscal program, opposed reform"
category sent to the General Court between 1780 and 1787 representatives who supported the commercial-cosmopolitan programs in
both cases with over two-thirds of their votes. The representatives
of the towns in the "Opposed fiscal program, favored reform" category took the opposite position. Delegates from towns in the "Divided over these questions" category took an intermediate position,
while towns in the "Not voting on these questions" category failed
to send representatives or their representatives failed to vote on
these questions.

gle over the Constitution fits relatively neatly into the developing
pattern of the commonwealth's preparty politics.

In addition to winning the support of the most commercial
towns and those communities that had favored the fiscal and repressive legislation of the 1780s and opposed reforms during the
Regulation, the Federalists also counted on the support of placeholders, judges, and ministers for their final victory. (See table 62.) The judges, justices, and ministers at the convention cast
over four-fifths of their votes for ratification, a figure which includes three-fourths of the placeholders and preachers representing
group B and C towns generally opposed to the new Constitution.
The combination of placeholders, ministers, and representatives
from the group A towns accounted for over three-fourths of the
total votes for the Constitution and only one-fifth of the opposition to ratification. Thus the placeholders and ministers were important to the success of the Federalists.

An analysis of three of these factors, the socioeconomic characteristics of the towns, the responses of the towns to the programs
of repression and reform, and the voting patterns of placeholders,
shows that the Constitution received its greatest support from the
most commercial-cosmopolitan towns, represented by placeholders,

TABLE 62
Vote on Ratification: The Role of Placeholders and Ministers

	Percentage Voting for Ratification		
Towns	Placeholders and Ministers	Others	Total
Group A	97%	53%	82%
Group B	83	36	51
Group C	62	23	29
Total vote	86%	30%	53%

SOURCES: *Proceedings in the Convention*, pp. 87–92, for the names and rankings of the delegates. Thomas Fleet and John Fleet, *Fleet's Pocket Almanack for the Year of Our Lord 1787 . . . to Which Is Annexed the Massachusetts Register* (Boston, 1786), pp. 86–105 (cited hereafter as Fleet, *Register*, with year and date of publication), lists the judges and justices of the peace. See ibid., pp. 51–58, for ministers who are also identified in the *Proceedings in the Convention*, pp. 87–92.

that had opposed reforms in 1786 and 1787. (See tables 63 and 64.) The most vigorous opposition came from the group C, least commercial-cosmopolitan communities, not represented by place-holders, that had favored reforms in the earlier sessions. There is a correlation between support for the Constitution and each of the three factors. The commercial towns tended to vote for the Consti-tution while the less commercial communities opposed it. Within each of the three commercial-cosmopolitan groups of towns, those communities that favored repression in 1786 and 1787 backed the new charter, and table 64 underlines the fact that regardless of a town's socioeconomic character or its political position in 1786

TABLE 63
Vote on Ratification by Groups and by Responses in the 1786-1787 General Court

	Percentage Voting for Ratification				
Towns	Favoring Repression	Divided	Not Voting	Opposed to Repression	Total
Group A	95%	75%	100%	50%	82%
Group B	59	50	100	38	51
Group C	52	47	44	7	29
Total	78%	52%	58%	28%	53%

SOURCES: Based on votes analyzed in table 60.

TABLE 64
Vote on Ratification by Groups, Responses, and Placeholders in the 1786-1787 General Court

| | Percentage Voting for Ratification | | | | | | | | |
| | Favoring Repression | | Divided | | Not Voting | | Opposed to Repression | | Total |
Towns	Ph[a]	Nph[b]	Ph[a]	Nph[b]	Ph[a]	Nph[b]	Ph[a]	Nph[b]	
Group A	100%[a]	80%[b]	100%[a]	0%[b]	100%[a]	0%[b]	86%[a]	19%[b]	84%
Group B	86	40	100	40	100	100	73	25	50
Group C	80	44	100	36	63	38	13	6	29
Total	96%	55%	100%	36%	79%	48%	65%	15%	

SOURCES: Based on table 60 and the sources for placeholders and ministers listed in table 62.
a. "Ph" stands for "Placeholders and ministers."
b. "Nph" stands for "Nonplaceholders and ministers."

and 1787, placeholding delegates supported the Constitution to a much greater degree than other representatives from the same class of towns.

Differences in the religious orientation of the various towns, which was also related to the commercial and social distinctions among them, also had some impact on the vote. (See table 65.)

TABLE 65
Vote on Ratification by Church Affiliations

Type of Town	Percentage of Total Delegates at Convention	Percentage of Delegates Voting for Ratification
Congregational church only	58%	52%
Congregational and other denominations	27	61
Other denominations only	7	29
No church or minister	8	48

SOURCE: Fleet, *Register, 1787* (1786), pp. 51–58.

Although there was practically no difference between the votes of towns with only Congregational ministers and all other communities, towns with more than one denomination tended to give more support to ratification. Just as these generally larger and more cosmopolitan communities supported the Constitution, the towns with no churches or with only non-Congregational ministers voted against ratification. These towns, relatively few in number, more isolated, and less integrated into a wider network of ecclesiastical relationships, probably voted against ratification because of their connections with the less commercial-cosmopolitan interests. At least religious differences were not crucial influences at the convention.

The final vote on ratification after all the speeches, pressure, compromises, and machinations still reflected the basic socio-economic divisions within the commonwealth, the political polarization developing from these divisions during the 1780s, and the social and political role of the placeholder which frequently made him unrepresentative of his community. After February 1788 the commonwealth seemed ready to enter a new era of party politics. The voters had been interested and mobilized, the important political leaders had shown signs of dividing on an important question, and the intense struggle over ratification had made citizens and politicians very conscious of the potential power of the new national government. For a brief time in 1788 and 1789 it seemed that the state would develop a viable party system but this was only the false dawn of party politics.

10

Federalists and Antifederalists

AFTER ratification, the pressure of debts and taxes relaxed, fiscal issues faded into the background and questions concerning the powers and programs of the new national government arising from the ratification controversies held the political spotlight. Since the questions of ratification had divided the interests along the commercial-cosmopolitan continuum, the former socioeconomic divisions remained, but the shift in issues brought about a gradual though noticeable change in the responses of the most and least commercial towns to these national questions. The other outstanding feature of the new political environment was the emergence of issue rather than personality-oriented factions. These factions, the Federalists, Antifederalists, and moderates, developed during 1787 and then by early 1788 had taken a position on the new Constitution and national government. Although not separated by hard and fast ideological or policy lines and often tending to merge with one another, the factions did sponsor different policies and use competing rhetoric to define and advertise their positions. The Federalists generally supported the new Constitution, preferably without amendments, and worked to create as powerful a national government as possible. Led by Archfederalists like Fisher Ames and Theodore Sedgwick and including more moderate members such as Caleb Strong and Benjamin Goodhue, most of whom had supported the most commercial-cosmopolitan policies during the 1780s, repression in 1786 and 1787, and ratification in 1788, this faction based in the most commercial-cosmopolitan towns and those communities that favored the Constitution attempted to control both the commonwealth and the Massachusetts delegation to the new national Congress. The Antifederalists, led by such convention stalwarts as Amos Singletary, Samuel Thompson, and Phanuel Bishop, opposed these new plans just as they had fought against the financial programs of the earlier 1780s and the ratification of the Constitution in 1788. The moderates, often taken for Antifederalists, occupied a position between the two other factions. Many of them had cooperated with Hancock's policy of moderate reforms in 1787 and others had been frightened by what they termed the national characteristics of the new Constitution. Led by such important politicians as Hancock, Samuel Adams, Elbridge Gerry, and James Sullivan, this moderate group wanted amendments to the new Constitution and as time passed became more and more Antifederalist. The Antifederalists drew their strength from the less commercial-cosmopolitan towns and from the communities that had opposed ratification of the Constitution, but the moderates' support cut across socioeconomic lines. By late 1788, for the first time during the 1780s, the political factions were basing their support on the significant differences among the various groups and types of towns. The lower house of the General Court was no longer the most sensitive political barometer because popular elections for both state and national offices would now be more indicative of changes than the roll calls in the house.

While the factions were beginning to relate to socioeconomic and ideological differences within the state, the Federalists mounted a vigorous campaign to destroy the political power of their moderate and Antifederalist opponents. At first they enjoyed great success. They elected Lincoln as lieutenant governor in 1788, increased their influence in the General Court and finally, in late 1788 and early 1789, carried the congressional elections which sent Federalists to the First Congress in New York City. But in early 1789 Hancock and Adams rallied the moderates and Antifederalists and took control of the two highest state offices. The Federalists countered by using their control of the congressional delegation and the plums of patronage to build up a political organization. Then the First Congress adopted measures so favorable to the commonwealth and dispelled the fears of the less commercial-cosmopolitan interests so completely that Antifederalist strength collapsed in the 1790-91 congressional elections. Ironically, because of the Federalists' success there was no longer a raison d'être for separate parties, so the commonwealth returned to a pre-Revolutionary state characterized by factionalism and personality politics.

The substructure of commonwealth politics, the continual divisions over fiscal policies between the most and least commercial-cosmopolitan interests, began to shift during 1788 as the twin problems of personal debts and state taxes began to disappear as political issues. The closure of the courts and the passage and extension of the law suspending suits for debt gave the less commercial-cosmopolitan interests time to pay their creditors. Thus when the courts began again to decide suits, the number of cases had declined tremendously from the 1785-1786 high. All but Bristol County had a fewer per-thousand poll number of complaint

TABLE 66
Reduction of Debts and Taxes in the West

	Debt Suits per 1,000 Polls		Taxes Levied per Poll	
County	1786	Total, 1787-91	1786	Total, 1787-91
Bristol	9.4	13.7	£2.98	£1.43
Middlesex	17.2	15.0	3.57	1.74
Worcester	29.8	11.1	3.27	1.55
Hampshire	5.8[a]	6.3	2.70	1.23
Berkshire	14.8[b]	7.8	2.87	1.38
State	12.7	13.1	3.17	1.47

SOURCES: For taxes see *Acts and Laws of the Commonwealth of Massachusetts, 1780-1797,* 11 vols. (Boston, 1890-1897), 23 Mar. 1786, 3:580-605; 27 Mar. 1788, 4:628-48; 14 Feb. 1789, 5:131-50; 3 Mar. 1790, 5:476-97 (cited hereafter as *Acts and Laws*).
NOTE: The following table gives the total taxes levied under four acts:

Date of Act	Levied for Expenses	Levied for Salaries of Representatives
23 Mar. 1786	£300,001	£11,001
27 Mar. 1788	65,000	13,362
14 Feb. 1789	32,605	4,839
3 Mar. 1790	25,360	4,155

The citations for suits concerning suits for debt are in the Docket Books of the Supreme Judicial Court, Office of the Clerk, Suffolk County Court House, Boston. The number of rateable polls are based on the Evaluation, 1784/86, vol. 163, of the unpublished Massachusetts Archives, Office of the Secretary, Boston (cited hereafter as Evaluation 1784/86), extrapolated for the period 1786-91 as explained in ch. 3.
a. This figure is for the year 1785, not 1786.
b. This figure is for the year 1787, not 1786.

cases in the entire 1787-1791 period than in the single year 1786. As individuals paid off their debts, towns retired their back taxes. Since the commonwealth levied no more heavy direct taxes after 1786 and used the funds from the impost and excise to pay general state expenses, the tax load on the western counties dropped considerably between 1787 and 1791. (See table 66.) No longer would actual loads of debts and taxes be political and economic problems. Yet despite this decline many in the less commercial-cosmopolitan towns feared that the new national government might levy heavy direct taxes on their polls and estates. This fear made many of these less commercial-cosmopolitan interests receptive to the reduction of national powers supported by the Antifederalists, and between 1788 and 1790 they tended to vote for moderate or Antifederalist candidates for national and state offices. But the alliance of the old anti-commercial-cosmopolitan interests and the ideological Antifederalists collapsed as soon as the less commercial-cosmopolitan interests realized that the new national government would not levy heavy taxes but would actually reduce their potential burdens by assuming the state debt which had, after all, been the central political point at issue of the earlier 1780s.

As conditions eased in the west, the Federalist political offensive in 1788 drove the Antifederalists and the moderates together. After defeating the anti-Constitutionalists at the convention, the Federalists, despite the fact that most of their opponents publicly announced their support of the new Constitution and government, moved to destroy the political power of the Antifederalists and moderates.[1] Jeremiah Hill, a Maine Federalist, expressed their attitude when he wrote that 108 of the 168 delegates voting against

1. *Debates and Proceedings in the Convention of the Commonwealth of Massachusetts, Held in the Year 1788, and Which Finally Ratified the Constitution of the United States* (Boston, 1856), 6 Feb. 1788, pp. 280-81; 7 Feb. 1788, pp. 281-82. See also *Worcester Magazine*, no. 23, Mar. 1788; *Hampshire Gazette*, 14 May 1788; Samuel Nasson to George Thatcher, 16 Mar. 1788, Thatcher Papers, Boston Public Library and Nasson to Thatcher, 26 Feb. 1788, ibid. Also see *Hampshire Gazette*, 9, 16 Apr. 1788; Rufus King to Alexander Hamilton, 12 June 1788, in Charles R. King, *The Life and Correspondence of Rufus King Comprising His Letters; Private and Official. His Public Documents and His Speeches*, 6 vols. (New York, 1894-1900), 1:332-33; T. B. Wait to George Thatcher, 14 Feb. 1788, Thatcher Papers; *Independent Chronicle*, 21 Feb. 1788.

ratification had been in league with the Regulators and felt it a
"pity . . . that civil society cannot be so well established as to
prevent such obnoxious beings from showing their spite to the
well disposed."[2] At first they had some difficulty implementing
their "well established" society. In the winter 1788 session of the
court Hancock, a moderate, reminded them of the proposed
amendments and assumed that "they will very early become part
of the Constitution," an eventuality that most Federalists found
rather frightening.[3] In the lower house John Coffin Jones of Boston objected to a further extension of the act suspending debt
suits but the opposition overruled him by a vote of 64 to 46. The
senate, as usual, resisted but eventually bowed to pressure and
passed the extension.[4] The court did pass a direct tax act, the
lowest one levied during the 1780s, to be used only for general
state expenses and passed a law prohibiting Massachusetts citizens
from taking part in the slave trade, legislation which at least one
Federalist feared would irritate South Carolina.[5] In order to make
some effort to retire the state debt, the court sold the commonwealth's interest to its lands in southwestern New York to Oliver
Phelps and Nathaniel Gorham for £300,000 in consolidated state
securities with the delegates from the most and least commercial
towns favoring passage while the representatives of the group B
towns voted against it.[6] The division merely underlines the fact

2. Jeremiah Hill to George Thatcher, 28 Feb. 1788, Thatcher Papers, and
Samuel P. Savage to Thatcher, 7 Mar. 1788 in ibid.

3. Hancock's address is in *Acts and Laws of the Commonwealth of Massachusetts, 1780-1797*, 11 vols. (Boston, 1890-1897), 27 Feb. 1788, 4:997-98;
"Hampden" in *Worcester Magazine*, Feb. 1788, pp. 245-46.

4. *Worcester Magazine*, Mar. 1788, no. 25; *Independent Chronicle*, 27 Mar.
1788, 5 Apr. 1788. *Acts and Laws*, 26 Mar. 1788, 4:622-23, gives the completed extension. William Widgery to Thatcher, 16 Mar. 1788, Thatcher Papers.

5. *Acts and Laws*, 27 Mar. 1788, 4:628-48. The law prohibiting the slave
trade is in ibid., 26 Mar. 1788, 4:615-17. For comments see *Independent
Chronicle*, 18 Apr. 1788; Jeremy Belknap to Hazard, 17 Feb., 2, 9 Mar.,
18 Apr. 1788 in Belknap Papers, Massachusetts Historical Society, *Collections*, 5th ser., vols. 2, 3 (1877), 6th ser., vol. 4 (1891), 5th ser., 3:19-20, 22,
27, 32. The court also passed a law on 31 Mar. 1788, *Acts and Laws*,
4:523-25, that prohibited alien blacks from residing in Massachusetts for
more than two months.

6. The legislation is in *Acts and Laws*, 1 Apr. 1788, 4:900-01. The vote is
from the unpublished Journals of the House of Representatives, available at
the Office of the Secretary, Boston, 31 Mar. 1788, pp. 523-25 (cited hereafter as House Journal).

that the least commercial towns had no hatred for speculators as long as they did not have to pay heavy taxes in order to retire their securities!

After being at least partially baffled by the court, the Federalists prepared for and performed well in the 1788 elections as they elected the lieutenant governor, cut down several Antifederalists and convention men in the state senate, and increased their strength in the lower house. The death of perennial lieutenant governor Thomas Cushing in early 1788 gave the Federalists a chance to secure that office whose occupant, due to Hancock's ill health, might well become the next governor. To increase their chances of success, or perhaps because of a previous deal, they ran no candidate against Hancock and in Boston attempted to gain moderate support by advertising a Hancock-Lincoln ticket. Meanwhile the Antifederalists organized a rather ineffectual campaign for Elbridge Gerry as governor and James Warren as lieutenant governor, and Samuel Adams became a candidate for lieutenant governor to appeal to the moderate voters.[7] By election time the voters, for once, had a rather clear choice—Hancock backed by the Federalists and moderates for governor against Gerry, the Antifederalist. And for lieutenant governor they could vote for a Federalist, Lincoln, an Antifederalist, Warren, or the moderate, Samuel Adams. The campaign rhetoric followed the usual pattern of personal abuse and conspiracy charges. Writers assailed Lincoln as the "artful, aristocratic Cincinnati hero" who would become a tool of the aristocratic juntos while Lincoln's friends pilloried Adams as a public defaulter and as an autocratic president of the senate.[8]

7. Henry Jackson to Henry Knox, 2 Mar. 1788, Knox Papers, Massachusetts Historical Society, already listed several candidates. Christopher Gore to Rufus King, 2 Mar. 1788, in King, *Rufus King*, 1:323-24; J. Q. Adams, diary entry of 7 Apr. 1788, Adams Papers, pt. 1, Adams Manuscript Trust. Also note Jackson to Knox, 10 Mar. 1788, Knox Papers.

8. *Worcester Magazine*, Mar. 1788, p. 342. The sons of Samuel Adams and Benjamin Lincoln both died in early 1788; see *American Herald*, 21 Jan. 1788. Thomas Cushing died in late February; see *Worcester Magazine*, Mar. 1788, p. 315, for the state funeral. For an attack on Higginson see *American Herald*, 24 Mar. 1788. See *Cumberland Gazette*, 2 Apr. 1788, in which a writer announced that the insurgents backed Warren. See also John Q. Adams, diary entry, 25 Apr. 1788, Adams Papers, pt. 1, for charges against Warren. For more election rhetoric see *Independent Chronicle*, 13, 20, 27 Mar. 1788; and *American Herald*, 27 Mar., 7 Apr. 1788. Henry Jackson to Henry Knox, 30 Mar. 1788, Knox Papers, gives election developments.

Despite the complexities of the campaign, the election returns showed that the various candidates received their strongest support from certain clearly definable groups and areas. Hancock eliminated Gerry who received only 19 percent of the vote, carrying forty three towns, only one of which had voted for the Constitution, a fact which illustrates Gerry's dependence on the anti-Constitutional communities. Gerry ran well in Bristol County, polling almost 50 percent of the vote because of a strong Antifederalist organization that also elected three state senators.[9] No candidate received a majority of the votes cast for lieutenant governor, but Federalist Benjamin Lincoln received 48 percent of the vote compared with 29 percent for Warren, the Antifederalist, and 17 percent for moderate Samuel Adams. (See table 67.) Benjamin Lincoln's strength reflected the alignment of pro-Constitutional and commercial-cosmopolitan support as he received 63 percent of the vote in the group A towns and 62 percent in the communities that had favored ratification. Warren, the Antifederalist, received a

TABLE 67
Election for Lieutenant Governor, 1788

				Percentage of Votes for Lincoln	
	Percentage of Votes for				
Towns	*Lincoln*	*Adams*	*Warren*	*1787*	*1788*
Group A	63%	19%	15%	37%	63%
Group B	42	17	37	26	42
Group C	36	17	36	30	36
Boston	44	56	1–	29	44
Other eastern group A	74	7	18	35	74
Western Group C	34	13	39	35	34
Federalist	62	22	12	38	62
Antifederalist	31	12	50+	23	31
State totals	48%	17%	29%	32%	48%

SOURCE: Election returns are from the unpublished Abstracts of Votes for Lieutenant-Governor, available at the Office of the Secretary, Boston, 1788 (cited hereafter as Abstracts-Lt.-Governor).

9. Election returns are in the unpublished Abstracts of Votes for Governor [1788], available at the Office of the Secretary, Boston (cited hereafter as Abstracts-Governor). Gerry carried 43 towns including 4 of the 7 Antifederalist towns in Bristol County and 12 of the 31 in Hampshire County.

FEDERALISTS AND ANTIFEDERALISTS

little over 50 percent of the vote in the anti-Constitutional towns but polled only 15 percent in the most commercial-cosmopolitan group A towns. Adams, the moderate, ran about the same in all three socioeconomic groups of towns but polled almost twice the percentage of the vote in the pro-Constitutional as compared with the anti-Constitutional towns. This election demonstrated the tendency toward polarization as Lincoln's proportion of the vote, compared with 1787, increased most rapidly in the group A and pro-Constitutional towns. The total vote of Lincoln and Warren tended to be concentrated in specific groups and types of towns with Lincoln polling 47 percent and 65 percent of his total vote from the group A and pro-Constitutional towns while Warren received 45 percent and 73 percent of his from the group C and anti-Constitutional towns. Adams received about one-third of his vote from each of the three socioeconomic groups of towns, but Federalist towns gave him almost two-thirds of his total support. Thus the three candidates ran best where their respective images of Federalism, Antifederalism, or moderation corresponded to the socioeconomic characteristics of the towns or their response to the ratification of the Constitution.

The Federalists also did relatively well in elections to the upper house; the voters returned seventeen men who had voted for ratification of the Constitution and only five opponents. Elections in six counties indicated marked differences between the Federalist and Antifederalist towns in their voting patterns for and against senatorial candidates. (See table 68.) In Berkshire County William Whiting, the former judge, sympathetic to the Shaysites, won election securing 56 percent of his total vote from the county's Antifederalist communities. Elijah Dwight and Thompson J. Skinner, two Federalist placeholders who ran behind Whiting, garnered only about one-fourth of their vote from the Antifederalist towns. In Lincoln County Dummer Sewall, a Federalist, prevented the popular election of Samuel Thompson, one of the leading antiratification spokesmen, when he received 55 percent of his total vote from the county's Federalist towns where his opponent gathered only about one-fourth of his total. In Bristol County a well-organized Antifederalist ticket composed of Abraham White, Holder Slocum, and Phanuel Bishop received almost two-thirds of its total vote from the Antifederalist towns while their opponents drew heavily from the Federalist communities. Even in commercially oriented Essex County Antifederalist Aaron Wood, although de-

TABLE 68
State Senatorial Elections Vote Profile, 1788

	Percentage of Votes from	
Counties and Candidates	Federalist Towns	Antifederalist Towns
Berkshire		
Whiting (AF)	32%	54%
Skinner (F)	65	28
Bristol		
Slocum (AF)	24	75
Durfee (F)	54	26
Essex		
Wood (AF)	49	32
Goodhue (F)	84	7
Hampshire		
Bodman (AF)	16	84
Strong (F)	51	46
Lincoln		
Thompson (AF)	25	63
Sewall (F)	55	18
Barnstable		
Smith (AF)	44	56
Freeman (F)	46	17
Worcester		
Singletary (AF)	4	94
Gill (F)	14	83

SOURCE: The vote of candidates on ratification is from *Debates and Proceedings in the Convention of the Commonwealth of Massachusetts, Held in the Year 1788, and Which Finally Ratified the Constitution of the United States* (Boston, 1856), pp. 87-92 (cited hereafter as *Proceedings in the Convention*). It gives the proportion of each candidate's vote that he received from Federalist or Antifederalist towns (towns whose delegates had either supported or opposed the ratification of the Constitution in February 1788). The vote is from the unpublished Abstracts of Votes for Senators, available in the Office of the Secretary, Boston, 1788 (cited hereafter as Abstracts-Senators).

feated, polled almost one-third of his vote from three towns whose representatives voted against ratification, while Benjamin Goodhue, a leading Federalist, polled less than one-tenth of his total from the same towns. In Worcester County the same division held true as Antifederalist Amos Singletary received only 4 percent of his vote from the seven Federalist towns, while Federalist placeholder Moses Gill got 14 percent of his total from the same communities. In Hampshire County William Bodman, an Antifederalist, secured 84 percent of his votes from the Antifederalist towns, while the popular Federalist Caleb Strong got less than half of his from the same group. Thus in many counties even the confused and unpublicized senatorial elections indicated the widening political divisions between the Federalist and Antifederalist towns.[10]

The elections for the lower house reflected a slight comeback for the most commercial-cosmopolitan and Federalist interests and towns. The combination of group A towns and justices from the group B and C towns accounted for 49 percent of the membership, an increase of more than six points over their 1787 showing but still not as high as the proportions of the earlier 1780s. The Federalist towns increased their representation almost five points and returned almost 50 percent of the total members.[11] This shift, although important, still did not give the commercial-placeholding interests or the pro-Constitutional towns as much power in the lower house as they had in the earlier 1780s, especially in 1786.

This slight shift in the membership of the General Court resulted in the selection of new officers for the senate and house and the election of Lincoln as lieutenant governor. The senate replaced Sam Adams with Samuel Phillips, Jr., a leading Federalist, as its president. The house selected Theodore Sedgwick, attorney, militant repressionist, and Federalist, as speaker to replace James Warren, one of the leading moderates during the summer of 1787. The house nominated Warren and Lincoln to the senate for the lieuten-

---

10. Returns for state senators are from the unpublished Abstracts of Votes for Senators [1788], available at the Office of the Secretary, Boston (cited hereafter as Abstracts-Senators). Candidates are identified as Federalists or Antifederalists depending upon their vote on ratification. *Worcester Magazine*, Mar. 1788, p. 342, gives a senatorial ticket for Worcester County. *American Herald*, 31 Mar. 1788, gives one for Suffolk County. In Christopher Gore to Rufus King, 9 Apr. 1788, in King, *Rufus King*, 1:327, Gore saw a much better senate for their policies. Also note Rufus King to James Madison, 25 May 1788, ibid., 1:329.

11. For a contemporary analysis see Theodore Sedgwick to George Washington, 31 May 1788, Benjamin Lincoln Papers, Massachusetts Historical Society. For some rhetoric see *Independent Chronicle*, 1 May 1788. For the Boston election see ibid., 8 May 1788.

The analysis of representation is based on the following sources: Federalist and Antifederalist towns are from the *Proceedings in the Convention*, pp. 87-92. Representatives are from the *Acts and Laws*, and House Journals, 1786-1788. Representation between 1780 and 1790 is from ch. 3.

ant governorship, and the senate, by a vote of 20 to 8, picked Lincoln to be Hancock's new assistant.[12]

The court made no sudden break with the programs hammered out in 1787. It did not again renew the act suspending debts but the act and its extensions had already relieved the westerners of much of their heavy burden of private debts. All groups apparently believed that credit conditions could once again return to normal. The summer session also finished with the Regulation as an important political issue and drew a "veil over the late unhappy commotions" by pardoning all citizens concerned in the riots. [13] The court made no effort to reestablish the commonwealth's now defunct financial system. It did order the comptroller general to prepare a funding bill for the state debt but seemed more interested in dredging up the commonwealth's old claims against the Continent in the hope that these would be settled by the new national government. [14] In order to retire some of the debt as painlessly as possible, the court established a gigantic lottery in Maine lands hoping to retire at least £163,000 worth of state securities. [15] Only one divisive issue marred the placid session—the question of pay increases for members of the lower house. On all three roll call votes the group A and pro-Constitutional towns cast over 70 percent of their votes against increases while over 55 per-

12. For actions in the house and senate see House Journal and the unpublished Journal of the Senate, available at the Office of the Secretary, Boston, 28, 29 May 1788 (cited hereafter as Senate Journal). For some comments see Theodore Sedgwick to Henry Van Schaack, 29 May 1788, Sedgwick Papers, Massachusetts Historical Society. For the story of how the Newburyport Federalists disposed of Dr. Kilham see John Q. Adams, diary entry of 4 Mar. 1788, Adams Papers, pt. 1.

13. For comment on the tender law (the law suspending suits for debt) see Theodore Sedgwick to Nathan Dane, 9 June 1788, Sedgwick Papers. The indemnity legislation is in *Acts and Laws*, 20 June 1788, 5:226-27. This act did not prevent the institution of civil proceedings against former Regulators. See *Berkshire Chronicle*, 26 June 1788, in which a writer is happy at the expiration of the law suspending suits for debts.

14. This financial legislation is in *Acts and Laws*, 5 June 1788, 5:189-90. The General Court, in its reply to Hancock's address, noted that the formation of the national government would lead to the loss of the state's impost revenues. On 6 June 1788, ibid., 5:178, and 16 June, ibid., 5:195-96, the court passed resolves providing for the auditing of accounts against the confederation and insisted upon the commonwealth's claims. On 20 June, ibid., 5:226-27, the court ordered the comptroller general to prepare a funding bill for the state debt.

15. For the Maine lottery, see ibid., 20 June 1788, 5:21-22 and 27-28.

cent of the anti-Constitutional and group C representatives voted for more money for house members.[16] The support from the less commercial-cosmopolitan and anti-Constitutional elements is an indication of their desire to increase the prestige of the lower house, which had been much more receptive to their demands, and to attract more delegates from the smaller towns by paying higher salaries.

While the court session remained peaceful, the Federalists made their plans for the first national elections. They considered these elections vital to their future since they foresaw that the first administration and Congress would implement the new Constitution and establish the policies that they had pursued since 1787. In addition they wanted to block the possibility of amendments or of a new constitutional convention that might amend or revoke important articles of the new Constitution.[17] They believed the best way to accomplish these goals would be to keep the moderates and Antifederalists out of the new national government. All of them backed Washington for the presidency and most supported favorite son John Adams for the vice-presidency. At the same time they attacked Hancock's efforts to become either president or vice president.[18] As they began to consider possible candidates for the Senate and House, the Antifederalists also began to stir. One writer calling himself "Solon" urged the election of rep-

16. Based on the roll call votes in House Journal, 17 June 1788, pp. 115-17; 6 June 1788, pp. 61-63; and 10 June 1788, pp. 73-75. The poorer towns would naturally want higher salaries and expense funds for their delegates.

17. The best recent account of these congressional elections is Kenneth R. Bowling, "Politics in the First Congress, 1789-1791" (Ph.D. diss., University of Wisconsin, 1968), see esp. pp. 16-19. For additional information about Massachusetts see Christopher Gore to Rufus King, 30 Aug. 1788, in King, *Rufus King*, 1:343; Benjamin Lincoln to George Washington, 24 Sept. 1788, Lincoln Papers; Theodore Sedgwick to Lincoln, 23 Sept. 1788, ibid. For the other side see William Widgery to George Thatcher, 14 Sept. 1788, Thatcher Papers. For some newspaper rhetoric see "A Republican," *Independent Chronicle*, 17 July 1788, and "Alfred" in ibid., 3 Oct., 9, 23 Nov. 1788.

18. In Sedgwick to Lincoln, 23 Sept. 1788, Lincoln Papers, Sedgwick hopes that "the amendment mongers, I trust in Heaven will be universally excluded." (Later, in order to win his election, Sedgwick became an amendment monger.) Also see Lincoln to George Washington, 24 Sept. 1788, Lincoln Papers. For activity in Maine see Jeremiah Hill to Thatcher, 9 Sept. 1788, Thatcher Papers. For some newspaper rhetoric see "A Farmer" in *Independent Chronicle*, 25 Sept. 1788.

resentatives who would support the amendments proposed by the
Massachusetts convention and a few even suggested a new convention, a specter that Theodore Sedgwick believed "would defeat
every beautiful effect to be expected from the unshackled operation of the system."[19]

The senatorial election caused a quarrel between the two houses
that almost resulted in an incomplete delegation. Since the new
Constitution specified only that the state legislatures elect the
senators, the house argued for election by a joint ballot of both
houses which would give the larger and more Antifederalist lower
chamber an advantage. The senate naturally opposed such a
scheme and suggested that both houses should vote separately. After almost three weeks of wrangling, the two houses pounded out
a compromise that permitted the house to nominate two candidates who would be voted on by the senate. If the upper chamber
refused to accept either or both choices, it could nominate other
candidates and return their names to the house. The nominations
would then proceed back and forth until both houses agreed on
the senators. This procedure gave the senate even more power over
the election of the national senators than it had over the election
of the governor or lieutenant governor who must be chosen from
the house's nominees.[20]

19. For feelers from Hancock see James Sullivan to Thatcher, 8 Oct. 1788,
Thatcher Papers. Also note "Honestus," 30 Oct., 25 Sept., and 6 Nov. 1788,
in *Independent Chronicle*; and Sedgwick to Lincoln, 23 Sept. 1788, Lincoln
Papers. Lincoln was already looking for a national job; see Lincoln to George
Washington, 24 Sept. 1788, in ibid. For other newspapers writers see "Al-
fred," 30 Oct. 1788; "Solon," 25 Sept., 3 Oct. 1788, all in *Independent
Chronicle*.

20. The election of senators was much more bitterly contested than noted
in Bowling, "Politics," p. 55. The struggle between the two houses over procedure may be followed in Senate Journal, 1, 4, 19, 20 Nov. 1788, and House
Journal, 10, 11, 20 Nov. 1788. On 1 Nov. 1788 the two houses appointed a
joint committee composed of three senators and five representatives to rec-
ommend legislation to both houses. Seven of these eight committeemen had
voted for ratification of the Constitution. See *Proceedings in the Convention*,
6 Feb. 1788, pp. 87-92. On 4 Nov. the senate accepted the report of this
committee and appointed another committee to draft the recommended legislation. See *Independent Chronicle*, 6, 13, 20 Nov., for additional details and
the outline of some of the debate. For other machinations see Nathan Dane
to George Thatcher, 10 Oct. 1788, Thatcher Papers; Christopher Gore to
Rufus King, 30 Oct., 23, 26 Nov., in King, *Rufus King*, 1:343, 345-47; Benjamin Lincoln to George Washington, 25 Oct. 1788, in George Bancroft, *History of the Formation of the Constitution of the United States of America*, 2
vols. (New York, 1882), 2:482, gives some discussion of the candidates.

The Federalists, thanks to their control of the senate, elected both senators. The house first nominated Caleb Strong, the Hampshire County Federalist, by a vote of 125 to 76, and the senate quickly ratified this choice by an overwhelming 27 to 2 margin, but the choice of the second senator produced serious differences. [21] With one seat allocated to a Federalist, the Antifederalists and moderates in the lower house attempted to balance the delegation by nominating Hancock's friend, Charles Jarvis, to the senate. The Federalist upper chamber refused to accept him and suggested James Lowell, a Boston Federalist, to the house. The house spurned this offer and by a vote of 108 to 77 renominated Jarvis. The senate, refusing to capitulate, suggested Azor Orne, a long-term Essex County senator and Federalist. The obstinate house again renominated Jarvis whom the senate rejected, this time suggesting Tristram Dalton, a Newburyport merchant and Federalist, to the house. [22] At this point the Antifederalists in the house attempted to stop the selection process by moving to postpone the choice of senators until the next session of the court. (See table 69.) The roll call vote on this measure shows the continuing importance of the older socioeconomic division and the newer pro- and anti-Constitutional one as 80 percent and 85 percent of the group A and pro-Constitutional towns voted against postpone-

TABLE 69
Vote to Postpone Election of Senators

Towns	Representatives Voting Against Postponement
Group A	80%
Group B	43
Group C	35
Federalist	85
Antifederalist	23
Total vote	53%

SOURCE: Roll call is in the unpublished Journals of the House of Representatives of the Commonwealth of Massachusetts, Office of the Secretary, Boston, 22 Nov. 1788, pp. 245-47 (cited hereafter as House Journal).

21. House Journal, 21 Nov. 1788. *Independent Chronicle*, 28 Nov. 1788, gives additional information.
22. House Journal, 21, 22 Nov. 1788; and Senate Journal, 21, 22 Nov. 1788.

ment while 65 percent and 77 percent of the group C and anti-Constitutional towns voted for the motion. After defeating postponement the Federalists rolled on to victory. Jarvis, in a lengthy speech, asked to be excused from further consideration, and the house submitted Nathan Dane, an Essex moderate, to the senate. The senate again refused the choice of the lower chamber and renominated Dalton. When the Federalists in the house then defeated another motion to postpone the election, the lower chamber gave up and elected Dalton. [23] Thus the entrenched Federalists' control of the senate gave them a decisive victory in the election of both national senators.

The house elections confirmed the fears of the anti-Constitutionalists about large election districts as the Federalists swept six of the eight seats in the national House of Representatives. The court created eight election districts, based on the counties, that varied in population from 96,500 for the District of Maine to 38,600 in Bristol and the Island counties. The four smallest, Bristol-Islands, Plymouth-Barnstable, Middlesex, and Suffolk, elected 50 percent of the representatives but contained only 35 percent of the total population. [24] These large districts increased the difficulties of the Antifederalists who had elected senators from counties in only two of the districts while the Federalists had elected their candidates to the upper house from every one except the Bristol District. [25]

Despite the lack of party organization, the fact that the districts were large and a successful candidate had to receive an absolute majority of the vote led to an extremely complex series of elec-

23. House Journal, 24 Nov. 1788; and *Independent Chronicle*, 28 Nov. 1788. Christopher Gore to Rufus King, 23, 26 Nov. 1788, in King, *Rufus King*, 1:345-46, was irritated at the Essex County members who supported Dalton.

24. The legislation is in *Acts and Laws*, 20 Nov. 1788, 5:256-58. Bowling, "Politics," p. 49, points out that Massachusetts had inequitable districts in comparison with other states. Jere[miah] Hill to George Thatcher, 25 Sept. 1788, Thatcher Papers.

25. Department of Commerce and Labor, Bureau of the Census, *Heads of Families at the First Census of the United States Taken in the Year 1790* (Washington, D.C., 1908), *Massachusetts*, pp. 9-10; *Maine*, pp. 9-10. Federalist or Antifederalist state senators are identified by their vote on ratification. The Maine district contained 20.4 percent of the total population and Hampshire-Berkshire held 19.0 percent while Bristol-Islands contained only 8.0 percent and Suffolk and Middlesex held 9.5 percent and 9.0 percent of the total.

TABLE 70
Congressional Elections, 1788-1789

| District and Winning Candidate | Percentage of Votes in Final Election | | | | Total Elections |
	Total	Federalist Towns	Anti-federalist Towns	Difference	
Suffolk					
Ames	51%	52%	20%	−32%	1
Essex					
Goodhue	67	62	100	+38	2
Plymouth					
Partridge	90	89	90	+ 1	1
Middlesex					
Gerry	61	43	76	+33	2
Worcester					
Grout	56	19	60	+41	3
Bristol					
Leonard	54	66	44	−22	1
Hampshire					
Sedgwick	50	69	34	−35	5
Maine					
Thatcher	62	53	75	+22	1

SOURCES: Unpublished Abstracts of Votes for National House of Representatives, available at the Office of the Secretary, Boston, 1788 and 1789 (cited hereafter as Abstracts-House). Federalist and Antifederalist towns are identified by the vote of their delegates at the ratification convention. The total elections column gives the number of elections that were required before a candidate secured a majority of the popular vote.

NOTE: For an overview of the elections see Kenneth R. Bowling, "Politics in the First Congress" (Ph.D. diss, University of Wisconsin, 1968), pp. 22-24. For a contemporary view see "A Real Republican," *Independent Chronicle*, 4 Dec. 1788. For biographical information about many of the candidates see *Biographical Congressional Directory*. Timothy Paine has a sketch in J. L. Sibley, ed., continued by C. K. Shipton, ed., *Harvard Graduates* (Boston, 1873-), 12:281-83.

tions. (See table 70.) Sectional differences within the districts played an important role in three of the contests and in one case the socioeconomic character of particular towns played the decisive role. Divisions based upon the response of the towns to the Constitution showed a difference of at least 22 percentage points between the voting patterns of Federalist and Antifederalist towns in seven of the eight districts.

In Plymouth district George Partridge, sheriff of the county, won an election completely unaffected by political, economic, or sectional differences. The former delegate to the Continental Congress secured 90 percent of the total vote, ran equally well in the pro- and anti-Constitutional towns, in all three socioeconomic groups of communities, and in both Barnstable and Plymouth counties. Partridge would become a moderate Federalist during the first session of the First Congress. His overwhelming victory which reflected his popularity with all groups and sections in his district was the exception to the divisions within the other districts. [26]

In Essex district the electors after two tries selected Benjamin Goodhue who, although a Federalist, seemed more moderate than his leading opponent, Jonathan Jackson. In the first election Goodhue, a resident of Salem and a long-term senator, received 41 percent of the vote; Jackson, a resident of Newburyport who had just published an extremely conservative pamphlet on political theory, polled 27 percent; Nathan Dane, a former member of the Confederation Congress, took 18 percent; and Samuel Holten, backed by the Antifederalists, a delegate who had failed to vote on ratification, polled only 14 percent of the total vote. Goodhue ran best in the less commercial group B and C towns, while Jackson received 50 percent of the vote from the three leading commercial centers of Newburyport, Salem, and Marblehead. In the second election most of the electors who voted for Holten and Dane shifted to Goodhue who received 100 percent of the vote in the anti-Constitutional and divided towns, over 80 percent of the vote in the group B and C communities, and about 64 percent in the group A towns. Jackson scored only in the three leading commercial centers where he picked up 52 percent of the total vote. Thus Goodhue, a solid Federalist, won his strongest support from the smaller, less commercial, and anti-Constitutional towns which voted against Jackson whom they considered too extreme. [27]

26. Partridge was not a nationally known figure, See Bowling, "Politics," p. 22; see Thomas and John Fleet, *Fleet's Pocket Almanack for the Year of Our Lord [1780-1790] . . . to Which Is Annexed the Massachusetts Register* (Boston, 1779-1789) for his local offices. The voting data is from the unpublished Abstracts of the Votes for House of Representatives [1788-1789], available at the Office of the Secretary, Boston (cited hereafter as Abstracts-House), Federalist and Antifederalist towns are determined by the vote of their delegates in *Proceedings in the Convention*, pp. 87-92.

27. For votes of the candidates at the ratification convention see *Proceedings in the Convention*, pp. 87-92. Jonathan Jackson's politically inept pamphlet was *Thoughts Upon the Political Situation of the United States. . .*

Antifederalists in the District of Maine also voted for a Federalist in an election marked by differences along sectional and pro- and anti-Constitutional lines. George Thatcher, Maine's only delegate to the Continental Congress during the 1780s, opposed Joshua Thatcher, a long-term Cumberland County senator, and Nathaniel Wells, a York County placeholder and senator. Only Wells had attended the ratification convention and voted for the new Constitution. George Thatcher won in the first election taking 62 percent of the total vote, 75 percent of the votes from the anti-Federalist towns, and 81 percent of the vote in Lincoln County. Joshua Thatcher ran best in Cumberland County and Wells received less than 10 percent of the total vote.[28] Thus George Thatcher, who would evolve into a moderate Federalist during the First Session, received his greatest support from both the anti-Constitutionalist and the frontier towns of Lincoln County.

The Federalist candidates did not manage to carry the anti-Constitutional towns in any of the other districts. In Suffolk County, thanks to a vigorous campaign and to his great appeal in the smaller group A, most commercial-cosmopolitan towns outside of Boston, arch Federalist Fisher Ames won a narrow victory. At first the Federalists feared that the multiplicity of candidates might lead to the election of moderate Samuel Adams but they finally united behind Ames, a young, articulate, Dedham attorney who had been one of their leading orators at the ratification con-

---

(Worcester, 1788). Goodhue's congressional record is described in ch. 11. For some of the flavor of the newspaper rhetoric see "An Observer," *Independent Chronicle*, 22 Jan. 1789; *Essex Journal*, 28 Jan. 1789; "An Elector," and "A Federal Elector," *Salem Mercury*, 27 Jan. 1789. Christopher Gore to Rufus King, 21 Dec. 1788, in King, *Rufus King*, 1:348 gives some informed gossip about the election.

   Returns are from Abstracts-House. Federalist and Antifederalist towns from *Proceedings in the Convention*, pp. 87-92. The three leading mercantile towns were Salem, Newburyport, and Marblehead.

   28. See Bowling, "Politics," p. 21 for some background on Thatcher. Thatcher corresponded with several of the Maine Antifederalist leaders, especially Samuel Nasson and William Widgery. For some background on the other candidates see *Acts and Laws*, 1780-1790, for legislative, and Fleet, *Register, 1780-1790* (1779-1789) for judicial and administrative offices. There is some information about the election in "Crazy Jonathan," *Cumberland Gazette*, 8 Jan. 1789; and in Daniel Cony to George Thatcher, 12 Mar. 1789, Thatcher Papers.

   Vote from Abstracts-House, 1788-1789; Federalist and Antifederalist towns from *Proceedings in the Convention*, pp. 87-92.

vention. The opposition divided their votes as the Antifederalists tended to support Benjamin Austin, Jr., of antilawyer, "Honestus" fame, and the moderates boosted Sam Adams. Ames won a very narrow majority of 50.7 percent of the vote, failed to carry Boston where he received only 49.4 percent, took 45 percent in the anti-Constitutional towns, but polled 72 percent in the seven group A towns outside Boston. Adams ran well in Boston, picking up 48.7 percent of the city's vote but drew only 14 percent in the seven other group A towns and did not receive a single ballot from the anti-Constitutional communities which gave 32 percent of their vote to Charles Jarvis, an associate of Hancock.[29] Ames thus won election because of his strength in the smaller commercial centers and because of Adams's weakness outside of Boston.

In Bristol County moderate Federalist George Leonard won election with 54 percent of the vote by carrying 66 percent of the vote in pro-Constitutional towns, 71 percent in the Island Counties, and a sizeable minority of 44 percent in the anti-Constitutional towns. David Cobb, a Cincinnati member, local judge, militia major general, and more extreme Federalist, received 18 percent of the total vote, 31 percent in the pro-Constitutional towns and 34 percent in the three group A towns located in the district. Phanuel Bishop, the Antifederalist state senator, ran strongest in the anti-Constitutional towns where he picked up 49 percent of the vote, while in the pro-Constitutional towns he secured a meagre 3 percent.[30] Although his support was based in the pro-

29. Bowling, "Politics," p. 22. E. A. Bernhard, *Fisher Ames, Federalist and Statesman, 1758-1808* (Chapel Hill, 1965), pp. 69-73 gives some excellent background. For an older account see William V. Wells, *The Life and Public Services of Samuel Adams*, 3 vols. (Boston, 1865), 3:277-82. For information about machinations and candidates see Christopher Gore to Rufus King, 26 Nov. 1788, in King, *Rufus King*, 1:347, who sees Lowell, Dawes, and Samuel A. Otis as the leading contenders. Gore to King, 14 Dec. 1788, ibid., 1:347, now views Adams, Ames, and Heath as the leaders. See also Gore to King, 21 Dec. 1788. 1:348, in which Gore claims that the Federalists preferred King but had to switch to Ames. For newspaper commentary see "Prudence" for Adams and "Justice" for Otis, both in *Independent Chronicle*, 11 Dec. 1788. Thomas Dawes, Jr., bows out in ibid., 4 Dec. 1788. "Marcus," ibid., 11 Dec. 1788, made a plea for Samuel Adams. "A Real Republican" wanted amendments and "A Countryman" backed Adams in ibid.
Voting is based on Abstracts-House, 1788. Federalist and Antifederalist towns from *Proceedings in the Convention*, pp. 87-92.
30. For backgrounds of candidates see Bowling, "Politics," p. 23. *Proceedings in the Convention*, pp. 87-92, gives the vote on ratification. Fleet, *Register, 1780-1790*, gives judicial positions. Bishop's involvement in the 1787

Constitutional towns, Leonard had polled enough votes in the anti-Constitutional towns to assure his victory.

In Middlesex County the withdrawal of Nathaniel Gorham, the leading candidate in the first election, and the shift of the anti-Constitutional towns to Elbridge Gerry gave the former Marblehead native a clear majority in the second election. In December Gorham led the field, securing 37 percent of the total vote which included 32 percent in the pro- and 39 percent in the anti-Constitutional towns. Gerry with 26 percent of the total ran second while Joseph B. Varnum, a Dracut Federalist, came in third with 17 percent. Gorham withdrew before the January election and Gerry, thanks to his 76 percent of the vote in the anti-Constitutional towns, carried the district with 61 percent. Varnum retained his former percentage and William Hull drew only 11 percent of the total.[31] Gerry's victory thus depended on Gorham's withdrawal and his excellent showing in the anti-Constitutional towns.

Worcester district voters from the anti-Constitutional towns elected Jonathan Grout, Antifederalist, convention leader, and state senator. After three elections he overcame Artemas Ward, Revolutionary major general and common pleas judge, and Timothy Paine, a former mandamus councillor in 1774 who had been accused of Toryism during the Revolution.[32] In the three elec-

---

election is noted in ch. 8. For early interest see Henry Knox to David Cobb, 20 Nov. 1788, Cobb Papers Massachusetts Historical Society. Voting is based on Abstracts-House, 1788-1789. (There were no group C towns in Bristol or the Island counties.) Federalist and Antifederalist towns from *Proceedings in the Convention*, pp. 87-92.

31. Varnum, who later became a leading Jeffersonian Republican, had voted for ratification. Gerry would become a strong Antifederalist during the First Session of the First Congress; see ch. 11. For newspaper rhetoric see "Adolphus," *Independent Chronicle*, 1 Jan. 1789, who backed amendments and Gerry; "A Middlesex Elector," in ibid., 15 Jan. 1789, wanted Wm. Hull, after Nathaniel Gorham and General Brooks had dropped out. He claimed that Hull also supported amendments. Elbridge Gerry, in ibid., 22 Jan. 1789, defended his position and charged that opposition to amendments was actually opposition to the Constitution and to the new government. "Countryman" in *Boston Gazette*, 26 Jan. 1789, claimed that Gorham backed Varnum. He accused Hull of being a militarist.

The voting analysis is based on Abstracts-House. Federalist and Antifederalist towns are from *Proceedings in the Convention*, pp. 87-92.

32. For the offices held by the candidates see *Acts and Laws*, 1780-1790, for legislative, and Fleet, *Register, 1780-1791* (1779-1790), for judicial positions. Also notice the activities and positions of Ward and Grout in Ch. 7 through 9. "Observer" in the *Independent Chronicle*, 22 Jan. 1789, gives some background.

tions Grout received 35 to 56 percent of the total vote and 40 to 60 percent in the anti-Constitutional towns but only 2 to 19 percent in the pro-Constitutional towns, while Paine, his leading competitor, carried the pro-Constitutional towns in all three elections. Grout's final victory in March 1789 reflected a 109 percent increase in his vote from the anti-Constitutional towns while Paine's rose by only 25 percent.[33] Grout, like Gerry, depended upon the support of the anti-Constitutional communities for his seat in the new national House.

In the huge Hampshire-Berkshire district a combination of support from the pro-Constitutional towns, the inability of the Antifederalists to find a candidate who could run well in both counties, and the timely and well-publicized concessions by Sedgwick enabled him to secure election after five trials. (See table 71.) The Berkshire County Antifederalists backed William Whiting, a former placeholder jailed for sedition in 1787 and since elected to the state senate, while the Hampshire group backed Samuel Lyman, a local Antifederalist. Thompson J. Skinner, a Berkshire Federalist, ran as a moderate and further confused the election by cutting down Sedgwick's Berkshire County vote. In the December election no single candidate secured a majority in either county, but Sedgwick showed his strength by taking 55 percent of the vote in the pro-Constitutional towns. In January 1789 Sedgwick, Lyman, and Whiting tied the vote with each receiving 24 to 28 percent of the total and again no single candidate carried both counties. In the early March election Lyman carried Hampshire County but received only 33 percent of the total district vote while Sedgwick received around one-third of the vote in both Hampshire and Berkshire. Skinner withdrew before the fourth election in late March and most of his vote went over to Sedgwick, permitting the latter to carry Berkshire County while Lyman continued to carry Hampshire. After these four elections marked by bitter attacks on all the leading candidates, Sedgwick published a letter promising the electors that he would support amendments to the Constitution and Whiting withdrew from the race.[34] The combination of the letter

33. Voting and turnout is based on Abstracts-House. Federalist and Antifederalist towns are from *Proceedings in the Convention*, pp. 87-92.

34. For general background see Bowling, "Politics," pp. 19, 24; Richard E. Welch, Jr., *Theodore Sedgwick, Federalist: A Political Portrait* (Middletown, Conn., 1965), pp. 66-70. For some examples of the flood of rhetoric that appeared in the western papers see the following attacking Sedgwick: "Monitor," *Hampshire Gazette*, 17 Dec. 1788; "An Elector," ibid., 22 Apr. 1789;

TABLE 71
Votes in Hampshire-Berkshire Elections

Candidate and Election	Federalist	Antifederalist	Towns Group A	B	C	Counties Hampshire	Berkshire	Berkshire Antifederalist	Total Vote
Sedgwick									
One	55%	19%	63%	27%	32%	38%	35%	22%	36%
Two	46	11	44	30	20	28	27	11	28
Three	49	18	52	30	26	31	31	18	31
Four	67	29	66	54	38	40	62	44	47
Five	69	34	64	56	44	41	71	69	50+
Lyman									
One	2	24	3	9	21	23	0	0	15
Three	19	42	25	17	42	55	1	1	33
Five	28	65	30	44	55	59	24	25	48
Skinner									
Three	14	12	1	18	13	1	21	34	13
Whiting									
Four	7	16	0	13	15	1	34	51	12

SOURCES: Abstracts-House, 1788-1789. Federalist and Antifederalist towns from *Proceedings in the Convention,* pp. 87-92.

and Whiting's withdrawal gave Sedgwick 71 percent of the vote in Berkshire County and 69 percent in the pro-Constitutional towns in both counties which overcame Lyman's margin of 59 percent in Hampshire County and 65 percent in the anti-Constitutional towns. Sedgwick, for the first time, carried the anti-Constitutional towns in Berkshire, a fact which indicates that the Berkshire Antifederalists preferred a local Federalist to an outside Antifederalist. The Hampshire-Berkshire election demonstrated the political problems of the Antifederalist and less commercial-cosmopolitan interests. They fought hard against the better organized Federalists and more commercial-cosmopolitan interests but their more localistic outlook made it difficult for them to unite behind a popular candidate who would carry a large and diverse district.

These elections, which reflected a shift toward alignments based upon reaction to the Constitution, resulted in Federalist control of the commonwealth's delegation to the First Congress. Dalton and Strong, firm Federalists residing in the most commercial-cosmopolitan towns and personally connected with the most commercial interests, would sit in the Senate. Goodhue, Ames, and Sedgwick, who would become staunch Federalists, all had commercial connections, while George Thatcher, Partridge, and Leonard, the three moderate Federalists, also resided in commercial towns, had served as placeholders, or had other connections with the most commercial-cosmopolitan interests and towns. Gerry was a member of these interests although he had become an ideological Antifederalist. Only Grout, the remaining Antifederalist, could be considered in any sense an outsider. The Federalists had been successful in their national plans; Hancock and Samuel Adams would not bother them at the national level, and convention leaders and other opponents such as Bishop, Lyman, and Whiting had been defeated. They could now roll on with their campaign to control the major state offices.

---

ibid., 6 May 1789; 22 Apr. 1789; 29 Apr. 1789; and 8 Apr. 1789. Other candidates received their share in *Hampshire Gazette*, 4, 25 Mar., 22 Apr. 1789. See also Sedgwick to Benjamin Lincoln, 6 Feb. 1789, Lincoln Papers in which Sedgwick expresses his irritation at the violence of the rhetoric. In the *Hampshire Gazette*, 6 May 1789, the editor published a letter of Sedgwick's dated 6 Apr. 1789, in which he announced his support of amendments to the Constitution, the assumption of the Massachusetts state debt by the national government, and lower land taxes. Sedgwick in a letter to William Henshaw, 15 May 1789, Miscellaneous Papers, Massachusetts Historical Society, blamed the entire contest on the machinations of the former Regulators.

But the Federalists were disappointed in their efforts to drive Hancock from office and to retain Lincoln as lieutenant governor. Hancock had been suspicious of his new lieutenant since 1787 because he believed Lincoln to be a dangerous political rival and an emissary of his most bitter opponents. Lincoln, to placate the governor, sent him a letter in June 1788 in which he contended that he had never intended any injury. But Hancock, evidently unconvinced, refused to appoint Lincoln to the lieutenant governor's financial sinecure, the governorship of Castle Island.[35] This placed Lincoln in a perilous financial situation since the lieutenant governor drew a very small salary which had been supplemented in Cushing's tenure by fees he collected as governor of Castle Island on all vessels entering the port of Boston. Hancock's refusal to appoint Lincoln led to recriminations by Lincoln's friends and political associates. Essays appeared in the papers that claimed Hancock had insulted Lincoln, while Hancock's supporters charged that the lieutenant governor had no legal right to the Castle.[36] In November 1788 the issue came before the General Court when it began to discuss the propriety of granting the lieutenant governor an annual salary. Samuel Breck, a Boston merchant and friend of Lincoln, chaired a special committee that recommended that the lieutenant governor be placed in command of the Castle. Charles Jarvis, Hancock's man on the Boston delegation, immediately attacked this proposal and the debate became warmer.[37] As the court pondered, the propagandists became even more inflamed. Lincoln attempted to reopen the old "S.H." letter affair and the governor's friends led by a writer who signed himself "Junius" pounced on the former general for defending the Tory Higginson. Higginson then took his revenge by publishing a lengthy series of "Laco" letters which attacked Hancock's honesty, morality, capacity, and intelligence, accused the governor of treason, peculation, demagoguery, weakness, extravagance, and

---

35. Benjamin Lincoln to John Hancock, 26 June 1788, Lincoln Papers. Lincoln needed this sinecure. His later correspondence with George Washington is filled with his financial problems which he hopes to correct through a lucrative national appointment. (He eventually becomes collector of the port of Boston.) For some additional background see "Fairplay" in *Independent Chronicle*, 7 Aug. 1788.

36. *Independent Chronicle*, 7, 14 Aug. 1788.

37. Ibid., 20 Nov., 4 Dec. 1788, gives the debates. Writers favoring Adams for the lieutenant governorship had appeared very early; see ibid., 4, 11 Sept. 1788.

incompetence, and sullied Hancock's reputation with future generations of historians.[38] Hancock's followers naturally responded by
identifying "Laco" as a political pimp soliciting for his idol Benjamin Lincoln.[39]

This affair came to a head when Theophilus Parsons and his cohorts introduced into the lower house of the court a motion censuring Hancock for his treatment of Lincoln. Moderate Federalists
such as Heath and Jarvis, joined by Antifederalists like Nasson,
defended the governor. The final vote shows the weakness of the
anti-Hancockites. The motion to censure won the approval of
62 percent of the delegates from the most commercial group A
towns and 60 percent of those from the pro-Constitutional towns,
but it secured only 31 percent of the votes in the house as 86 percent of the representatives of the anti-Constitutional towns voted
against it together with 72 percent and 84 percent of those from
the group B and C communities. This vote indicates that the violent anti-Hancockites had strength only in the group A and pro-
Constitutional towns.[40]

The vote was a sign of things to come. In the 1789 spring election campaign the Hancock moderates, now united behind a ticket
of Hancock and Samuel Adams, accused their enemies, Bowdoin
and Lincoln, of being involved in the typical, tired aristocratic
plots and juntos that could be ended only by the election of the
"Patriot Ticket."[41] The election resulted in an overwhelming vic-

_____

38. *Boston Gazette*, 12 Jan. 1789. "The Letters of Laco" appeared in the
Massachusetts Centinel, during early 1789 and were also published in pamphlet form as [Stephen Higginson], *The Writings of Laco* (Boston, 1789) See
Thomas W. Higginson, *Life and Times of Stephen Higginson* (Boston, 1907),
pp. 128-37.

39. See *Boston Gazette*, 12, 19 Jan., 2 Feb. 1789. Other allies of Hancock
argued that the governor had saved state funds by refusing Lincoln a sinecure;
see *Independent Chronicle*, 15 Jan., 19, 26 Feb. 1789. "To Laco the Pimp of
Aristides," appeared in the *Boston Gazette*, 19 Jan. 1789.

40. Based on the roll call in House Journal, 7 Feb. 1789, pp. 369-72. *Boston Gazette*, 16 Feb. 1789, and *Independent Chronicle*, 12 Feb. 1789, give
additional details. Daniel Cony to George Thatcher, 9 April 1789, Thatcher
Papers, saw the vote as a defeat of the *"Star Chamber Junto."*

41. For some examples of the election rhetoric and its varied impact in
various sections see Jeremy Hill to George Thatcher, 4 Feb. 1789, Thatcher
Papers, in which Hill claimed there was a plot afoot to replace Hancock with
Lincoln. "Ironicus," *Boston Gazette*, 16 Feb. 1789, urged the defeat of the
"Aristocratical Cincinnatical" Lincoln. Violent attacks on "Laco" continued
in which he (Higginson) was accused of being the penman for the anti-
Republican, aristocratic junto. See *Boston Gazette*, 23 Feb. 1789, and *Inde-*

TABLE 72
Votes in Gubernatorial Elections, 1787 and 1789

Towns	Bowdoin		Hancock	
	1787	*1789*	*1787*	*1789*
Group A	33%	27%	66%	69%
Group B	17	12	81	85
Group C	15	9	80	89
Eastern group A	33	28	66	69
Western group C	19	12	76	85
Federalist	29	24	68	72
Antifederalist	14	8	84	89
Total vote	22%	16%	75%	81%

SOURCES: Unpublished Abstracts of Votes for Governor, available at the Office of the Secretary, Boston, 1787 and 1789. Federalist and Antifederalist towns from *Proceedings in the Convention*, pp. 87-92.

tory for the Hancock-Adams team, underlining the reorientation of politics within the commonwealth. The vote for governor was very similar to that in 1787. (See table 72.) Bowdoin's proportion of the vote declined 6 percent and while he received 27 percent of the vote in the group A and 24 percent of the vote in the pro-Constitutional towns, he garnered only 9 percent in the group C and 8 percent in the anti-Constitutional communities.

But the much closer contest for lieutenant governor, in which Samuel Adams won with 55 percent of the total vote, showed a considerable realignment since 1788. (See table 73.) Lincoln's total vote declined by only two percentage points between the

pendent Chronicle, 19, 26 Feb. 1789. One writer accused the *Massachusetts Centinel* of being the vehicle for the aristocrats; see *Independent Chronicle*, 26 Feb. 1789. In March writers continued to attack "Laco" and also took aim at the "high flying Federalists;" see ibid., 26 Feb., 5, 12 Mar. 1789, and *Boston Gazette*, 2, 9, 23 Mar. 1789. One writer, "Consistency," unmasked Higginson as the author of the "Laco" articles and accused him of being a Tory till 1777 and of attempting to sabotage the moderate policies of the General Court in 1787. See *Independent Chronicle*, 2 Apr. 1789. Despite these assaults some of Lincoln's supporters still believed that Bowdoin and Lincoln would win; see Caleb Davis to John Derby, 4 Apr. 1789, Caleb Davis Papers, Massachusetts Historical Society. Wells, 3:282-86 has an overview. For activities at the town and county levels see J. Bridger to John Q. Adams, 28 Feb. 1789, Adams Papers, pt. 4. *Essex Journal*, 1 Apr. 1789, and *Independent Chronicle*, 2 Apr. 1789, ran tickets for the senatorial elections.

TABLE 73
Votes in Elections for Lieutenant Governor, 1788 and 1789

	Adams		Lincoln	
Towns	*1788*	*1789*	*1788*	*1789*
Group A	19%	52%	64%	47%
Group B	17	54	42	43
Group C	17	59	36	37
Eastern group A	21	53	65	46
Western group C	13	48	34	45
Federalist	22	45	62	53
Antifederalist	12	68	31	28
Total vote	17%	55%	48%	46%

SOURCES: Abstracts-Lt.-Governor, 1788 and 1789. Federalist and Anti-federalist towns from *Proceedings in the Convention*, pp. 87-92.

elections, but he lost 17 points in the group A towns, and gained one point in the group B and group C towns. Thus Lincoln's support from the three different groups of towns tended to bunch together. The twenty-five point spread in 1789 between his performance in the pro- and anti-Constitutional towns shows that in this election the older socioeconomic differences had become less important than the newer ideological divisions over the Constitution and the new national government. Samuel Adams's base of support also changed totally during the twelve-month period. In 1788 he ran best in the pro-Constitutional towns, while in 1789 he gained the highest proportion of his votes in the anti-Constitutional. In 1788 he had only a two-point spread between his performance in the group A and C towns; by 1789 he ran best in the group C towns where he had performed worst the previous year. The western C towns that voted heavily for Warren in 1788 did not shift completely over to Adams because he, after all, had favored militant anti-Regulator measures as late as early 1787. Adams's victory seemed to augur a new coalition and a new pattern for politics. He had run well in Boston and other eastern port centers. He had captured the anti-Constitutional vote and had retained enough of the old less commercial-cosmopolitan strength to hammer together a winning combination. But such a strange assortment of bedfellows could be kept together only within the framework of an organized political party. Without such an organization, the coalition would quickly collapse.

11

Toward a New Order
of Politics

THE established alignments based on the socioeconomic differences among the interests and towns, their positions on the fiscal
programs of the earlier 1780s, and their attitudes towards the new
national government disintegrated rapidly and completely after
1789. In the General Court the old divisions over state fiscal policy held firm through early 1790, but with the passage of national
assumption this issue finally disappeared from state politics. Economic and financial improvements in the conditions of the group C
towns and the less commercial-cosmopolitan farmers also eased
the tensions on fiscal policy. As debt cases became rarer, taxes
decreased; as towns and farmers caught up with their outstanding
taxes, they became less concerned with fiscal policies and many
swung over to support a national government that had removed
their burden of direct taxes. As these issues disappeared throughout the state, the Federalist-Antifederalist division also evaporated. During the first session of the First Congress the Federalist
and Antifederalist members of the Massachusetts congressional
delegation divided along partisan lines. But during the second session the Antifederalists joined with their opponents to support
Hamilton's assumption and funding schemes which together relieved the General Court of the thorny problems of funding, servicing, and taxing. By the time the electors voted for their representatives to the Second Congress, this division had also practically
disappeared. In the 1790 state and 1790 and 1791 national elections fewer voters turned out, fewer towns sent delegates to the
General Court, the placeholders returned to both houses, Hancock
and Adams faced almost no opposition for the state's two highest
offices, and the divisions so significant in 1788-1789 were of consequence in the elections in only two of the congressional districts.

Thus it seemed that the commonwealth had returned to a brand of preparty politics revolving around the intricate maneuvers by factions and individual politicians for power and place which bore little relationship to issues or to underlying social, cultural, or economic differences. Yet the raw materials for a new political system that would eventually result in the creation of highly organized parties were present. By 1790-91, bitter ideological debates over the French Revolution had already broken out among leading politicians, Maine representatives began to revive the secession movement, and Antifederalist strength persisted in pockets such as Bristol County. But the parties that emerged in the 1790s and the first decade of the nineteenth century were based on essentially new alignments. The Worcester and Hampshire farmers and towns that had vehemently opposed the fiscal program and the Constitution would become a vital component of the Federalist party, while the residents of the rapidly growing District of Maine who had supported the financial measures of the 1780s and the Constitution would become a bulwark of the Jeffersonian Republicans. This seeming change occurred because the issues of the 1780s were resolved before any organized or institutionalized party, which could have maintained the earlier divisions, had emerged. Lacking the stabilizing effect of organized parties, the voters naturally related to either personalities or issues. When the issues changed, as they did in the 1790s, the new divisions were naturally different from the ones of the earlier decade.

The establishment of the new national government resulted in a period of political peace in the General Court. Between February 1789 and January 1790 no question even came to a roll call vote in the lower house and no new fiscal policies were approved. In February 1789 the house defeated a senate-sponsored specie tax designed to meet some of the needs of the state's creditors.[1] With no new tax revenues and the income from the state's impost declining the court did not even bother to keep up with interest payments on the consolidated debt. To meet current needs it borrowed from the Massachusetts Bank, tried to speed up the collection of the small March 1788 tax, levied a new tax of £32,605 to meet current expenses, and gave Phelps and Gorham some addi-

1. There was some discussion about the state's fiscal problems in *Boston Gazette*, 5 Jan., 9 Mar. 1789; *Hampshire Gazette*, 4 Mar. 1789; *Independent Chronicle*, 19 Feb. 1789; Cotton Tufts to Abigail Adams, 10 Feb. 1789, Adams Papers, Adams Manuscript Trust, pt. 4.

tional time to meet their commitments.[2] During the summer of 1789, Hancock urged the court to take action on the state debt and a finance committee reported a bill levying a specie tax to support state credit. The court defeated the proposal after debates that reflected the old division in the house between the most and least commercial-cosmopolitan towns and interests. The senate then rejected a house-sponsored lottery bill designed to retire part of the principal of the state debt. By early 1790 it was obvious that the court would await congressional action on assumption before considering the future of its own consolidated debt.[3]

The actual voting patterns on state fiscal questions remained almost identical to those of the earlier 1780s. (See table 74.) In

TABLE 74
General Court Voting on Financial Issues in Early 1790

Towns	Representatives Opposing Payment in Securities	Representatives Opposing Postponement
Group A	90%	89%
Group B	57	47
Group C	31	13
Federalist	86	82
Divided and not voting	87	45
Antifederalist	30	25
Total vote	58%	49.6%

SOURCES: Unpublished Journal of the House of Representatives of the Commonwealth of Massachusetts, Office of the Secretary, Boston, 19 Feb. 1790, pp. 262-64, and 3 Mar. 1790, pp. 301-03 (cited hereafter as House Journal). The first vote was on a provision that "whatever taxes may be appropriated the present session, to pay any particular demands against the Government [the consolidated debt], these demands shall be received in payment of those taxes." The second vote concerned the postponement of the repayment of outstanding warrants.

2. For borrowing from the bank see *Acts and Laws of the Commonwealth of Massachusetts, 1780-1790*, 11 vols. (Boston, 1890-1897), 19 Nov. 1788, 5:255-56; 17 Jan. 1789, 5:309; 16 Feb. 1789, 5:347. For speeding up collections see ibid., 14 Feb. 1789, 5:345-46. Jere[miah] Hill to George Thatcher, 7 Feb. 1789, Thatcher Papers, Boston Public Library, mentioned that the state could no longer pay interest on the consolidated debt. For the extension of the Phelps-Gorham contract see *Acts and Laws*, 22 Nov. 1788, 5:263; also notice the material filed in the unpublished Public Papers for this legislation, available in the Office of the Secretary, Boston.

3. Hancock's message is in the *Acts and Laws*, 8 June 1789, 5:567-69. The

February 1790, the house, thanks to the heavy vote of the Federalist and most commercial-cosmopolitan towns, rejected a bill that would have permitted taxes to be paid in state securities and in March the same groups and towns voted against postponing consideration of the servicing of the consolidated debt until the next session of the court. In February 1790, Boston instructed its representatives to repeal the state excise, the commonwealth's last resource for paying off her creditors. But instead of repealing these duties the court placed additional ones on certain imports, established a new enforcement system, provided that the revenue would be allocated to fund the consolidated debt, and thus served notice on Congress that the state would and could continue to service her debt unless the national government took action. Actually the court was bluffing. It had no intention of levying heavy taxes that would aggravate the less commercial-cosmopolitan towns and interests and it rejected a bill that would have levied a tax of £25,000 a year to meet interest charges on the debt. It passed only a small direct tax of £25,360 designed to meet general state expenses.[4] The court finally surrendered on 4 June 1790 when it resolved that "it will not only be just and reasonable but highly expedient that the Government of the United States should assume and provide for the payment of those debts which the several states contracted" and informed the senators and representatives that they had been instructed to have the national government assume the debts of the commonwealth.[5] The court then

debates are covered in the *Independent Chronicle*, 18 June 1789. According to John Q. Adams to John Adams, 28 June 1789, in Worthington C. Ford, ed., *Writings of John Quincy Adams*, 7 vols. (New York, 1913-1917), 1:41, the court debated finances for almost a month. John Q. Adams reported that Parsons planned to pay off the state debt with a lottery scheme and that this measure actually passed the house but failed in the senate. Adams's report is substantiated by "Equity" in the *Independent Chronicle*, 20 Aug. 1789. The court continued to borrow from the Massachusetts Bank; see *Acts and Laws*, 20 June 1789, 5:571.

4. *Reports of the Record Commissioners of the City of Boston*, 39 vols. (Boston, 1876-1900), 10 Feb. 1790, 31:215-16. The new excise system is in *Acts and Laws*, 3 Mar. 1790, 5:462-76. The tax act is in ibid., 3 Mar. 1790, 5:476-97. Other proposals for paying the debt were mentioned in the *Independent Chronicle*, 25 Feb., 4 Mar. 1790.

5. *Acts and Laws*, 4 June 1790, 6:101-02. Hancock in his address in ibid., 1 June 1790, 6:547-51, had stated: "I am not convinced of the propriety of the General Government assuming to pay debts of this Commonwealth without the request of consent of this government." The court, as noted, quickly gave its consent.

resolved that the Massachusetts impost and excise acts would expire when the United States assumed the state's debt.[6]

The formation of the national government, the cooling off of the fiscal issue, and the passage of the Assumption Act changed the character of state politics by 1791. The Federalists gave little resistance to the Hancock-Adams ticket in the April 1790 state elections and the turnout declined substantially from the 1789 figures. The votes for governor declined by almost 23 percent and over 26 percent fewer electors bothered to vote for the lieutenant governor. Hancock picked up 86 percent of the vote, compared with 81 percent in 1789, and carried all but eight towns. Samuel Adams, who had won with only 55 percent of the vote in 1789, increased his proportion to 84 percent of the total. Adams ran poorest in Plymouth County with 57 percent of the vote and in Berkshire where he picked up 74 percent of the total.[7] Turnout also dropped in the senate elections. Between 1789 and 1790 voting for the state senate increased only in Lincoln and the Island counties.[8] The decline in voting gave the combination of place-holders and residents of the most commercial-cosmopolitan towns control of 76 percent of the seats in the upper house. Senators who had voted for ratification of the Constitution held 55 percent of the seats while its opponents claimed only 9 percent.[9] Thus

6. *Independent Chronicle*, 10 June 1790. Nathaniel Wells to George Thatcher, 4 June 1790, Thatcher Papers. *Acts and Laws*, 24 June 1790, 6:20-21, provided for the expiration of the state's impost system. The Federalists approved these actions. See Fisher Ames to George R. Minot, 11 June 1790, in Seth Ames, ed., *Works of Fisher Ames With A Selection From His Speeches and Correspondence*, 2 vols. (Boston, 1854), 1:81, and Ames to Minot, 23 June 1790, ibid., 1:83.

7. Turnout figures and the percentage of vote comes from the unpublished Abstract of Votes for Governor and Abstract of Votes for Lieutenant-Governor, available in the Office of the Secretary, Boston, for 1790. The senate returns are from the Abstract of Votes for Senators, also available in the Office of the Secretary, Boston (cited hereafter as Abstracts-Senators), for 1790 and from returns in the unpublished Journals of the Senate, available in the Office of the Secretary, Boston (cited hereafter as Senate Journal).

8. Senate returns are from Abstracts-Senators, 1790.

9. Membership in the house and senate may be determined from the *Acts and Laws*, 1790, the unpublished Journals of the House of Representatives, available in the Office of the Secretary, Boston (cited hereafter as House Journal), and the Senate Journal. See also *The Debates and Proceedings in the Convention of the Commonwealth of Massachusetts, Held in the Year 1788, and Which Finally Ratified the Constitution of the United States* (Boston, 1856), 6 Feb. 1788, pp. 87-92.

despite the uncontested election of Hancock and Adams, the decline in political interest and the disappearance of important state issues gave the control of the senate to a Federalist, commercial-cosmopolitan, placeholding combination. The elections to the house also increased the strength of the most commercial-cosmopolitan placeholding interests. The percentage of representatives who resided in the group A towns or served as justices in the less commercial-cosmopolitan communities increased from about 49 percent of the house in 1788 to about 53 percent in 1789 and 1790. Representation in the lower house fell by 14 percent between 1788 and 1789 and by almost 17 percent between 1789 and 1790.[10] The lower house, as apathetic as the voters, took only two roll call votes between June 1790 and May 1791, neither of which reflected a close contest.[11] None of the new issues had the impact of nor could they be related to the old financial and constitutional questions that had been a staple of house politics during the 1780s. In early 1789 a controversy arose as to whether George Leonard could serve as register of probate and Partridge as sheriff while sitting in the national Congress. The court decided to continue Partridge as sheriff but forced Leonard to resign his regis-

10. *Acts and Laws*, House Journal, and *Proceedings in the Convention* for membership in the house. "An Elector" in *Independent Chronicle*, 10 June 1790, noticed the tendency of many towns to avoid sending representatives to the lower house. The election appeared unexciting. Daniel Cony to George Thatcher, 7 Feb. and 6 Mar. 1790, Thatcher Papers, noted complete silence and suspected that Hancock and Adams would win. John Q. Adams to John Adams, 19 Mar. 1790, in Ford, ed., *John Q. Adams*, 1:48-49, stated that politics were tranquil and that Hancock would be left in quiet possession of the governorship. Stephen Higginson to John Adams, 24 Mar. 1790, Adams Papers, pt. 4, noted no contest in the election. Higginson wanted some changes in the senate, since it contained too many Hancock supporters or in Higginson's terms, "the insurgent spirit was often a little too virile in a majority of them." *Independent Chronicle*, 1 Apr. 1790, had some propaganda. "A Republican" warned the electors that the "Laconian" party was active and tickets were printed for the senators running with Hancock and Adams in Suffolk County. In ibid., "A Republican" claimed that the junto really had wished to defeat Hancock and Adams.

11. The first incident was on 28 Jan. 1791, House Journal, pp. 175-76, when the house by a vote of 112 to 5 decided that federal judge David Sewall could not sit in the house. The second on 12 Mar. 1791, ibid., pp. 324-25, concerned a vote on a petition submitted by Elizabeth and James Bowdoin, Jr. Hancock vetoed a resolve granting their petition and the house by a vote of 6 to 59 decided not to override his veto.

try.[12] In early 1790 the court, by an overwhelming vote, decided that federal officers could not sit in the state legislature and some debate developed over ceding the commonwealth's lighthouses to the national government and the use of local jails to house federal prisoners.[13] Piqued by the national government's failure to consider or discuss Massachusetts proposals, the court refused to ratify the twelve amendments proposed by Congress until its recommendations had been considered.[14] Thus the court failed to ratify the famous Bill of Rights but also failed to force Congress to consider the commonwealth's amendments. After early 1790 it was evident that the amendments would be ratified without Massachusetts so the entire controversy became a dead issue.

Two new developments did create some political interest. By 1791 the Maine secessionist movement was active again. The other matter involved John Gardner's proposed legal reforms. Gardner, accused of Toryism during the Revolution, returned to Maine, resumed his career at the bar, and drafted some legal reforms designed to simplify the commonwealth's legal and judicial systems and reduce the powers of attorneys. Unlike "Honestus," he advocated basic law reforms, including a new code. Hoping to replace the English common law with his new codification, he soon ran afoul of prominent politicians and important placeholders.[15] Charles Jarvis attacked both Gardner and his proposals in

12. *Acts and Laws*, 6 Jan., 16 Feb. 1789, 6:296, 353; *Independent Chronicle*, 8, 29 Jan. 1789. Memorandum dated Jan. 1789 in Hancock Papers, Massachusetts Historical Society.

13. House Journal, 22 Jan. 1790, pp. 183-85. The vote was 137 to 24. *Independent Chronicle*, 7, 21, 28 Jan., 4 Feb. 1790. For lighthouses, jails, etc., see *Acts and Laws*, 10 June 1790, 6:7-9; 26 Feb. 1790, 5:455-56. The court also laid the fisheries problem before Congress; see ibid., 24 Feb. 1790, 5:675; 9 Mar. 1790, 5:698 and 715-16.

14. The best material on this is in Herbert V. Ames, ed., "Report of a Committee of the Massachusetts Legislature on Additional Amendments to the Federal Constitution, 1790," *American Historical Review* 2:99-105. There is also a Report of the Joint Committee of Senate and House of Representatives of the Commonwealth of Massachusetts, dated 24 Feb. 1790, in Adams Papers. Stephen Higginson to John Adams, 24 Mar. 1790, in ibid., gives some details. Also see *Acts and Laws*, 14 Jan. 1790, 5:449-53 for Hancock's support of amendments. The reply of the court is in ibid., 27 Jan 1790, 5:626-28, where they assure the governor that they will consider the amendments.

15. For some background see the *Independent Chronicle*, 21, 28 Jan., 4 Feb. 1790. For comments see William Cranch to John Adams, 24 Jan. 1790, Adams Papers.

the lower house and the editor of the *Herald of Freedom* published a vicious personal attack on the reformer which, among
other things, accused Gardner of murdering his wife by ill treatment.[16] When Gardner attempted to have the editor arrested for
libel, his opponents raised a cry about freedom of the press. The
jury eventually refused to convict the editor after a trial for criminal libel so Gardner filed a civil suit which dragged on throughout
the year.[17] Gardner's ideas aroused some stir in the press and
"Impartialis" and "Fabius" rushed to his defense. Some antilawyer agitation continued throughout the summer and fall of
1790 but resulted only in the passage of an innocuous law that
gave any person who possessed a power of attorney the power to
serve as a lawyer.[18] The lawyers, horrified by Gardner's dangerous
ideas, accused him of radicalism in their letters and publications.

The lack of political controversy was underlined by the absence
of any roll call votes in the lower house between March 1790 and
January 1791. In the entire year of 1791, the house took only
three roll call votes. Only one of these, which dealt with a state
subscription to the Bank of United States, related to financial
questions and it failed by a three-to-one margin.[19] In February
1792 the house approved the incorporation of the Boston Tontine
Association but the old divisive issues of taxes, consolidated securities, and suspension of suits for debts that had been central to
politics in the 1780s had simply disappeared by 1791 and 1792.[20]

16. *Independent Chronicle*, 4 Feb. 1790; and James Sullivan to Elbridge
Gerry, 3 Feb. 1790, Gerry Papers, Massachusetts Historical Society.

17. Daniel Cony to George Thatcher, 7, 13 Feb.; Samuel Emerson to
Thatcher, 16 Feb. 1790; all in Thatcher Papers.

18. For discussion see "Junius," *Independent Chronicle*, 11 Feb. 1790.
"Fabius" in *Western Star*, Mar. 1790, claimed that lawyers had too much
power and charged exorbitant fees. "Impartialis," *Hampshire Gazette*, 17, 24,
31 Mar., 7 Apr. 1790, argued that justice had been purchased by the wealthy
while the poor did without, and assailed imprisonment for debt and the use
of oaths. The law is in *Acts and Laws*, 6 Mar. 1790, 5:511. For responses see
Daniel Cony to Thatcher, 24 Feb. 1790, Thatcher Papers, and "Robert
Brock" in *Hampshire Gazette*, 31 Mar. 1790.

19. These votes were: to determine whether Judge David Sewall had a right
to a seat in the house, House Journal, 28 Jan. 1791, pp. 175-77, a vote of
5 Yes and 112 No; to pass a resolve on the petition of Elizabeth Bowdoin
over Hancock's veto, ibid., 12 Mar. 1791, pp. 324-25, a vote of 6 Yes and
59 No; the vote concerning the Bank of the United States is in ibid., 14 June
1791, pp. 101-03, a vote of 35 Yes and 112 No.

20. The Tontine vote is in ibid., 7 Feb. 1792, pp. 208-09, with a vote of
83 Yes and 51 No.

Meanwhile congressional actions, the activities of the Massachusetts delegation, and the responses of the commonwealth's voters all blurred the divisions between Federalists and Antifederalists that had become important in 1788 and 1789. During the first session of the First Congress a serious Federalist versus Antifederalist division occurred in the Massachusetts delegation. On questions that involved the organization of the new national government and the amendment of the Constitution, Gerry and Grout took a solidly Antifederalist position while Ames, Goodhue, and Sedgwick stood at the other extreme and Leonard, George Thatcher, and Partridge occupied the middle ground.

Despite these differences the delegation united behind legislation that they believed would benefit the commonwealth. All of them favored an impost for revenue purposes only and argued against duties on imported raw materials including molasses. Gerry agreed with Ames that higher duties would encourage smuggling and damage the state's economy.[21] The congressmen also wanted heavy tonnage duties laid on foreign ships but opposed Madison's proposal to discriminate against British vessels. Ames feared that Madison's plan would lead to British reprisals against vulnerable American shipping.[22]

The delegation did divide over the temporary or permanent grant of a customs revenue to the national government. Ames opposed any time limitation on the operation of the law arguing that a permanent impost would prove that the government would possess sufficient revenue to fund the national debt and would thus reassure the speculators and security holders. Goodhue at first expressed doubts about a permanent system and Gerry con-

21. Speeches on these subjects are found in *Debates and Proceedings in the Congress of the United States, 1789-1824*, 42 vols., (Washington, D.C., 1834-1856), 1st Cong., 1st sess. (cited hereafter as *Annals*). See especially 14 Apr. 1789, p. 138, for George Partridge; 27 Apr. 1789, p. 211 for Thatcher; 28 Apr. 1789, pp. 228-29, for Goodhue; 28 Apr. 1789, pp. 221-24, 228-29, for Ames; 9 May 1789, pp. 296-300, for Ames and pp. 315-16 for Gerry. For the senators see E. S. Maclay, ed., *William Maclay, Journal... 1789-1791* (New York, 1927), 27 May 1789, p. 51; 28 May 1789, pp. 54-55; 4 June 1789, pp. 63-65.

22. For higher tonnage duties see *Annals*, 21 Apr. 1789, pp. 176-77, 188; 5 May 1789, pp. 253-56, 257, 261, for Ames; and 7 May 1789, pp. 282-83, for Goodhue. For resistance to discrimination see ibid., 1 July 1789, p. 616, for Sedgwick. Maclay, ed., *Journal*, 26 May 1789, p. 50, for action in the Senate. Fisher Ames to George R. Minot, 27 May 1789, in Ames, *Fisher Ames*, 1:45, and Ames to Minot, 2 July 1789, ibid., 1:57-60.

tended that a series of temporary acts would reduce the dangers of the rapid expansion of national power.[23] This debate over the permanent or temporary nature of the impost foreshadowed the division in the delegation regarding organizational and constitutional questions.

The congressmen were divided on several important organizational matters considered during the first session. (See table 75.)

TABLE 75
Massachusetts Congressmen and the Organizational and Salary Issues

| | Vote on 5 Issues | | | | | *Federalist* |
Congressman	*1*	*2*	*3*	*4*	*5*	Support Score[a]
Ames	F	F	F	F	F	100
Goodhue	F	F	F	F	F	100
Sedgwick	F	F	F	—	—	80
Leonard	F	AF	—	F	F	70
Thatcher	F	AF	AF	F	F	60
Partridge	AF	AF	AF	F	F	40
Gerry	AF	AF	AF	AF	AF	0
Grout	AF	AF	AF	AF	AF	0

SOURCES: Vote One: Passage of a bill to establish executive departments. A Yes vote is a Federalist vote (House Journal, 22 June 1789, pp. 50-51).

Vote Two: To pass a bill establishing the State Department. A Yes vote is a Federalist vote (Ibid, 24 June 1789, pp. 52-53).

Vote Three: Passage of the salary bill. A Yes vote is a Federalist vote (Ibid., 29 Aug. 1789, p. 93).

Vote Four: To regulate processes in courts. A No vote is a Federalist vote (Ibid., 24 Sept. 1789, pp. 122-23).

Vote Five: To accept the Senate amendments to the above measure. A Yes vote is a Federalist vote (Ibid., 28 Sept. 1789, p. 128).

a. I have given each congressman twenty points for a Federalist vote, ten points if he failed to vote, and zero points for an Antifederalist vote. Kenneth R. Bowling, "Politics in the First Congress, 1789-1791" (Ph.D. diss, University of Wisconsin, 1968), p. 119, classifies all of the congressmen into governmental or opposition members. In his analysis Goodhue was a total supporter, Ames was a secondary core member of the administrative party, Leonard was a fringe member, and Sedgwick, Thatcher, and Partridge were moderate supporters. Gerry and Grout stood in opposition. Sedgwick's absence from one-half the votes probably made him more moderate on Bowling's scale than on mine. Considering the fact that Bowling was analyzing the behavior of all the congressmen, the similarities between the two scales are rather impressive.

23. *Annals*, 11 Apr. 1789, p. 116, for Goodhue. Fisher Ames to Minot, 16 May 1789, in Ames, *Fisher Ames*, 1:39, and Ames to Minot, 19 May 1789, 1:42. The vote on limiting the impost to a specified term of years is in *Journal of the House of Representatives of the United States of America,*

Gerry opposed having a single secretary of the treasury and advocated the creation of a board to handle fiscal affairs. Gerry also wanted the house to draw up its own financial programs without any executive leadership and opposed Ames's and Sedgwick's motions to have the secretary of the treasury report financial plans to the house.[24] Gerry also worried about the President's power to remove executive officials and argued that the senate should agree to removals, a position that Sedgwick and Ames assailed. Specifically, Sedgwick and Ames wanted to grant the President power to remove the secretary of state, a recommendation which Gerry opposed.[25] The representatives also divided over the question of salaries for executive and judicial officials. Gerry wanted lower salaries for federal judges and voted against the final salary bill, while Ames worked feverishly for high salaries.[26] On these related issues of organization and salaries, the delegation split into three groups. Gerry and Grout voted against executive powers and for

1789 (New York, 1789), 16 May 1789, p. 36 (cited hereafter as *House Journal*). The measure passed by a vote of 41 to 8. Ames and Thatcher voted No; Gerry, Goodhue, Grout, Leonard, and Partridge voted Yes. Sedgwick had not yet arrived in New York.

24. For an excellent discussion of the divisions in the House see Kenneth R. Bowling, "Politics in the First Congress, 1789-1791" (Ph.D. diss., University of Wisconsin, 1968), passim, and E. A. Bernhard, *Fisher Ames, Federalist and Statesman, 1752-1808* (Chapel Hill, 1965), pp. 76-118, which gives an overview of the first session. Gerry's comments are in the *Annals*, 19 May 1789, p. 383, and 20 May 1789, pp. 391, 393, and 396. The responses of Ames and Sedgwick are in ibid., 25 June 1789, pp. 595-97. 598-99, 601-03.

25. For some general comments by Gerry see *Annals*, 19 May 1789, pp. 376-77, 380. For Ames's feelings see Fisher Ames to George R. Minot, 29 May 1789, in Ames, *Fisher Ames*, 1:51. For the debate over the removal of the secretary of state see *Annals*, 16 June 1789, pp. 460-61, 472-77; 17 June 1789, pp. 501-05; 18 June 1789, pp. 520-23. The final vote is in *House Journal*, 22 June 1789, pp. 50-51.

26. Sedgwick worked hard for high salaries for the executive and judicial branches; see *Annals*, 13 July 1789, p. 634; 16 July 1789, pp. 646-47, 649, 651-52, 656-57. Theodore Sedgwick to Mrs. Sedgwick, 23 July and 8 Aug. 1789, Sedgwick Papers, Massachusetts Historical Society; Sedgwick to Benjamin Lincoln, 19 July 1789, Lincoln Papers, Massachusetts Historical Society. Gerry's attack on judicial salaries is in *Annals*, 18 Sept. 1789. pp. 899-900, 901. The two men took the reverse positions on legislative salaries. Gerry wanted higher pay for legislators (see *Annals*, 6 Aug. 1789, pp. 680-83) while Sedgwick opposed these in ibid., 6 Aug. 1789, p. 683. Gerry's support of higher congressional salaries drew a warning from James Sullivan; see Sullivan to Gerry, 16, 18 Aug. 1789, Gerry Papers.

lower salaries opposing Ames, Goodhue, and Sedgwick, while Leonard and Thatcher tended to side with the Federalists and Partridge with the Antifederalists.

The debates over amending the Constitution exposed a similar division. The Antifederalists throughout the nation had insisted on either basic amendments or a new convention. Hancock threw himself behind this movement when, in his January 1789 address to the General Court, he opposed a new convention but strongly recommended the passage of several amendments that would make important structural changes in the national government. The General Court backed the governor and announced that it had "full confidence that the representatives of this Commonwealth, will not fail, to exert their utmost influence and use all reasonable and legal measures that the alterations and provisions aforesaid [the amendments recommended by the Massachusetts convention] be duly considered in Congress and recommended by that honorable body agreeably to the true spirit and letter of the aforesaid resolution." Samuel Adams openly announced support for this proposal and the Antifederalist press began a campaign favoring the proposed amendments.[27]

The Massachusetts Federalists found themselves in a ticklish position. They had drafted the proposals in order to win over moderate support at the ratification convention, so they had to appear to work for changes while making certain that these would be relatively unimportant. Belknap believed that a bill of rights would make Sam Adams happy, and Ames and Sedgwick both favored amendments that might lure North Carolina into the union.[28] In order to make these changes as minor as possible Ames and Sedgwick favored a proposal to discuss the amendments in a select committee whose deliberations would be secret.

27. Bowling, "Politics," pp. 121-36, underlines the importance of these amendments. The account of the elections in ch. 10 also illustrates the importance of amendments in several of the congressional contests in Massachusetts. Hancock's address is in *Acts and Laws*, 27 Jan. 1789, 5:321-23. For the newspapers see *Independent Chronicle*, 26 Feb., 5, 19 Mar. 1789; *Salem Mercury*, 3 Mar. 1789. For Federalist fears see Benjamin Lincoln to George Washington, 15 Apr. 1789, Lincoln Papers.

28. Jeremy Belknap to Hazard, 14 June 1789, Belknap Papers, Massachusetts Historical Society, *Collections*, 5th ser., 3:140; Fisher Ames to George R. Minot, 23 July 1789, in Ames, *Fisher Ames*, 1:65; Theodore Sedgwick to Benjamin Lincoln, 19 July 1789, Lincoln Papers.

TABLE 76

Massachusetts Congressmen and the Amendment Issue

Congressman	Vote on 5 Issues					Federalist Support Score[a]
	1	2	3	4	5	
Ames	F	F	F	F	F	100
Goodhue	F	F	F	F	F	100
Sedgwick	F	F	F	F	—	90
Partridge	F	AF	AF	F	F	60
Thatcher	F	AF	AF	F	F	60
Leonard	—	—	—	—	F	60
Gerry	AF	AF	AF	AF	F	20
Grout	AF	AF	AF	AF	AF	0

SOURCES: Vote One: To include all the amendments proposed by the states for consideration by the Committee of the Whole. A Federalist vote is a No vote (House Journal, 18 Aug. 1789, p. 81).

Vote Two: To weaken the proposed amendment limiting power of the national government. A Federalist vote is a Yes vote (Ibid., 21 Aug. 1789, p. 86).

Vote Three: To limit congressional power over elections. A Federalist vote is a No vote (Ibid., 21 Aug. 1789, p. 86).

Vote Four: To limit the power of Congress to impost direct taxes. A Federalist vote is a No vote (Ibid., 22 Aug. 1789, pp. 87-88).

Vote Five: House to agree to Senate amendments. Federalist vote is a Yes vote (Ibid., 24 Sept. 1789, p. 124).

a. Each congressman was given twenty points for each Federalist vote, ten points for not voting, and zero points for an Antifederalist vote. Bowling, "Politics," p. 137, gives a scale for all members of the House that shows Ames, Goodhue, Leonard, and Sedgwick as members of the Madison coalition favoring the adopted amendments. Thatcher and Partridge were listed as nonaligned and Gerry and Grout were listed as being in favor of stronger amendments. Leonard, who had an extremely poor voting record, was the only individual located differently on the two scales. Again this shows the impressive similarity between Bowling's analysis of the entire House and this description of the divisions within a single delegation.

Gerry opposed this move and taunted the Federalists by accusing them of fearing the public and wishing for secrecy.[29]

The debate over amendments soon divided the delegation. (See table 76.) Gerry wanted smaller congressional districts, a total House membership of at least 200, a guarantee of freedom of assembly, and the right of the electors to instruct their representatives, and proposed that all the amendments submitted by the

29. For some early interchanges between Gerry and Goodhue see *Annals*, 8 June 1789, pp. 426, 444-46. For the debate among Gerry, Ames, Partridge, and Sedgwick, see ibid., 21 July 1789, pp. 660-62, 664.

state ratifying conventions should be considered on the floor of the House.[30] Ames in reply favored even larger districts; Sedgwick opposed any special protection for the right of assembly, gibing that the Constitution might have to be changed to protect the rights of men to wear hats or to get out of bed; and Ames moved to prevent the committee of the whole House from considering all of the proposed amendments that had been submitted by the conventions.[31] On 18 August 1789 Gerry called for a showdown by moving that the House should consider all the proposed amendments. His motion lost 34 to 16 with only Grout and himself favoring it among the Massachusetts delegation.[32] Gerry continued to hack away at the Federalists and on 21 August moved an amendment to limit the national government to the powers expressly granted to it by the Constitution. Although the motion was defeated 32 to 17, Grout, Partridge, and Thatcher joined Gerry in favoring it.[33] Other votes involved motions to increase the power of the states over elections and to limit the power of the national government to levy direct taxes. On the latter question only Grout, the Worcester County representative and former county convention member, voted in the affirmative.[34] An analysis of the various votes on amendments again shows a divided delegation. Ames, Goodhue, and Sedgwick voted together against any major changes; Gerry and Grout supported change; and Partridge, Thatcher, and Leonard tended to shift from side to side. In the Senate, Strong followed a strict Federalist line, but Dalton weakened and voted for an amendment to hold the ratio of representatives at one for every 34,000 people until the House reached 200 members.

Many Massachusetts citizens bitterly criticized the results of this first session since it had not solved the fiscal problems confronting the commonwealth and the nation. Congress had passed an impost, had established executive departments, a judicial system, a customs service, and had submitted twelve proposed amendments to the states for their consideration and approval, but it had failed

30. For the debate among the Massachusetts delegation over these issues, see ibid., 14 Aug. 1789, pp. 720-24, 726; 15 Aug. 1789, pp. 731-35, 736-43, 747-49.

31. Ibid.

32. *House Journal*, 18 Aug. 1789, p. 81.

33. Ibid., 21 Aug. 1789, p. 86.

34. Ibid., 22 Aug. 1789, pp. 87-88.

to take any action on the state or national debts. John Avery warned the Federalists in April 1789 that since the new nation would absorb the commonwealth's impost revenues it would have to take action to assume the debt or "many of those who are now highly federal when they see the operations of the Continental impost and excise will become anti-federal."[35] Benjamin Lincoln also raised storm warnings informing Sedgwick that the national government must assume the state debt to win popular support. If the commonwealth had to fund her own debt, "that affection and support which should be attached to the one government will be transferred to the other."[36] Christopher Gore, soon to be the new federal district attorney, also urged Congress to fund the state and national debts since that would be "very favorable to many of the most influential men of this commonwealth, and engage them warmly to promote the operation of this government."[37] The lack of action on debts combined with the imposition of an impost and the creation of national offices made many persons uneasy about the new government. Sullivan reported that high salaries had alienated many, while several important merchants believed that the impost had harmed shipbuilding and commerce. Sullivan predicted that the people "will demand of the high Feds some of the blessings so lavishly promised and what the consequences of their disappointment will be time will discover."[38]

During the winter of 1789-1790 pressure for the assumption of state debts continued to grow. As it became more and more obvious that the commonwealth could not or would not service its debt, even papers in the western part of the state pressed for assumption without direct taxes. Antifederalist writers predicted that the national government would waste the customs revenues on large salaries and would eventually levy a direct tax collected by "haughty" national officials.[39] Federalists warned their congress-

---

35. John Avery to George Thatcher, 22 Apr. 1789, Thatcher Papers. Also see an earlier letter from Samuel P. Savage to Thatcher, 7 Mar. 1789, ibid., in which Savage already hoped for quick action on refunding the national debt.

36. Benjamin Lincoln to Theodore Sedgwick, 1 July 1789, Lincoln Papers.

37. Christopher Gore to Rufus King, 29 July 1789, in Charles R. King, *The Life and Correspondence of Rufus King*, 6 vols. (New York, 1894-1900), 1:364.

38. James Sullivan to Elbridge Gerry, 31 July, 13 Sept. 1789, Gerry Papers.

39. For examples of this rhetoric see *Independent Chronicle*, 3, 17 Dec. 1789; *Western Star*, 3 Jan., 16 Mar. 1789; *Hampshire Gazette*, 20 Jan. 1790.

men that influential politicians such as Bowdoin, Phillips, Breck, and Jonathan Mason would shift over to the opposition if the state debt were not assumed, with favorable terms, by the national government.[40]

The increasing pressure for assumption and for refunding the national debt placed both the Federalists and Antifederalists in a hazardous political situation. The Federalists realized that their political futures depended upon both funding and assumption, for if either of these schemes failed, the Antifederalists could gather the disappointed security holders to their party. In addition many of the Federalist politicians were security holders themselves. The Antifederalists occupied an even more uncomfortable position. They could not openly oppose either funding or assumption, but they could not claim credit for their passage since Antifederalists in other states with no large debts campaigned against assumption. A few Antifederalists wanted the state to fund its own debt, but this program had absolutely no appeal for the Antifederalist and least commercial farming communities that had opposed ratification. Finally, of course, the Federalists won their gamble. Congress accepted both assumption and funding, the security holders beamed, the burden of the state debt disappeared, and the less commercial-cosmopolitan interests breathed easier when the national government failed to levy direct taxes to finance the new program.

The Massachusetts congressmen, needled by personal and official pressures from the commonwealth, worked together to force both assumption and funding through the House and Senate. Ames and Sedgwick quickly supported Hamilton's report and Gerry played a leading role in the debate against Madison's proposal to discriminate against speculators.[41] Some speculators in the commonwealth complained that Hamilton's plan did not provide high enough in-

40. Christopher Gore to Rufus King, 24 Jan. 1790, in King, *Rufus King*, 1:385.

41. For early actions see *Annals*, 1st Cong., 2d sess., 21 Jan. 1790, pp. 1097, 1102. For the debates in February see ibid., 9 Feb. 1790, pp. 1153-58, 1163; 10 Feb. 1790, pp. 1172-73; 15 Feb. 1790, pp. 1205-08, 1216-22; 16 Feb. 1790, pp. 1239-40; 18 Feb. 1790, pp. 1279-87; 23 Feb. 1790, pp. 1319, 1324-26. For an overview see Bernhard, *Fisher Ames*, pp. 119-39; Richard E. Welch, Jr., *Theodore Sedgwick, Federalist: A Political Portrait* (Middletown, Conn., 1965), pp. 81-105; Bowling, "Politics," pp. 224 ff.; and Jacob E. Cooke, "The Compromise of 1790," *William and Mary Quarterly*, 3d ser., 27:523-45.

terest payments, but most apparently believed it would be the best politically practicable proposal.[42] After defeating discrimination, the congressmen campaigned for assumption. Goodhue, Gerry, and Sedgwick argued that a defeat of the assumption proposal would result in heavy direct taxes, the outbreak of new rebellions, and the rapid formation of parties and factions built around the national and state creditors. Sedgwick warned the House that he would be unable to support the funding of the national debt unless Congress also approved the assumption of the state debts.[43] Despite these efforts the initial attempt to pass assumption failed in the House. On 29 March 1790 the House recommitted the sections on assumption to the committee of the whole by a close vote of 29 to 27 and on 12 April the House defeated the assumption scheme. According to Maclay, Sedgwick broke into tears as a result of the failure while Ames sat "torpid as if his faculties were deranged."[44]

After the apparent defeat of the assumption proposal, all sorts of groups and individuals and the General Court put additional pressure on the Massachusetts congressmen. "A Landholder" warned the farmers that defeat of assumption would result in heavy direct taxes; "Jack Tarpaulin," an Antifederalist essayist, pictured the federal ship crashing into the breakers because the officers busily counted their wages instead of navigating their vessel; and a "Real Republican" claimed that the Constitution had

42. Jonathan Jackson to Fisher Ames, 7 Feb. 1790, Sedgwick Papers. Daniel Cony to George Thatcher, 7 Feb. 1790, Thatcher Papers, warned Thatcher against the Antifederalist use of the assumption question.

43. The efforts of the Massachusetts congressmen may be followed in the *Annals*, 23 Feb. 1790, p. 1319, which gives the argument that the failure of assumption would force the levying of heavy state taxes. Gerry, on the same day, in ibid., pp. 1324-26, argued that failure to assume the state debts would create two parties. Sedgwick on 24 Feb. 1790, ibid., pp. 1332-38, stated that the insurrection had been caused by the imposition of direct taxes and argued that assumption would end such taxes and would thus make the national government the center of affection of the Massachusetts farmers. Gerry on 24 Feb. 1790, ibid., pp. 1341, 1348-52, argued against any settlement of accounts between the states and the national government until the state debts had been assumed. E. James Ferguson, *The Power of the Purse: A History of American Public Finance, 1776-1790* (Chapel Hill, 1961), pp. 289-305, gives a good overview of the debate. Sedgwick's warnings came in *Annals*, 2 Mar. 1790, pp. 1405-08, and 3 Mar. 1790, pp. 1410, 1412.

44. *Annals*, 12 Apr. 1790, pp. 1525-26; and Maclay, *Journal*, 12 Apr. 1790, p. 231.

produced none of the benefits promised by its supporters.[45] In the west, "A.Z." warned that any failure to assume the state debt would lead to an exodus of Massachusetts farmers into states with lower taxes.[46] Important Federalists also took up their cudgels. Cabot warned Goodhue that the failure of assumption would convert the state creditors into Antifederalists.[47] Gore informed King that unless the impost could be used to pay off the state debt, it would become as unpopular as the infamous Townshend duties. Summing up the general frustration, Thomas B. Wait asked George Thatcher, *"what in God's name have you been doing Gentlemen?"*[48] The court tightened the screws by refusing to return Dalton to the United States Senate. Dalton had drawn a two-year term and the house, irritated by high salaries and the apparent lack of action, didn't even submit his name to the senate. The court selected George Cabot, a leading Federalist merchant, in his place and served notice on the congressional delegation that they could either produce or retire.[49]

In Congress the entire Massachusetts delegation continued to work for assumption. Gerry and Ames worked together to have the committee of the whole reconsider the question and Gore warned King, practically a third senator from Massachusetts, that the merchants of Salem would oppose the revenue laws unless assumption passed.[50] Meanwhile other groups were formulating a

45. *Independent Chronicle*, 15, 22, 29 Apr. 1790, 6 May 1790.

46. *Western Star*, 11, 25 May, 1 June 1790.

47. George Cabot to Goodhue, 6 Apr. 1790, in Henry Cabot Lodge, *The Life and Letters of George Cabot* (Boston, 1877), pp. 35-36.

48. Christopher Gore to Rufus King, 25 Apr. 1790, in King, *Rufus King*, 1:386. Gore to King, 6 May 1790, ibid., 1:386-87; Thomas B. Wait to George Thatcher, 21 Apr. 1790, Thatcher Papers. For additional pressures see John Q. Adams to John Adams, 5 Apr. 1790, in Ford. ed., *John Q. Adams*, 1:53-54; Nathaniel Wells to George Thatcher, 27 Apr. 1790, Thatcher Papers; John Carnes to Thatcher, 20 Apr. 1790, ibid.; George Cabot to Goodhue, 2 May 1790, in Lodge, *Cabot*, pp. 37-38.

49. Christopher Gore to Rufus King, 28, 30 June 1790, in King, *Rufus King*, 1:389, 390; Theodore Sedgwick to Mrs. Sedgwick, 27 June 1790, Sedgwick Papers. According to the tables in Bowling, "Politics," pp. 120 and 137, Dalton had been a softer Federalist than Caleb Strong.

50. Christopher Gore to Rufus King, 30 May 1790, in King, *Rufus King*, 1:388. There had been a strong movement in Massachusetts to elect King as a senator or as the Suffolk County representative in the House. For Gerry and Ames see *Annals*, 24 May 1790, pp. 1587-90, 1591; 25 May 1790, pp. 1592-1603, 1613-16.

solution that would trade assumption for the location of the national capital. All the Massachusetts congressmen were against Philadelphia. But, although the eventual choice mortified Gore, Ames hoped that placing the capital so far south would lead Congress to meet the Commonwealth's demands for assumption.[51]

The Senate resurrected the issue and between 12 and 21 July hammered out a new fiscal measure that included assumption. In a series of eleven roll call votes, Dalton and Strong consistently voted for the package and against any crippling amendments. Their only defeat came in their efforts to secure a higher interest rate for the state security holders.[52] Between 24 and 29 July the House took five roll call votes on whether it would agree with the Senate amendments. The entire Massachusetts delegation from Goodhue to Grout stood as a monolithic bloc for assumption.[53] The issue that had divided Congress, fractured the Federalists, and may have spurred the foundation of the Jeffersonian Republican party solidified the Massachusetts delegation because the commonwealth needed assumption to solve its fiscal and political problems. (See table 77.)

While attention focused on assumption and funding, a few minor issues did divide the delegates. They voted as a group to table the Quaker petitions on slavery and usually voted together on the location of the new capital.[54] Grout alone opposed the excise on

51. Bowling, "Politics," has an excellent chapter dealing with the political importance of locating the capital. The Massachusetts congressmen were not excited by a southern location. See Theodore Sedgwick to Mrs. Sedgwick, 22 June 1790, Sedgwick Papers. See also Fisher Ames to Thomas Dwight, 27 June 1790, Ames Papers, Dedham Historical Society, Dedham, Mass.; Ames to George R. Minot, 27 June 1790, in Ames, *Fisher Ames*, 1:85; Christopher Gore to Rufus King, 11 July 1790, in King, *Rufus King*, 1:390-91.

52. For some of the Senate roll calls see *Senate Journal*, 14 July 1790, p. 180; 16 July 1790, p. 181; 19 July 1790, p. 183; 20 July 1790, pp. 185-86; and 21 July 1790, p. 187.

53. The votes are in *House Journal*, 24 July 1790, pp. 277-78, when a motion to disagree with the Senate amendment [the addition of assumption] failed by a vote of 29 to 32. On 26 July 1790, p. 281, the House agreed to the Senate amendment by a vote of 34 to 28, and on 29 July 1790, pp. 282-84, by a vote of 33 to 27 the House receded from its disagreement with certain Senate amendments. Gerry and Ames backed a motion to increase the interest payments on the assumed debt. This was defeated 33 to 27 and the other six members of the Massachusetts delegation voted against the motion. See ibid., 29 July 1790, pp. 283-85.

54. *House Journal*, 12 Feb. 1790, pp. 157-58. All eight of the Massachu-

distilled liquor and the division over the payment of a pension to
Baron Von Steuben did not follow the former Federalist versus
Antifederalist alignments.[55] In a brief struggle over the salaries to

TABLE 77
Roll Call Votes on Assumption

Congressman	1	2	3	4	5	6	7	8	9	10
Ames	No	No	Yes	Yes	No	No	No	No	Yes	Yes
Gerry	No	No	Yes	Yes	No	No	No	No	Yes	Yes
Grout	No	No	Yes	Yes	No	No	No	No	Yes	Yes
Thatcher	No	No	Yes	Yes	No	No	No	No	Yes	Yes
Goodhue	No	No	Yes	Yes	No	No	No	No	Yes	Yes
Leonard	No	—	Yes	Yes	No	No	No	No	Yes	Yes
Partridge	No	—	Yes	Yes	No	No	No	No	Yes	Yes
Sedgwick	—	—	Yes	Yes	No	No	No	No	Yes	Yes
Total vote										
Yes	33	32	31	18	40	29	15	13	34	33
No	23	18	25	36	15	32	45	47	28	27

SOURCES: Vote 1, House Journal, 15 Apr. 1790, pp. 194-95; vote 2, ibid.,
26 Apr. 1790, pp. 233-34; vote 3, ibid., 26 May 1790, pp. 223-24; vote 4,
ibid., 26 May 1790, pp. 224-25; vote 5, ibid., 19 July 1790, pp. 272-73; vote
6, ibid., 24 July 1790, pp. 277-78; vote 7, ibid., 26 July 1790, pp. 279-80;
vote 8, ibid., 26 July 1790, p. 280; vote 9, ibid., 26 July 1790, p. 281; vote
10, ibid., 29 July 1790, pp. 283-84.
NOTE: Compare this table with tables 75 and 76 and notice the tremendous changes in voting patterns.

---

setts congressmen voted to submit the Quaker petition to a special committee. On 23 Mar. 1790 (ibid., pp. 179-80), Ames, Grout, and Thatcher voted
against inserting the committee report into the journal. Between 31 May and
9 July 1790, the House took a total of twenty-two roll call votes on the
location of the temporary and permanent capital of the United States. On
thirteen of these votes all voting members of the delegation voted together.
On four other votes only one member voted in a minority. On the five
remaining votes there was a division among the delegates. Four of these roll
calls came on 31 May 1790 (House Journal, pp. 228-31). The fifth came on
9 July 1790 (ibid., pp. 265-66).
    55. Gerry, Goodhue, and Sedgwick all opposed an excise on distilled spirits
until Congress assumed the state debts. See *Annals*, 8 Feb. 1790, p. 1129;
9 June 1790, p. 1624; 14 June 1790, p. 1638; 18 June 1790, p. 1642;
21 June 1790, p. 1643. Knox's militia plan also ran into some difficulties.
Daniel Cony to Thatcher, 12 Feb. 1790, Thatcher Papers, and Henry Sewall
to Thatcher, 20 Mar. 1790, ibid., both claimed that the plan had little popularity in Massachusetts. Massachusetts papers attacked both the Knox plan
and the land grant to Baron Von Steuben. See *Independent Chronicle*,
29 Apr., 17 June 1790; *Berkshire Chronicle*, 15 Aug. 1790.
    On the excise on distilled liquor the House on 11 June 1790 (ibid.,

be paid to American ministers abroad, Partridge, Ames, and Goodhue opposed the rest of the delegation, as they had in the first
session, in voting for higher salaries.[56]

The decline of partisanship in the delegation, the victory of
assumption, the disappearance of the financial question as a state
issue, and better conditions in the west led to a sudden and basic
change in political patterns during 1790. With the debt assumed,
amendments passed, and no evidence of federal tyranny, the Antifederalists lacked issues. They tried to inflate some from the
Steuben pension, Knox's plans for an army, or from the complexities of the funding and assumption act, but by the fall of 1790 it
was evident that the Federalists were firmly in control.

In June 1790 the court established the same districts and procedures for the elections to the Second Congress that had served in
the elections of 1788 and 1789.[57] The Antifederalists scratched
for issues. They accused the new government of being too expensive, of paying exorbitant salaries, of being unwilling to aid commerce and manufacturing, of neglecting the fisheries, and of drafting a complex and intricate funding and assumption act. Others
attempted to fan popular resentment by writing of shadowy juntos whose members hoped to consolidate the states into a unified
and aristocratic national government. But the less commercial-
cosmopolitan interests remained unconvinced. In their eyes the
new government had reduced taxes, removed the threat of supporting a heavy state debt, and had not destroyed their local institutions or their political rights. After all, no direct taxes had been
levied, conditions had improved, the country had not been overrun
by placeholders and a federal army.[58] Friction continued between

---

pp. 238-39) voted not to resolve itself into a committee of the whole on the
subject of levying duties on domestic spirits. Only Grout among the Massachusetts representatives voted against this motion. On 21 June 1791 (ibid.,
pp. 245-46), the entire delegation voted against engrossing the liquor excise
bill.

56. *House Journal*, 28 May 1790, p. 227. But this division was still unlike
most of those in the First Session. See tables 74 and 75.

57. The legislation is in *Acts and Laws*, 18 June 1790, 6:117-20.

58. For the improvement in conditions see the first part of ch. 10. For
some of the Antifederalist charges see *Independent Chronicle*, 1, 8, 15 July
1790, for claims that the new government wished to copy European models
and that it was controlled by a junto who wished to destroy state and local
power. Ibid., 15, 22 July 1790, attacked the Congress for not aiding manufacturing or commerce. Ibid., 22 July, 12, 19 Aug. 1790, charged that the fund-

the commonwealth and the nation, but the fears of the typical anticommercial-anticosmopolitan and anti-Constitutional farmer simply had not materialized. The Federalists claimed that their funding and assumption plan had ended the danger of direct taxes, that they, at least, had worked hard to protect manufacturing and commerce, and that they had provided government officials with small salaries.[59] Since both sides agreed on the basic issue of funding and assumption, the campaign had the air of a peaceful morning after a decade of political nightmares.

The congressional elections for the eight districts fell into three general patterns. In Suffolk, Essex, and Hampshire-Berkshire, the incumbent had little opposition, and Ames, Goodhue, and Sedgwick won easy victories. In the districts where voting patterns changed, Gerry, nevertheless, won reelection in Middlesex, but Artemas Ward replaced Grout in Worcester, and Sherashrub Bourne won in Plymouth-Barnstable thanks to a heavy turnout in his native Barnstable County. The two districts, Maine and Bristol-Islands, in which alignments were most consistent with the 1788-1789 patterns held several elections before any single candidate secured a majority.

In Suffolk and Essex districts, Ames and Goodhue won easily. Ames carried both the Federalist and Antifederalist towns in Suffolk and, unlike 1788, ran extremely well in Boston. Goodhue's support in Essex County changed somewhat from 1788 as he carried the three leading mercantile towns of Salem, Newburyport, and Marblehead very handily but failed to run as strongly in the less commercial and Antifederalist towns as he had in the earlier election. Samuel Holten's candidacy cut into Goodhue's strength in these areas, but Goodhue had no problem as he polled over four-fifths of the total vote.[60]

---

ing legislation was too complex, protested the expenses of a seven-month congressional session, and accused Congress of defrauding the original holders of state and national securities. "Rusticus" in ibid., 26 Aug. 1790, argued that the national government was more expensive than state governments and on 2 Sept. 1790, in ibid., he charged the new government of incompetence. Some Antifederalists appealed to the artisans and pointed out that the establishment of a national government had resulted in less protection against imports: see ibid., 2 Sept. 1790.

59. See *Western Star*, 2, 31 Aug. 1790, for examples of this rhetoric in the west.

60. For background to the elections see Cotton Tufts to John Adams, 28 Sept. 1790, Adams Papers, pt. 4, in which Tufts worried about Ames's

Theodore Sedgwick won reelection quite easily in Hampshire and Berkshire counties in results that show a considerable across-the-board increase in his support. The Berkshire County Federalist carried all three groups of towns in the two counties and secured a majority in both counties in the Federalist and Antifederalist communities. Samuel Lyman, Sedgwick's leading opponent in 1788-1789, ran poorly in all the groups of towns and in both counties.[61]

Elbridge Gerry had more difficulty winning the election in Middlesex County where his base of support had changed considerably. (See table 78.) In 1789 he ran much stronger in the group C than in the group A communities and he carried the Antifederalist towns by a much greater margin than the Federalist communities. In 1790 he ran better in the most commercial-cosmopolitan towns and received an almost identical percentage of support from the Antifederalist and Federalist communities.[62]

---

reelection. See *Independent Chronicle*, 19, 26 Aug. 1790, for some early attacks on Ames. Ibid., 9 Sept. 1790, lists Benjamin Austin, Jr., Thomas Dawes, and Ames as the candidates. In ibid., 23 Sept. 1790, Ames was attacked for opposing amendments and favoring direct taxes. In ibid., 30 Sept. 1790, "Elector" favored Dawes while "A Suffolk Farmer" criticized Ames for voting for high salaries for government officials. John Q. Adams to Abigail Adams, 17 Oct. 1790, in Ford, ed., *John Q. Adams*, 1:59, noted that Ames's victory surpassed even the expectations of his friends. Christopher Gore to Rufus King, 23 Oct. 1790, in King, *Rufus King*, 1:393, was also pleasantly surprised by the Suffolk election.

In the Essex district an article in the *Independent Chronicle*, 23 Sept. 1790, foresaw an easy Goodhue victory. William Bently, *The Diary of William Bently, D. D., Pastor of the East Church, Salem, Massachusetts*, 4 vols. (Salem, 1905-1914), 28 Sept., 4 Oct., 1790, 1:201-02, noted the quietness of the election. Voting returns are from the unpublished Abstracts of Votes for the House of Representatives, available at the Office of the Secretary, Boston, for the years 1790-1792 (cited hereafter as Abstracts-House). Federalist and Antifederalist towns are from *Proceedings in the Convention*, pp. 87-92.

61. See Ames to Timothy Dwight, 18 July 1790, Ames Papers, Dedham Historical Society, in which Ames expresses some concern about Sedgwick's reelection. *Hampshire Chronicle*, 18 Aug., 8, 15 Sept. 1790 has some election rhetoric. *Independent Chronicle*, 9 Sept. 1790, stated that Thompson J. Skinner might win in Berkshire. John Q. Adams, 19 Oct. 1790, in Ford, ed., *J. Q. Adams*, 1:61, noted that Sedgwick was chosen by a surprising majority. Returns are from Abstracts-House, 1790-1792. Federalist and Antifederalist towns are from the *Proceedings in the Convention*, pp. 87-92.

62. Cotton Tufts to John Adams, 28 Sept. 1790, Adams Papers, informed Adams that great efforts would be made for Gorham in the Middlesex dis-

TABLE 78
Votes for Gerry in Middlesex District, 1788–1789 and 1790

Year	Group A	Group B	Group C	Federal-ist	Antifed-eralist	Total
1788–89	52%	67%	64%	43%	76%	61%
1790	62	65	51	60	60	60

SOURCES: Unpublished Abstracts of Votes for House of Representatives, available at the Office of the Secretary, Boston, 1790-1792 (cited hereafter as Abstracts-House). Federalist and Antifederalist towns are from *Debates and Proceedings in the Convention of the Commonwealth of Massachusetts, Held in the Year 1788, and Which Finally Ratified the Constitution of the United States* (Boston, 1856), pp. 87-92 (cited hereafter as *Proceedings in the Convention*).

In the Plymouth-Barnstable district, the socioeconomic pattern of previous elections had little relevance. Sherashrub Bourne, accused of Toryism during the Revolution, won in the second attempt at election because his native Barnstable County electors cast more ballots than their Plymouth County cousins and 97 percent of their votes went to Bourne. He carried the district with 58 percent of the vote despite the fact that he garnered only 12 percent of the total Plymouth County vote.[63] Partridge, the incumbent, failed to run for reelection, Plymouth County divided its vote among three major candidates, and in November the Barnstable electors turned out to vote for a local resident. It was a simple case of friends-and-neighbors politics.

The Antifederalists met their gravest defeat in Worcester County as the Federalist placeholder Artemas Ward defeated incumbent Jonathan Grout after two tries. Grout lost the election because Ward cut into his former majorities in the Antifederalist communities and the placeholder did especially well in the Antifederalist group B towns.[64] Table 79 shows the significant shift away

---

trict. Apparently Tufts believed that Gorham might win. The *Independent Chronicle* published several supporters of Gerry on 23 Sept. 1790. "A Middlesex Elector" backed Gorham in ibid. John Q. Adams to Abigail Adams, 17 Oct. 1790, in Ford, ed., *John Q. Adams*, 1:60, claimed that Gorham had been working for election for two years. In John Q. to John Adams 19 Oct. 1790, ibid., 1:62, he points out that Gerry won despite Gorham's best efforts.

63. Voting and turnout based on Abstracts-House, 1790; Federalist and Antifederalist towns from *Proceedings in the Convention*, pp. 87-92.

64. Abstracts-House; Federalist and Antifederalist towns from *Proceedings in the Convention*, pp. 87-92.

TABLE 79
Votes for Grout in Worcester District, 1789 and 1790

Year	Group A	Group B	Group C	Federal-ist	Antifed-eralist	Total
1789	56%	64%	50%	19%	60%	56%
1790	53	38	46	20	48	45

SOURCES: Abstracts-House, 1790, and *Proceedings in the Convention*, pp. 87-92.

from Grout in these Antifederalist communities, another indication of the changing nature of the state's politics.

In two elections the old Federalist and Antifederalist divisions played an important role. In Maine, thanks to the support of the Antifederalist towns, the less commercial-cosmopolitan communities, and the towns that had divided or neglected to vote on the ratification of the Constitution, George Thatcher won reelection after four attempts. (See table 80.) His opponents, Wells and Lithgow, ran stronger in the Federalist towns, and Lithgow also secured the support of his native Lincoln County.[65] Thus in Maine a combination of older political patterns and friends-and-neighbors voting eventually led to the reelection of the moderate Federalist incumbent.

The nine elections in Bristol-Islands district revolved around the Federalist-Antifederalist division and finally resulted in the reelection of George Leonard. Leonard, who had a moderate Federalist record, found himself in a five-way race with Phanuel Bishop, the former county convention leader and opponent of ratification, David Cobb, the Bristol County placeholder and high Federalist, Peleg Coffin, a Nantucket politician, and Walter Spooner, a New Bedford Federalist. Despite the chaotic nature of the race, Bishop carried the Antifederalist towns in all but one of the nine elections, and Leonard ran much stronger than any of the other Federalist candidates in the same group of communities. (See table 81.) Spooner, Coffin, and Cobb always did best in the Federalist

65. *Proceedings in the Convention*, pp. 87-92. There is a massive amount of material on this lengthy election in the Thatcher Papers and the *Cumberland Gazette*. As early as July 1790, Thatcher's friends warned him of opposition; see Nasson to Thatcher, 7 July 1790; Nathaniel Barrell to Thatcher, 10 July 1790; and T. B. Wait to Thatcher, 17 July 1790, all in Thatcher Papers.

TABLE 80
Votes in Maine District, 1790 and 1791

| | Thatcher | | | | Lithgow, Apr. 1791 |
	Oct. 1790	Nov. 1790	Jan. 1791	Apr. 1791	
Towns					
Group A	29%	47%	39%	46%	51%
Group B	25	24	32	31	43
Group C	43	70	57	57	38
Federalist	32	23	20	35	51
Antifederalist	35	86	65	63	30
Counties					
York	45	49	62	66	6
Cumberland	24	48	52	65	32
Lincoln	21	NR	32	37	62
Total	37%	48%	48%	51%	41%

SOURCES: Abstracts-House, 1790. Federalist and Antifederalist towns are from *Proceedings in the Convention*, pp. 87-92.
NR = No response.

group A towns.[66] The election closely resembled the earlier 1788 election since Leonard, the moderate Federalist, finally won because of his support in the Antifederalist towns.

Thus the congressional elections resulted in Federalist victories and reflected a shift in political alignments. Goodhue, Ames, and Sedgwick, the three most extreme Federalists, won reelection handily. In Sedgwick's case the ease of his victory resulted from his increased support from the Antifederalist and the less commercial-cosmopolitan towns. Grout's defeat in Worcester, the most dramatic Federalist victory, depended upon Ward's success in picking up strength in the county's Antifederalist towns and served as another example of the political realignments occurring throughout the commonwealth. Gerry, the Middlesex Antifederalist, won, but his support now came equally from the Federalist and Antifederalist towns. Out on the Cape, Bourne won an election which turned on his success in his own county of Barnstable. Only in

66. Fisher Ames to Timothy Dwight, 1 June 1791, Ames Papers, in which Ames states that there "are now symptoms of accommodation to keep out the common enemy." [Phanuel Bishop], *Independent Chronicle*, 14 July 1791, had an essay favoring Bishop. This election took so long to complete that no one represented this district in the Second Congress.

TABLE 81
Votes in Bristol District, 1790-1792

Election and Candidate	Group A	Federalist	Antifed-eralist	Total
October 1790				
Leonard	6%	27%	29%	22%
Bishop	2	8	55	24
Cobb, Spooner, Coffin	92	65	16	54
November 1790				
Leonard	4	23	13	13
Bishop	11	15	69	28
Cobb, Spooner, Coffin	85	62	18	59
April 1791				
Leonard	5	7	6	5
Bishop	18	27	68	39
Cobb, Spooner, Coffin	77	66	26	56
September 1791				
Leonard	11	48	29	29
Bishop	13	35	68	42
Cobb, Spooner, Coffin	76	17	3	29
December 1791				
Leonard	21	70	43	45
Bishop	8	27	56	32
Cobb, Spooner, Coffin	71	3	1	23
April 1792				
Leonard	28	69	51	54
Bishop	7	15	49	27
Cobb, Spooner, Coffin	65	16	0	19

SOURCES: Abstracts-House, and *Proceedings in the Convention*, pp. 87-92.

Maine and the Bristol-Islands district did the former political patterns remain relatively firm and in those two districts, it took four and nine attempts to elect a congressman.

A temporary lull in late 1791 marked the commonwealth's survival of a decade of bitter and divisive preparty politics. The Revolution had raised expectations and had created issues that divided the state along social and economic lines. The absence of well-organized, ideologically oriented, bureaucratic parties intensified these differences as the towns and interests fought to control policies in response to the new issues. Between 1780 and 1786 the most commercial-cosmopolitan interests and towns seemed to have the political situation under control. The political system and social structure when related with the constitution of 1780 enabled them to control the senate, the judiciary, and the congressional delegation and gave them a considerable amount of influence in the lower house. These towns and interests parlayed this control into a political program that involved refunding and consolidating the state's debt at a high specie value, the eventual repayment of these securities in gold and silver, the abolition of legal tender paper currency, the continued rapid collection of private debts, and the levying and collection of heavy direct taxes. The less commercial-cosmopolitan interests and towns bitterly opposed this entire program. But this opposition had relatively little success. Although they blocked some of the programs in the house, held conventions to mobilize sentiment, and some resorted to violence, they accomplished very little. During the summer of 1786 the most commercial-cosmopolitan interests increased the pressure when they passed legislation levying direct taxes to pay the supplemental funds to the confederation and refused to permit the revenues from the state's impost and excise to be used for general expenses. At this point the pressure of debts, taxes, and constant political failure pushed many westerners to the breaking point. Some met in conventions in which they demanded new policies while others forced reform by preventing court sessions which would enforce the collection of debts. The General Court in the fall of 1786 attempted to compromise. It suspended suits for debt and permitted the lapse of direct tax collections while at the same time it opposed the activities of the Regulators. These policies satisfied neither the commercial-cosmopolitan militants nor the Regulators. In early 1787 Benjamin Lincoln and the militia, financed by important merchants, smashed the Regulation and the court and the judicial authorities cracked down on the defeated rebels. But in the spring of 1787 the tide of politics turned. James Bowdoin lost the governorship, long-term placeholding senators lost their seats, and the less commercial-cosmopolitan towns and interests increased their power in the lower house. This resulted in Hancock's pardoning of the convicted Regulators and the court's extension of the suspension of debts, easing of pressure on former Regulators, and its decision not to support the state's credit by new taxation schemes.

The double shock of Shays's Rebellion and political defeat drove most of the commercial-cosmopolitan towns over to a nationalistic position that they had frequently opposed in the earlier 1780s. By the end of 1787 the battle lines over ratification of the new Constitution resembled the old divisions over consolidation, debts, taxes, and Regulation. Thanks to a few tactical compromises and intense pressure, the most commercial-cosmopolitan groups and towns forced ratification through the convention. But then they again overreached themselves. Their efforts to seize control of the executive branch failed dismally as Bowdoin lost to Hancock and Samuel Adams defeated Benjamin Lincoln in 1789. But at the same time the placeholders returned to the senate and the less commercial-cosmopolitan interests sent fewer members to the lower house.

While these towns and interests continued their struggle for mastery, it seemed that a new division of Federalist and Antifederalist closely interrelated with the older divisions was coming to the fore. Leading Antifederalists such as Elbridge Gerry, Samuel Adams, and other politicians gave the less commercial-cosmopolitan towns the elite leadership they had lacked during the earlier 1780s. Although the Federalists did well in the 1788 and 1789 congressional elections, the first session of the First Congress indicated that a serious ideological split had occurred within the Massachusetts delegation. For a while it seemed that parties might result from the complex patterns of new issues, old divisions, and new leaders. But the agitation for and passage of assumption and funding knocked the props out from under the old politics and by the end of 1790 and 1791 the commonwealth found itself no longer divided along either the lines of the socioeconomic continuum or the Antifederalist versus Federalist debate. So in 1791 and 1792 it seemed that the commonwealth could easily revert to a simpler era of preparty factional politics in which small groups of politicians would machinate for power and privilege with few issues developing that could divide the state along socioeconomic or even ideological lines. This, of course, was a temporary situation since organized parties responding to new issues did develop in the commonwealth especially between 1794 and 1808. But that is another story.

A decade of preparty politics had passed. The events of that decade showed that if voters or voting units recognized the importance of issues, especially economic ones, and had some control over their elected representatives political divisions resembled the socioeconomic differences among groups, individuals, and communities. Throughout the 1780s the less commercial-cosmopolitan groups and towns opposed the financial programs of the most commercial-cosmopolitan communities and groups and this opposition colored their reception of the new national Constitution. Nevertheless many political decisions were not influenced by these specific and narrow interests. All groups and towns seemed to unite on certain issues and questions and until 1787 the important political leaders strove for positions of power and profit while paying little attention to the issues and problems that divided the communities in the General Court. Finally after 1787 protoparties began to emerge. The leaders divided into Federal and Antifederal factions and communities and individuals tended to support certain leaders for socioeconomic or ideological reasons. But these protoparties failed to develop their own identities and when the economic and ideological issues disappeared in 1790 and 1791 the new groups quickly disintegrated.

The events of the decade also demonstrated that politics based on socioeconomic and ideological distinctions among communities and individuals did not depend upon a functioning party system. Indeed during the period it sometimes seemed that the direct reaction of towns and individuals to important issues, without the interposition of political parties, might and could result in an absolute disaster for a commonwealth founded on the principles of eighteenth-century political thought. More divisive than mere faction, less susceptible to compromise than party, the struggles in preparty Massachusetts illustrated the explosive potential of politics operating through popular and direct responses to hotly debated issues.

INDEX

BIBLIOGRAPHICAL INDEX

Index

Bibliographical Index